URBAN SOCIAL GEOGRAPHY
AN INTRODUCTION

THIRD EDITION

Urban Social Geography

an Introduction

Paul Knox

Longman Scientific & Technical
Longman Group Limited
Longman House, Burnt Mill, Harlow
Essex CM20 2JE, England
and Associated Companies throughout the world

Copublished in the United States with
John Wiley & Sons, Inc., 605 Third Avenue, New York
NY 10158

First published 1982
Second edition 1987
Third edition 1995

British Library Cataloguing in Publication Data
A catalogue entry for this title is available from the British Library.

ISBN 0-582-22937-5

Library of Congress Cataloging-in-Publication data
Knox, Paul L.
    Urban social geography: an introduction/Paul Knox. — 3rd ed.
      p.   cm.
    Includes bibliographical references and index.
    ISBN 0-582-22937-5 (Longman). — ISBN 0-470-23414-8 (Wiley)
    1. Sociology, Urban. 2. Human geography. 3. Cities and towns.
    I. Title.
    HT151.K57   1994
    307.76—dc20
    94-7618
     CIP

Set by 14 in 12/14pt Times

Produced by Longman Singapore Publishers (Pte) Ltd.
Printed in Singapore

Contents

Acknowledgements

We are grateful to the following for permission to reproduce copyright material:

Academic Press Ltd. and the author, Professor Agocs for Table 6.1 (Agocs, 1981); Architecture and Behaviour (Ecole Polytechnic Federale de Lausanne) for Fig. 7.6 (Knox, 1984); Edward Arnold (Publishers) Ltd for Figs 4.1 and 4.2 (Bourne, 1981); Belhaven Press for Figs 2.5 and 4.7 (MacLaren, 1992); Blackwell Publishers for Table 7.1 (Harvey, 1989); Carfax Publishing Company for Fig. 9.6 (Clarke and Onaka, 1983); Centre for Urban and Regional Studies for Table 2.3 (Duncan, 1971); the authors, Professor R M Downs and Professor D Stea for Fig. 8.10 compiled from Figs 7.2, 7.3, 7.4 and 7.5 (Downs and Stea, 1973); Duke University Press for Figs 6.2, 6.5 and 6.6 (Huttman, 1991); Economic Geography (Clark University) for Figs 2.21 (*Economic Geography*, 1971) and 8.2 (*Economic Geography*, 1982); Fig. 10.1 reprinted from *Geoforum*, 14, Humphrys, Mason and Pinch, S, The externality fields of football grounds: a case study of The Dell Southampton, 401–12, Copyright © (1983), with kind permission from Elsevier Science Ltd, The Boulevard, Langford Lane, Kidlington OX5 1GB, UK; Glasgow City Council for Fig. 2.29 (Rae, 1983); Institute of British Geographers for Figs 2.8 (Whitehand, 1992), 2.17 (Pacione, 1987) and 6.1 (Waterman, 1988); The Johns Hopkins University Press, Baltimore/London for Fig. 2.10 (Hart, John Fraser (ed.) *Our Changing Cities*, 1991); Koninklijk Nederlands Aardrijkskundig Genootschap for Fig. 2.11 (Musterd, 1991); Longman Group Ltd. for Tables 9.1 (White, 1984) and 10.1 and Figs 10.5 and 10.6 (Knox, 1982) and Figs 4.6 and 4.10 (Taylor and Hadfield, 1982); New Zealand Geographical Society (Inc.) for Fig. 5.4 (Kearsley, 1983); Office of Population Censuses and Surveys for Table 9.2 (*General Household Survey*, 1976) Crown Copyright; Oxford University Press, Oxford for Table 3.1 and Fig. 3.1 (Pinch, 1979); Table 9.3 from *Environmental Choice, Human Behaviour and Residential Satisfaction* by William Michelson. Copyright 1977 by Oxford University Press Inc.

Reprinted by permission; Pion Limited, London for Fig 6.3 (Jackson and Smith, 1981); Pion Limited, London and the author, M Dear for Fig. 7.4 (Moos and Dear, 1986); Pion Limited, London and the author, E Feitelson for Fig. 9.3 (Feitelson, 1993); Pion Limited, London and the authors, S Pinch for Table 10.2 (Pinch, 1989), G Pratt for Fig. 2.19 (Pratt and Hanson, 1988), K Simonsen for Figs 7.1 and 7.2 (Simonsen, 1991), R Wallace for Fig. 2.13 (Wallace, 1989), B Warf for Fig. 5.5 (Warf, 1990) and P White for Fig. 2.18 (Winchester and White, 1988); Roof (Shelter Publications) for Fig. 4.8 (Weir, 1976); Routledge for Figs 2.3, 2.4 (Whitehand, 1992), 8.1 (Werlen, 1993), 8.6 (De Evans *et al.*, 1992) and 10.9 (Bennett and Estall, 1991); Royal Scottish Geographical Society for Figs 2.14 (Knox, 1976) and 8.3 (Williams, 1985); Southwark Council, Planning and Economic Development Division for 4.3, 4.4 and 4.5 (Southwark Development Department, 1973); The University of Chicago Press for Fig. 5.3 (Park *et al.*, 1925); V H Winston and Sons, Inc. for Fig. 2.12 (White and Winchester, 1991).

Whilst every effort has been made to trace the owners of copyright material, in a few cases this has proved impossible and we take this opportunity to offer our apologies to any copyright holders whose rights we may have unwittingly infringed.

"As people live and work in urban spaces, they gradually impose themselves on their environment…"
Community art in a Berlin neighbourhood. Photograph by Ruth Rohr-Zanker.

1 *Social geography and the sociospatial dialectic*

The Sociospatial Dialectic • Urban Spaces: Some Preliminary Characterizations •
The Macro-geographical Context

At one point in his essay on Boston, Jonathan Raban stops to ask:

> Why should the Italians all cram themselves behind the expressway in
> the North End? Why should [African-Americans] live in Roxbury and
> Jews in Chelsea? By what law do Boston suburbs turn into rigidly
> circumscribed ghettos when they look so much alike, so quaintly
> attractive, so prim, so dull? For it is as if someone had taken a map of
> the city and, resolutely blind to its topography, had coloured in
> irregularly-shaped lumps labelled 'Blacks', 'Jews', 'Irish', 'Academics',
> 'Gentry', 'Italians', 'Chinese', 'Assorted Others'.[1]

For the geographer, such questions present themselves in more general
terms, so that the major issues become: why do city populations get sifted
out according to race and social class to produce distinctive neighbourhoods? And how? In addition, the geographer is interested in a number of
supplementary issues. Are there, for example, any other criteria by which
individuals and households become physically segregated within the city?
To what extent is territory relevant to the operation of local social systems?
How does a person's area of residence affect his or her behaviour? How do
people choose where to live, and what are the constraints on their choices?
What groups, if any, are able to manipulate the 'geography' of the city, and
to whose advantage?

As many writers now acknowledge, the answer to most of these questions
is ultimately to be found in the wider context of social, economic and

political organization. In short, the city must be seen as reflection of the society which maintains it. It follows that the study of the city should not be abstracted from its historical, cultural and economic matrix. It also follows that a proper understanding of the city requires a cross-disciplinary approach, whatever the ultimate focus of attention. In the city, everything is connected to everything else, and the deficiencies of one academic specialism must be compensated for by the emphases of others.

This need for eclecticism is compounded by the coexistence, within geography as a whole, of several different approaches to knowledge and understanding. Four main approaches have been identifiable in the recent literature of urban geography:

- The first is a quantitative and descriptive approach, based on a philosophy in which the geographer's role is to document the spatial organization of society. Its explanatory concepts are derived partly from neoclassical economics and partly from the functional sociology of Talcott Parsons.
- Second is the so-called behavioural approach, which emerged in the mid-1960s as a reaction to the normative assumptions of neoclassical–functional description. The emphasis here is on the study of people's activities and decision-making processes (where to live, for example) within their perceived worlds. Many of the explanatory concepts are derived from social psychology although phenomenological philosophy, with its emphasis on the ways in which people experience the world around them, has also exerted a considerable influence on behavioural research.
- Third there is the structuralist approach, which stresses the constraints on the behaviour of individuals that are imposed by the organization of society as a whole and by the activities of powerful groups and institutions within it. At its broadest level, this approach looks to political science for its explanatory concepts, focusing on the idea of power and conflict as the main determinants of locational behaviour and resource allocation. In this context, the chief source of inspiration has been Marxian theory and its modern derivatives.
- Finally, there are poststructuralist approaches that accommodate difference and ambiguity, contingency and uncertainty. At the heart of such approaches are attempts to reconcile the interaction of meta-structures (economic, political, etc.) with human agency within a cohesive theoretical framework. This has resulted in, among other things, greater attention to moral philosophies, and to the nature of self/other relationships. The effect on urban social geography has been substantial, to the point where the subdiscipline has taken a clear 'cultural turn'.[2] This, it should be emphasized, is not a turn towards the superorganic notion of culture inherent to traditional cultural geography, but to the anthropological idea of cultures as systems of shared meanings. An important objective here is to examine how such cultures 'enter into struggle over

the distribution of goods, rights, needs, and so on between different groups and spaces'.[3]

1.1 The Sociospatial Dialectic

Geography's traditional concern with inter-relationships between people and their physical and social environments provides the basis for the study of urban social geography. Urban spaces are created by people, and they draw their character from the people that inhabit them. As people live and work in urban spaces, they gradually impose themselves on their environment, modifying and adjusting it, as best they can, to suit their needs and express their values. Yet at the same time people themselves gradually accommodate both to their physical environment and to the people around them. There is thus a continuous two-way process, a *sociospatial dialectic,*[4] in which people create and modify urban spaces while at the same time being conditioned in various ways by the spaces in which they live and work. Neighbourhoods and communities are created, maintained and modified; the values, attitudes and behaviour of their inhabitants, meanwhile, cannot help but be influenced by their surroundings and by the values, attitudes and behaviour of the people around them. At the same time, the ongoing processes of urbanization make for a context of change in which economic, demographic, social and cultural forces are continuously interacting with these urban spaces.[5]

It is helpful to follow Dear and Wolch in recognizing three principal aspects to the sociospatial dialectic:[6]

1. Instances wherein social relations are *constituted* through space, as when site characteristics influence the arrangements for settlement.
2. Instances wherein social relations are *constrained* by space, such as the inertia imposed by an obsolete built environment, or the degree to which the physical environment facilitates or hinders human activity.
3. Instances wherein social relations are *mediated* by space, as when the general action of the 'friction of distance' facilitates the development of a wide variety of social practices, including patterns of everyday life.

Space, then, cannot be regarded simply as a medium in which social, economic and political processes are expressed. It is of importance in its own right in contributing both to the pattern of urban development and to the nature of the relationships between different social groups within the city. While not necessarily the dominant factor in shaping patterns of social interaction, spatial organization is undeniably important as a determinant of social networks, friendships and marriages. Similarly, territoriality is frequently the basis for the development of distinctive social milieux which, as well as being of interest in themselves, are important because of their capacity to mould the attitudes and shape the behaviour of their inhabitants. Distance also emerges as a significant determinant of the quality of life in different parts of the city because of variations in physical accessibility to opportunities and amenities such as jobs, shops, schools, clinics, parks and sports centres. Because the benefits conferred by proximity to these amenities contribute so much to people's welfare, locational issues also often form the focus of inter-class conflict within the city, thus giving the spatial perspective a key role in the analysis of urban politics. The partitioning of space through the establishment of *de jure* territorial boundaries also represents an important spatial attribute which has direct repercussions on several spheres of urban life. The location of local authority boundaries helps to determine their fiscal standing, for example; while the boundaries of school catchment areas have important implications for community status and welfare; and the configuration of electoral districts is crucial to the outcome of formal political contests in the city.

The geographer therefore has a considerable contribution to make to urban social studies. Moreover, the geographer is uniquely placed to provide descriptive analyses of cities. Although it is fashionable to play down the 'mapping' role of geography, the identification of spatial patterns and spatial linkages within the city provides a basic source of material both for educationalists and policy-makers. Similarly, the geographer's traditional concern with the 'distinctiveness of place' and areal differentiation is very relevant to the study of the city, for it is widely accepted that, while cities must be seen as wholes and, ultimately, as part of the wider social and economic system, they comprise a 'mosaic' of different neighbourhoods and districts. Here, the geographer's ability to synthesize a wide variety of environmental, social and economic characteristics and to identify distinctive regions is germane to both theory and practice in urban analysis. Thus, for example, the identification of urban 'problem regions' and their salient characteristics has occupied an increasing number of geographers ever since the concern for 'relevance' in geographic research emerged as a major issue within the discipline in the early 1970s. More recently, there has been a revival of interest in regionalism as an academic approach, emphasizing the locally unique factors which modify the more general forces that shape urban residential structure.

1.2 Urban Spaces: Some Preliminary Characterizations

Certainly it is the distinctiveness of particular neighbourhoods and districts and the 'sense of place' associated with them that gives the city its fascination not only to geographers but also to writers from a wide variety of disciplines. Take, for example, the variety of neighbourhoods one finds in a 'typical' medium-sized British city.[7] At one end of the spectrum is the rundown inner-city neighbourhood of old terraces where the dwellings, some of them without an inside lavatory, look out on the blackened remains of dead and dying factories. Children play games in the street amid roaming dogs and old women beating carpets, cleaning windows, or just gossiping. Similar, and yet very different, are the nearby neighbourhoods of terraced housing jammed between railway lines and now occupied by Asian or West Indian immigrants and their families. Even the shops here are immigrant-owned, apart from those run by a few diehard white corner-shopkeepers whose premises betray the poor state of their trade. The houses, having been inherited from the city's indigenous working classes, are now orientalized and caribbeanized by exotic colour schemes: bright pink and dull turquoise, ochre and cobalt blue. Further along the socio-economic spectrum and on the outer edges of the inner city are neighbourhoods of mixed tenure and varied character, where an ageing population struggles to maintain respectability in the midst of a steadily deteriorating environment. Here and there are groups of two or three newer houses, squeezed into gaps in the urban fabric and sporting imitation coach lamps, frosted-glass porches and some young rose bushes in a brave attempt to elevate their status against all the evidence of their surroundings. At about the same distance from the city centre there may be a small neighbourhood of formerly artisan houses that have been 'gentrified' by an influx of prosperous young professionals. The character of such areas is derived more from the life-style of their new inhabitants than from anything else:

> Their cars are grimly economic and ecological, as near to bicycles as four wheels and the internal combustion engine will allow – the Deux Cheveaux, the Renault 4L, the baby Fiat and the Volkswagen. Here children play with chunky allwood Abbatt toys; here girl-wives grill anaemic escalopes of veal; everyone takes the *Guardian*.[8]

For the most part though, the more prosperous neighbourhoods are suburban. At the top end of the socio-economic scale there is usually a sequestered area of soundly-built, older houses standing in their own plots amid an abundance of trees and shrubbery. With increasing distance from this core of affluence and respectability is a series of neighbourhoods of diminishing status whose individuality is to be found in subtle variations of garage space, garden size and the architectural detail of the houses – all of which are owned, or are at least in the process of being purchased, by their inhabitants. In these neighbourhoods, children definitely do not play in the streets, and the shopping centres are dotted with freezer food centres, fashion shops and boutiques selling cane chairs, paper lamp-shades, herb racks and reproduction tea caddies. Finally, and sharing the fringe of the city with most recent of the middle-class neighbourhoods, there is a series of public housing estates, graded into distinctive neighbourhoods through a combination of landscape architecture and the age structure, public comportment and social reputation of their inhabitants. Like the newer privately-built estates, they have few shops or pubs, probably no doctor's surgery, no playgrounds, and a poor bus service into town.

This picture is by no means exhaustive; a full listing would have to include student bed-sitter neighbourhoods, redeveloped inner-city areas, red light districts, and so on. It is also important to remember that although a similar variety of neighbourhoods exists in cities of other countries, their character and *raison d'être* may be quite different. Compare, for example, the description of the typical medium-sized British city given above with this description of 'Anycity USA':

> Anycity, USA is laid out on a grid street pattern. At its centre are new glass and steel corporate towers. . . . One of its main retail streets has been converted to a brick surfaced pedestrian mall. It is lined by a mixture of large department stores, older establishments catering to lower income consumers, and a scattering of new boutiques, record stores, health clubs and bookstores with racks of greeting cards. . . . Within the city centre is an imposing city hall, county headquarters, or domed State capitol building surrounded by green lawns and sporting the appropriate flags. Adjacent to downtown are several old industrial districts located near rail lines or canalized rivers. There are still a few active mills, factories and warehouses, but others are boarded up, awaiting 'adaptive reuse' or demolition. Some signs of redevelopment appear in warehouses converted to residential condominium apartments or artists' lofts. Nearby is skid row where homeless people (including an increasing number of women) drink from bottles in paper bags and varieties of 'adult' entertainment are purveyed. Not far from the city centre is an historic district of renovated Victorian homes with shady trees, olive green doors, brass fittings and wrought iron lamp standards. But most of the inner city housing is in apartment blocks and terraced or semi-detached houses in various stages of deterioration and renovation.
>
> Perhaps the most quintessentially American part of Anycity is its postwar suburbs. Sprawling in most directions for several miles are single family ranch style or split level homes on lots of an eighth of an acre. Most have garages, with the second family car (or boat or pickup truck) parked in the driveway. The grid iron street pattern is replaced by a curvilinear one in more affluent neighbourhoods. There are few fences or hedges, nor, compared to the equivalent European neighbourhoods, many flower beds. . . . Anycity's suburbs have local shopping centres with convenience stores and fast food outlets, often close by some apartment complexes. . . . The suburban fringe is also the location of large 'regional' shopping centres . . . surrounded by an ocean of parking lots. Increasingly, industrial parks, seeking cheaper land and lower taxes, locate in suburban tracts—especially those adjacent to interstate highways. The parks are both the site of manufacturing industries and of corporate office buildings. As the outer suburbs or the rural–urban fringe is reached, the lots are larger and land once farmed lies unworked, awaiting the best offer from a developer.[9]

1.3 The Macro-geographical Context

This book is concerned with cities in developed countries that have 'post-industrial' societies, particularly those of Europe and North America, where levels of urbanization are among the highest anywhere. References to cities elsewhere are included not to redress this bias but to provide contrasting or complementary examples and to place arguments within a wider setting. The principal focus of attention is upon European and North American cities, reflecting the weight and distribution of published research in urban social geography as well as the origins of much of the relevant social, economic and urban theory. Even within this relatively narrow cultural and geographical realm, however, there are important differences in the nature of the urban environment. These will be elaborated in the body of the text but it is important to guard against 'cultural myopia' from the beginning of any discussion of urban geography. It is, therefore, important to acknowledge the principal differences between European and North American cities. For one thing, European cities are generally much older, with a tangible legacy of earlier modes of economic and social organization embedded within their physical structure. Another contrast is in the composition of urban populations, for in Europe the significance of minority groups is generally much less than in North America. A third major difference stems from the way in which urban government has evolved. Whereas North American cities tend to be fragmented into a number of quite separate and independent municipalities, European cities are less so and their public services are funded to a significant level by the central government, making for a potentially more even-handed allocation of resources within the city as a whole. This is not unrelated to yet another important source of contrast – the existence of better-developed welfare states in Europe. This not only affects the size and allocation of the 'social wage' within cities but also has had profound effects on the social geography of the city through the operation of the housing market. Whereas fewer than 5 per cent of US urban families live in public housing, over 30 per cent of the families in many British cities live in dwellings rented from public authorities.

Finally, it is worth noting that in Europe, where the general ideology of privatism is less pronounced and where there has for some time been an acute awareness of the pressures of urban sprawl on prime agricultural land, the power and influence of the city planning machine is much more extensive. As a result, the morphology and social structure of European cities owe much to planning codes and philosophies. Thus, for example, the decentralization of jobs and homes and the proliferation of out-of-town hypermarkets and shopping malls has been much less pronounced in Europe than in North America, mainly because of European planners' policy of urban containment. The corollary of this, of course, is that the central business districts (CBDs) of European cities have tended to retain a greater commercial vitality than many of their North American counterparts. Finally, it should be noted that there are important *regional* and *functional* differences in the social geography of cities. The cities of the American northeast, for example, are significantly different, in some ways, from those of the 'Sunbelt', as are those of Canada and the United States.[10]

A Changing Context for Urban Social Geography

> Cities have become impossible to describe. Their centers are not as central as they used to be, their edges are ambiguous, they have no beginnings and apparently no end. Neither words, numbers, nor pictures can adequately comprehend their complex forms and social structures (Richard Ingersoll)[11]

> Just when we'd learned to see, and even love, the peculiar order beneath what earlier generations had dismissed as the chaos of the industrial city ... along came a tidal wave of look-alike corporate office parks, mansarded all-suite hotels, and stuccoed town houses to throw us for another monstrous, clover-leaf loop (Eric Sandweiss)[12]

It is now clear that cities throughout the developed world have recently entered a new phase – or, at least, begun a distinctive transitional phase – with important implications for the trajectory of urbanization and the nature of urban development.[13] This new phase has its roots in the dynamics of capitalism and, in particular, the globalization of the capitalist economy, the increasing dominance of big conglomerate corporations, and the steady shift within the world's core economies away from manufacturing industries towards service activities. Yet, as this fundamental economic transition has been gathering momentum, other shifts – in demographic composition, and in cultural and political life – have also begun to crystallize.

Economic Change and Urban Restructuring

Since the 1960s, the world's core economies have entered a substantially different phase in terms of *what* they produce, *how* they produce it, and *where* they produce it. In terms of *what* they produce, the dominant trend has been a shift away from agriculture and manufacturing industries towards service activities. There have been, however, substantial differences in the performance of different *types* of services. Contrary to the popular view of retail and consumer services as a driving force in advanced economies, they have not in fact grown very rapidly. Rather, it has been producer services, public sector services and non-profit services (mainly higher education and certain aspects of health care) that have contributed most to the expansion in service-sector employment. As we shall see in subsequent chapters, these economic shifts have been written into the social geography of contemporary cities in a variety of ways as labour markets have been restructured.

In terms of *how* production is organized, there have been two major trends. The first has been towards oligopoly as larger and more efficient corporations have driven out their competitors and sought to diversify their activities. The second has been a shift away from mass production towards flexible production systems. This trend has had much greater significance for urban social geography, since the flexibility of economic activity has imprinted itself on to the social organization and social life of cities, creating new cleavages as well as exploiting old ones.

In terms of *where* production takes place, the major trend has been a redeployment of activity at metropolitan, national and international scales – largely in response to the restructuring of the big conglomerates. As the big new conglomerates have evolved, they have rationalized their operations in a variety of ways, eliminating the duplication of activities between regions and nations, moving routine production and assembly operations to regions with lower labour costs, moving 'back office' operations to suburbs with lower rents and taxes, and consolidating head-office functions and R&D laboratories in key settings. As a result, a complex and contradictory set of processes has begun to recast many of the world's economic landscapes. One of the major outcomes in relation to urban social geography has been the *deindustrialization* of many of the cities and urban regions of the industrial heartlands in Europe and North America. Another has been the accelerated *decentralization* of both manufacturing and service employment within metropolitan regions. A third has been the transformation of a few of the largest cities into '*world cities*' specializing in the production, processing and trading of specialized information and intelligence. And a fourth has been the *recentralization* of high-order producer-service employment.

While these structural transformations were taking place, the international economic system has been restructured – the result of the conjunction of several factors (including slowed economic growth, rising inflation, increased international monetary instability, suddenly increased energy prices, increased international competition, a resurgence of political volatility and intensified problems of indebtedness among less developed nations). The response has been characterized by a new model of economic accumulation, social organization and political legitimation. Under this new scheme of things, new relationships between capital and labour are being forged, with capital recapturing the initiative over wages and regulations. New roles for the public sector have been established, reducing levels of government intervention and support while shifting the emphasis from collective consumption (the term given to various mechanisms of public-sector provision of medical, educational, sports, cultural and transport facilities) to capital accumulation and from legitimation to domination.

Quite clearly, changes this fundamental are likely to precipitate major changes in the social geography of every city, affecting everything from class structure and community organization to urban service delivery and the structure of urban politics. Meanwhile, economic restructuring and transition have already produced some important changes in the composition of urban labour markets, not least of which is a tendency towards *economic polarization.* One obvious outcome has been a decisive increase in unemployment in the cities of the world's industrial core regions. Another important outcome has been that the shift away from manufacturing has resulted in a substantial decrease in blue-collar employment and a commensurate increase in white-collar employment. White-collar employment itself has been increasingly dichotomized between professional and managerial jobs on the one hand and routine clerical jobs on the other. Within the manufacturing sector, meanwhile, advances in technology and automation have begun to polarize employment opportunities between those for engineers/technicians and those for unskilled/semi-skilled operatives. Within the service sector, retailing and consumer services have come to be dominated by part-time jobs and 'secondary' jobs (jobs in small firms or in the small shops or offices of large firms, where few skills are required, levels of pay are low and there is little opportunity for advancement.[14] Government services, on the other hand, tend to have increased the pool of 'primary' jobs (jobs with higher levels of pay and security).

One important consequence of these changes, from the point of view of urban social geography, is that a growing proportion of both working- and middle-class families find it increasingly difficult to achieve what they had come to regard as an acceptable level of living on only one income. One response to this has been the expansion of the two-paycheck household; another has been the growth and sophistication of the informal economy; which in turn has begun to create new kinds of household organization, new divisions of domestic and urban space and new forms of communal relations.[15]

Finally, it is important to bear in mind that many of the changes emanating from economic transformation are taking place simultaneously within most large cities. Thus we see, side by side, the growth of advanced corporate services and the development of sweatshops operated by undocumented workers, the emergence of newly affluent groups of manager-technocrats and the marginalization of newly disadvantaged groups. As a result, the emerging geography of larger cities is complex. It is creating distinct new social spheres, yet it has to link these spheres within the same functional unit. As Manuel Castells puts it:

> This trend is different from the old phenomenon of social inequality and spatial segregation in the big city. There is something else than the distinction between rich and poor or white and non-white. It is the formation of different systems of production and social organization, which are equally dynamic and equally new, yet profoundly different in the wealth, power and prestige that they accumulate . . . Yet these different worlds (the high tech world, the advanced services world, the auxiliary services world, the various immigrant worlds, the traditional black ghettoes, the protected middle-class suburbs, etc.) develop along

separate lines in terms of their own dynamics, while still contributing altogether to the complex picture of the new supercity. The new labor market is at the basis of this newly polarized sociospatial structure. We witness the rise of dualized supercities that segregate internally their activities, social groups and cultures while reconnecting them in terms of their structural interdependency. These metropolises are magnets on a world level, attracting people, capital, minds, information, materials and energy while keeping separate the channels of operation for all these elements in the actual fabric of the metropolis . . . We are witnessing the rise of urban schizophrenia. Or, in other words, the contradictory coexistence of different social, cultural and economic logics within the same spatial structure.[16]

The Imprint of Demographic Change

In the past 15 or so years, some important demographic changes have occurred which have already begun to be translated into the social geography of the late twentieth-century city. The storybook family in Dick-and-Jane readers (with an aproned mother baking cakes for the two children as they await father's return from a day of breadwinning) has by no means disappeared, but it is fast being outnumbered by other kinds of families. In the United States, for instance, most people live in households where there are two wage-earners. The single-parent family is the fastest-growing of all household types, and one in every four households consists of a person living alone (Table 1.1). Similar changes are occurring in most other Western societies in response to the same complex of factors.

Central to all these changes is the experience of the generation born after the Second World War (the baby boomers). The peak birth rate of this population boom occurred in the mid-1960s, creating a 'disadvantaged cohort' of population which entered the labour market at a time of economic recession (the mid-1980s) and which seems likely to experience much greater competition not only in the labour market but also in housing

Table 1.1 Household composition, United States, 1950–1990 (percentages)

	Married couples		Headed by women	Primary individuals	Other	Total
	Home-making wife	Working wife				
1950	59.4	19.6	8.4	10.8	1.8	100
1955	54.2	21.7	8.8	12.8	2.5	100
1960	51.2	23.3	8.5	14.9	2.5	100
1965	47.0	25.6	8.7	16.7	2.0	100
1970	41.6	28.9	8.8	18.8	1.9	100
1975	36.6	29.2	10.0	21.9	2.3	100
1980	30.3	30.6	10.8	26.1	2.2	100
1990	23.0	32.2	11.6	29.8	3.4	100

markets and many other spheres of life for the next 15 years at least. This has already shown up in aggregate statistics. In the United States, for example, after-tax income for families headed by a person aged 25–34 was almost 3 per cent lower, in real terms, in 1992 than it had been in 1961. This fall is actually worse than it seems at face value, since many more of the households in 1992 were two-paycheck households.

The end of the baby boom was marked in the mid-1960s as fertility levels fell significantly. In some cases this resulted in net decreases of population. This was most pronounced in West Germany, where a natural increase of over 420 000 a year in the mid-1960s had been converted to a natural decrease of 150 000 a year by 1975. The reasons for this shift are several. There appears to have been a widespread change in life-style preferences away from familism towards consumerism. Sociologists Young and Willmott wrote of the 'mid-century alliance of family and technology' and suggested that the family should now be regarded not so much as a unit of production as a unit of *consumption*.[17] The advent of reliable methods of birth control also fostered the growth of consumerism and the postponement of childbearing. Meanwhile, the demise of the 'living wage', noted above, prompted still more women to take up full-time employment and to postpone childbearing or to return to work soon after childbirth.

These trends have some important consequences for urban social geography. We seem to be witnessing a significant change in urbanism as a way of life. In addition to (i) the implications of an increasingly consumerist urban life-style, (ii) the effects of reduced birth rates on many aspects of collective consumption, and (iii) the effects of higher proportions of working women on the demand for child care facilities, there are (iv) the implications of the changes in social attitudes that have occurred. It has been established, for example, that dual-career couples in the United States are less religious than other couples, less concerned about their own relatives, more inclined to change jobs and/or move house, and less concerned about making or keeping friends.[18]

All these changes, in turn, have contributed to the *instability of household units*. Studies in the United States have shown that nuclear families now average less than seven years before experiencing a significant change in composition, while for persons living alone the figure is less than five years; and for couples without children and for single parents it is closer to four years.[19] This instability, as we shall see, has some important consequences for (v) patterns of residential mobility and sociospatial segregation. Perhaps most important change of all is (vi) the general, if gradual and incomplete, change in attitudes towards women that has accompanied consumerism, birth control and increased female participation in the labour market. Already, changing attitudes about the status of women have come to be reflected in improved educational opportunities and a wider choice of employment, both of which have fostered the development of non-traditional family structures and life-styles. In addition, once the proposition that sex need not be aimed primarily or solely at procreation had become generally accepted, further trends were set in motion. The social value of marriage decreased, with a consequent decline in the rate of marriage, an increase in divorce, and an increase in cohabitation without marriage – all conspiring to depress the fertility rate still further and to create large numbers of non-traditional households (single-parent households, in particular) with non-traditional housing needs, non-traditional residential behaviour and non-tradititional demands on urban services. Meanwhile, the effects of economic restructuring, combined with the increased number of female-headed households and the generally inferior role allocated to women in the labour market, have precipitated yet another set of changes with important implications for urban social geography: the economic marginalization of women and the 'feminization of poverty'.[20]

The City and Cultural Change
The rise of consumerism and the propagation of materialistic values has been one of the dominant cultural trends within the sociospatial dialectic. In crude terms, people have been made more materialistic as capitalism has, in its search for profits, had to turn away from the increasingly regulated realm of production towards the more easily exploited realm of consumption. Meanwhile, the relative affluence of the postwar period allowed many households to be more attentive to consumerism, and people soon came to be schooled in the sophistry of conspicuous consumption. One of the pivotal aspects of this trend, from the point of view of urban social geography, was the demand for home ownership and the consequent emphasis on the home as an expression of self and social identity.

Against the background of this overall trend towards consumerism there emerged in the 1960s a distinctive middle-class youth counterculture based on a reaction against materialism, scale and high technology. These ideas can be seen, for example, in the politicization of liberal/ecological values in relation to urban development and collective consumption,[21] and in the realm of postmodernist, neo-romantic architecture and urban design. It should be noted, however, that the spread of these values has not, for the most part, displaced materialism. Rather, they have grown up alongside. The middle classes have come to have their cake and eat it too, facilitated by the commercial development of products and services geared to liberal/ecological tastes.

Meanwhile, economic and technological change has induced a certain amount of cultural change which is likely to feed back, in turn, to social behaviour and community organization.[22] New modes of telecommunication ('telematics') and innovative forms of electronic representation have allowed the rearrangement of geography and the editing of history in ways never before conceivable. Studies of the effects of mass communications have found that a homogenized cultural mainstream is emerging, reconstructing the collective conscience. One consequence of this trend is the attenuation of the meaning of place in people's lives. 'The outer experience is cut off from the inner experience. The new attempted urban meaning is the spatial and cultural separation of people from their product and from their history. It is the space of collective alienation and of individual violence. . . . Life is transformed into abstraction, cities into shadows.'[23] The corollary of *this*, in turn, is an increased concern with conserving and developing the urban sense of place:[24] another aspect of change which is related to the liberal/ecological legacy of the 1960s counterculture.

Political Change and the Sociospatial Dialectic

The complex and intertwined trends outlined above are pregnant with problems and predicaments that inevitably figure among the dominant political issues of the 1990s. The new spatial division of labour is forging a realignment of class relations which are being drawn increasingly along geographical (as well as structural) lines, with the polarization of social well-being in large metropolitan areas creating the preconditions for incendiary urban disturbances. In addition, the unfinished restructuring of the space-economy continues to provoke a constant stream of political tensions as labour markets become more segmented, as differential processes of growth and decline work themselves out, and as shifts in the balance of economic and social power reshape the political landscape.

Especially significant in this context was the spread in the 1980s of the idea that welfare states had not only generated unreasonably high levels of taxation, budget deficits, disincentives to work and save, and a bloated class of unproductive workers, but also that they may have fostered 'soft' attitudes towards 'problem' groups in society. Ironically, the electoral appeal of this ideology can be attributed to the very success of welfare states in erasing from the minds of the electorate the immediate spectre of material deprivation. Consequently, the priority accorded to welfare expenditures receded (though the logic and, critically, the costs of maintaining them did not). The retrenchment of the public sector has already brought some important changes to the urban scene as, for example, in the privatization of housing and public services. In broader perspective, these changes can be interpreted as part of the shift in emphasis from collective consumption to capital accumulation that is in turn one of the mechanisms through which the lead economies of the world-system have attempted to steer themselves out of an episode of 'stagflation'.[25]

Meanwhile, deindustrialization and economic recession mean that sociospatial disparities have been reinforced. Even the US President's *Commission for a National Agenda for the Eighties* accepted the inevitability of a 'nearly permanent' urban 'underclass'. As this class has grown and become immiserated, the landscape of inner-city politics has inevitably changed. At the same time, there is evidence of a more general shift in urban politics as 'traditional' working-class politics, having lost much of its momentum and even more of its appeal, is being displaced by a 'new wave' of local politics (Chapter 3).

SUGGESTED
READING

An excellent guide to contemporary theoretical debates is provided by Paul Cloke, Chris Philo and David Sadler in their book *Approaching Human Geography* (1991: Guilford Press, London). Another useful review, with more of an historical perspective on the development of ideas, is *Exploring Social Geography*, by Peter Jackson and Susan Smith (1984: Allen & Unwin, London). Both of these books go well beyond the introductory remarks of this chapter and will provide a depth and breadth of coverage that carries over to many of the themes discussed in subsequent chapters of this book. The key reference on the concept of the sociospatial dialectic is the essay by Edward Soja in the *Annals of the Association of American Geographers* (**70**, 1980, 207–225). Also useful is the introductory essay, 'How territory shapes social life', by Michael Dear and Jennifer Wolch in their edited volume *The Power of Geography* (1989: Unwin Hyman, London). On the question of the distinctiveness of European cities in comparison with those of North America, see pp. 102–106 in *Cities of the World*, edited by Stanley Brunn and Jack Williams (2nd edition, 1993: HarperCollins, New York). A more extended discussion of the changing economic and sociocultural context for urban social geography can be found in my introductory essay to *The Restless Urban Landscape* (P. L. Knox, ed., 1993: Prentice-Hall, New York).

NOTES

1. Raban, J., *Soft City*. London: Fontana, 1975, p. 216.

2. Philo, C., De-limiting human geography: new social and cultural perspectives. In C. Philo, (ed.), *New Words, New Worlds: Reconceptualizing Social and Cultural Geography*. Lampeter: Social and Cultural Geography Study Group, Institute of British Geographers, 1991, pp. 14–27.

3. *Ibid.*, p. 19.

4. Soja, E., The socio-spatial dialectic, *Annals, Association of American Geographers*, **70**, 1980, 207–225.

5. Knox, P. L., *Urbanization*. Englewood Cliffs, NJ: Prentice-Hall, 1994.

6. Dear, M. and J. Wolch, How territory shapes social life. In J. Wolch and M. Dear (eds), *The Power of Geography. How Territory Shapes Social Life*. Boston: Unwin Hyman, 1989, p. 9.

7. Harrison, P., The life of cities, *New Society*, **30**, 1974, 559–604.

8. *Ibid.*, p. 88.

9. Holcomb, B., Metropolitan development. In P. Knox *et al.* (eds), *The United States: A Contemporary Human Geography*. London: Longman, 1988, pp. 194–195.

10. Goldberg, M. A. and J. Mercer, *The Myth of the North American City*. Vancouver: University of British Columbia Press, 1985.

11. Ingersoll, R., The disappearing suburb, *Design Book Review*, **26**, 1992, 5.

12. Sandweiss, E., *Design Book Review*, **26**, 1992, 38.

13. Knox, P. L. (ed.), *The Restless Urban Landscape*. Englewood Cliffs, NJ: Prentice-Hall, 1993.

14. Gordon, D. M., *The Working Poor: Toward a New State Agenda*. Washington, DC: The Council of State planning Agencies, 1979

15. Pahl, R., Employment, work, and the domestic division of labour. In M. Harloe and E. Lebas (eds), *City, Class, and Capital*. London: Arnold, 1981.

16. Castells, M. High technology, economic restructuring, and the urban–regional process in the United States. In M. Castells (ed.), *High Technology, Space, and Society*. Beverly Hills: Sage, 1985, p. 24.

17. Young, M. and P. Willmott, *The Symmetrical Family*. New York: Pantheon, 1973.

18. Spain, D. and S. Nock, Two-career couples: a portrait. *American Demographics*, **6**, 24–27.

19. Gober, P., Urban housing demography, *Progress in Human Geography*, **16**, 1992, 171–189.

20. McDowell, L., Restructuring production and reproduction: some theoretical and empirical issues relating to gender. In M. Gottdiener and C. G. Pickvance (eds), *Urban Life in Transition*. Newbury Park: Sage, 1991, pp. 77–105; R.M. Law and J. Wolch, Social reproduction in the city: restructuring time and space. In P. L. Knox (ed.), *The Restless Urban Landscape*. Englewood Cliffs, NJ: Prentice-Hall, 1993, pp.165–206.

21. Ley, D., Liberal ideology and the postindustrial city, *Annals, Association of American Geographers*, **70**, 238–258, 1980.

22. Fischer, C. S., Studying technology and social life. In M. Castells (ed.), *High Technology, Space, and Society*. Beverly Hills: Sage, 1985, pp. 284–300.

23. Castells, M., Crisis, planning, and the quality of life, *Society and Space*, **1**, 1983, 7.

24. Appleyard, D., *The Conservation of European Cities*. Cambridge, Mass.: MIT Press, 1979.

25. Castells, *High Technology*.

First-tier suburbs, South Boston. Photograph by Paul Knox.

2 *Patterns of sociospatial differentiation*

Urban Morphology and the Physical Structure of Cities • Difference and Inequality: Socio-economic and Sociocultural Patterns

Following the tradition of regionalization within the discipline as a whole, urban social geographers have sought to 'regionalize' towns and cities in attempts to produce high-level generalizations about urban form and structure. These generalizations can be thought of as capturing the outcome, at a particular point in time, of the sociospatial dialectic. They provide useful models with which to generate and test hypotheses and theories concerning urban growth processes and patterns of social interaction in cities. Moreover, many geographers regard the analysis of areal differentiation within cities as a basic task of geographical analysis (like regionalizations of countries or continents), providing an overall descriptive synthesis which is of fundamental utility in its own right. Whatever the perspective, the initial objective is to identify areas within cities which exhibit distinctive characteristics and which can be shown to be relatively homogeneous. Such areas may be termed morphological regions, neighbourhoods, neighbourhood types, residential areas, urban social areas, or urban regions, according to the type of approach and the semantic tastes of the researcher. In this chapter, we shall establish the fundamental patterns that occur in both the physical and the socio-economic dimensions of contemporary cities and describe them from a variety of perspectives.

2.1 Urban Morphology and the Physical Structure of Cities

The study of the physical qualities of the urban environment is one of the longest-established branches of urban geography, especially in Europe, where the study of 'townscapes' and 'morphological regions' has occupied a prominent place in urban studies.

House Types, Building Lots and Street Layouts

To a large extent, morphological patterns are based on two fundamental elements: the size and shape of plots of land, and the layout of streets. Both vary according to historical period, economics and sociocultural ideals. Where there is a shortage of building land, or where as many buildings as possible have to be accommodated along a given frontage (as on a water-front or around a market square), small, deep plots tend to result. Elsewhere, the size and form of the plot tend to be determined by the predominant house type (for example, the towns of England, The Nether-lands, and the north German coast were historically characterized by small, rational house types that required small plots with only a narrow (5 metre) frontage; the standard nineteenth-century tenement building of American cities required only a 9-metre frontage; whereas the standard apartment house needed 32 metres of frontage).[1]

In general, just a few major forms have come to be dominant:[2]

1. The fundamental morphological framework provided by plots of land has traditionally been *rectilinear*, because of the ease of surveying, the efficiency of use of space and the ease of laying out streets (Fig. 2.1). It follows that city blocks and street layouts have also tended to be rectili-near (Fig. 2.2). The dominance of this form eventually provoked a reaction.

2. The continuous *curvilinear* form, with wide, shallow plots that reinforce the impression of spaciousness (Fig. 2.3). The origins of this form can be traced to the Romantic suburbs of the mid- to late nineteenth-century

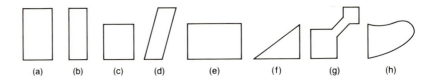

(a)   (b)   (c)   (d)   (e)   (f)   (g)   (h)

Figure 2.1
Plot forms in European cities, in order of frequency: (a) rectangular-deep, (b) narrow-deep, (c) square, (d) parallelogram-deep, (e) rectangular-wide, (f) triangular, (g) many-sided, different combinations, (h) irregular
Source: G. Curdes, Fig. 14.1, p. 282, in A. Montanari, G. Curdes and L. Forsyth (eds), *Urban Landscape Dynamics*, Avebury, Aldershot, 1993.

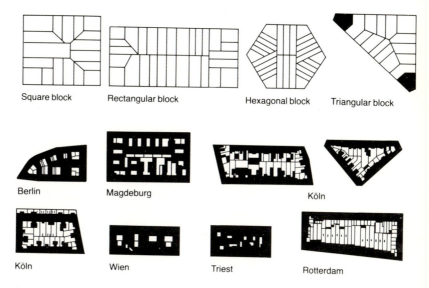

Figure 2.2
Block forms in European cities
Source: G. Curdes, Figs 14.2 and 14.3, p. 282, in A. Montanari, G. Curdes and L. Forsyth (eds),
Urban Landscape Dynamics, Avebury, Aldershot, 1993.

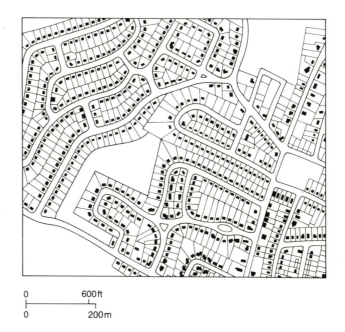

Figure 2.3
An example of the continuous curvilinear form of street network, with wide, shallow plots
Source: A. Moudon, Fig. 7.4, p. 176, in J. W. R. Whitehand and P.J. Larkham (eds),
Urban Landscapes: International Perspectives, Routledge, London, 1992.

(e.g. the Chicago suburb of Riverside, designed by F. L. Olmsted); it became widespread in the United States in the 1930s (as the newly-created Federal Housing Administration promoted its virtues) and in Europe in the 1950s (as developers of suburbia copied the American model to which consumers aspired).

3. A refinement of the curvilinear form is the *loop road with culs-de-sac* (Fig. 2.4), an attempt to retain the aesthetics of curvilinear layouts while mitigating the nuisance and dangers of automobile traffic. Such sub-divisions can be traced to the Radburn garden city model in New Jersey that was sponsored in the 1930s by the Regional Planning Association of America; since the 1970s, they have been the dominant form of suburban morphology in most developed countries. The loop road provides access to arterial through-streets, while the houses (typically

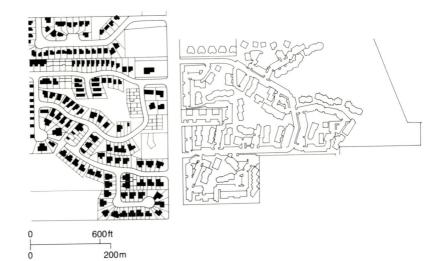

```
0              600ft
├──────────────┤
0              200m
```

Figure 2.4
An example of the loop road street network, with (left) zero lot-line plots and (right) garden apartments
Source: A. Moudon, Fig. 7.5, p. 177, in J. W. R. Whitehand and P.J. Larkham (eds),
Urban Landscapes: International Perspectives, Routledge, London, 1992.

semi-detached dwellings on zero-lot-line plots or garden apartments with no internal plot boundaries) face away from the loop, served by culs-de-sac.

Morphogenesis

Morphogenesis refers to the processes that create and reshape the physical fabric of urban form. Over time, urban morphology changes, not only as new urban fabric is added but also as existing fabric is modified. Basic forms, consisting of house, plot and street types of a given period, become hybridized as new buildings replace old, plots are amalgamated or subdivided and street layouts are modified. Arthur Smailes, writing about British cities in the postwar growth era, pointed out that the tracts of residential development surrounding downtown areas – what he called the 'integuments' of the city–were already the product of successive phases of urban growth, each of which had been subject to the influence of different social, economic and cultural forces. He also identified the fundamental processes of morphological change within the city. The growth of every town, he suggested, 'is a *twin process* of outward *extension* and internal *reorganization*. Each phase adds new fabric–outside in the form of accretions, within in the form of replacements. At any time, many of the existing structures are obsolescent and in their deterioration are subject to functional changes; they are converted for new uses'.[3] The process of outward extension typically results in the kind of annular patterns of accretion shown in Figs. 2.5 and 2.6. The process of reorganization is illustrated by Fig. 2.7, which shows the changes that occurred in part of Liverpool as institutional land users (including the University, the Roman Catholic Cathedral, and hospitals and clinics) encroached into the nineteenth-century street pattern, replacing the fine grain of residential streets with a much coarser fabric of towers and slab blocks. As Table 2.1 suggests, such reorganization involves a variety of processes of change that operate at different spatial scales, with small-scale changes to individual buildings eventually leading to morphological transformations at the level of city blocks, neighbourhoods and quarters.

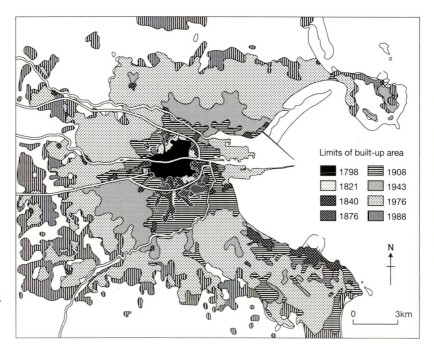

Limits of built-up area

■	1798	☰	1908
□	1821	▦	1943
▨	1840	▨	1976
▦	1876	⦀	1988

N

0   3km

Figure 2.5
Growth phases in Dublin
Source: A. MacLaran, Fig. 2.9, p. 42 in *Dublin*, Belhaven Press, London, 1993.

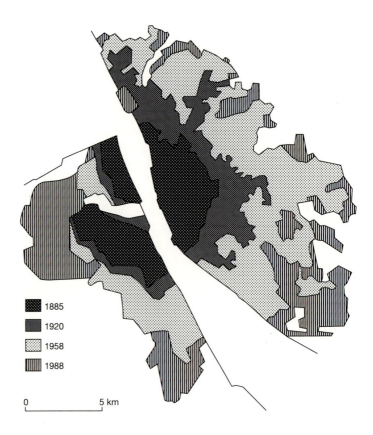

Figure 2.6
Growth phases in Liverpool
Source: B. Chandler et al., Fig. 5.2, p. 101, in A. Montanari, G. Curdes and L. Forsyth
(eds), *Urban Landscape Dynamics*, Avebury, Aldershot, 1993.

The oldest, innermost zones of the city are especially subject to internal reorganization, with the result that a distinctive morphological element is created, containing a mixture of residential, commercial and industrial functions, often within physically deteriorating structures. Small factories and workshops make an important contribution to the ambience of such areas. Some of these factories may be residual, having resisted the centrifugal tendency to move out to new sites, but a majority are 'invaders' that have colonized sites vacated by earlier industries or residents. Typically, they occupy old property that has become available in side streets off the shopping thoroughfares in the crowded but decaying residential zone surrounding the CBD.

Beyond this inner zone, Smailes suggested, industrial, commercial and residential morphological elements tend to be clearly differentiated,

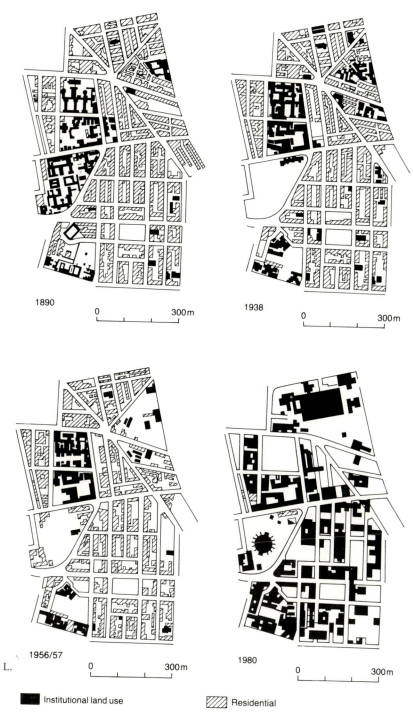

1890

0   300m

1938

0   300m

Figure 2.7
Morphological
reorganization of the
university district in
Liverpool, 1890-1980
Source: B. Chandler et al.,
Fig. 5.3, p. 112, in A.
Montanari, G. Curdes and L.
Forsyth (eds), *Urban
Landscape Dynamics*,
Avebury, Aldershot, 1993.

1956/57

0   300m

1980

0   300m

█ Institutional land use   ▨ Residential

Table 2.1 A hierarchy of morpholological transformation

1. Change of uses on sites and in buildings
2. Reorganization within the building
3. Extension into the unbuilt areas of plots and blocks, densification
4. Increase in the number of storeys
5. Linking of plots
6. Alteration of the whole or relevant part of a block
7. Changes to the size of blocks through alterations to the street network
8. Alterations to a large area consisting of a number of blocks
9. Changes to a whole quarter or part of the town

Source: G. Curdes, Table 14.1, p. 287, in A. Montanari, G. Curdes and L. Forsyth (eds), *Urban Landscape Dynamics*, Avebury, Aldershot, 1993

although typically arranged in an imperfect zonation, interrupted by radial arteries of commercial and industrial development and by major roads and railway tracks, and distorted by the peculiarities of site and situation. In addition, he pointed out that most urban development is characterized by the persistence of *enclaves of relict morphological units* (e.g. castles,

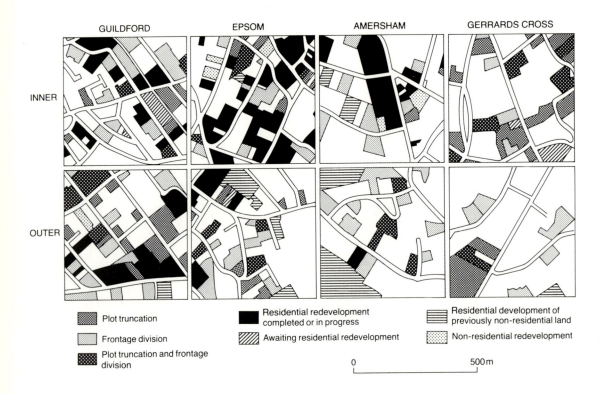

Figure 2.8
Plot subdivision and redevelopment in low-density residential areas in sample towns in south-east England, c. 1955-1986
Source: J. W. R. Whitehand, Fig. 4.4, p. 141 in *The Making of the Urban Landscape,* Blackwell, Oxford, 1992.

cathedrals, university precincts, boulevards, public parks and common lands, all of which tend to resist the logic of market forces and so survive as vestigial features amid newly developed or redeveloped neighbour-hoods). These relict units tend to impair the symmetrical pattern which may otherwise emerge. What Smailes failed to anticipate was that even in relatively new and homogeneous suburban residential areas a good deal of morphological reorganization can take place. Figure 2.8 shows the extent of morphological reorganization (between the mid-1950s and the late 1980s) in sample sites taken from both the inner and the outer reaches of suburban neighbourhoods of towns in southeast England. In this case, reorganization resulted from pressure for more intensive residential devel-opment that arose because of a combination of a reduction in the average size of households and increases in population, employment opportunities and incomes in southeast England.[4] The result, reflected in all of the sample sites shown in Fig. 2.8, is a considerable degree of plot subdivision (the truncation of corner plots, the subdivision of original parcels, or both) and

Table 2.2   Innovations in urban design

Time	Innovation	Location
1100–1500	Medieval irregular towns	Middle Europe
1200–1400	Medieval regular towns	France, south west Germany, Baltic Sea, east of Elbe
1500–1700	Renaissance town concepts	Italy, France, Germany, USA
1600–1900	Baroque town concepts	Rome, Paris
1800–1830	Classical grid/block reverting to renaissance principles	Krefeld, Prussia
1800–1880	Geometric town design	Middle Europe
1850–1900	Haussmann: axis concept, circus, triangle, boulevard, point de vue	Paris
1857	Ring concept	Vienna, Cologne
1889–1930	Sitte, Henrici, Unwin: artistic movement	Austria, Germany, UK
1898–1903	Howard, Parker and Unwin: Garden city	Letchworth
1902–1970	Garden city movement	World-wide
1900–1930	Modern blocks	Netherlands, Germany
1920–1930	Corbusier, Taut, May, Gropius: Rationalism and 'Neues Bauen'	France, Germany
1930–1945	Fascist neoclassicism	Italy, Germany
1945–1975	Flowing space and free	
1975 to date	Reurbanization: reverting to block systems	Europe
1975 to date	Postmodernism	World-wide
1985 to date	Deconstructivism	Western world

Source: G. Curdes, Table 14.2, p. 287, in A. Montanari, G. Curdes and L. Forsyth (eds), *Urban Landscape Dynamics*, Avebury, Aldershot, 1993.

redevelopment (including the residential development of previously non-residential land). Such patterns represent an important dimension of change – piecemeal infill and redevelopment – that is central to the sociospatial dialectic of the ageing suburbs of cities throughout the developed world.

The sociospatial dialectic is indeed an important aspect of morphogenesis, which must be seen as more than the sum of detailed processes of extension and reorganization. Over the broader sweep of time, morphogenesis is caught up in the continual evolution of norms and aesthetics of power, space and design. Successive innovations in urban design (Table 2.2) are not only written into the landscape in the form of extensions and reorganizations but also come to be symbolic of particular values and attitudes that can be evoked or manipulated by subsequent revivals or modifications. Within this context, innovations in transport technology are of particular importance, since they not only contribute to the evolution of the norms and aesthetics of power, space and design (as in the development of subdivisions based on culs-de-sac and loop roads in response to the intrusiveness of automobiles) but also exert a direct influence on the overall physical structure of urban areas. The overall relationship between transport and urban structure is illustrated by Fig. 2.9, where (1) the spatial structure of the region determines the distribution of activities in space, (2) these activities generate traffic flows in the transport system, (3) the response of the transport system affects the relative accessibility of specific locations, and (4) locations with high accessibility attract more develop-

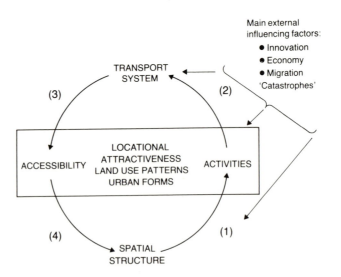

Figure 2.9
The relationship between transport systems and urban structure
Source: G. A. Giannopoulos, Fig. 12.1, p. 239, in A. Montanari, G. Curdes and L. Forsyth (eds.), *Urban Landscape Dynamics,* Avebury, Aldershot, 1993.

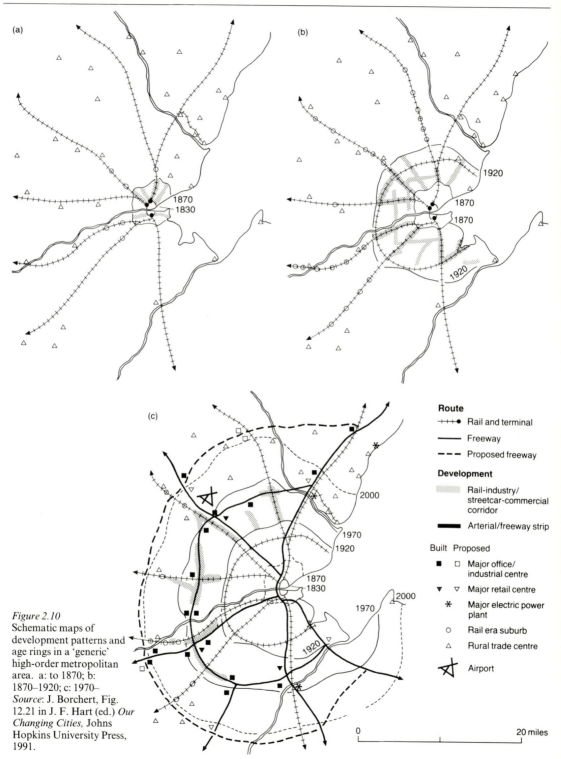

Figure 2.10
Schematic maps of development patterns and age rings in a 'generic' high-order metropolitan area. a: to 1870; b: 1870–1920; c: 1970–
Source: J. Borchert, Fig. 12.21 in J. F. Hart (ed.) *Our Changing Cities,* Johns Hopkins University Press, 1991.

Route
+++• Rail and terminal
—— Freeway
– – – Proposed freeway

Development
▓ Rail-industry/ streetcar-commercial corridor
▬ Arterial/freeway strip

Built Proposed
■ □ Major office/ industrial centre
▼ ▽ Major retail centre
✳ Major electric power plant
○ Rail era suburb
△ Rural trade centre
⋈ Airport

0 _____ 20 miles

ment than less accessible ones, thus changing the overall spatial structure. Major innovations in transport technology (the railway, the streetcar, rapid transit, automobiles, trucks and buses) have the effect of revolutionizing this relationship because they allow for radical changes in patterns of relative accessibility. The result is a pattern of physical development that is the product of successive epochs of transport technology. These have been identified in US cities (Fig. 2.10) as: (a) the pre-rail (before 1830) and 'iron horse' (1830–70) epochs; (b) the streetcar epoch (1870–1920); (c) the auto-air-cheap oil epoch (1920–70) and jet propulsion–electronic communication epoch (1970–).[5]

Environmental Quality

One specific dimension of the built environment that is worth special consideration from a social perspective is that of spatial variations in environmental quality. Implicit in the previous sections is the fact that not only are different urban sub-areas built to different levels of quality and with different aesthetics, but that at any given moment some will be physically deteriorating while others are being renovated and upgraded. Because they are closely tied in to the sociospatial dialectic through patterns and processes of investment and disinvestment (Chapter 4) and of social segregation (Chapter 6), the qualitative dimension of the built environment tends to exhibit a considerable degree of spatial cohesion. Take, for example, the patterns of physical upgrading and downgrading in Amsterdam (Fig. 2.11), where the stability of the outermost sub-areas contrasts with the renewal and upgrading of much of the inner, nineteenth-century residential districts and in most of the central neighbourhoods along the canals, where private housing predominates.[6] In this example, downgrading is very limited in extent, being restricted to four small sub-areas adjacent to older industrial works. In some cities and metropolitan areas, however, physical decay and substandard housing is a serious problem. Figure 2.12 shows the extent to which the northeastern sector of inner Paris is riven with substandard housing; while Fig. 2.13a shows the highly localized impact of urban decay in New York City, where in parts of the Bronx (Fig. 2.13b) some sub-areas lost between 50 and 80 per cent of their occupied housing units within a brief (ten-year) but devastating period.

The actual condition of streets and buildings is an aspect of the built environment that has been of increasing interest to town planners and community groups as well as to geographers. Indeed, much of the methodology appropriate to such studies has been developed by planning agencies in Europe and North America in preparing strategic plans and delimiting environmental 'action areas' of various sorts. In a majority of cases, the 'quality' of residential environments is evaluated by field survey and involves the allocation of points to buildings or groups of buildings according to the presence or absence of environmental *defects* of various sorts, and

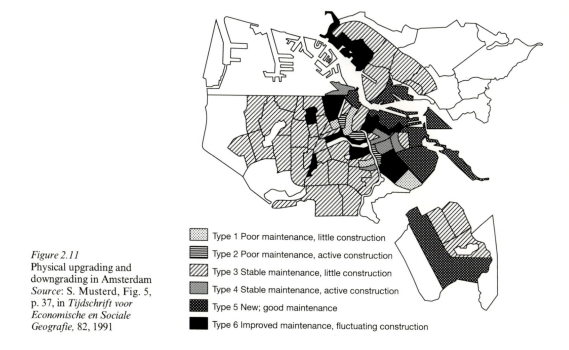

Figure 2.11
Physical upgrading and
downgrading in Amsterdam
Source: S. Musterd, Fig. 5,
p. 37, in *Tijdschrift voor
Economische en Sociale
Geografie,* 82, 1991

Type 1 Poor maintenance, little construction
Type 2 Poor maintenance, active construction
Type 3 Stable maintenance, little construction
Type 4 Stable maintenance, active construction
Type 5 New; good maintenance
Type 6 Improved maintenance, fluctuating construction

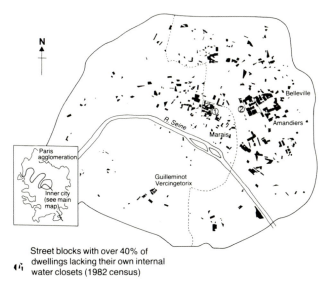

Figure 2.12
Substandard housing in
Paris: street blocks with over
40 per cent of dwellings
lacking their own WCs
Source: P. White and H.
Winchester, Fig. 1, p. 41 in
Urban Geography, 12, 1991

Street blocks with over 40% of
dwellings lacking their own internal
water closets (1982 census)

Boundary of the 'East of Paris'
in the 1983–7 plan

① Bonne Nouvelle
② Folie–Mericourt east

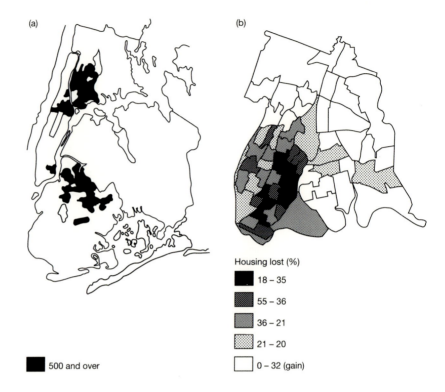

Housing lost (%)

■ 18 – 35

▨ 55 – 36

▨ 36 – 21

░ 21 – 20

□ 0 – 32 (gain)

■ 500 and over

Figure 2.13
Urban decay. (a) Census tracts in New York City that each lost 500 or more occupied
housing units between 1970 and 1980; (b) Percentage loss of occupied housing units in the
Bronx, 1970-1980
Source: R. Wallace, Fig. 4 (part), p. 1590, in *Environment & Planning A,* 21, 1989; and R.
Wallace and M. T. Fullilove, Fig.2, p. 1703, in *Environment & Planning A*, 23, 1991.

these points are subsequently summed to give an overall index score for the
location. A good example of the technique is represented in Table 2.3.

Although such schedules are employed most frequently in detailed
surveys of perhaps just a few city blocks, it is possible to employ sampling
procedures in order to cover a much larger area, either to provide a
background for more detailed investigations or simply to obtain a generalized picture of intra-urban patterns of environmental quality. Such an
approach was employed in a study of environmental quality in Sheffield,
using a schedule designed to award up to 100 penalty points according to
the relative degree of deficiency in a number of specific aspects of the
environment (including the visual quality of houses, streets and gardens,
the separation of pedestrians and traffic, access to public open space, and
the presence of 'street furniture' such as bus shelters, post boxes, street
lighting and telephone kiosks).[7] The resulting map and transects reveal a
large variation in the quality of the environment (from less than 10 to nearly
90 defect points), with a clear spatial patterning (Fig. 2.14). Environmental

Table 2.3 Extract from an environmental quality assessment schedule

	Penalty points	Maximum
Traffic:		
normal residential traffic	0	
above normal residential traffic	3	6
large amount ind. and through traffic	6	
Visual quality:		
higher standard than environment	0	
same standard as environment	1	3
lower standard than environment	3	
Access to public open space:		
park/POS within 5 min walk	0	3
no park/POS within 5 min walk	3	
Access to shops and primary schools:		
primary school and shops within 5 min walk	0	
primary school but no shops in 5 min walk	2	
shops but no primary school in 5 min walk	5	
no primary school or shops in 5 min walk	7	7
Access to public transportation to major centres:		
less than 3 min walk	0	3
more than 3 min walk	3	
Landscape quality:		
mature, good quality abundant landscape	0	
immature, insufficient amounts	2	
total or almost total lack of landscape	5	5
Air pollution:		
negligible	0	
light	3	9
heavy	9	
Privacy:		
no overlooking on either side	0	
overlooking on one side	2	5
overlooking on both sides	5	
Noise:		
normal residential standard	0	
above residential but not ind./comm. std.	2	5
ind./comm., e.g. main street standard	5	

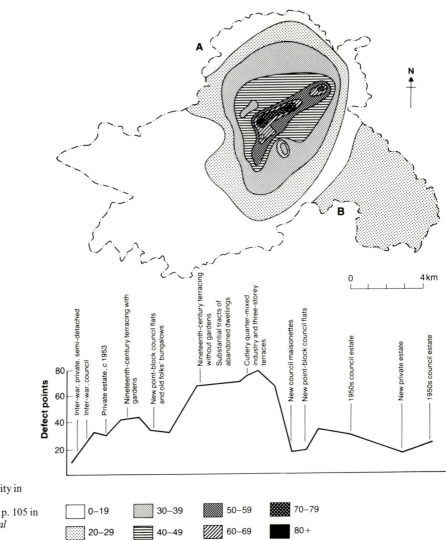

Figure 2.14
Environmental quality in
Sheffield
Source: P. L. Knox, p. 105 in
*Scottish Geographical
Magazine*, 92, 1976.

☐ 0–19	▨ 30–39	▦ 50–59	▨ 70–79
▨ 20–29	▤ 40–49	▨ 60–69	■ 80+

quality is positively associated with distance from the city centre and with owner-occupied and local authority housing; and negatively associated with the occurrence of industrial land use and the age of the built environment. In terms of its spatial configuration, the index exhibits a markedly zonal pattern, with a steady improvement from the highly defective inner areas to the high quality suburban environments: a pattern which, it is worth noting, bears only a loose resemblance to the pattern of socioeconomic status in the city. Deviations from the zonal pattern were found to be related principally to the effects of topography, local authority redevelopment schemes and industrial location. To the west of the city centre, for example, the high quality environment of the suburbs intrudes markedly inwards, following the high-status housing associated with the Hallam Ridge. Conversely, the 'islands' of better environmental quality to the southeast and northwest of the city centre are associated with recent local authority developments. The areas which show up most clearly on the map are those in the Norfolk Park and Netherthorpe districts, although it is likely that a finer mesh of sampling points (only 100 were used in the survey) would have highlighted more such areas. Finally, the greatest distortion of the concentric pattern is represented by the extensive area of low-quality environment stretching northeastwards from the cutlery quarter near the CBD, along the floor of the Don valley to Attercliffe and Carbrook. Here, the inhabitants of the terrace houses that were contemporary with and adjacent to the older cutlery factories and steelworks must live with the dereliction, noise, fumes and congestion associated with present concentrations of traffic and industry.

It is difficult to generalize about such patterns because of the paucity of empirical research. Moreover, it should be acknowledged that the available measurement techniques are far from perfect. In particular, it would be fallacious to assume that assessment techniques carry any real degree of objectivity, since the choice of the aspects of 'quality' to be measured and the weightings assigned to different degrees of quality (or defectiveness) are always dependent on the subjectivity of those who design the schedule. We therefore have to rely to a great extent on the experience and expertise of those 'who know best' (or who think they do) about measuring environmental quality, and their decisions will always be debatable. Weightings, for example, can only be justified by assuming the researcher's awareness of the consensus of values among the people whose environment is being measured. What is really needed, of course, is some comprehensive attitudinal survey of what components of environmental quality people think are important, and how important they feel they are in relation to one another. In reality, however, people's opinions will differ widely, for environmental quality is highly income-elastic. The less well-off, with more urgent needs to satisfy, may well be relatively unconcerned about many aspects of environmental quality; while the rich, having satisfied their own material needs, may be particularly sensitive to environmental factors such as the appearance of houses, streets and gardens. This problem, together with the magnitude of the task involved in evaluating community preferences, must mean that such surveys will be regarded as impracticable for all but the most intensive of studies. Perhaps the solution is simply to ask the residents of each street or neighbourhood to rate their own level of satisfaction with the quality of their environment on some numerical or semantic scale. But here we should necessarily become involved in awkward questions of definition. Thus if two people each give a score of 9 out of 10 for environmental quality, how do we know that they are both evaluating the same concept? One may be thinking more of noise and pollution while the other sees the question in terms of the visual qualities of the built environment. If we try to standardize the response by offering a comprehensive definition of what environmental quality is, we are back to the problem of subjective definitions on the part of the researcher.

Despite such problems, some researchers have attempted to analyse the determinants and patterns of environmental quality using questionnaire data. A study of a low-status public housing district in Glasgow concluded that residents' satisfaction with the quality of their neighbourhood was largely a product of their perceptions of the following:

- Traffic problems
- Street cleanliness and maintenance
- Accessibility to open space
- Antisocial activity (e.g. vandalism, roving dogs)
- Accessibility within the city as a whole
- Social interaction
- Landscaping.[8]

Meanwhile, an analysis of data from the US Annual Housing Survey has shown overall satisfaction with neighbourhood environmental quality to be inversely related to centrality and to city size, with low levels of satisfaction being a function, in particular, of the presence of rundown housing units, abandoned buildings, litter, street crime, air pollution, street noise and heavy traffic.[9] These, of course, are aggregate findings: different *types* of household, with different backgrounds and values, react in different ways to the same kind of environment. Younger, married female heads, blacks, and people with many children, for example, tend to express significantly lower levels of satisfaction in any residential context.[10]

Townscapes and the Genius Loci *of the Built Environment*

Morphological regions are not simply the sum of the attributes of building style and function, plot and street layout, and environmental quality: it is the form in which these morphological elements and attributes are set in relation to each other and to unbuilt spaces that creates the *genius loci* which lends distinctiveness to one morphological region in comparison with another. In many ways, this distinctiveness can only be captured subjectively, articulated by written descriptions rather than formal analysis.

The strength of written description in conveying the flavour and character of particular parts of the city is illustrated in these brief extracts from Jonathan Raban's *Soft City*. Of Kentish Town, in London, he writes:

> Most of the houses are survivals of the most notorious period of Victorian speculative jerry-building. They were erected in short terraces of what were accurately described by their builders as 'fourth-rate residences' . . . Their doors and windows are cheaply gabled and scalloped, and in line on the terrace they look like brick railway carriages, their decorations skimped, their narrow front strips of garden

> a long balding patch of tarry grass with motor scooters parked under flapping tarpaulines with holes in them.[11]

And of Roxbury, in Boston:

> Roxbury was the first and the sweetest of the nineteenth-century 'streetcar suburbs' of Boston . . . The churches, the houses, the tall trees on the streets, are there still. The paint is pocky, much of the wood is rotten, and slats of shingling have fallen away exposing the skeletal frames, but the basic lineaments of the old dream are clear enough even now. It takes a few minutes before you notice that the windows are mostly gone and only a few shutters are left. Each house stares blindly through eyes of cardboard and torn newspaper. Burn marks run in tongues up their sides, and on most blocks there is a gutted shell, sinking onto its knees in flapping ruin of blackened lath and tar-paper. Our own century has added rows of single-storey brick shacks, where bail-bondsmen and pawnbrokers do their business. What were once front lawns are now oily patches of bare earth. The carcasses of wrecked Buicks, Chevrolets and Fords are jacked up on bricks, their hoods open like mouths, their guts looted. No one is white.[12]

Reyner Banham is another writer who was able to capture the 'feel' of a townscape in this way. He provides an evocative description of the principal townscapes of a whole city in his exposition of the architecture of Los Angeles. Unconstrained by the jargon and conventions of urban geography, Banham divided Los Angeles into three major morphological regions, or 'architectural ecologies' (Fig. 2.15).[13]

1. *Surfurbia* – the coastal strip of Los Angeles stretching from Malibu to Balboa, and typified by the Beach Cities of Playa del Rey, El Segundo, Manhattan Beach, Redondo Beach and, further south, Huntingdon Beach. The townscape here consists of a narrow strip of four or five streets deep and draws its distinctive character from beach houses, fantasy architecture, surfboard art and beautified oil rigs.
2. *The Foothills* – stretching along the lower slopes of the Hollywood Hills and the Santa Monica Mountains between Pacific Palisades and Highland Park, with an exclave on the slopes of Palos Verdes, the morphology of the Foothills reflects the marked correlation in Los Angeles between altitude and socio-economic status. It is characterized by:

> narrow, tortuous residential roads serving precipitous house plots that often back up directly on unimproved wilderness . . . The fat life of the delectable mountains is well known around the world, wherever television re-runs old movies . . . it is the life, factual and fictional, of Hollywood's classic years . . . Where would the private eyes of the forties have been without laurel shrubberies to lurk in, sweeping front drives to turn the car in, terraces from which to observe the garden below, massive Spanish Colonial Revival doors at which to knock, . . . or rambling split-level ranch house plans in which to lose the opposition, . . . and the essential swimming pool for the bodies?

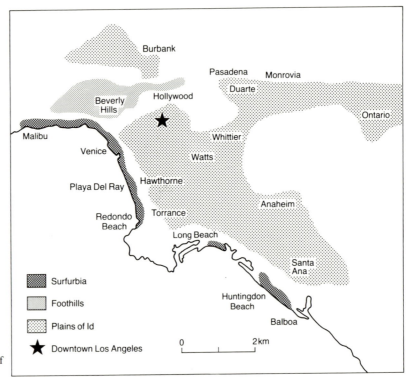

Figure 2.15
The architectural ecologies of
Los Angeles

3. *The Plains of Id* – the greater part of the Los Angeles metropolitan area,
   also familiar to television viewers and part of the popular image of the
   city:

> an endless plain endlessly gridded with endless streets, peppered
> endlessly with ticky-tacky houses clustered in indistinguishable
> neighbourhoods, slashed across by endless freeways that have destroyed
> any community spirit that may once have existed, and so on . . .
> endlessly.

Although encompassing a wide variety of socio-economic neighbourhoods, the whole area, Banham suggests, is characterized by the
'dingbat' – a two-storey walk-up apartment block built of wood and
stuccoed over, with simple rectangular forms and flush smooth surfaces
to the sides and rear but with an eclectic façade containing all kinds of
architectural styles and fantasies:

> a statement about the culture of individualism . . . the true symptom of
> Los Angeles's urban Id trying to cope with . . . residential densities too
> high to be subsumed within the illusions of homestead living.

Superimposed on these three major morphological regions is a fourth
'ecology', *Autopia*: the built environment of the freeway system which,
Banham suggested, is physically large enough and functionally important

enough to amount to 'a single comprehensible place, a coherent state of mind, a complete way of life, the fourth ecology of the Angeleno'.[14] Other distinctive morphological elements in the city include the downtown area – distinctive because of its relative lack of high density commercial development and historic 'centrality' – and various enclaves of West Coast architecture scattered around the city, from the pioneer architecture of Frank Lloyd Wright and Irving Gill to the fantasy architecture of restaurants, fast food outlets and shopping centres and residential indulgences like Venice – built complete with lagoon and canal bridges and now a counterculture haven.

While Banham was attempting to generalize from the somewhat Olympian view of an architectural critic, another author, Richard Sennett, emphasizes *diversity* and the *subjectivity* of his own responses to places. The following extracts are from his description of his regular walk from his apartment, in New York's Greenwich Village, to the restaurants in midtown on the East Side, where he likes to eat:[15]

> To reach the French restaurants I have to pass from my house through a drug preserve just to the east of Washington Square. Ten years ago junkie used to sell to junkie in the square and these blocks east to Third Avenue. In the morning stoned men lay on park benches, or in doorways; they slept immobile under the influence of the drugs, sometimes having spread newspapers out on the pavement as mattresses. . . . The dulled heroin addicts are now gone, replaced by addict-dealers in cocaine. The cocaine dealers are never still, their arms are jerky, they pace and pace; in their electric nervousness, they radiate more danger than the old stoned men. . . .
>
> Along Third Avenue, abruptly above Fourteenth Street, there appear six blocks or so of white brick apartment houses built in the 1950s and 1960s on the edges of the Grammercy Park area; the people who live here are buyers for department stores, women who began in New York as secretaries and may or may not have become something more but kept their jobs. Until very recently, seldom would one see in an American city, drinking casually in bars alone or dining quietly with one another, these women of a certain age, women who do not attempt to disguise the crowsfeet at the edge of their eyes; for generations the blocks here have been their shelter. It is a neighborhood also of single bald men, in commerce and sales, not at the top but walking confidently through to the delis and tobacco stands lining Third Avenue. All the food sold in shops here is sold in small cans and single portions; it is possible in the Korean groceries to buy half a lettuce. . . .
>
> Unfortunately, in a few minutes of walking this scene too has disappeared, and my walk now takes an unexpected turn. The middle Twenties between Third and Lexington is the equestrian center of New York, where several stores sell saddles and Western apparel. The clientele is varied: polo players from the lusher suburbs, Argentines, people who ride in Central Park, and then another group, more delicate connoisseurs of harnesses, crops, and saddles. The middle Twenties play host as well to a group of bars that cater to these leather fetishists, bars

> in run-down townhouses with no signs and blacked-out windows. . . .
> The last lap of my walk passes through Murray Hill. The townhouses here are dirty limestone or brownstone; the apartment buildings have no imposing entrance lobbies. There is a uniform of fashion in Murray Hill: elderly women in black silk dresses and equally elderly men sporting pencil-thin mustaches and malacca canes, their clothes visibly decades old. This is a quarter of the old elite in New York. . . . The center of Murray Hill is the Morgan Library, housed in the mansion at Thirtysixth and Madison of the capitalist whose vigor appalled old New York at the turn of the century. . . . Near the Morgan Library is B. Altman's, an enormous store recently closed which was regularly open in the evenings so that people could shop after work. One often saw women, of the sort who live nearby in Grammercy Park, shopping for sheets there; the sheet-shoppers had clipped the advertisement for a white sale out of the newspaper and still carried it in their unscuffed calf handbags; they were hardworking, thrifty.

What is most striking about these extracts is the importance of *people* in giving character to place. To Sennett's eye, the squares, streets, apartment houses, townhouses, bars, stores and institutions along his walk are given character and meaning by people – the 'addict-dealers', the 'single bald men' and the 'women of a certain age' – and vice versa. This is a theme that we shall explore systematically in Chapters 5 and 7.

2.2 Difference and Inequality: Socio-economic and Sociocultural Patterns

A major theme of urban social geography is the spatial patterning of difference and inequality. In detail, such patterns can present a kaleidoscope of segregation, juxtaposition and polarization:

> At one end of Canon St Road, London E1, you can pay £4 for a two-course meal. At the other end of the street, less than 500 metres away, the same amount of money will buy a single cocktail in Henry's wine bar in a postmodern shopping mall come upmarket residential development. The very urban fabric here, as in so many other cities across the globe, has altered at a feverish rate in the past decade.
> The street runs south from the heartland of the rag trade and clutter of manufacturing, retail and wholesale garment showrooms on Commercial Road. Residentially, the north end is occupied almost exclusively by the Bengali community in one of the poorest parts of any British city. Three hundred yards south, the road crosses Cable Street, a short distance away from a mural commemorating a defiant Jewish community confronting Moseley's fascist Blackshirts in 1926, the caption 'they shall not pass' now addressed to the adjacent gentrified terrace. A few hundred yards further and the microcosm is completed by Tobacco Dock, cast as the 'Covent Garden of the East End', although suffering badly in the depression of the early 1990s.

> The leitmotif of social polarization is unavoidable. Golf GTIs share the streets uneasily with untaxed Ford Cortinas. Poverty is manifest, affluence is ostentatious. Gentrification sits beside the devalorization of old property. The appeals for information in the police posters tell of yet another racist attack, just as the graffiti with which they are decorated demonstrate the credence given locally to the powers of police investigation.[16]

Seen in broader perspective, patterns of inequality and spatial differentiation exhibit a certain regularity that is often consistent from one city to another. In societies based on the competition and rewards of the marketplace, personal income is probably the single most significant indicator, implicated as it is with people's education, occupation, purchasing power (especially of housing), and with their values and attitudes towards others. It has long been recognized that the geography of income within cities is characterized not only by steep gradients and fragmented juxtapositions at the micro-level but also by clear sectors dominated by high-income households and by sinks of inner-city poverty. Consider, for example, the map of incomes in the Oklahoma City metropolitan area (Fig. 2.16), where in 1989 the median family income in the affluent northwestern suburbs was between four and six times the median family income of inner-city census tracts.

While socio-economic differentiation is arguably the most important cleavage within contemporary cities, it is by no means the only one. Demographic attributes such as age and family structure are also of central importance to social life yet are only loosely related, if at all, to differences in socio-economic status. There are, however, clear patterns to the geo-demographics of cities – in large part because of the tendency for certain household types to occupy particular niches within the urban fabric. Thus, for example, families with pre-school children are typically found in disproportionately high numbers in new, peripheral suburban subdivisions and apartment complexes, as in the case of Naples, Italy (Fig. 2.17a); the elderly, on the other hand, typically tend to be concentrated as a residual population in older, inner-city residential neighbourhoods (Fig. 2.17b).

Embedded in the sociospatial framework delineated by the major stratifications of money and demographics are the marginalized subgroups of contemporary society. The idea of marginality is of course a relative concept, and depends on some perceived norm or standard. Hilary Winchester and Paul White have suggested that these norms and standards can be economic, social and/or legal.[17] They identify four groups of the *economically marginal*:

1. The unemployed, particularly the long-term unemployed
2. The impoverished elderly
3. Students
4. Single-parent families.

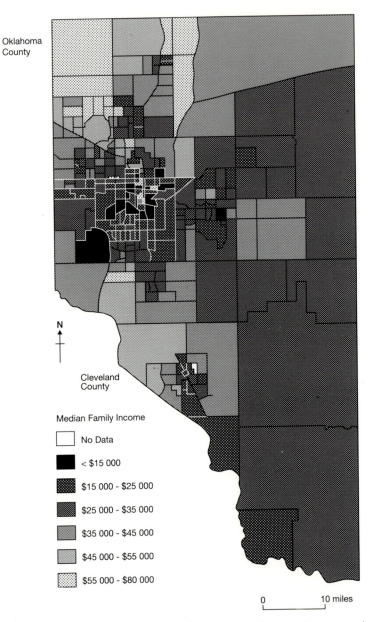

Figure 2.16
Median family income, by
census tract, in Oklahoma
City metropolitan area, 1989.

In addition, they identify another three groups that can be categorized as *both economically and socially marginal*, the two dimensions generally reinforcing one another:

5. Ethnic minorities
6. Refugees
7. The handicapped (either mentally or physically), and the chronically sick (notably including people with AIDS).

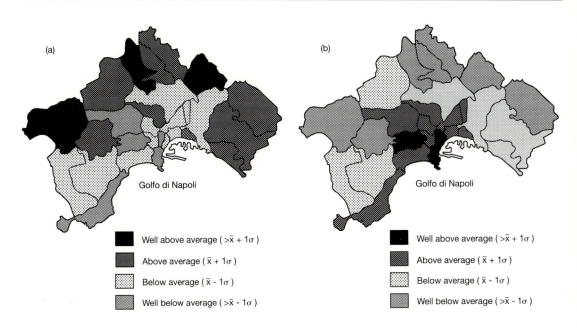

Figure 2.17
Demographic patterns in Naples. (a) proportion of total population aged 0-4 years; (b) proportion of total population aged 65 and over
Source: M. Pacione, Figs 6 and 7, p. 445, in *Transactions, Institute of British Geographers*, 12, 1987.

The remaining marginalized groups are marked by elements of *legal* as well as economic and/or social marginality:

8. Illegal immigrants
9. Down-and-outs
10. Participants in drug cultures
11. Petty criminals
12. Prostitutes
13. Homosexuals (both male and female).

Not surprisingly, these groups also tend to be marginalized spatially, both in terms of their residential locations and in terms of their activity spaces. In general, this translates into fractured, isolated and localized clusters – though with some numerically larger groups, such as the impoverished lone elderly (Fig. 2.18), the clustering tends to be somewhat less pronounced. With the possible exception of some criminals, prostitutes and homosexuals, this localization is determined by niches of the most economically and socially marginal housing: older, residual inner-city blocks, blighted and abandoned spaces, and lower-grade social (public) housing. The high degree of localization of female headed households within the inner city of Worcester, Mass., for example (Fig. 2.19), is largely a product of their concentration in inner-city public housing projects.[18] In many cases, such

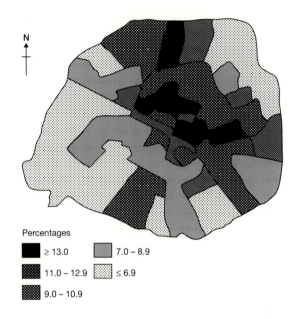

Percentages

■	≥ 13.0	▨	7.0 – 8.9
▦	11.0 – 12.9	▨	≤ 6.9
▨	9.0 – 10.9		

Figure 2.18
Impoverished elderly living alone in Paris
Source: H. Winchester and P. White, Fig. 1, p. 47, in *Environment & Planning D: Society and Space*, 6, 1988.

(a)   (b)

Percentage

■	50 – 70
▦	25 – 50
▨	20 – 25
░	15 – 20
▨	10 – 15
▨	6 – 10

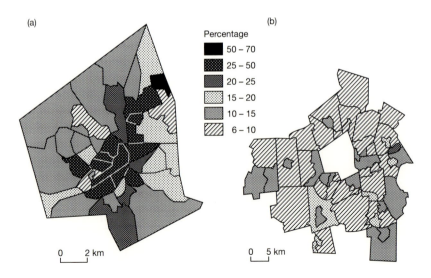

0   2 km

0   5 km

Figure 2.19
Families headed by women: (a) Worcester City, (b) Worcester Metropolitan Statistical Area
Source: G. Pratt and S. Hanson, Fig. 6, p. 31, in *Environment & Planning D: Society and Space*, 6, 1988.

clusters are in fact shared spaces for several marginal subgroups (the subgroups listed above being by no means mutually exclusive, in any case), so that specific sub-areas can take on a very definite character – bohemia, ghetto, slum, drug market – according to the mix of inhabitants. This, of course, begs the more general question of how cities are patterned according to the attributes and relative homogeneity of their neighbourhoods. It is a question that is most effectively addressed empirically through the study of factorial ecology.

Studies of Factorial Ecology

Factor analysis, together with the associated family of multivariate statistical techniques which includes principal components analysis, has become one of the most widely used techniques in social research of all kinds; and it is now generally the preferred approach for dealing with the complex question of measuring urban sociospatial differentiation. In this context, factor analysis is used primarily as an inductive device with which to analyse the relationships between a wide range of social, economic, demographic and housing characteristics, with the objective of establishing what common patterns, if any, exist in the data. The approach stems directly from attempts to validate the hypotheses implicit in Social Area Analysis, a deductive methodology for classifying census tracts that was developed on the basis of early theories of urban social differentiation.[19] Subsequently, innovations in computer technology and programming encouraged the use of a larger selection of input variables and so led to a more explicitly inductive approach. The bandwagon effect generated by the 'quantitative revolution' in geography led to factorial ecology studies of a wide range of cities, thus forming the basis for reliable high-level generalizations about urban sociospatial structure.

The Method
It is not within the scope of this book to discuss details of the methodology of factor analysis and related techniques. Essentially, they can be regarded as summarizing or synthesizing techniques which are able to identify groups of variables with similar patterns of variation. These are expressed in terms of new, hybrid variables called factors or components. Each factor accounts for measurable amounts of the variance in the input data and, like 'ordinary' variables, can be mapped or used as input data for other statistical analyses. The relationships and spatial patterns which the factors describe are known collectively as a *factorial ecology*. The usual factoring procedure produces a series of hybrid variables (factors), each statistically independent of one another and each successively accounting for a smaller proportion of the total variance in the input data. Since the objective of the technique is to identify only the major dimensions of covariance in the data, it is usual to retain only those factors which account for a greater proportion

of the total variance than could any one of the original variables. These are identifiable through the relevant *eigenvalues*, which should have a minimum value of 1.0 and whose magnitude is in direct proportion to the explanatory power of the factor to which it relates. The composition of the factors is reflected in another part of the output: the *loadings*, which are simply correlation coefficients computed between the new hybrid variables (factors) and each of the original input variables. The spatial expression of the factors is derived from the respective vectors of *scores*, computed as the sum of the products of the original (standardized) variables and the relevant loadings.

In addition to these basic outputs there are certain refinements which are frequently used. The most important of these is the *rotation* of the factor axes in an attempt to maximize their fit to patterns in the original data. The most frequently used method of rotation in factorial ecology studies is the Varimax procedure, which retains the orthogonality (i.e. the statistical independence) of the factors. It is possible, however, to relax the orthogonality constraint in order to search for separate yet related dimensions of covariance in the data. Rotation procedures of this kind are referred to as *oblique* solutions, and are regarded by many as being the most sensitive approach when factoring socio-economic data of any kind. Relatively few such solutions have been used in factorial ecology studies, however; partly because they require a series of intuitive decisions from the analyst.

An Example

The typical approach is illustrated here using the example of the city of Baltimore and employing the areal framework (census tracts) and data source (the census) most often used in factorial ecology studies. The 21 variables used in this example (Table 2.4) have also been selected to be representative of the 'typical' input of studies of North American cities, although the choice of certain variables relates to a preliminary inspection of census data. Thus the proportion of persons of Italian origin is included because such persons constitute a sizeable minority of the city's population; Mexican Americans, on the other hand, are numerically unimportant in Baltimore and so are excluded from the analysis. Using a Varimax rotation of a principal axes solution, the input variables collapse to four major dimensions which together account for 72.2 per cent of the variance in the initial data set (Table 2.5). By far the most important of these is factor I, which alone accounts for over 30 per cent of the variance. An examination of the highest loadings on this factor (Table 2.5) suggests that it is strongly and positively associated with extreme poverty and disadvantage, rented accommodation, and single-person households (but, interestingly, not with the general population of black or working-class households). It thus appears to be differentiating an 'underclass' of impoverished neighbourhoods from the rest of the city. Factor II represents a combination of variables reflecting socio-economic status: income, education, occupation and material possessions. This differentiation between high- and low-status

Table 2.4 Input variables for factorial ecology of Baltimore, 1980

1. Per cent aged 19–30
2. Per cent aged 65 or over
3. Per cent persons never married
4. Sex ratio
5. Per cent adults with a college degree
6. Per cent Italian origin
7. Per cent Spanish speaking
8. Per cent black
9. Per cent recent migrants
10. Per cent unemployed
11. Per cent managers, administrators and professionals
12. Per cent operatives
13. Median family income
14. Per cent families below poverty level
15. Per cent dwellings vacant
16. Per cent dwellings privately rented
17. Per cent dwellings with 2 or more bathrooms
18. Per cent dwellings with less than 2 bedrooms
19. Per cent dwellings without complete kitchen facilities
20. Per cent single-parent households

areas explains just over 18 per cent of the total variance. Factor III (which explains over 14 per cent of the variance) is equally distinctive, representing an ethnic/migrant dimension which identifies census tracts with high proportions of in-migrants, young people, Spanish-speaking people, and a predominance of males. Factor IV is associated with African-American households, families living in poverty (but not extreme poverty), and single-parent families, and accounts for just over 7 per cent of the total variance.

Figure 2.20 shows the spatial expression of the two leading dimensions of residential differentiation in Baltimore. While a detailed examination of the social geography of Baltimore need not detain us here, it is worth noting the principal features of these maps, particularly the solid block of census tracts in the inner city that is associated with the 'underclass' dimension and the equally cohesive group of tracts in the northern and western suburbs that is associated with the socio-economic status dimension.

The Generality of Factorial Ecologies

By far the major finding of factorial ecology studies has been that residential differentiation in the great majority of cities of the developed, industrial world is dominated by a socio-economic status dimension, with a second dimension characterized by family status/life-cycle characteristics and a third dimension relating to segregation along ethnic divisions.[20] Moreover, these dimensions appear to be consistent even in the face of variations in input variables and in the statistical solution employed; and evidence from the limited number of studies of factorial ecology *change* which have been undertaken shows that these major dimensions tend to persist over periods

Table 2.5 Baltimore City: factor structure in 1980

(A) Explanatory power of each factor

Factor	Per cent variance explained	Cumulative (%)	Eigenvalue
I	32.5	32.5	6.8
II	18.2	50.7	3.8
III	14.4	65.1	3.0
IV	7.1	72.2	1.5

(B) The nature of the factors

Factor		Loadings	
I.	'Underclass'	Rented housing	0.88
		Extreme poverty	0.79
		Vacant dwellings	0.70
		Inadequate kitchens	0.68
		Single persons	0.68
		Unemployment	0.65
II.	'Socio-economic status'	Two or more bathrooms	0.85
		Family income	0.84
		College degree	0.78
		Managers, administrators and professionals	0.75
III.	'Youth/migrants'	Migrants	0.88
		Age 19-30	0.88
		Sex ratio	0.84
		Spanish speaking	0.57
IV.	'Black poverty'	Blacks	0.82
		Italian origin	−0.68
		Single-parent families	0.55
		Poverty	0.54

of two or three decades at least.[21] There also appears to be a consistent pattern in the *spatial expression* of these dimensions, both from city to city and from one census year to the next. Salins, for example, showed how the socio-economic status dimension of four US cities – Buffalo, Indianapolis, Kansas City and Spokane – was reflected in an essentially sectoral pattern through 1940, 1950 and 1960, while the family status dimension exhibited a zonal gradient over the same period (Fig. 2.21); patterns of ethnicity were subject to greater change, although they were consistent in exhibiting a clustered pattern with a tendency to extend in a sectoral fashion.[22] Cross-

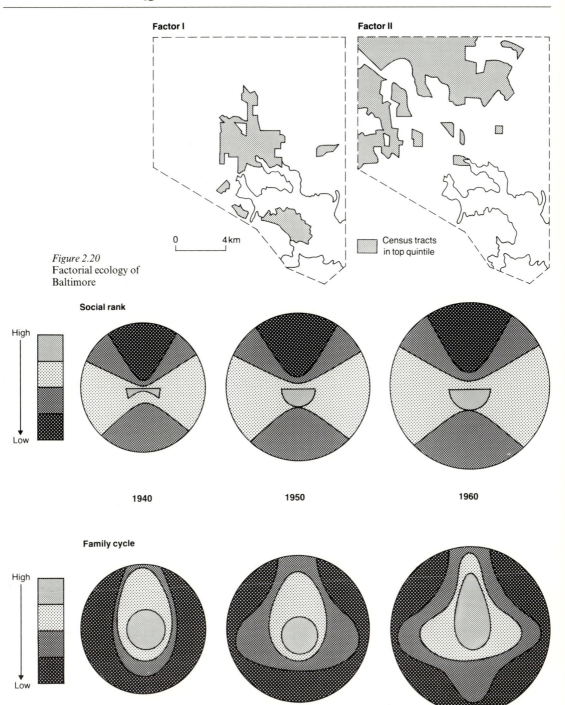

Figure 2.20
Factorial ecology of
Baltimore

Figure 2.21
Changing patterns of social rank and family status in American cities, 1940-1960
Source: P. D. Salins, pp. 243 and 245 in Economic Geography, 47, 1971.

reference with other studies confirms the generality of these findings, and the significance of sectoral and zonal configuration of the two leading dimensions has been further substantiated by analysis of variance tests conducted on the relevant sets of factor scores.

Murdie suggested that socio-economic status, family status and ethnicity should be regarded as representing major dimensions of social space which, when superimposed on the physical space of the city, serve to isolate areas of social homogeneity 'in cells defined by the spider's web of the sectoral–zonal lattice'.[23] The resultant idealized model of urban ecological structure is shown in Fig. 2.22. Yet, as Murdie acknowledged, these sectors and zones are not simply superimposed on the city's morphology: they result from detailed interactions with it. Radial transport routes, for example, are likely to govern the positioning of sectors and to distort zonal patterns. Similarly, the configuration of both sectors and zones is likely to be influenced by specific patterns of land use and by patterns of urban growth. By introducing such features to the idealized model it is possible to provide a closer approximation to the real world.

In addition to (and sometimes instead of) the three 'classic' dimensions represented in Murdie's model, it is quite common for factor–ecological

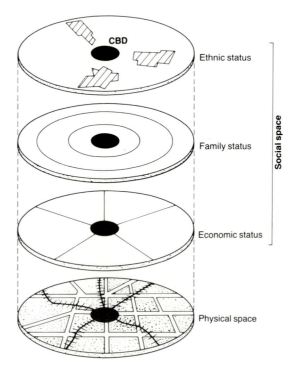

Figure 2.22
Idealized model of urban ecological structure
Source: R. A. Murdie, p. 8, in *Factorial Ecology of Metropolitan Toronto, 1951–1961*, Department of Geography, University of Chicago, 1969.

analyses to identify *other* dimensions of residential differentiation. Often, these are related to particular local conditions, but the occurrence of some of them is quite widespread. Davies recognizes six: migration status, housing substandardness/skid row, pre-family, late/established family, tenure (public housing tenure, usually associated with family life-cycle characteristics), and urban fringes – each with a characteristic spatial pattern (Fig. 2.23).[24] A thorough and comprehensive study of Canadian cities found, in addition to the three dimensions of the Murdie model, widespread occurrence of several additional axes of differentiation, including a socio-economic polarization

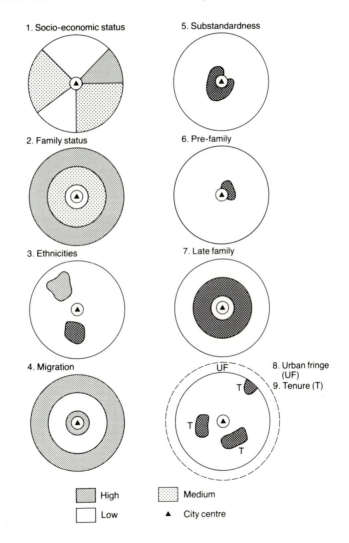

Figure 2.23
Spatial patterns associated with major dimensions of urban structure
Source: W. Davies, Fig. 9.6, p. 323, in *Factorial Ecology*, Gower, Aldershot, 1984.

('impoverishment') axis and several axes related to family structure.[25] A comparative study of 24 US metropolitan areas showed how the third dimension of the Murdie model – ethnicity – varies a great deal by region, establishing in particular that the spatial clustering of the African-American population is most pronounced where African Americans constitute the largest single minority population. In such cities, an important additional axis tends to emerge: one that is based on the ecology of single-parent families, African-American households, and poverty.[26]

It is important to emphasize that the Murdie model represents a high level of generalization and that the results of many studies are ambiguous or even contradictory. In Montreal, for example, the socio-economic status dimension is not 'pure', for it contains some 'ethnic' elements.[27] Nevertheless, many geographers have suggested that the idealized three-factor model has substantial generality throughout the Western culture area. This is certainly borne out by factorial ecologies of cities in Canada, Australia and New Zealand, but evidence from studies of European cities tends to be less conclusive. Overall, residential differentiation in continental European cities does tend to be dominated by a socio-economic status dimension (as in the example of Geneva: Fig. 2.24), though it is often associated with housing status and the localization of self-employed workers. Continental cities like Geneva also tend to conform to the 'classical' ecological model in that family status figures prominently (though often in a complex manner) in the factor structure. Ethnicity, however, does not generally occur as an independent dimension, partly because of the absence of substantial ethnic minorities, and partly because those which do exist appear to be more integrated – at census tract level – with the indigenous population. British cities, however, do not conform so closely to the general Western model. Indeed, British cities exhibit a somewhat distinctive ecological structure, with the principal dimensions of the classical model being modified by the construction and letting policies associated with the large public housing sector. Figure 2.25 shows the typical outcome.

Factorial Ecologies as a Product of Social Structure
If there is such a thing as a general model of Western city structure, then these modifications must be viewed as the product of special conditions, or of the absence or attenuation of the basic conditions necessary for the classic dimensions to emerge. But what are these necessary conditions? Janet Abu-Lughod attempted to answer this question in relation to the socio-economic status and family status dimensions. She suggested that residential differentiation in terms of socio-economic status will only occur in the following instances:

1. Where there is an effective ranking system in society as a whole which differentiates population groups according to status or prestige.

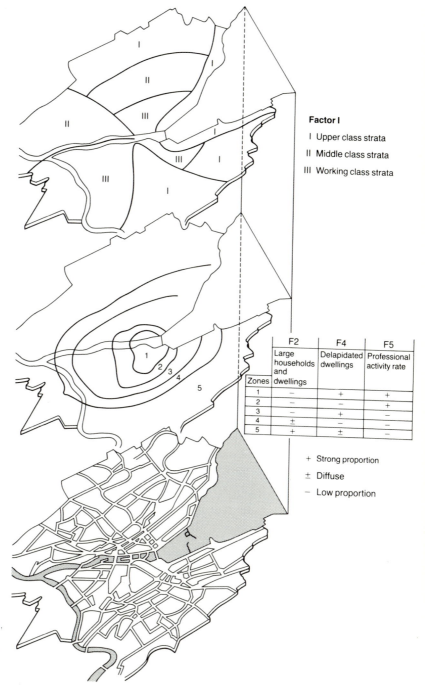

Factor I

I Upper class strata

II Middle class strata

III Working class strata

Zones	F2 Large households and dwellings	F4 Delapidated dwellings	F5 Professional activity rate
1	−	+	+
2	−	−	+
3	−	+	−
4	±	−	−
5	+	±	−

+ Strong proportion

± Diffuse

− Low proportion

Figure 2.24
The factorial ecology of
Geneva
Source: M. Bassand, Map 1.
p. 73, in *Urbanization:
Appropriation of Space and
Culture,* Graduate School,
City University of New
York, 1990.

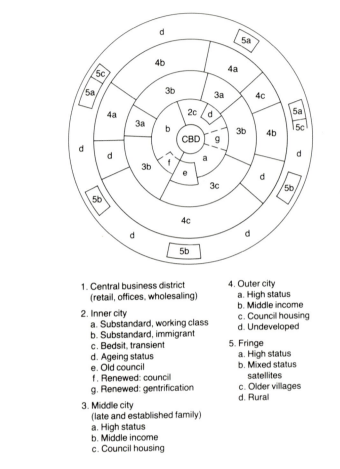

1. Central business district
   (retail, offices, wholesaling)

2. Inner city
   a. Substandard, working class
   b. Substandard, immigrant
   c. Bedsit, transient
   d. Ageing status
   e. Old council
   f. Renewed: council
   g. Renewed: gentrification

3. Middle city
   (late and established family)
   a. High status
   b. Middle income
   c. Council housing

4. Outer city
   a. High status
   b. Middle income
   c. Council housing
   d. Undeveloped

5. Fringe
   a. High status
   b. Mixed status
      satellites
   c. Older villages
   d. Rural

Figure 2.25
A model of social regions for
British cities
Source: W. Davies, Fig. 9.8,
p. 341, in *Factorial Ecology*,
Gower, Aldershot, 1984.

2. Where this ranking system is matched by corresponding subdivisions of the housing market.[28]

Similarly, she suggested that a family status dimension will occur where families at different stages of the family life cycle exhibit different residential needs *and* where the nature and spatial arrangement of the housing stock is able to fulfil these needs. Implicit in these conditions is the important assumption that the population is sufficiently mobile to match up social status and life-cycle needs to existing housing opportunities. Abu-Lughod points out that these conditions are characteristic of contemporary North American society: a pre-welfare state in which people are geographically very mobile, and where social status is ascribed principally by occupation and income.

Accepting the validity of these ideas, it is clearly possible to relate factorial ecologies to a wider view of society and to begin to build a body of theory around the generalized model of the Western city. Little attempt has been made to do this, however; researchers have been preoccupied more with the technical pros and cons of different aspects of factor analysis. Nevertheless, Abu-Lughod's work provides a useful framework against which deviations from the general model can be explained. In Montreal, for example, where the socio-economic status dimension overlaps with ethnicity, the explanation can be found in the unusually large minority population of French-speakers which occupies most of the lower part of the social ladder with the result that ethnicity and social status are not independent phenomena.[29] In Swedish cities, the existence of three separate family status dimensions can be attributed to the relative immobility of Swedes, compared to American norms.[30] In Geneva, the fact that three factors exhibit a strong concentric zonal pattern (Fig. 2.24) can be explained by the two main stages of the city's growth. The first, pre-industrial phase, established a commercial core (zone 1) surrounded by fortifications that, when demolished, formed the template for zone 2; zones 3 and 4, meanwhile, emerged as the result of early suburban growth. In the second stage, the innermost zone was reaffirmed by commercial redevelopment and the recentralization of tertiary activities, while manufacturing industry and working-class housing shifted to the periphery (zone 5). At the same time, the zonal structure of the city was consolidated by the pattern of investment in road and public transport circuits and by a series of town planning decisions concerning the legal regulation of construction in different zones of the city.[31]

The tendency for the ecology of English cities to be dominated by housing market characteristics can be seen as a reflection of the country's more highly developed public sector. The association between the family status dimension and measures of crowding found in most British studies, for example, can be related to the letting policies of local authority housing departments, many of which allocate public housing on the basis of family size, among other things, as an indicant of housing need. Similarly, the use of economic criteria of housing need in determining people's eligibility for council houses ensures that there is a close association between socio-economic status and housing tenure.

Davies provides a different framework for explaining variations in urban structure.[32] He suggests that, historically, four major dimensions of social differentiation have dominated cities everywhere – social rank, family status, ethnicity and migration status – and that these are *combined in different ways in different types of society* to produce varying urban structures (Fig. 2.26). In traditional or feudal societies, family-related considerations dominated the social structure, since prestige and status were based primarily on kinship. In the 'feudal' city, therefore, a single axis of differentiation can be expected, combining social rank and family status as well as the limited amount of ethnic and migrant variation. With economic specialization and the development of external economic linkages, division of labour intensifies, a merchant class is added to the political élite, and selective migration streams add to the social and ethnic complexity of

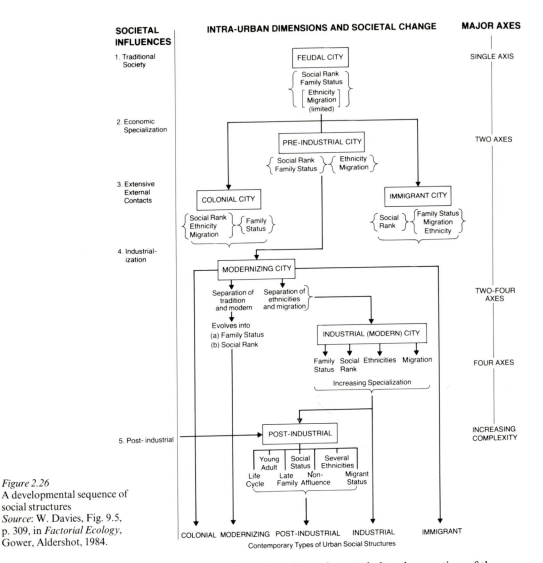

Figure 2.26
A developmental sequence of
social structures
Source: W. Davies, Fig. 9.5,
p. 309, in *Factorial Ecology*,
Gower, Aldershot, 1984.

cities. Davies postulates that these changes led to the creation of three very different types of urban structure, each composed of two dominant axes of differentiation that combined the four basic dimensions in different ways. In 'pre-industrial' cities, the perpetuation of family kinship patterns and the continued importance of the established élite combined to produce a single axis of differentiation (social rank/family status), while the arrival of migrant groups of different ethnic origins created a second major axis of differentiation. In 'colonial' cities that were located in previously-settled areas, immigrants would be politically and socially dominant, so that social rank, ethnicity and migration status would be collapsed into a single dimension. Meanwhile, family status characteristics would represent an independent dimension of differentiation. In 'immigrant' cities, the indigenous political élite remained dominant, while the age-, ethnic- and sex-selective process of in-migration tended to overwhelm residential variations in family status. As a result, social rank and migration/ ethnicity/family status emerge as the major dimensions of residential structure. The onset of industrialization brought a great increase in specialization, while income and wealth became more important as yardsticks of social prestige. As transport technologies made large-scale suburbanization possible, these changes produced a transformation in the characteristics of social prestige and in family organization, eventually leading to quite distinct patterns of differentiation in terms of social rank and family status. Similarly, processes of segregation led to the separation of various ethnic and migrant groups in different parts of cities, thus completing the 'classic' structure of the modern industrial city.

The Fragmentation of Urban Space?

Recently, it has been suggested that this classical model of urban structure is in the process of being overwritten. As we saw in Chapter 1, cities of the developed world have entered a new phase as a fundamental economic transition has gathered momentum, accompanied by demographic, cultural, political and technological changes. Advances in telecommunications have already begun to remove many of the traditional frictions of space for households as well as for economic activities, opening up the possibility of the dissolution of traditional urban spaces and the irruption of a diversity of new ones.[33] This is not to suggest that residential differentiation and segregation will disappear, but that they will be manifest *in more complex ways and at a finer level of resolution* than the sectors, zones and clusters that have been associated with socio-economic status, family status and ethnicity.

Davies, reviewing the implications of economic, technological, demographic and social change for ecological structure, concludes that 'the increasing complexity of society means that there are likely to be many more axes of differentiation, some of which are derived from the fission of the . . . constructs identified in previous societies'.[34] Among these are:

1. The emergence of *migrant* status as a potent source of differentiation.
2. The reinforcement of *ethnic* differentiation with the arrival of new immigrant groups.
3. The emergence of new dimensions of *occupational differentiation* related to the expansion of service jobs.
4. The appearance of significant distinctions in the degree of *welfare dependency*.
5. A relative increase in the importance of *poverty* and *substandard housing* as a result of the consolidation of the urban underclass.
6. The increased sociospatial differentiation of *young adults* and of the *elderly* as a result of changes in household organization.

7. The emergence of a distinctive *urban fringe* milieux.

There is already some evidence that the ecological structure of central city areas in America is becoming more finely differentiated into specialized dimensions that were formerly part of more general constructs, while suburban space is becoming homogenized around more general constructs.[35] At the same time, longstanding differences between suburban and central city areas have begun to disappear as the suburbs have become the hub of daily economic activity and sections of central cities have been renewed, upgraded or gentrified, bringing some 'suburban' socio-economic and demographic profiles to some inner-city neighbourhoods.

Some Limitations

Notwithstanding the considerable potential of factorial ecologies, several important methodological issues remain as stumbling blocks in the pursuit of a more sophisticated theory of residential differentiation. These issues have been the subject of extensive debate. Among the chief limitations is the fact that most analyses rely almost exclusively on decennial or quinquennial censuses for their data. This means that research is often constrained by a lack of data covering a full range of socio-economic characteristics, since many census authorities have been chary of demanding information on sensitive subjects such as religion and have been unwilling to expend limited resources collecting information on complex phenomena such as people's life-style or activity patterns.

This may help to explain the interesting finding that the geography of 'communities of interest' in Minneapolis–St Paul, as reflected by patterns of newspaper and magazine readership, was quite different from the factorial ecology of the city.[36] Indeed, the generality of factorial ecology results may be partly attributable to similarities in the input variables used in different studies. The territorial units for which aggregate census data are published may also have a considerable effect upon the analysis. Despite the probability that the boundaries of census sub-areas will not match actual patterns of residential variation on the ground, the implicit assumption in the methodology is that these territories are homogeneous. Research has shown, however, that not only do census sub-areas tend to be relatively heterogeneous, but that the incorporation of measures of homogeneity in the data matrix can suggest important qualifications to 'classical' factorial ecologies.[37] Another, more intractable problem arising from the boundary locations of census sub-areas is that of spatial autocorrelation, although the *extent* to which this distorts the results of factorial ecologies is a matter of debate. It should also be recognized that census sub-areas represent only one of the very large number of ways that a city can be subdivided, thus raising the question as to whether the same factorial ecology would result from different spatial frameworks; and, if not, whether the difference is a product of scale-specific processes or merely an artefact of the data set.

A further issue, and one with particularly important implications for comparative studies, concerns the degree to which factorial ecologies cover functional, as opposed to administrative, urban areas. Most research has been conducted at the level of administratively-defined *cities*. Yet it is clear that, as urbanization produces larger metropolitan areas, the scale of residential differentiation is likely to change. Much therefore depends on the researcher's definition of what constitutes the ecological 'universe'. It has been suggested that central city and suburban ecologies can be viewed as separate phenomena, with central city ecological structure becoming more differentiated over time, and suburbia developing a more general ecology that is dominated by status dimensions.[38]

Patterns of Social Well-being

As we have seen, one of the major shortcomings of traditional factorial ecology studies is that the mix of input variables overlooks many important aspects of urban life, including environmental quality, accessibility to facilities like hospitals, shopping centres, libraries and parks, and the local incidence of social pathologies such as crime, delinquency and drug addiction. The emergence of 'quality of life' and 'territorial justice' as important concerns within human geography has meant that much more attention has been given to such issues, demanding a rather different perspective on patterns of socio-economic differentiation.

Rather ironically, the initial impetus for research into social indicators came from the North American Space Administration, which sought to develop quantitative measures of the 'social spin-off' of its activities. Within a short time, however, social indicators had established a firm footing in federal administrative thinking. Official interest was first declared in a document produced by the United States Department of Health, Education and Welfare, which went on to define a social indicator as:

> a statistic of direct normative interest which facilitates concise, comprehensive and balanced judgements about the conditions of major aspects of a society. It is in all cases a direct measure of welfare and it is subject to the interpretation that, if it changes in the 'right' direction, while other things remain equal, things have gotten better, or people are 'better off'.[39]

As David Smith has shown, *territorial* social indicators provide a very useful descriptive device in the context of geographical analysis. Smith has made a case for a 'welfare approach' to human geography, with the central concern being 'who gets what, where, and how?' Following this approach, territorial social indicators are seen as fundamental to 'the major and immediate research task' of describing the geography of social well-being at different spatial scales. This, it is argued, will not only provide the context for empirical research concerned with *explaining* the mechanisms and processes which create and sustain territorial disparities in well-being but will also facilitate the *evaluation* of these disparities in the light of prevailing societal values and, if necessary, the *prescription* of remedial policies.[40] Two kinds of study are of particular interest here: those which attempt to describe variations in the overall level of local social well-being – 'quality of life' studies – and those which attempt to identify particular sub-areas whose residents are relatively disadvantaged – studies of 'deprivation'.

Intra-urban Variations in the Quality of Life

Quality of life studies are of interest here because they offer the possibility of portraying the essential sociogeographical expression of urban communities on a conceptual scale that ranges along a continuum from 'good' to 'bad', thus providing a potent index with which to regionalize the city. The construction of such an index presents a number of difficulties, however. The first task is to set out a definition of social well-being that can be translated into a composite statistical measure: something that has taxed social scientists a great deal. The range of factors which potentially influence people's well-being for better or worse is enormous. Moreover, opinions about the importance of different contributory factors often vary between sociogeographical groups; and factors that might be important at one geographic scale can be completely irrelevant at another. Smith concludes that 'we are apparently faced with the problem of trying to measure something which is not directly observable, for which there is no generally accepted *numeraire*, and which theory tells us is some function of things which ultimately rest on societal values'.[41] Any search for conclusive or universal definitions of social well-being is therefore futile. Nevertheless, as Smith himself argues, 'the imperative of empirical analysis in welfare geography means that we must be prepared to move in where the angels fear to tread'.[42]

Smith's original analysis of Tampa, Florida, provides a good case study of intra-urban variations in the quality of life. In operationalizing the concept Smith drew on measures of welfare dependency, air pollution, recreational facilities, drug offences, family stability and public participation in local affairs – a marked contrast to the conventional spectrum of variables deployed in studies of factorial ecology. Smith acknowledged that his selection of variables was 'a compromise between the ideal and what was possible given the constraints of time and resources', but maintained that 'the data assembled provide a satisfactory reflection of the general concept of social well-being and embody many important conditions which have a bearing on the quality of individual life'.[43]

An overall measure of social well-being was derived from these data using the relatively simple procedure of aggregating, for each census tract, the standardized scores on all the variables. The resultant index is mapped in Fig. 2.27. Despite the rather peculiar shape of the city, with its CBD close to the bay and its southern suburbs surrounded on three sides by water, there is a clear pattern: a sink of ill-being occupies the inner city area, with relatively poor areas extending towards the city limits in a northeasterly direction. The best areas occupy the opposite sector of the city, although most suburban neighbourhoods enjoy a quality of life which is well above the average. Similar results have emerged from other quality of life studies: they typically describe a sharply bi-polar society, in which the geography of social well-being exhibits both sectoral and zonal elements.[44] In addition, most studies have revealed a close association between race and the quality of life.

One of the major potential weaknesses of this kind of approach is the implicit assumption that the aggregation of a series of measures of different aspects of social well-being will produce a meaningful statistic. Although this procedure may be an acceptable expedient in many circumstances, it is clear that social well-being should in fact be regarded as the product of a series of contributory factors which are *weighted* according to their relative importance to the people whose well-being is under consideration. It is evident from social surveys, for example, that British and American people do not regard housing conditions as being as important to their well-being

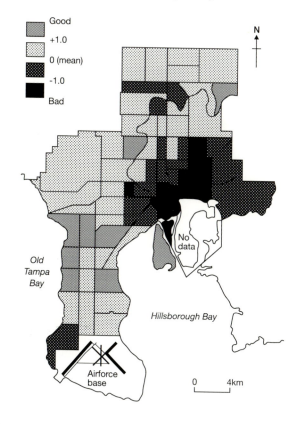

Figure 2.27
Standard scores on a general indicator of social well-being for Tampa, Florida
Source: D. M. Smith, p. 126, in *The Geography of Social Well-Being in the United States*, McGraw-Hill, New York, 1973.

as their health, whereas both factors are felt to be much more important than accessibility to recreational facilities. Moreover, these values tend to vary significantly between sociogeographical groups: in Britain, for example, intra-urban variations in attitudes to education have become part of the conventional wisdom of a whole generation of educationalists. There are plenty of reasons for such variations. To begin with, some aspects of social well-being (leisure and material consumption, for example) are highly income-elastic, so that successive increases in expendable income will bring about marked increases in the intensity with which they are valued. This conforms neatly with Maslow's suggestion that human motivation is related to a hierarchy of human needs, so that as people's basic needs – for nutrition, shelter and personal safety – are satisfied, motivation turns towards higher goals such as the attainment of social status, prestige, and self-expression.[45] Accepting this model of behaviour, it follows that people with low levels of material well-being will attach more importance to materialistic than to aesthetic, spiritual or cultural aspects of life. People's values also vary according to their stage in the family life cycle, and to their membership of particular religious or cultural groups. Moreover, the social geography of the city is itself likely to generate or reinforce differences in values from one neighbourhood to another, for the sociodemographic composition of different neighbourhoods creates distinctive local reference groups which contribute significantly to people's attitudes to life (see Chapter 5).

The crucial issue for quality of life studies is whether these variations in people's values are great enough to blunt the effectiveness of unweighted bundles of statistics such as those used by Smith. Unfortunately, few studies have pursued this question in any detail, largely because of the difficulties involved in obtaining reliable data on people's values: the cost of properly conducted surveys is simply too great for most research projects. Nevertheless, the available evidence suggests that weighting indicators of local well-being according to prevailing local values does not make a significant difference to overall patterns of the quality of life. One source of evidence for this conclusion is a study of the geography of social well-being in Dundee, Scotland. In this study, an overall index of 'level of living' was computed for each of 14 neighbourhood types using survey data on 50 variables relating to 11 'domains' of life: health, housing, employment opportunities, education, personal security, income and consumption, leisure, social and political participation, access to amenities, environmental quality, and social stability.[46]

According to this unweighted index, the owner-occupied neighbourhoods to the east and west of the city were by far the best-off, followed by more central neighbourhoods containing the most stable and sought-after of the city's older public housing estates. At the other end of the spectrum were most of the inner-city neighbourhoods, together with a few of the outlying suburbs of more recent public housing. Data on people's values collected in the same survey showed that there were statistically

significant differences between the 14 neighbourhood types in the importance attached to all but two of the domains (income/finance and leisure);
but when these data were used to weight the level of living index it was found
that 'The results of these calculations show that weighted description,
although it is arguably more sensitive to variations in well-being . . .
produces much the same picture, ecologically, as the conventional unweighted approach.'[47] Interestingly, the survey results also showed that
people tended to attach most value to the things they found themselves to
be best at, or had most of – thus helping to explain the close relationship
between the weighted and unweighted index values.

The Geography of Deprivation and Disadvantage
Patterns of deprivation represent a particularly important facet of the social
geography of the city. In this context, it is useful to regard deprivation as
multi-dimensional, directing attention to the spatial configuration and
inter-relationships of different aspects of deprivation. These patterns may
be of four different kinds:[48]

1. *Random*, with no observable covariance between different aspects of
   deprivation.
2. *Compensatory*, where the local occurrence of particular aspects of deprivation is accompanied by above-average conditions in relation to other
   aspects of life.
3. *Accumulative*, where there is a high degree of spatial overlap in the
   distribution of deprivations, resulting in areas of 'multiple deprivation'.
4. Distributions of deprivations that form distinctive constellations of
   problems, thus reflecting different *kinds* of deprived areas containing
   different combinations of deprivation.

The tendency within many cities is for the accumulative distribution of
deprivations. In the Norwegian city of Trondheim, for example, low-status
neighbourhoods tend to fare badly on most of the 19 indicators used to
measure relative levels of deprivation and prosperity (Fig. 2.28). The same
tendency for the accumulative distribution of deprivations has been evident
in other studies, and this has encouraged the development of overall
measures of deprivation: if the distribution of deprivations is accumulative,
it seems fair to aggregate indicators to produce a single index of 'multiple
deprivation'. A good example of this approach is provided by the work of
the City of Glasgow Planning Department.[49] Working at enumeration
district level, ten census indicators of deprivation – covering housing
amenities, overcrowding, vacant dwellings, child density (children as a
proportion of all persons living above ground-floor level), low-income
occupations, unemployment, handicapped/permanently sick persons,
single-parent families, and large households – were used to compute an
overall index derived from the scores on the dominant dimension of a factor
analysis of the data. Figure 2.29 shows that, in Glasgow, pockets of
deprivation are found throughout the city, not only in central areas of older,

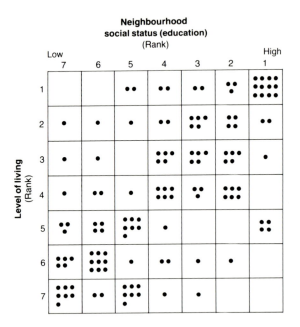

Figure 2.28
The localization of deprivation in Trondheim, Norway: rankings for 19 level-of-living
indicators among 7 areas
Source: A. Aase and B. Dale, p. 49 in 'Interregional and interurban variations in levels of
living', mimeo, 1978.

private, tenemental housing, but also–and indeed predominantly – in some
of the newer, peripheral public housing estates.

This kind of approach can be criticized on several grounds, however,
including the desirability of aggregating indicators of several different
aspects of deprivation and the validity of assigning them equal weight in
the overall index (recall the discussion of quality-of-life indicators). It is also
necessary to guard against the dangers of *ecological fallacy*: not everyone
in a deprived area is necessarily deprived; and not every deprived person in
an area of 'multiple deprivation' is necessarily multiply deprived. Consider
Fig. 2.30, for example, which shows the results of a special tabulation of
census data that allowed the overlap of 'multiple deprivation' to be identified at the level of individual households,[50] thus avoiding the dangers of
ecological fallacy. Multiple deprivation is shown to be a very widespread
phenomenon, with significant levels in nearly every part of the city (although it should be acknowledged that Glasgow is a city with an unusually
high overall level of multiple deprivation).

Aggregate measures based on small-area (rather than household) data
may also mask distinctive combinations of deprivations in one part of the
city or another. Although the examples outlined above suggest that the
general trend is for an accumulative distribution of deprivations, detailed
statistical analysis sometimes reveals significant localized constellations of

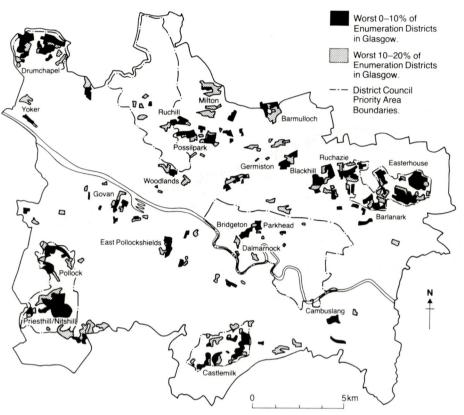

Figure 2.29
Social deprivation in Glasgow
Source: J. Rae, Map 1, p. 20, in *Social Deprivation in Glasgow*, Glasgow district Council,
1983.

particular aspects of deprivation. It has been suggested that there are in fact
three broad types of disadvantaged urban sub-areas, each with rather
different population compositions:[51]

1. Spatially marginal areas in peripheral districts, where commercially
    undesirable sites are allocated to public housing to cater for low-income
    families.
2. Socially marginal areas in inner-city districts, where the degree of physi-
    cal deterioration and a poor social reputation are sufficient to deter any
    attempt at upgrading. Such areas are typically dominated by the im-
    mobile, long-term poor of the city's unskilled working classes, with a
    high incidence of elderly persons.
3. Inner-city areas that have become 'blighted' by imminent major
    environmental and/or social change. These areas represent short-term,
    low-cost niches that become dominated by transient populations such
    as single unemployed men and immigrants.

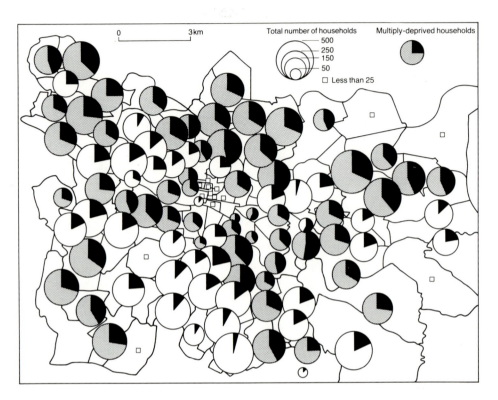

Figure 2.30
The distribution of multiply deprived households in Glasgow
Source: P. L. Knox, Fig. 19-2, p. 261, in *The Take-Off of Suburbia and the Crisis of the Central City,* Steiner, Stuttgart, 1986.

SUGGESTED
READING

A thorough and comprehensive treatment of morphologenesis and the physical structure of British cities can be found in Jeremy Whitehand's book, *The Making of the Urban Landscape* (1992: Blackwell, Oxford). The evolution of twentieth-century residential forms in America is reviewed and analysed in an essay by Anne Moudon in *Urban Landscapes: International Perspectives*, edited by Jeremy Whitehand and Peter Larkham (1992: Routledge, London), while both the physical landscapes and the social ecology of the 'postmodern urban matrix' in American cities are described in Chapter 8 (pp. 207–236) of my edited book, *The Restless Urban Landscape* (1993: Prentice-Hall, New York). *A Glossary of Urban Form*, edited by Peter Larkham and Andrew Jones (1991: Historical Geography Research Series No. 26, Urban Morphology Research Group, University of

Birmingham), is a very useful resource that contains examples and commentaries as well as dictionary-type entries. Every student will also find *The Dictionary of Human Geography* (Ron Johnston, Derek Gregory and David Smith, editors; 3rd edition, 1994: Blackwell, Oxford) an invaluable resource, not just for the material in this chapter but also for the entire subject-area of the book. A thorough review of geographical approaches to urban residential patterns is provided by Ron Johnston in his extended essay (pp. 193–236) in *Social Areas in Cities*, edited by Ron Johnston and David Herbert (1976: Wiley, London). More detailed and specific treatments of factorial ecology and patterns of residential differentiation are provided by Wayne Davies in *Factorial Ecology* (1984: Gower, Aldershot) and by Michael White in *American Neighborhoods and Residential Differentiation* (1987: Russell Sage Foundation, New York). The key reference to patterns of social well-being is David Smith's *The Geography of Social Well-Being in the United States* (1973: McGraw-Hill, New York), while the geography of deprivation and disadvantage is introduced in my review essay (pp. 32–47) in *Social Problems and the City. New Perspectives* (David Herbert and David Smith, editors; 1989: Oxford University Press, Oxford).

NOTES

1. Curdes, G., Spatial organization of towns at the level of the smallest urban unit: plots and buildings. In A. Montanari, G. Curdes and L. Forsyth (eds), *Urban Landscape Dynamics. A Multi-level Innovation Process*. Aldershot: Avebury, 1993, pp. 281–294.

2. Moudon, A. V., The evolution of twentieth-century residential forms: an American case study. In J. W. R. Whitehand and P. J. Larkham (eds), *Urban Landscapes: International Perspectives*, London: Routledge, 1992, pp. 170–206. See also M. Southworth and P. M. Owens, Studies of community, neighborhood and street form at the urban edge, *Journal of the American Planning Association*, **59**, 1993, 271–287.

3. Smailes, A., *The Geography of Towns*. London: Hutchinson, 1966, p.87; emphasis added.

4. Whitehand, J. W. R., *The Making of the Urban Landscape*. Oxford: Blackwell, 1992, p. 138.

5. Borchert, J., Futures of American cities. In J. F. Hart (ed.), *Our Changing Cities*. Baltimore: Johns Hopkins University Press, 1991, pp. 218–250.

6. Musterd, S., Neighbourhood change in Amsterdam, *Tidschrift voor Economische en Sociale Geographie*, **82**, 1991, 37.

7. Knox, P. L., Fieldwork in urban geography: assessing urban environmental quality, *Scottish Geographical Magazine*, **92**, 1976, 101–107.

8. Pacione, M., Evaluating the quality of the residential environment in a deprived council estate, *Geoforum*, **13**, 1982, 45–55.

9. Dahmann, D., Assessments of neighbourhood quality in metropolitan America, *Urban Affairs Quarterly*, **20**, 1985, 511–536.

10. Galster, G. C. and G. W. Hester, Residential satisfaction: compositional and contextual correlates, *Environment and Behavior*, **13**, 1981, 735–758.

11. Raban, J., *Soft City*. London: Fontana, 1975, p. 109.

12. *Ibid.*, p. 215.

13. Banham, R., *Los Angeles: The Architecture of Four Ecologies*. Harmondsworth: Penguin, 1973, pp. 101, 161, 175–177.

14. *Ibid.*, p. 213.

15. Sennett, R., *The Conscience of the Eye. The Design and Social Life of Cities*. New York: Knopf, 1990, pp. 123–124, 125, 130.

16. Keith, M. and M. Cross, Racism and the postmodern city. In M. Cross and M. Keith (eds), *Racism, The City and the State*. London: Routledge, 1992, p. 1.

17. Winchester, H. P. M. and P. White, The location of marginalised groups in the inner city, *Environment & Planning D: Society and Space*, **6**, 1988, 37–54.

18. Pratt, G. and S. Hanson, Gender, class, and space, *Environment & Planning D: Society and Space*, **6**, 1988, 15–35.

19. Shevky, E. and M. Williams, *The Social Areas of Los Angeles*. Los Angeles: University of Los Angeles Press, 1949; see also R. J. Johnston, Residential area characteristics: research methods for identifying urban sub-areas – social area analysis and factorial ecology. In D. Herbert and R. J. Johnston (eds), *Social Areas in Cities*. London: Wiley, 1976, pp. 193–236.

20. Rees, P, *Residential Patterns in American Cities*. Research Paper No. 189, Department of Geography, University of Chicago, 1979.

21. See, for example, R. J. Johnston, Social area change in Melbourne, 1961–1966, *Australian Geographical Studies*, **11**, 1973, 79–98.

22. Salins, P. D., Household location patterns in American metropolitan areas, *Economic Geography*, **47**, 1971, 234–248.

23. R. A. Murdie, *Factorial Ecology of Metropolitan Toronto, 1951–1961*, Research Paper No. 116, Department of Geography, University of Chicago, 1969.

24. Davies, W. K. D., *Factorial Ecology*. Gower: Aldershot, 1984.

25. Davies, W. K. and R. A. Murdie, Consistency and differential impact in urban social dimensionality: intra-urban variations in the 24 metropolitan areas of Canada, *Urban Geography*, **12**, 1991, 55–79.

26. White, M., *American Neighborhoods and Residential Differentiation*. New York: Sage Foundation, 1987.

27. Foggin, P. and M. Polese, *The Social Geography of Montreal in 1971*. Research Paper No. 88, Center for Urban and Community Studies, University of Toronto, 1977.

28. Abu-Lughod, J., Testing the theory of Social Area Analysis: the ecology of Cairo, Egypt, *American Sociological Review*, **34**, 1969, 198–12.

29. Foggin and Polese, *Social Geography*.

30. Janson, C-G., A preliminary report on Swedish urban spatial structure, *Economic Geography*, **47**, 1971, 249–257.

31. Bassand, M., *Urbanization: Appropriation of Space and Culture*. New York: Graduate School and University Center, CUNY, 1990.

32. Davies, *Factorial Ecology*.

33. Virilio, P., *Lost Dimension*. New York: Semiotext(e), 1991.

34. Davies, *Factorial Ecology*, p. 311.

35. Perle, E. D., Perspectives on the changing ecological structure of suburbia, *Urban Geography*, **2**, 1981, 237–254.

36. Palm, R., Factorial ecology and the community of outlook, *Annals, Association of American Geographers*, **63,** 1973, 341–346.

37. Newton, P. W. and R. J. Johnston, Residential area characteristics and residential area homogeneity: further thoughts on extensions to the factorial ecology method, *Environment and Planning A*, **8**, 1976, 543–552.

38. Perle, *Urban Geography*.

39. US Department of Health, Education, and Welfare, *Toward a Social Report*. Washington, DC: USGPO, 1969, p. 97.

40. Smith, D. M., *Human Geography: A Welfare Approach*. London: Edward Arnold, 1977.

41. Smith, D. M., *The Geography of Social Well-Being in the United States*. New York: McGraw-Hill, 1973, p. 46.

42. *Ibid.*, p. 47.

43. *Ibid.*, p. 125.

44. Stimpson, R. J., *The Australian City: A Welfare Geography*. Melbourne: Longman Cheshire, 1982.

45. Maslow, A. H., *Motivation and Personality*, New York: Harper & Row, 1970.

46. Knox, P. L. and A. MacLaran. Values and perceptions in descriptive approaches to urban social geography. In D. Herbert and R. J. Johnston (eds), *Geography and the Urban Environment*, Vol. 1. Chichester: Wiley, 1978, pp. 197–247.

47. *Ibid.*, p. 224.

48. The first three were identified by A. Aase in his work on levels of living in Norway.

49. Rae, J. J., *Social Deprivation in Glasgow*. Glasgow: City of Glasgow District Council, 1983.

50. According to the criterion used, a household is 'Multiply deprived' if it has two or more of the following: head of household seeking work, permanently sick, or disabled; overcrowded; low social status; single-parent family with dependent children; four or more dependent children in the household; only persons of pensionable age. See P. L. Knox, Disadvantaged households and service provisions in the inner city, pp. 253–265 in G. Heinritz and E. Lichtenberger (eds), *The Take-off of Suburbia and the Crisis of the Central City*. Stuttgart: Steiner, 1986.

51. White, P. E. and H. P. M. Winchester, The poor in the inner city: stability and change in two Parisian neighbourhoods, *Urban Geography*, **12**, 1991, 35–54.

Pro-choice rally,
Washington, D.C.
Photograph by Paul Knox.

3 Spatial and institutional frameworks: citizens, the state, and civil society

> The Interdependence of Public Institutions and Private Life • *De Jure* Urban Spaces • The Democratic Base and its Spatial Framework • Community Power Structures and the Role of the Local State • The Question of Social Justice in the City

In this chapter, we explore some fundamental components of the socio-spatial dialectic: the social, legal and political structures surrounding citizenship, democracy, and civil society. The physical and socio-economic patterns described in Chapter 2 are all outcomes of complex, interlayered processes in which social and spatial phenomena are dialectically inter-meshed – the *sociospatial dialectic* described in Chapter 1. These processes are all played out, moreover, within spatial and intitutional frameworks – electoral districts, school catchment areas, legal codes, homeowner associ-ation deeds, and so on – that are themselves both outcome and medium of social action. Individually and collectively, we act out our lives and pursue our interests both *in* and *through* these institutional and spatial frameworks. Our lives and our lifeworlds are facilitated, shaped, and constrained by these frameworks but we also, consciously and unconsciously, contribute to their shape and character.

3.1 The Interdependence of Public Institutions and Private Life

It was the emergence of capitalist democracies that forged the basis for modern urban society. The scale, rhythm and fragmentation of life required by the new logic of industrial capitalism meant that traditional societies had to be completely restructured. Local and informal practices had to be increasingly standardized and codified in order to sustain the unprecedentedly large and complex matrix of an urbanized and industrialized system. At the heart of this process was the growth and transformation of public institutions in order to be able to facilitate and regulate the new political economy. This was the era when many new nation states were established and most of the old ones were recast with modern institutions of governance, democracy and judicial process.

Yet these institutions did not simply emerge, autonomous, from the flux of change in the eighteenth and nineteenth centuries. The public sphere that came to encapsulate the realms of private life derived its *raison d'être* from the changing needs (and demands) of citizens who 'freely join[ed] together to create a public, which forms the critical functional element of the political realm'.[1] According to social theorist Jurgen Habermas, the *public sphere* and the citizens who populate it can be seen as one of four fundamental categories of social organization characteristic of modern societies. The others are *the economy, civil society* and *the state*.[2] The emergence of these categories, Habermas points out, requires the working-through of an established relationship of the public to the private spheres of life. He has suggested that in most instances this relationship has come to rest on the recognition of three sets of common rights:[3]

1. Those related to rational critical public debate (freedom of speech and opinion, freedom of the press, freedom of assembly and association, etc.).
2. Those related to individual freedoms, 'grounded in the sphere of the patriarchal conjugal family' (personal freedom, inviolability of the home, etc.).
3. Those related to the transactions of private owners of property in the sphere of civil society (equality before the law, protection of private property, etc.).

The way these rights are articulated and upheld in particular locales determines, among other things, the nature of access to economic and political power and to social and cultural legitimacy. It follows that issues of citizenship, legal codes and the roles claimed by (or given to) urban governments have a great deal to do with the unfolding of the sociospatial dialectic.

Citizenship, Patriarchy and Racism

The idea of citizenship 'refers to relationships between individuals and the community (or State) which impinges on their lives because of who they are and where they live'.[4] In contrast to the pre-modern hierarchies of rights and privileges tied to the notion of the allegiance of subjects to a monarch, citizenship implies a rationality that is accompanied by mutual obligations. The citizenship that emerged with the onset of modernity was tied to the territorial boundaries of new and reconstituted nation states rather than to the divine authority of nobility. It was the construct through which political and civil rights were embedded in national constitutions. Later, there developed in most of the economically more-developed countries an ideal of citizenship that embraced social as well as political and civil rights – the right to a minimum level of personal security and of economic welfare, for example.

The process of constructing this modern idea of citizenship inevitably provoked a running debate over who is and who is not a citizen, especially in countries like Australia and the United States which drew demographic and economic strength on the basis of immigration. The result was that the social construction of citizenship has been mediated through deep-seated prejudices and entrenched cultural practices. Sexism and racism, in short, found their way into conceptions of citizenship and from there into the relationship between the public sphere and private life and to the very heart of the sociospatial dialectic through which contemporary cities have been forged.

In the first instance, of course, citizenship was available only to white, property-owning males. Women and minority populations 'in essence retained their subject status'.[5] The exclusion of women can be traced, in large measure, to the paternalism of Western culture: in particular, to naturalistic assumptions about the social roles of men and women. The basic assumptions are (i) that the dominance of husband over wife is a 'law of nature', and (ii) that men by nature are more suited to the aggressive pursuits of economic and public life while women by nature are more suited to the nurturing activities of the domestic sphere. In addition, the social philosophers of the transition to modernity cultivated the assumption that women are by nature sentimental rather than rational, and so incapable of developing the proper sense of justice required for participation in civil society. The idea of 'Public Man' (whose corollary was 'Private Woman') persisted even after the franchise was extended to women and indeed still persists, well after the 'women's liberation' of the 1960s. Even in Australia, a comparatively progressive country in terms of incorporating women's issues into mainstream policymaking, gender inequalities persist in the form of 'discriminatory controls on the availability of social citizenship rights which determine how women are defined in Australian social policy. . . . State policies, from social security and income tax to industrial and family law, construct women as wives, mothers and carers, regulating their social role and reinforcing women's dependency on men'.[6]

The exclusion of minority populations has in general been more explicit, not least in antebellum America, where black slavery represented the very antithesis of citizenship. The inherent racism of 'mainstream' society overtly circumscribed the participation of Native American, Chinese and black populations in the full rights of citizenship all through the 'melting-pot' of American urbanization in the late nineteenth and early twentieth centuries, until the Civil Rights legislation of the late 1960s. In Europe, racism was focused on Jews and gypsies until after the Second World War, when immigration brought large numbers of Asians and Africans to the cities of Britain, France and Germany. In addition to the overt and formal limits imposed on these immigrants in terms of the civil and political rights of citizenship, systematic discrimination has circumscribed their social rights of citizenship, so that, for example:

> ... despite the theoretical eligibility of black Britons for welfare benefits, and despite their disproportionate contribution to the welfare state (through labour and taxation), their ability to secure State-subsidized services and resources may actually be deteriorating relative to that of whites.[7]

We shall see in Chapter 5 how these consequences of racism come into play in the social production of space and the maintenance of sociospatial segregation.

The Law and Civil Society

The law stands as an important link between the public and private spheres, and between the State and the economy. As a key component of the sociospatial dialectic, the law must be seen as both a product of social forces and spatial settings and as an agent of sociospatial production and reproduction. There are several specific elements to the law in this context. It is *formulated* (usually in quite abstract and general ways) by elected legislatures that in turn draw on citizens' conceptions of justice, equity, etc. It is subsequently *applied* in specific places and circumstances by a variety of agencies (such as the police, social workers, housing authorities, etc.) to whom responsibility is delegated by the national state. Where problems and disputes emerge as to the specific meaning of law, it is *interpreted* through other mechanisms of civil society, principally the courts.[8]

It is now acknowledged that all of these elements are deeply geographic in that they involve the interpenetration of place and power.[9] Indeed, recent research on law and geography has been explicitly framed within the concept of the sociospatial dialectic through which the spatiality of social life is reproduced, reinforced or transformed.[10] Among the best-documented examples of the interpenetration of law, civil society and urban geography are the decisions of the US Supreme Court in cases involving voting rights, school desegregation, open housing and land use zoning. To take just a few examples, these include decisions on *Brown* v. *Board of Education* (1954), which declared school segregation unconstitutional; *Shelley* v. *Kraemer* (1948), which ruled that racially restricted covenants on property sales are illegal; *Euclid* v. *Ambler* (1926), which established the right of municipalities to zone land use in order to protect the public interest; and *NAACP* v. *Mt Laurel* (1972), which struck down an exclusionary zoning ordinance.[11]

Through such cases, particular social values and moral judgements are mapped on to the urban landscape while others are deflected or eradicated. This, of course, is by no means straightforward. Apart from anything else, the formulation, application and interpretation of law take place not only at the national scale but also at the level of the municipality (or 'local state'), making for a complex and sometimes contradictory framework of legal spaces that are superimposed on, and interpenetrated with, the social spaces of the city. At the same time, the continual evolution and reorganization of society introduces elements of change that cumulatively modify the tenor of civil society itself, alter the relationships between central and local states, and raise new challenges for law and urban governance. Legal practice and discourse, observes Nicholas Blomley,

> . . . contain multiple representations of the spaces of social and political life. . . . Spatial representations play a vital role in legal reasoning: legal categories – property, the public and the private, the individual, the municipal corporation – are all spatially conceived and defined. The spaces of local discretion and autonomy, for example, are frequently cast as problematic within formal legal practice by virtue of their contextuality and 'communality'. Indeed, in much the way that geography as a discipline is unsure how to map theoretically the sociospatial world, so legal actors struggle and quarrel over the spatiality of the law. The city, for example, can be cast as a dangerously collectivized agency that, by virtue of its semi-autonomous location within the interstices of the state, poses a threat to individual liberty, or it can be hailed as the epitome of democratic participation and political life.[12]

The Changing Nature of Urban Governance

As the economic base of cities has shifted, the fortunes of different groups have changed, cities themselves have thrown up new problems and challenges, and urban government has attracted different types of people with different motivations and objectives. The ethos and orientations of urban government, reflecting these changes, has in turn provided the catalyst for further changes in the nature and direction of urban development. Today, the scope of urban governance has broadened to the point where it now includes the regulation and provision of all kinds of goods and services, from roads, storm drainage channels, street lighting, water supplies and sewage systems to law enforcement, fire prevention, schools, clinics, transport systems and housing. All these activities have a direct and often fundamental effect on the social geography as well as on the physical morphology of cities, as we shall see in Chapter 10. Moreover, the economic and legislative power of modern local authorities makes them a potent factor in moulding and recasting the urban environment. In general terms, it is useful to distinguish five principal phases in the evolution of urban governance.

1. The earliest phase, dating to the first half of the nineteenth century, was a phase of virtual non-government, based on the doctrine of utilitarianism. This *laissez-faire* philosophy rested on the assumption that the maximum public benefit will arise from unfettered market forces. In practice, an oligarchy of merchants and patricians presided over urban affairs but did little to modify the organic growth of cities.

2. The second phase, dating between 1850 and 1910, saw the introduction of 'municipal socialism' by social leaders in response to the epidemics, urban disorder and congestion of the Victorian city. The law and urban governance in this period was based on a strong ethos of public service and paternalism, and the result was a wide range of liberal reforms. At the same time, the increasing power and responsibility of political office-holders facilitated the widespread development of corruption in urban affairs.

3. Between 1910 and 1940 there occurred a critical event – the Depression – that finally swung public opinion in favour of a permanent and more fundamental municipal role in shaping many aspects of social life and well-being. Cities everywhere expanded their activities in health, welfare, housing, education, security and leisure. At the same time, the composition and character of city councils shifted once more. In Britain, the 75 per cent de-rating of industry by the Local Government Act (1929) and the central government's policy of industrial protection in the 1930s combined to remove from many businessmen the incentive to participate in local affairs.[13] In contrast, members of the working and lower-middle classes found a new rationale for being on the council: to speak for the city's growing number of salaried officials and blue-collar employees. These developments led to the replacement of paternalistic businessmen and social leaders by 'public persons' drawn from a wider social spectrum. In addition, representatives of the working class were installed on city councils through the agency of the Labour party, and *party politics* soon became an important new facet of urban governance.

4. Between 1940 and 1975, the many roles of urban government generated large, vertically segregated bureaucracies of professional administrators geared to managing the city and its environment. The professional and the party politician came to rule as a duumvirate, the balance of power between the two being variable from function to function and from city to city. By this time, however, a deep paradox had clearly emerged to confront all those concerned with urban affairs. The paradox was this. *Although urbanization was the vehicle that capitalism needed in order to marshal goods and labour efficiently, it created dangerous conditions under which the losers and the exploited could organize themselves and consolidate.* Urban governance and management, facing this paradox, became

hybrid creatures, dedicated on the one hand to humanistic and democratic reform, but charged on the other with the management of cities according to a particular kind of economic and social organization. Inevitably, the demands of this task led to an escalation in the number of professional personnel employed to assist councillors in their decision-making. At the same time, however, the effective power of councillors to formulate policy initiatives decreased. As the technical complexities of municipal finance, public health, educational administration and city planning increased, councillors became more and more dependent on the expertise of professional personnel and their staff. Consequently, most cities have become permanently dependent on large bureaucracies staffed by specialist professionals.

5. In the most recent phase, from the mid-1970s, radical economic transformation at the national and international scale has set in motion a pronounced bout of metropolitan restructuring that has been accompanied, in most large cities, by chronic problems of physical deterioration and fiscal stress. Faced with the rapid decentralization of jobs and residents, and with an increasingly externalized and distant control of their economies, local governments lost a good deal of power and autonomy to central governments. In their weakened and somewhat desperate position, they began to 'privatize' many of the functions and responsibilities that they had acquired in previous phases. In the vacuum left by the retreat of the local state, voluntarism became a principal means of providing for the needs of the indigent, while in more affluent communities various forms of 'stealthy', 'private' governments, such as homeowner associations, have proliferated. Meanwhile, local governments themselves turned increasingly to the private sector for capital for economic and social investment through public–private partnerships of various kinds, and gave much greater priority to economic development than to the traditional service-providing and regulating functions of the local state. This 'civic entrepreneurialism'[14] has fostered a speculative and piecemeal approach to the management of cities, with a good deal of emphasis on set-piece projects such as downtown shopping centres, festival market places, conference and exhibition centres and the like, which are seen as having the greatest capacity to enhance property values (and so revivify the local tax base) and generate retail turnover and employment growth. Meanwhile, economic restructuring and the decentralization of manufacturing changed the complexion of urban politics, undermining the former strength of working-class constituencies. At the same time, the growth and recentralization of producer-service jobs has created (in some cities, at least) a new bourgeoisie with a distinctively materialistic sort of liberal ideology that has come into play in urban politics and policymaking.[15]

3.2 De Jure Urban Spaces

The geopolitical organization of metropolitan areas is an important element in the sociospatial dialectic. The *de jure* territories in which urban governments operate can be seen as both outcome and continuing framework for the sociospatial dialectic. In this section we examine the evolution of *de jure* spaces at the intra-metropolitan level and discuss some of the major implications of the way in which urban space has been partitioned for political and administrative purposes.

Metropolitan Fragmentation and its Spatial Consequences

Modern metropolitan areas are characterized by a complex partitioning of space into multi-purpose local government jurisdictions and a wide variety of special administrative districts responsible for single functions such as the provision of schools, hospitals, water and sewage facilities. This complexity is greatest in Australia and North America, where the ethic of local autonomy is stronger, and it reaches a peak in the United States, where the largest metropolitan areas each have hundreds of separate jurisdictions.[16] While never reaching these levels of complexity, the same phenomenon can be found in Europe. In Britain, for example, the Birmingham, Manchester, Merseyside and Tyneside conurbations were all under the control of at least four major multi-purpose local authorities until the whole system of local government was reorganized in the mid-1970s; the government of London is still fragmented between 32 boroughs; and in every city there are special district authorities which are responsible for the provision of health services and water supplies.

Much of this complexity can be seen as the response of political and administrative systems to the changing economic and social structure of the metropolis. In short, the decentralization of jobs and residences from the urban core has brought about a corresponding decentralization and proliferation of local jurisdictions. New local governments have been created to service the populations of new suburban and exurban dormitory communities, resulting in the 'balkanization' of metropolitan areas into competing jurisdictions. In the United States, this process has been accelerated by policies which, guided by the principle of local autonomy, made the annexation of territory by existing cities more difficult while keeping incorporation procedures very easy.

New single-function special districts, on the other hand, have proliferated throughout metropolitan areas, largely in response to the failure of existing political and administrative systems to cope with the changing needs and demands of the population. Between 1942 and 1972, the number of non-school special districts in the United States increased from 6299 to 23 885. By 1992, Cook County, Illinois, contained 516 separate jurisdictions, one for every 10 000 residents. Special districts are an attractive solution to a wide range of problems because they are able to avoid the statutory limitations on financial and legal powers that apply to local governments. In particular, a community can increase its debt or tax revenue by creating an additional layer of government for a specific purpose. Special districts also have the advantage of corresponding more closely to functional areas and, therefore, of being more finely tuned to local social organization and participation. Another reason for their proliferation has been the influence of special interest groups, including citizen groups concerned with a particular function or issue and business enterprises which stand to benefit economically from the creation of a special district.

Yet, although spatial fragmentation can be defended on the grounds of fostering the sensitivity of politicians and administrators to local preferences, it can also be shown to have spawned administrative complexity, political disorganization, and an inefficient distribution of public goods and services. Not least of these problems is the sheer confusion resulting from the functional and spatial overlapping of different jurisdictions. Decentralized decision-making leads to the growth of costly bureaucracies, the duplication of services and the pursuit of conflicting policies. Of course, not all public services require metropolitan-wide organization: some urban problems are of a purely local nature. But for many services – such as water supply, planning, transport, health care, housing and welfare – economies of scale make large areal units with large populations a more efficient and equitable base.

The balkanization of general-purpose government in the United States has also led to the suppression of political conflict between social groups:

> Social groups can confront each other when they are in the same political arena, but this possibility is reduced when they are separated into different arenas. Political differences are easier to express when groups occupy the same political system and share the same political institutions, but this is more difficult when the groups are divided by political boundaries and do not contest the same elections, do not fight for control of the same elected offices, do not contest public polities for the same political units, or do not argue about the same municipal budgets.[17]
>
> This subversion of democracy means in turn that community politics tends to be low-key, while the politics of the whole metropolitan area are often notable for their absence. The balkanization of the city means that it is difficult to make, or even think about, area-wide decisions for area-wide problems. 'The result is a series of parish-pump and parochial politics in which small issues rule the day for want of a political structure which could handle anything larger'.[18]

Fiscal Imbalance and Sociospatial Inequality
One of the most detrimental consequences of metropolitan fragmentation

is the *fiscal imbalance* which leaves central city governments with insufficient funds and resources relative to the demands for the services for which they are responsible. The decentralization of jobs and homes, the inevitable ageing of inner-city environments and the concentration of a residuum of elderly and low-income households in inner-city neighbourhoods has led to a narrowing tax base accompanied by rising demands for public services. The ageing, high-density housing typical of inner-city areas, for example, requires high levels of fire protection; high crime rates mean higher policing costs; and high levels of unemployment and ill-health mean high levels of need for welfare services and health care facilities. As a result of these pressures, many central cities in the United States have experienced a *fiscal squeeze* of the type which led to the near-bankruptcy of New York City in 1975. Some have suggested that such problems are aggravated by additional demands for public services in central city areas which stem from suburbanites working or shopping there. This is the so-called *suburban exploitation* thesis. There is no question that the presence of suburban commuters and shoppers precipitates higher expenditures on roads, parking space, public utilities, policing, and so on; on the other hand, it is equally clear that the patronage of downtown businesses by suburbanites enhances the central city tax base while their own suburban governments have to bear the cost of educating their children. The extent to which these costs and benefits balance out has not yet been conclusively demonstrated.

A more compelling argument interprets fiscal squeeze as a product of the nature of economic change.[19] In this interpretation, it has been the growth of new kinds of *private* economic activity that has imposed high costs on the *public* sector. In general, the growth of new kinds of urban economic activity has been expensive because it has failed to provide employment and income for central city residents, and it has made demands on the public sector for infrastructure expenditures which were not self-financing:

> On the one hand, new economic growth in the central cities did not provide sufficient employment and income benefits to the central city's residents. Industrial jobs were taken by suburbanized union workers. Construction work was dominated by restrictive craft unions. And the new office economy was drawing on the better educated, better heeled, suburban workforce. Industrial investments were now part of vast multilocational networks of plants, thus weakening the local multipliers from local plant investments. This export of the income benefits of local economic growth meant a continuous reservoir of poor, structurally unemployed people who turned to city governments for jobs and services.
>
> On the other hand, the rising office economy of the central city required a restructuring of urban space to move people and information most efficiently. This required a massive investment in public capital for mass transit, parking, urban renewal, and the more traditional forms of infrastructure.[20]

These infrastructural investments were insulated from conflict through the exploitation of new forms of administration and financing: autonomous special districts, banker committees, and new forms of revenue and tax increment bonding. As a result there emerged two worlds of local expenditure: one oriented to providing services and public employment for the city's residents, the other to constructing the infrastructure necessary to profitable private development. 'These two worlds–of social wage and social capital–were structurally segregated. The former was governed by electoral politics and the excesses of patronage. The latter was housed in bureaucratic agencies, dominated by men in business who survived by their efficiency.'[21]

Fiscal crises of the sort epitomized by the plight of New York City in the mid-1970s (and again in the early 1990s) are seen by some commentators as an important catalyst for change in the political economy of central cities. Few, however, are optimistic as to the eventual outcomes. One particularly gloomy scenario, which Richard Hill suggests can be recognized in the central areas of cities like Newark and St Louis, is the emergence of what he calls a *pariah city*, a form of 'geographical and political apartheid – a "reservation" for the economically disenfranchised labour force'.[22] Those left behind in the 'pariah city', he suggests, will be the poor, the deviant, and the unwanted, together with those who make a business or career of managing them for the rest of society.

Fiscal Mercantilism

In a classic economic interpretation of urban public economies, Tiebout, noting the different 'bundles' of public goods provided by different metropolitan jurisdictions, suggested that households will tend to sort themselves naturally along municipal lines according to their ability to pay for them.[23] It is now increasingly recognized, however, that a good deal of sociospatial sorting is deliberately engineered by local governments. This unfortunate aspect of metropolitan political fragmentation arises from the competition between neighbouring governments seeking to increase revenue by attracting lucrative taxable land users. The phenomenon has been called *fiscal mercantilism*.[24] Its outcome has important implications for residential segregation as well as the geography of public service provision.

In a fiscal context, desirable households include those owning a large amount of taxable capital (in the form of housing) relative to the size of the household and the extent of its need for public services. Low-income households are seen as imposing a fiscal burden, since they not only possess relatively little taxable capital but also tend to be in greatest need of public services. Moreover, their presence in an area inevitably lowers the social status of the community, thus making it less attractive to high-income households. In competing for desirable residents, therefore, jurisdictions must offer low tax rates while providing good schools, high levels of public safety and environmental quality and pursuing policies that somehow keep out the socially and fiscally undesirable.

The most widespread strategy in the United States involves the manipulation of land-use *zoning powers*, which can be employed to exclude the fiscally undesirable in several ways. Perhaps the most common is 'large lot zoning', whereby land within a jurisdiction is set aside for housing standing on individual plots of a minimum size – usually at least half an acre (0.2 ha) – which precludes all but the more expensive housing developments and so keeps out the fiscally and socially undesirable. It is not at all uncommon, in fact, for American suburban subdivisions to be zoned for occupation at not less than one acre per dwelling. Other exclusionary tactics include zoning out apartments, the imposition of moratoria on sewage hook-ups, and the introduction of building codes calling for expensive construction techniques.

The existence of large tracts of undeveloped land within a jurisdiction represents a major asset, since it can be zoned to keep out the poor and attract either affluent households or fiscally lucrative commercial activities such as offices and shopping centres. Inner metropolitan jurisdictions, lacking developable land, have to turn to other, more expensive strategies in order to enhance their tax base. These include the encouragement of gentrification and/or urban redevelopment projects designed to replace low-yielding slum dwellings with high-yielding office developments – both of which also have the effect of displacing low-income families to other parts of the city, often to other jurisdictions.

The result is that central city populations are left the privilege of voting to impose disproportionate costs of social maintenance and control upon themselves. Markusen, pursuing a Marxian analysis, goes further:

> . . . the salient function of suburban governments is to insulate class consumption and capital from the costs of social accumulation and social expenses in the central city, thereby forcing the poor to finance their own oppressive police force and welfare system. The suburban government actually constructs its own public-service market by employing policy tools such as zoning in which class aims for levels and types of social consumption and class reproduction can be achieved by excluding high-cost residents and attracting those with ample resources. At the same time, the independence of the suburban government allows it to use these same exclusionary tools to *enhance the private-sector functions of suburbia* – the class assimilation of children by restricting their playmates and experience, the removal of class conflict from living situations, and the preservation of asset value of housing.[25]

In short, and in crude terms, different social sub-classes reproduce themselves in different types of juridical areas. This is a point to which we shall return in considering the role of the local state (p. 102).

Municipal Service Delivery and Sociospatial Inequality
The conflicts over resources that are embodied in the issues surrounding metropolitan fragmentation, fiscal imbalance and fiscal mercantilism are at once the cause and the effect of significant inter-jurisdictional disparities

in public service provision. Here, then, we see another facet of the socio-spatial dialectic: spatial inequalities that stem from legal and institutional frameworks and sociopolitical processes, inequalities that in turn are constitutive of the relations of power and status.

The extent of these disparities in a fragmented metropolitan area can be illustrated with reference to the example of social services for the elderly in Greater London. From a geographical point of view, the 'ideal' distribution of such resources might be one that is in direct proportion to the levels of need in each of the 32 Greater London boroughs: a situation that represents 'territorial justice'. An examination of the provision of home help, meals-on-wheels, home nurses and residential accommodation for the elderly, however, found evidence of considerable variability in the extent to which territorial justice is achieved.[26] In order to quantify local levels of need for social services for the elderly, the study used an index of social conditions based on a mixture of variables measuring local levels of health, housing conditions, unemployment and socio-economic status, as well as the incidence of pensioners living alone. Levels of provision were measured both in terms of *financial input* committed to each service by the local authorities and in terms of the *extensiveness* and *intensity* of the services provided by this expenditure. The extensiveness of service provision is taken to be the proportion of those eligible for a service who actually receive it (e.g. the percentage of the elderly who receive home help or meals-on-wheels), while the intensity of service provision is evaluated in terms of the average amount of monetary or physical resources provided per recipient of the service.

Correlations between the index of need and a series of measures of service provision (Table 3.1) shows that although the overall trend is for a positive relationship between need and provision, the situation fell a long way short of the criterion of territorial justice. Indeed, there were some aspects of the home nursing and health visiting services for the elderly for which the overall spatial distribution was regressive, as shown by the negative correlation coefficients in Table 3.1. Most of the domiciliary services for the aged were distributed more equitably, although the correlation between needs and provision is far from perfect. This is illustrated by Fig. 3.1, which shows the relationship between the index of social conditions and the average net expenditures on residential accommodation for the elderly. Not surprisingly, several of the boroughs with poor social conditions (i.e high levels of need) and relatively low levels of provision were inner-city jurisdictions – the likes of Islington, Lambeth and Lewisham, where fiscal problems were most severe. On the other hand, there were several needy inner-city boroughs that provided a relatively high standard of service – Camden, Hammersmith and Southwark, for example. The explanation for this seems to be rooted in local political disparities which, like the local resource base, are very closely influenced by the spatial configuration of local government boundaries.

Table 3.1 Correlations between Social Conditions Index and indexes of provision of social services for the elderly in Greater London boroughs

	Correlations with Social Conditions Index		Correlations with Social Conditions Index
(A) Residential accommodation		**(C) continued**	
1. Average net expenditure on residential accommodation for the elderly and disabled provided directly by London boroughs and registered voluntary and private agencies on their behalf between 1965 and 1968 (per 1000 populations)	0.45	on-wheels by London boroughs and voluntary agencies in a one-week period in 1970 per 1000 population aged 65 and over	0.67
2. Number of persons (excludung staff) in residential accommodation for the elderly and disabled provided directly by London boroughs and registered voluntary and private agencies on their behalf on 31 December 1971 per 1000 population of pensionable age in 1971	0.65	7. Number of meals-on-wheels served to persons aged 65 and over by London boroughs and voluntary agencies in a one-week period in 1970 per 1000 population aged 65 and over	0.72
(B) Home-helps service		**(D) Home nursing**	
3. Average net expenditure by London boroughs on home helps between 1971 to 1972 per 1000 population	0.76	8. Average net expenditure on home nursing by London boroughs between 1965 and 1968 per 1000 population	0.15
4. Number of home helps employed by London boroughs per 1000 population of pensionable age in 1971	0.68	9. Number of home nurses employed by London boroughs in 1969 per 1000 population aged 65 and over	-0.03
5. Number of persons aged 65 or over on first visit by a home-help during 1971 per 1000 population aged 65 and over	0.81	10. Number of persons aged 65 and over first visited by a home nurse during the year 1971 per 1000 population aged 65 and over	-0.25
(C) Meals-on-wheels service		**(E) Health visiting**	
6. Number of persons aged 65 and over served with meals-		11. Average net expenditure on health visiting by London boroughs between 1965 and 1968 per 1000 population	0.65
		12. Number of persons aged 65 and over first visited by a health visitor in 1971 per 1000 population aged 55 and over	-0.44

Source: S. Pinch, p. 213 in D. T. Herbert and D. M. Smith (eds), *Social Problems and the City*, Oxford University Press, Oxford, 1979.

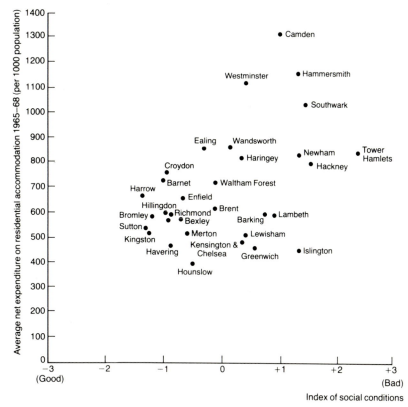

Figure 3.1
The relationship between social conditions and expenditure on residential accommodation for the elderly in Greater London
Source: S. Pinch, p. 214 in D. T. Herbert and D. M. Smith (eds) *Social Problems and the City,* Oxford University Press, Oxford, 1979.

3.3 The Democratic Base and its Spatial Framework

In all Western cities, the political framework is structured around the democratic idea of power resting, ultimately, with an electorate in which all citizens have equal status. A distinctive feature of urban politics in practice, however, is the low turnout of voters at election time. Seldom do more than 50 per cent of the registered voters go to the polls in municipal elections: the more likely figure is 30 per cent, and it is not uncommon for the vote to drop to less than 25 per cent of the electorate. Moreover, although data on voting behaviour at municipal elections are rather fragmentary, it seems probable that about one-fifth of the electorate never vote at all. This passivity can be attributed to two very different perspectives on life. On the one hand there are those who feel that their interests are well served by the existing power structure and who therefore do not feel the need to act; and on the other there are those who feel that their interests are consistently neglected or sacrificed by government but who feel they can do little about it.

Such passivity is clearly undesirable from the standpoint of civic vitality; even more serious is the consequent lack of sensitivity of the political system to the interests of all sectors of society, since non-voters are by no means distributed randomly throughout the population. People living in rented accommodation tend to vote less than homeowners; women tend to vote less than men; young people and retired people are less likely to go to the polls than are people in intervening age groups; people with lower incomes and lower educational qualifications tend to vote less than the rich and the well educated; and recent in-migrants are less inclined to vote than long-term residents.[27] This represents another important facet of the sociospatial dialectic. It amounts to a distortion of the democratic base which inevitably leads to a bias in the political complexion of elected representatives; and, given the overall composition of voters compared with non-voters, it is logical to expect that this bias will find expression in municipal policies which are conservative rather than liberal.

At the same time, the *spatial organization* of the electoral process is itself also a source and an outcome of conflict. Electoral results, in other words, can be influenced by the size and shape of electoral districts in relation to the distribution of the electorate. Put another way, a vote can be regarded as a resource whose value varies according to the degree to which it permits the voter to secure preferred policies. This value tends to vary from one neighbourhood to another according to the individual voter's relative numerical importance within his own constituency. At the same time, it is a function of the marginality of his or her constituency in terms of the balance between the major conflicting social groups and political parties.

Evaluating the effects of geopolitical organization on urban affairs in this context is not easy, since systems of electoral representation and their associated spatial frameworks can be very complex. This complexity is compounded by the existence, in most countries, of a hierarchy of governments responsible for a variety of different functions. The Greater London boroughs discussed above, for example, have been both independent multi-purpose jurisdictions and constituencies for the Greater London Council, which was (until its abolition by the Thatcher government) responsible for certain aspects of strategic planning, housing management and slum clearance. They also happen to be constituencies for the House of Commons and they are themselves divided into wards for the election of their own political office-holders. A person may therefore find his or her vote much more effective in influencing policy at one level of government than at another. A further complicating factor is the electoral system itself which, for any given set of constituencies may operate on the basis of: (1) a single-member plurality system; (2) a multi-member plurality system; (3) a weighted plurality system; (4) preferential voting in single-member constituencies; (5) preferential voting in multi-member constituencies; or (6) a list system in multi-member constituencies. It is not possible to do justice here to the potential effect of each of these systems on the sociospatial dialectic. Rather, attention is directed towards two of the more widespread ways in which the spatial organization of electoral districts has been engineered in favour of particular communities, social groups and political parties: malapportionment and gerrymandering.

Malapportionment refers to the unequal population sizes of electoral subdivisions. Quite simply, the electorate in smaller constituencies will be over-represented in most electoral systems, while voters in larger-than-average constituencies will be under-represented. Deliberate malapportionment involves creating larger-than-average constituencies in the areas where opposing groups have an electoral majority. In the United States, malapportionment of congressional, state senatorial and state assembly districts was ended by the Supreme Court in a series of decisions between 1962 and 1965 which began the so-called 'reapportionment revolution'. But malapportionment continues to exist at the city council level, and deviations in constituency size as large as 30 per cent are not unusual. Deviations of this magnitude also exist at the intra-metropolitan level in Britain, effectively disenfranchising large numbers of citizens. If, as is often the case, the malapportioned group involves the inner-city poor, 'the problem assumes an even more serious nature. Policies such as rent control and garbage collection, and questions such as the location of noxious facilities or the imposition of a commuter tax will be decided in favour of the outer city'.[28]

Gerrymandering occurs where a specific group or political party gains an electoral advantage through the spatial configuration of constituency boundaries–by drawing irregular-shaped boundaries so as to encompass known pockets of support and exclude opposition supporters, for example; or by drawing boundaries that cut through areas of opposition supporters, leaving them in a minority in each constituency. Not all gerrymanders are deliberate, however: some groups may suffer as a result of any system of spatial partitioning because of their geographical concentration or dispersal. Gerrymandering by a party for its own ends is usually termed 'partisan gerrymandering' and it occurs most frequently where – as in the United States – the power to redraw constituency boundaries lies in the hands of incumbent political parties.

It is very difficult to prove that gerrymandering has taken place: all that is usually possible is to produce strong circumstantial evidence, although there is considerable evidence of gerrymandering against African Americans in US cities.[29] Finally, it should be noted that although the definition of constituency boundaries in Britain and some other countries is left to non-partisan Boundary Commissions, their efforts often result in an *unintentional* gerrymander which favours the majority party, thus reinforcing its dominance in the electoral assembly. It has been shown, for example, that the application of the rules for the creation of parliamentary constituencies from an amalgamation of city wards by the fiercely neutral English Boundary Commission has tended to produce a packed gerrymander in

favour of the majority party simply because of the marked spatial segregation of the social classes which provide the support for the principal political
parties.[30]

The Spatiality of Key Actors in Urban Governance: Elected Officials and City Bureaucrats

The formal democracy of urban affairs is also subject to imperfections in
the behaviour of the elected holders of political office. Although city
councillors are ostensibly representative of their local communities, there
are several reasons for doubting their effectiveness in pursuing their constituents' interests within the corridors of power. Apart from anything else,
councillors are by no means representative in the sense that their personal
attributes, characteristics and attitudes reflect those of the electorate at
large. Even in large cities the number of people who engage actively in local
politics is small and they tend to form a community of interest of their own:
'they meet each other regularly, share common interests, and denounce
public apathy towards their activities with a vehemence only matched by
the suspicion they sometimes evidence towards those who seek to contest
their authority'.[31] Moreover, those who end up as councillors tend to be
markedly more middle class and older than the electorate as a whole, and
a large majority are men.

Notwithstanding these differences between councillors and their constituents, it is in any case doubtful whether many councillors are able – or,
indeed, willing – to act in the best interests of their constituents. Councillors
with party political affiliations, for example, may often find that official
party policy conflicts with constituency feelings. Alternatively, some councillors' behaviour may be influenced by the urge for personal gain or
political glory. A graphic though perhaps extreme example of this is
provided by the politicians of the Democratic 'machine' in Chicago. Their
approach to politics and public office, coloured heavily by economic
self-interest and the desire for power, leaves little room for the broader
considerations of community well-being:

> They have little concept of broad social problems and social
> movements. They deal with each other, and with the problems of the
> community, on a person-to-person, individual basis. They shrink from
> striking out in new directions, have no interest in blazing new trails,
> abhor radical solutions to problems, and, in general, resist activism of
> any sort about anything. 'I got two rules', 29th Ward Committeeman
> Bernard Neistein confided when asked how he operated so successfully
> in politics in Chicago for most of his adult life. 'The first one is "Don't
> make no waves". The second one is "Don't back no losers".'[32]

Another doubt about the effectiveness of councillors as local representatives stems from the conflicting demands of public office. In
particular, it is evident that many councillors soon come to view their public
role mainly in terms of responsibility for the city as a whole or in terms of

their duties as committee members rather than general spokespersons for specific communities. Moreover, after election, 'a councillor's perceptions become increasingly socialized into ways of looking at things dominated by other councillors, and his views become more similar to others in his stratum of the political élite'.[33] It is therefore not surprising to find that empirical evidence suggests that there is a marked discrepancy between the priorities and preoccupations of local electorates and those of their representatives (Table 3.2). At least part of this gap between councillors' perceptions and those of their constituents must be attributable to the dearth of mutual contact: one survey of 1235 local councillors in England and Wales found that almost half of them had contact with less than nine electors over a four-week period.[34] Moveover, the bulk of this contact tends to take place in the rather uneasy atmosphere of councillors' advice bureaux and clinics, where discussion is focused almost exclusively on personal grievances of one sort of another – usually connected with housing. Personal links within the constituency also appear to be weak. In a survey of Sheffield councillors for instance, only one-third were found to live within their own constituency, while less than one-sixth reported that a majority of their friends lived in their constituency.[35]

Table 3.2 Assessment by councillors and electors of the importance of local issues in Sheffield

Issue	Base	Total Cllrs. 108 %	Electors 584 %	Cons.supporters Cllrs. 48 %	Electors 198 %	Lab. supporters Cllrs 59 %	Electors 300 %	Others Electors 86 %
Provison of housing		62	49	46	55	76	45	52
Comprehensive education		52	25	35	22	66	26	29
Rent rebate scheme		43	37	54	30	34	43	31
Provision of education		35	27	38	29	34	24	31
Redevelopment		32	42	31	38	34	44	49
Roads and traffic		19	53	31	56	10	53	50
Recreation and social facilities		15	13	2	11	25	14	12
Utility services		11	21	15	26	8	18	21
Closed shop for council employees		11	4	23	4	2	5	5
Local airport		7	16	17	21	0	13	12
Local radio station		1	6	2	6	0	6	3

Column header note: *Proportion placing issue 1st, 2nd, or 3rd in importance:*

Source: W. Hampton, *Democracy and Community,* Oxford University Press, Oxford, 1970, p. 207.

Bureaucracy and Sociospatial (Re)production

In theory, the expert professional is 'on tap' but not 'on top', but there are many who believe, like Max Weber, that the sheer complexity of governmental procedure has brought about a 'dictatorship of the official'.[36] Lineberry, for instance, has argued that the influence of professional personnel can be so great and the decision rules by which they operate so complex as to effectively remove the allocation of most public services from the control of even the strongest political power groups.[37] The crucial point here is that the objectives and motivations of professional officers are not always coincident with the best interests of the public nor in accordance with the views of their elected representatives. Although it would be unfair to suggest that bureaucrats do not have the 'public interest' at heart, it is clear that *they are all subject to distinctive professional ideologies and conventions*; and their success in conforming to these may be more valuable to them in career terms than how they accomplish their tasks as defined by their clientele.

There are several techniques which bureaucrats are able to use in getting their own way. Among the more widely recognized are: (1) 'swamping' councillors with a large number of long reports; (2) 'blinding councillors with science' – mainly by writing reports which are full of technicalities and statistics; (3) presenting reports which make only one conclusion possible; (4) withholding information or bringing it forward too late to affect decisions; (5) rewriting but not changing a rejected plan, and submitting it after a decent interval; and (6) introducing deliberate errors in the first few paragraphs of a report in the hope that councillors will be so pleased at finding them that they let the rest go through. In the graphic words of one councillor in Birmingham:

> It's a subtle blend of bullshit and flannel and making sure things go their way. And writing reports. Report writing, I would say, is the most important part of their job. They put out so many reports that you get swamped by it all . . . Just look at this lot. That's for one committee. It's – what – about two inches thick. Well this thing may cost £200, and the other lot may cost three million. It may all be on the same size paper. Same small print. You've got to be on the watch for what's going on . . . It's all protective confetti to the officers.[38]

But there is by no means common agreement as to the degree of autonomy enjoyed by professional officers. There are broad economic and social forces which are completely beyond the control of any bureaucrat, as well as strong constraints on their activities which derive from central government directives. In addition, it can be argued that the highest stakes in urban politics are won and lost in the budgetary process, to which few professional officers are privy. Thus, 'having set the rules of the game', politicians 'can leave the calling of the plays to the bureaucratic referees'.[39]

Key actors like city officials should not simply be seen, however, in terms of resource allocation and their direct interventions in the democratic process. As David Wilson points out, they are 'complex carriers of spatiality, mediating past and present sociospatial configurations through the lens of evolving biographies. They . . . proceed through life paths, producing value orientations rooted in encounters with distinctive sociospatial landscapes. These values, imported into the current organization, inform role interpretation, worker regulation, and resource allocation'.[40] Like everyone else, city officials are caught up in the sociospatial dialectic; they are different only in the degree to which their experience and interpretation of space and place carries over into values and attitudes (as well as resource-allocating decisions and direct interventions in civic affairs) that (re)produce the spatiality of urban life.

The Parapolitical Structure

Bureaucrats as well as politicians may in turn be influenced by elements of what has been called the *parapolitical structure* – informal groups that serve as mediating agencies between the individual household and the machinery of institutional politics.[41] These include business organizations, trade unions and voluntary groups of all kinds, such as tenants' associations and conservation societies. Although relatively few such organizations are explicitly 'political' in nature, many of them are 'politicized' inasmuch as they occasionally pursue group activities through the medium of government. Indeed, there is a school of thought among political scientists which argues that, in American cities at least, private groups are highly influential in raising and defining issues for public debate.[42] According to this school of thought, politicians and officials tend to back off until it is clear what the alignment of groups on any particular issue will be and whether any official decision-making will be required. In essence, this gives urban government the role of umpiring the struggle among private and partial interests, leaving these outsiders to decide the outcome of major issues in all but a formal sense. The idea of a strong parapolitical structure is also central to the school of thought which subscribes to what is known as the *manipulated city hypothesis*.[43] Here, the city is regarded as a distributive system in which coalitions of major private interests are able to operate the legal and institutional framework in order to obtain favourable resource allocations.

Business

Business leaders and business organizations have of course long been active in urban affairs. One of the more active and influential business organizations in most towns is the Chamber of Commerce, but it is by no means the only vehicle for private business interests. Business itself typically engages in *coalition building*. Business executives take a leading part in forming and guiding a number of civic organizations, they often play a major role in fund raising for cultural and charitable activities, and they hold many of the board positions of educational, medical and religious institutions. The leading business families of Detroit, for example, were able to influence policy-makers and exercise social control through their presence on university, hospital and library committees, and as prominent members of civic organizations such as the Detroit Urban League and New Detroit Inc.[44] Because of its contribution to the city's economic health in the form of employment and tax revenues, the business community is in an extremely strong bargaining position and, as a result, its interests are often not so much directly expressed as *anticipated* by politicians and senior bureaucrats, many of whom seek the prestige, legitimacy and patronage that the business élite is able to confer.

The basic reason for business organizations' interest in urban affairs is clearly related to their desire to influence the allocation of public resources in favour of their localized investments. In general, the most influential nexus of interests is often the 'downtown business élite': directors of real estate companies, department stores and banks, together with retail merchants and the owners and directors of local newspapers who rely heavily on central city business fortunes for the maintenance of their advertising revenue. The policies for which this group lobbies are those which can be expected to sustain and increase the commercial vitality of the central city. Given the widespread trend towards the decentralization of jobs and residences, one of their chief objectives has been to increase the accessibility and attractiveness of the CBD as a place in which to work and shop, and this has led business interests to support urban motorway programmes, improvements to public transport systems, urban renewal schemes and the construction of major amenities such as convention centres and theatres from public funds. In Washington, DC, for example, merchants formed a Downtown Retail Merchants Association to fight for what they described as the 'survival of small retailers'.

Labour

Organized labour, in the form of trades unions, represents the obvious counterbalance to the influence of the business élite in urban affairs. But, while organized labour is a major component of the parapolitical structure at the national level, it has traditionally exercised little influence on urban affairs. It is true that union representation on civic organizations has been widespread, and many union officials have been actively engaged in local party political activities; but organized labour in general has been unwilling to use its *power* (the withdrawal of labour) over issues that are not directly related to members' wages and conditions. In Britain, Trades Councils have provided a more community-based forum for trade unionists and have taken a direct interest in housing and broader social problems, but they are concerned primarily with bread-and-butter industrial issues rather than those related to the size and allocation of the 'social wage'. The point is that organized labour in most countries (France and Italy being the important exceptions) is essentially and inherently reformist. Occasionally, however, union activity does have direct repercussions on the urban environment. In Australia, for example, the Builders' Labourers Federation has organized 'Green Bans' that have held up development projects on the grounds that they were environmentally undesirable; construction unions in the United States have resisted changes to building regulations which threatened to reduce the job potential of their members; and the pressures of local government fiscal retrenchment have drawn public-employee unions directly into the local political arena.

Citizen Organizations and Special Interest Groups

It is commonly claimed in the literature of political sociology that voluntary associations are an essential component of the democratic infrastructure, helping to articulate and direct the feelings of individuals into the relevant government channel. The most graphic examples can be seen where grand plans for urban change have failed to take account of the complexity of local feelings. Ravetz, for example, recounts the case of Chesterfield market, where local opposition was mounted against the local authority's scheme to demolish listed buildings and an open-air market to make way for a speculative developer's shopping complex. The proposal successfully found its way through the various statutory stages, only to be shelved after a protest march of several thousand citizens and a petition signed by over 30 000 persons.[45] A similar example is provided by the proposed redevelopment of Covent Garden in London.[46] But relatively little is actually known about the number of citizen organizations of different kinds in cities, whose interests they represent, and how many of them are ever politically active. There have been numerous case studies of pressure group activity over controversial issues such as urban renewal, transportation and school organization, but these represent only the tip of the pressure-group iceberg, leaving the remaining nine-tenths unexplored. This other nine-tenths encompasses a vast range of organizations, including work-based clubs and associations, church clubs, welfare organizations, community groups such as tenants' associations and parents' associations, sports clubs, social clubs, cause-oriented groups such as Shelter, Help the Aged, and the Child Poverty Action Group, groups which emerge over particular local issues (e.g. the 'Save Covent Garden' campaign), as well as political organizations *per se*.

Given the nature of local government decision-making, many of these are able to influence policy and resource allocation on the 'squeaky wheel' principle. This need not necessarily involve vociferous and demonstrative campaigns. The Los Angeles system of landscaped parkways, for example, is widely recognized as the result of steady lobbying by *Sunset* magazine, the official organ of obsessive gardening and planting in southern California. But not all organizations are politically active in any sense of the word. A study of Birmingham found over 4000 formally organized voluntary associations, from the local branch of Alcoholics Anonymous to the Zoroastrian society. Of these, only 30 per cent were considered to have been at all politically active, with social welfare, youth- and health-related organizations and trades unions being most active of all.[47] It appears, therefore, that the bulk of the 'pressure-group iceberg' is in fact fairly passive. A typical example is provided by working-men's clubs, one of the most popular types of local voluntary organization in British industrial cities. They firmly reject the idea of involvement in community issues: 'It's not our job to get involved in politics. The members wouldn't stand for it.' Club committees are expected 'not so much to provide leadership as to manage the existing and traditional activities of the clubs. Even members' often-asserted pride in the cooperative self-government of their clubs seemed to carry with it a rejection of the outside world in which they were not masters'.[48] Such passivity is of course a reflection of the passivity of the community at large. It should not be confused with neutrality, however, since passivity is effectively conservative, serving to reinforce the *status quo* of urban affairs.

Homeowners' Associations: Private Governments
In contrast to this passivity, affluent homeowners have come to represent an increasingly important element within the parapolitical structure. This has been achieved through homeowners' associations (also known as residential community associations and property owners' associations). Legally, these are simply private organizations that are established to regulate or manage a residential subdivision or condominium development. In practice, they constitute a form of private government whose rules, financial practices and other decisions can be a powerful force within the sociospatial dialectic. Through boards of directors elected by a group of homeowners, they levy taxes (through assessments), control and regulate the physical environment (through covenants, controls and restrictions attached to each home's deed), enact development controls, maintain commonly-owned amenities (such as meeting rooms, exercise centres, squash courts and picnic areas) and organize service delivery (such as garbage collection, water and sewer services, street maintenance, snow removal and neighbourhood security).

The private nature of these associations means that they are an unusually 'stealthy' element of the parapolitical structure. In most of the developed industrial nations, homeowners' associations have proliferated, but their numbers and activities remain largely undocumented. In the United States, where the phenomenon is probably most pronounced, homeowners' associations range in size and composition from a few homes on a single city street to thousands of homes and condominiums covering hundreds of acres. Altogether, it is estimated that there are over 130 000 homeowners' associations in the United States (compared with fewer than 500 in the early 1960s and around 20 000 in the mid-1970s), together covering more than 12 per cent of the nation's households and 30 million people. At least half of all housing currently on the market in the 50 largest metropolitan areas and nearly all new residential development in California, Florida, New York, Texas and suburban Washington, DC, is subject to mandatory governance by a homeowners' association.[49]

The earliest homeowners' associations, from the first examples in the 1920s to the point in the mid-1960s when a new wave of suburbanization provided the platform for the proliferation of a new breed of associations, were chiefly directed toward exclusionary segregation. They were, as Mike Davis puts it, 'overwhelmingly concerned with the *establishment* of what Robert Fishman has called "bourgeois utopia": that is, with the creation of racially and economically homogeneous residential enclaves glorifying the single-family home'.[50] Their activities involved crude and straightforward legal–spatial tactics. At first, the most popular instrument was the *racially restrictive covenant*. This was a response to the Supreme Court's judgement against segregation ordinances enacted by public municipalities (*Buchanan v. Warley*, 1917); it was, in turn, outlawed by a Supreme Court case (*Shelley v. Kraemer*, 1948). Later, they turned to campaigns for *incorporation* that would enable them, in their metamorphosis to a public government, to deploy 'fiscal zoning' (e.g. limiting the construction of multi-family dwellings, raising the minimum lot size of new housing) as a means of enhancing residential exclusivity.

The explosive growth of homeowners' associations in the last 25 years has been driven by the logic of the real-estate industry, which saw mandatory membership in pre-established homeowners' associations as the best way to ensure that ever-larger and more elaborately packaged subdivisions and residential complexes would maintain their character until 'build-out' and beyond. Initially concerned chiefly with the preservation of the aesthetics and overall design vision of 'high end' developments, these common-interest associations soon moved to defend their residential niches against unwanted development (such as industry, apartments and offices) and then, as environmental quality became an increasingly important social value, against *any* kind of development. This 'Sunbelt Bolshevism', as Davis calls it in the context of southern California, became an important element in the no-growth/slow-growth politics of American suburbs: 'the latest incarnation of a middle-class political subjectivity that fitfully constitutes and reconstitutes itself every few years around the defense of household equity and residential privilege'.[52] At the same time, homeowners' associations established themselves as regular participants at public meetings of city councils, school districts and planning boards. Complaining about encroachment and undesirable development, they represent the vanguard of the NIMBY (Not In My BackYard) movement.

Urban Social Movements

The impact of affluent homeowner groups raises the question of whether it is possible for disadvantaged groups to sidestep the traditional institutions of urban affairs so that they too can somehow achieve greater power. The conventional answer has been negative. The leaders and organizers of the lower classes 'act in the end to facilitate the efforts of the élite to channel the insurgent masses into normal politics, believing all the while that they are taking the long and arduous but certain road to power'.[53] According to some observers, however, a distinctive *new* form of urban social movement was precipitated in the 1970s by fiscal stress that in turn led to crises in the provision of various elements of collective consumption. The critical point here is that these shortcomings had a serious impact on many of the skilled working classes and the lower middle and younger middle classes as well as on disadvantaged and marginalized groups. Thus, it is argued, concern over access to hospitals, public transport (especially commuter rail links), schools, and so on, together with frustration at the growing power of technocratic bureaucracies and disillusionment with the formal institutions of civil society, gave rise to a new kind of urban social movement that was based on a broad alliance of anti-establishment interests.

Supporters of this interpretation found encouragement in a series of events during the 1970s in continental Europe. In Paris, lower-class groups mobilized against evictions and the commercial redevelopment of their neighbourhoods;[54] in Copenhagen, citizens organized to force the city authorities to increase facilities and initiate improvements; in Amsterdam, a spate of social movements centred on housing issues;[55] and in the major industrial cities of Italy there was widespread occupation of newly built public housing as well as the 'autoreduction' of public utility rates by users – that is, the refusal to pay more than a proportion of the price of public transport, telephones, rents, etc.[56]

Nevertheless, urban social movements have generally been sporadic and isolated, and some observers have questioned the initial expectation that community consciousness, activated by issues related to collective consumption, can in fact lead to the kind of *class* consciousness that is assumed to be a prerequisite to achieving a degree of power on a more permanent basis. The answer here seems to be contingent: it depends on whether a community can mobilize an awareness of the structural causes of local problems. This caveat is the basis of the typology of political movements shown in Fig. 3.2. Two of these categories represent urban social movements. *Community-defined* movements are those that are purely local: issue-oriented movements that are bounded by particular context and circumstance. *Community-based* movements are those that transcend the initial issue, context, and circumstance to form the basis of alliances that are able to achieve a broader and more permanent measure of power.[57] A good example is provided by some of the African-American communities in Baltimore, where during the late 1980s and early 1990s a 'community-based' movement, modelled on the liberation theology movement in Latin America, created a particularly successful alliance.[58]

		Community consciousness	
		low	high
Class consciousness	low	competitive individualism	community-defined movement
	high	class struggle	community-based movement

Figure 3.2
A typology of political movements
Source: J Fitzgerald, Fig. 1, p. 120, *Environment & Planning D: Society and Space,* 9, 1991

3.4 Community Power Structures and the Role of the Local State

How are the relationships between these various groups and decision-makers structured? Who really runs the community and what difference does it make to the local quality of life? These are questions which have concerned political scientists and urban sociologists for some time and which have now caught the attention of urban social geographers because of their implications for the sociospatial dialectic. There are two 'classic' types of urban power structure – monolithic and pluralistic – each of which has been identified in a wide range of cities since their 'discovery' by Hunter (in 1953) and Dahl (in 1961) respectively.[59] In his study of 'Regional City' (Atlanta), Hunter found that nearly all decisions were made by a handful of individuals who stood at the top of a stable power hierarchy. These people, drawn largely from business and industrial circles, constituted a strongly entrenched and select group: with their blessing, projects could move ahead, but without their express or tacit consent little of significance was ever accomplished.

In contrast, the pluralistic model of community power advanced by Dahl in the light of his analysis of decision-making in New Haven, Connecticut, holds that power tends to be dispersed, with different élites dominant at different times over different issues. Thus, if the issue involves public housing, one set of participants will control the outcome; if it involves the construction of a new health centre, a different coalition of leaders will dominate. In Dahl's model, therefore, business élites of the kind Hunter found to be in control of Atlanta are only one among many influential 'power clusters'. As Dahl puts it, 'The Economic Notables, far from being a ruling group, are simply one of many groups out of which individuals sporadically emerge to influence the politics and acts of city officials. Almost anything one might say about the influence of the Economic Notables could be said with equal justice about half a dozen other groups in the New Haven community.'[60] Dahl argued that the system as a whole is democratic, drawing on a wide spectrum of the parapolitical structure and ensuring political freedom through the competition of élites for mass loyalty. When the policies and activities of existing power structures depart from the values of the electorate, he suggested, people will be motivated to voice their concerns and a new power cluster will emerge. According to the pluralist model, therefore, we may expect the interplay of views and interests within a city to produce, in the long run, an allocation of resources which satisfies, to a degree, the needs of all interest groups and neighbourhoods: problems such as neighbourhood decay are seen merely as short-term failures of participation in the political process. On the other hand, we might expect monolithic power structures to lead to polarization of well-being, with few concessions to the long-term interests of the controlling élite.

More recently, it has been suggested that US urban politics should be seen not in terms of monolithic versus pluralistic power structures but in terms of the evolution and succession of a series of *regimes*, each of which is dominated by 'pro-growth coalitions' put together by political entrepreneurs in order to achieve concrete solutions to particular problems.[61] In the context of economic restructuring and metropolitan change, city officials seek alliances, it is argued, that will enhance their ability to achieve visible policy results. These alliances between public officials and private actors constitute regimes through which governance rests less on formal authority than on loosely structured arrangements and dealmaking. With an intensification of economic and social change in the 'post-industrial' city, new sociopolitical cleavages – green, yuppie, populist, neo-liberal – have been added to traditional class- and race-based cleavages, so that these regimes have become more complex and, potentially, more volatile. Meanwhile, the scale and extent of economic restructuring have meant that greater competition for economic development investments *between* municipalities has established a new dynamic whereby the intensity of political conflict *within* them is muted.[62]

The Political Economy of Contemporary Cities

Such considerations require us to take a broader view of urban politics. In recent years an increasing number of scholars have turned to Marxian theories of political economy in response to the need to relate urban spatial structure to the institutions of urban society. At its most fundamental level, Marxian theory turns on the contention that all social phenomena are linked to the prevailing mode of production. This is the material economic *base* from which everything else – the social *superstructure* – derives. In historical terms, the economic base is the product of a dialectical process in which the prevailing ideology, or 'thesis', of successive modes of production is overthrown by contradictory forces (the 'antithesis'), thus bringing about a *transformation* of society to a higher stage of development: from subsistence tribalism through feudalism to capitalism and eventually, Marx believed, to socialism. The base in Western society is of course the capitalist mode of production and, like other bases, it is characterized by conflict between opposing social classes inherent in the economic order. The superstructure of capitalism encompasses everything that stems from and relates to this economic order, including tangible features such as the morphology of the city as well as more nebulous phenomena like legal and political institutions, the ideology of capitalism and the counter-ideology of its antithesis.

As part of this superstructure, one of the major functions of the city is to fulfil the imperatives of capitalism, the most important of which is the *circulation and accumulation* of capital. Thus the spatial form of the city, by reducing indirect costs of production and costs of circulation and consumption, speeds up the rotation of capital, leading to its greater accumulation. Another important role of the city, according to Marxian theory, is to provide the conditions necessary for the perpetuation of the economic base. In short, this entails the *reproduction* of the relationship between labour and capital and, therefore, the stabilization of the associated social structure. One aspect of this is the perpetuation of the economic class relationships through ecological processes, particularly the development of a variety of suburban settings with differential access to different kinds of services, amenities and resources. The role of government is particularly important in this respect because of its control over the patterns and conditions of provision of schools, housing, shopping, leisure facilities and the whole spectrum of collective consumption. Moreover, it can also be argued that urban neighbourhoods provide distinctive milieux from which individuals derive many of their consumption habits, moral codes, values and expectations. The resulting homogenization of life-experiences within different neighbourhoods 'reinforces the tendency for relatively permanent social groupings to emerge within a relatively permanent structure of residential differentiation'.[63] The division of the proletariat into distinctive, locality-based communities through the process of residential differentiation also serves to fragment class consciousness and solidarity while reinforcing the traditional authority of élite groups, something that is also strengthened by the symbolic power of the built environment. In short, the city is at once an expression of capitalism and a means of its perpetuation. It is here that we can see the notion of a sociospatial dialectic in its broadest terms.

Meanwhile, it is also recognized that the structure of the city reflects and incorporates many of the *contradictions* in capitalist society, thus leading to local friction and conflict. This is intensified as the city's economic landscape is continually altered in response to the 'creative destruction' of capital's drive towards the accumulation of profits. Residential neighbourhoods are cleared to make way for new office developments; disinvestment in privately rented accommodation leads to the dissolution of inner-city communities; the switch of capital to more profitable investment in private housing leads to an expansion of the suburbs; and so on. This continual tearing down, re-creation and transformation of spatial arrangements brings about locational conflict in several ways. Big capital comes into conflict with small capital in the form of retailers, property developers and small businesses. Meanwhile, conflict also arises locally between, on the one hand, capitalists (both large and small) and, on the other, those obtaining important use- and exchange-values from existing spatial arrangements. This includes conflict over the nature and location of new urban development, over urban renewal, road construction, conservation, land-use zoning, and so on: over the whole spectrum, in fact, of urban affairs.

Underlying most Marxian analyses of the political economy of cities is the additional hypothesis involving the role of the state as a *legitimating agent*, helping to fulfil the imperatives of capitalism in a number of ways. These include defusing discontent through the pursuit of welfare policies, the provision of a stable and predictable environment for business through the legal and judicial system, and the propagation of an ideology conducive to the operation and maintenance of the economic base through its control and penetration of socializing agencies such as the educational system, the armed forces and the civil service.

A major criticism of Marxian theory is that it does not give sufficient recognition to the influence of human agency: the actions of individuals are seen in Marxian theory as a direct function of economic and socio-political structures. It has been argued, however, that there are elemental and universal human drives and behavioural responses which give life and structure to the city and that people are capable of generating, independently, important ideas and behaviours. Furthermore, it is argued that these products of the human spirit can sometimes contribute to the economic and sociopolitical structures that Marxian theory attributes exclusively to the material economic base. These ideas are the basis of the poststructuralist approaches described in Chapter 1; we will encounter them in subsequent chapters. Nevertheless, the overall contribution of Marxian theory is clearly significant. It provides a clear break with earlier, narrower conceptions of urban sociospatial relationships and a flexible theoretical framework for a wide range of phenomena. As we shall see, it has been deployed in the analysis of a variety of issues.

The Local State and the Sociospatial Dialectic

Despite the clear importance of local government – even simply in terms of the magnitude of expenditure on public services – there is no properly developed and generally accepted theory of the behaviour and objectives of local government, or the 'local state'. Within the debate on this question, however, three principal positions have emerged, two of which stem directly from Marxian interpretations of urban political economy:

1. That the local state is controlled by officials, and that their goals and values are crucial in determining policy outcomes (the 'managerialist' view).
2. That the local state is an adjunct of the national state, with both acting in response to the prevailing balance of class forces within society (the 'structuralist' view).
3. That the local state is an instrument of the business élite (the 'instrumentalist' view).

The *managerialist view* has generated widespread interest and support, and it is clear that a focus on the activities and ideologies of professional decision-makers can contribute a lot to the understanding of urban sociospatial processes (as we shall see in Chapter 4 in relation to the social production of the built environment). We shall also see, however, that the managerialist approach does not give adequate recognition either to the influence of local élites and pressure groups or to the economic and political constraints stemming from the national level.

Because of such shortcomings, attention has recently been focused on the structuralist and instrumentalist positions, both of which stem directly from Marxian theory and therefore share certain views on the role of the local state. These may be summarized in terms of three broad functions: facilitating private production and capital accumulation (through, for example, the provision of the urban infrastructure; through planning processes that ease the spatial aspects of economic restructuring; through the provision of technical education; and through 'demand orchestration' which, through public works contracts, etc., brings stability and security to markets), facilitating the reproduction of labour power through collective consumption (through, for example, subsidized housing), and facilitating the maintenance of social order and social cohesion (through, for example, the police, welfare programmes and social services, and 'agencies of legitimation' such as schools and public participation schemes). Where the structuralist view differs from the instrumentalist view is not so much in the identification of the functions of the state as in the question of for whom or for what the functions operate, whether they are class-biased, and the extent to which they reflect external political forces.[64]

One of the first detailed empirical analyses of the local state from a *structuralist* perspective was Cockburn's study of Lambeth, in London. She identified two dominant trends within the borough – corporate management and community development – and interpreted these as a reflection of the position of the local state in relation both to the national state and to business interests. As she points out, the trend toward corporate management was initiated by the central government in an attempt to replace the fragmented administrative structure of local authorities with a corporate approach borrowed from business. This meant the establishment of an integrated senior management team and a shift of power away from junior administrators and back-bench councillors. But, while municipal efficiency was increased, the concentration of power at the top meant a decrease in contact between the local population and the power-holders. Apart from anything else, this reduced the feedback of information essential to the effective management of the corporate-style system. Moreover, the erosion of democracy, both real and perceived, tended to undermine the legitimacy of the local authority and encourage 'the managed' to seek sources of power outside the orthodox system of representative democracy. It was in order to remedy this situation, she argues, that 'community development' (i.e. public participation) was encouraged, with the initiative again coming from central government. Meanwhile, the onset of economic recession revealed that the power of the corporate decision-makers in the town hall was strictly limited, especially in comparison with the power of local property speculators and industrialists. Cockburn's interpretation of events thus generally supports the structuralist view that the local state, as a relatively autonomous adjunct of the national state, tends to safeguard the long-term interests of the dominant class (in this case, monopoly capital) while 'buying off' the working class through reformist strategies.[66]

The *instrumentalist* view of the local state derives largely from Miliband's work, in which he emphasizes the significance of the class backgrounds of top decision-makers, presenting evidence to show that the social composition of senior positions in government, the civil service, the judiciary, the police, legislative assemblies and local governments is such as generally to ensure that the interests of capital will receive a sympathetic hearing.[67] He also argues that the state itself is dependent upon continued capitalist accumulation, which it is therefore constrained to support. This, in turn, serves to enhance the leverage of the already powerful business élite which represents the interests of capital. These ideas have found some support in a study of community power in the London borough of Croydon, where 'the local authority's commitment to private profitability is mediated by an interpersonal "community of interest and sentiment" which exists between leading politicians and top business leaders in the town'.[68]

Some theorists have attempted to reconcile elements of all three models – managerialist, structuralist and instrumentalist.[69] This, in turn, has led to the suggestion that *Regulation Theory* provides the most appropriate framework for understanding the local state.[70] Regulation theory is based on the concept of successive *regimes of accumulation* that represent particular organizational forms of capitalism (e.g. Fordism), with distinctive patterns and structures of economic organization, income distribution and collective consumption. Each such regime develops an accompanying *mode of regulation* that is a collection of structural forms (political, economic, social, cultural) and institutional arrangements which define the 'rules of the game' for individual and collective behaviour. The mode of regulation thus gives expression to, and serves to reproduce, fundamental social relations. It also serves to guide and to accommodate change within the political economy as a whole. In this context, the local state can be seen as both an object and an agent of regulation, a semi-autonomous institution that is itself regulated so that its strategies and structures can be used to help forge new social, political and economic relations within urban space.

3.5 *The Question of Social Justice in the City*

The issues of citizenship, patriarchy, racism, collective consumption, the law, the state and civil society reviewed in this chapter all raise, in one way or another, the question of social justice in the city. David Harvey, following Engels, recognizes that conceptions of justice vary not only with time and place, but also with the persons concerned.[71] It follows that it is essential to examine the material and moral bases for the production of the lifeworlds from which divergent concepts of social justice emerge. This we shall do in subsequent chapters. Meanwhile, however, it is useful to clarify some basic concepts and principles with respect to social justice: no student of social geography will be able to avoid confrontation with the moral (or theoretical) dilemmas of social justice for long.[72]

There are, as Harvey points out, many competing concepts of social justice. Among them are: the positive law view (that justice is simply a matter of law); the utilitarian view (allowing us to discriminate between good and bad law on the basis of the greatest good of the greatest number); and the natural rights view (that no amount of greater good for a greater number can justify the violation of certain inalienable rights). Making clear sense of these concepts and understanding the 'moral geographies' of post-industrial cities and post-modern societies (that contain fragmented sociocultural groups and a variety of social movements, all eager to articulate their own definitions of social justice) is a task that even Harvey finds challenging. Having wrestled with the fundamental issues ever since writing the immensely influential volume on *Social Justice and the City*, published in 1973,[73] Harvey avoids the fruitless task of reconciling competing claims to conceptions of social justice in different contexts. Rather, he follows Iris Young[74] in focusing on sources of *oppression*, from which he draws six propositions in relation to just planning and policy practices:

1. They must confront directly the problem of creating forms of social and political organization and systems of production and consumption that minimize the exploitation of labour power both in the workplace and the living place.
2. They must confront the phenomenon of marginalization in a non-paternalistic mode and find ways to organize and militate within the politics of marginalization in such a way as to liberate captive groups from this distinctive form of oppression.
3. They must empower rather than deprive the oppressed of access to political power and the ability to engage in self-expression.
4. They must be sensitive to issues of cultural imperialism and seek, by a variety of means, to eliminate the imperialist attitude both in the design of urban projects and modes of popular consultation.
5. They must seek out non-exclusionary and non-militarized forms of social control to contain the increasing levels of institutionalized violence without destroying capacities for empowerment and self-expression.
6. They must recognize that the necessary ecological consequences of all social projects have impacts on future generations as well as upon distant peoples, and take steps to ensure a reasonable mitigation of negative impacts.

As Harvey recognizes, this still leaves a great deal for us to struggle with in interpreting the moral geographies of contemporary cities. Real-world geographies demand that we consider all six dimensions of social justice rather than applying them in isolation from one another; and this means developing some sense of consensus over priorities and acquiring some rationality in dealing with place- and context-specific oppression.

SUGGESTED
READING

The author who has contributed most to the understanding of the spatial and institutional frameworks of the law and the state is Gordon Clark. His essay, 'Geography and law', in *New Models in Geography*, edited by R. Peet and N. Thrift (1990: Unwin Hyman, London) provides a good review of the interface between law and spatial change; while his co-authored book (with Michael Dear), *State Apparatus: Structures and Language of Legitimacy* (1984: Allen and Unwin, London) provides both breadth and depth of coverage on the question of how to theorize the state from a geographical perspective. Another authoritative author in this field is Ron Johnston: see his essay, 'The territorriality of law' (*Urban Geography*, **11**, 1990, 548–565); his review of the local state, local government, and local administration, in *The State in Action*, edited by J. Simmie and R. King (1990: Belhaven Press, London); and his book, *Political, Electoral, and Spatial Systems* (1979: Clarendon Press, Oxford), which also deals with the spatial organization of political boundaries in cities. An excellent review of the inter-relationships between class and community in contemporary cities can be found in Kevin Cox's essay, 'The politics of turf and the question of class', in *The Power of Geography*, edited by Jennifer Wolch and Michael Dear (1989: Unwin Hyman, London). An extensive review of the changes that occurred in British and American metropolitan areas in the 1980s with respect to socio-economic change, political change and metropolitan restructuring can be found in Brian Jacobs's book: *Fractured Cities: Capitalism, Community and Empowerment in Britain and America* (1992: Routledge, Chapman, and Hall, Andover); a more theoretical approach to the same issues can be found in Michael Peter Smith's book, *City, State and Market* (1988: Blackwell, Oxford). The question of social justice is considered in David Harvey's essay, 'Social justice, postmodernism, and the city', in the *International Journal of Urban and Regional Research* (1992: 588–601). Finally, Mike Davis provides a very readable account of the political biography of one city – Los Angeles – in the second chapter ('Power Lines') of his *City of Quartz: Excavating the Future in Los Angeles* (1990: Verso, London). The third chapter of this book ('Homegrown revolution') has an absorbing account of homeowners' associations; the rest of the book is in fact equally absorbing and provides an excellent stimulus and accompaniment to the study of urban social geography.

NOTES

1. Marston, S., Who are 'the people'?: gender, citizenship, and the making of the American nation, *Environment & Planning D: Society and Space*, **8,** 1990, 455.

2. Habermas, J., *The Structural Transformation of the Public Sphere*. Cambridge, Mass.: MIT Press, 1989.

3. Habermas, J. *Structural Transformation*, p. 83; cited in Marston, Who are 'the people'?

4. Smith, S. J. Society, space and citizenship: a human geography for the 'new times'?, *Transactions, Institute of British Geographers*, **14,** 1989, p. 147.

5. Marston, Who are 'the people'?, p. 450.

6. Smith, Society, space and citizenship, p. 150.

7. Smith, Society, space and citizenship, p. 149.

8. Blomley, N., Interpretive practices, the state and the locale. In J. Wolch and M. Dear (eds.), *The Power of Geography*. London: Unwin Hyman, 1989, pp. 175–196.

9. Clark, G., The geography of law. In R. Peet and N. Thrift, (eds), *New Models in Geography*, London: Unwin Hyman, 1990, pp. 310–337.

10. See, for example, Clark, Geography of law; Delaney, D., Geographies of judgement: the doctrine of changed conditions and the geopolitics of race, *Annals, Association of American Geographers*, **83,** 1993, 48–65; and Blomley, N. and G. Clark, Law, theory and geography, *Urban Geography*, **11,** 1990, 433–446.

11. See Clark, W. A. V., Problems of integrating an urban society. In J. Hart (ed.), *Our Changing Cities*. Baltimore: Johns Hopkins University Press, 1991, pp. 127–145.

12. Blomley, N., Editorial: Making space for law, *Urban Geography*, **14,** 1993, 6.

13. Cox, W. H., *Cities: The Public Dimension*. Harmondsworth: Penguin, 1976.

14. Harvey, D. W., From managerialism to entrepreneurialism: the transformation in urban governance in late capitalism, *Geografiska Annaler*, **71B,** 1989, 3–17.

15. See, for example, D. Ley, Liberal ideology and the postindustrial city, *Annals, Association of American Geographers*, **70,** 1980, 238–258.

16. US Advisory Commission on Intergovernmental Relations, *The Organization of Local Public Economies*. Washington, DC: ACIR, 1987.

17. Newton, K., Conflict avoidance and conflict suppression. In K. Cox (ed.), *Urbanization and Conflict in Market Societies*. London: Methuen, 1978, p. 84.

18. *Ibid.*, p. 86.

19. Friedland, R. Central city fiscal stress: the public costs of private growth, *International Journal of Urban and Regional Research*, **5,** 1981, 356–375.

20. *Ibid.*, pp. 370–1.

21. *Ibid.*, p. 371.

22. Hill, R., Fiscal crisis, austerity, and alternative urban policies. In W. K. Tabb and L. Sawers (eds), *Marxism and the Metropolis*, 2nd edn. Oxford: Oxford University Press, 1984, p. 311.

23. Tiebout, C. M., A pure theory of local expenditures, *Journal of Political Economy*, **64,** 1956, 416–424.

24. Cox, K. and M. Dear, *Jurisdictional Organization and Urban Welfare*, Occasional Paper No. 47, Department of Geography, Ohio State University, Columbus, 1975.

25. Markusen, A., Class and urban social expenditure. In W. K. Tabb and L. Sawers, (eds), *Marxism and the Metropolis*, 2nd ed. Oxford: Oxford University Press, 1984, p. 93, emphasis added.

26. Pinch, S., Territorial justice in the city: a case study of social services for the elderly in Greater London. In D. Herbert and D. Smith (eds), *Social Problems and the City: Geographical Perspectives*. Oxford: Oxford University Press, 1979, 201–223.

27. Wolfinger, R. E. and S. J. Rosenstone, *Who Votes?* New Haven: Yale University Press, 1980.

28. O'Loughlin, J., Malapportionment and gerrymandering in the ghetto. In J. S. Adams, (ed.), *Policymaking and Metropolitan Dynamics*. Cambridge, Mass.: Ballinger, 1976, p. 540.

29. O'Loughlin, J., The identification and evaluation of racial gerrymandering, *Annals, Association of American Geographers*, **72,** 1982, 165–184.

30. Taylor, P. J. and G. Gudgin, The myth of non-partisan cartography: a study of electoral biases in the English Boundary Commission's Redistribution for 1955–1970, *Urban Studies*, **13,** 1976, 13–25.

31. Hampton, W, *Democracy and Community*. Oxford: Oxford University Press, 1970, p. 49.

32. Rakove, M. L., *Don't Make No Waves, Don't Back No Losers*. Bloomington: Indiana University Press, 1975, p. 11.

33. Davies, B., Territorial injustice, *New Society*, **36,** 1976, 352.

34. Committee on the Management of Local Government, *The Local Government Councillor*. London: HMSO, 1967.

35. Hampton, *Democracy and Community*.

36. Weber, M., *The Theory of Social and Economic Organization*. Glencoe, Illinois: Free Press, 1947.

37. Lineberry, R. L., *Equality and Urban Policy*. Beverly Hills: Sage, 1977.

38. Newton, K., *Second City Politics*. London: Oxford University Press, 1976, pp. 156–157.

39. Rich, R., Neglected issues in the study of urban service distributions, *Urban Studies*, **16,** 1979, 143–156.

40. Wilson, D., Space and social reproduction in local organizations: a social

constructionist perspective, *Environment & Planning D: Society and Space*, **10,** 1992, 215–230.

41. Greer, S. and P. Orleans, The mass society and the parapolitical structure, *American Sociological Review*, **27,** 1962, 634–646.

42. See, for example, Banfield, E. C. and J. Q. Wilson, *City Politics*. Cambridge, Mass.: Harvard University Press, 1963.

43. Gale, S. and E. G. Moore (eds), *The Manipulated City*. Chicago: Maaroufa Press, 1975.

44. Ewen, L., *Corporate Power and Urban Crisis in Detroit*. Princeton: Princeton University Press, 1978.

45. Ravetz, A., *Remaking Cities*. London: Croom Helm, 1980.

46. Christensen, J., The politics of redevelopment: Covent Garden. In D. T. Herbert and R. J. Johnston (eds), *Geography and the Urban Environment*, vol. 4. Chichester: Wiley, 1982, pp. 129–151.

47. Newton, *Second City Politics*.

48. Batley, R., An explanation of non-participation in planning, *Policy and Politics*, **1,** 1972, 103.

49. Dilger, R. J., Residential community associations: issues, impacts, and relevance for local government, *State and Local Government Review*, **23,** 1991, 17–23.

50. Davis, M., *City of Quartz*. London: Verso, 1990, pp. 169–170.

51. Delaney, Geographies of judgement.

52. Davis, *City of Quartz*, p. 159.

53. Piven, F. F. and R. A. Cloward, *Poor People's Movements: Why They Succeed, How They Fail*. New York: Pantheon Books, 1977, p. 12.

54. Olives, J., The struggle against urban renewal in the 'Cité d'Aliarte' (Paris). In C. Pickvance (ed.), *Urban Sociology*. London: Tavistock, 1976, pp. 174–197; Castells, M., *The Urban Question*. London: Arnold, 1977.

55. Draaisma, J. and P. Hoogstraten, The squatter movement in Amsterdam, *International Journal of Urban and Regional Research*, **7,** 1983, 406–416.

56. Marcelloni, M., Urban movements and political struggles in Italy, *International Journal of Urban and Regional Research*, **3,** 1979, 251–268.

57. Fitzgerald, J., Class as community: the new dynamics of social change, *Environment & Planning D: Society and Space*, **9,** 1991, 117–128.

58. McDougall, H. A., *Black Baltimore. A New Theory of Community*. Philadelphia: Temple University Press, 1993.

59. Hunter, F. *Community Power Structure: A Study of Decision Makers*, Chapel Hill: University of North Carolina Press, 1953; Dahl, R., *Who Governs?* New Haven: Yale University Press, 1961.

60. Dahl, *Who Governs?*, p. 72.

61. Stone, C. N., *Regime Politics: Governing Atlanta 1946–1988*. Lawrence: University Press of Kansas, 1989; Mollenkopf, J. H., *The Contested City*. Princeton: Princeton University Press, 1983.

62. Cox, K. R. and A. Mair, Locality and community in the politics of economic development, *Annals, Association of American Geographers*, **78,** 1988, 307–325.

63. Harvey, D., Class structure in a capitalist society and the theory of residential differentiation. In R. Peel, M. Chisholm, and P. Haggett (eds), *Processes in Physical and Human Geography*. London: Heinemann, 1975, p. 364.

64. Duncan, S.S. and M. Goodwin, The local state: functionalism, autonomy and class relations in Cockburn and Saunders. *Political Geography Quarterly*, **1,** 1982, 77–96.

65. Cockburn, C., *The Local State*. London: Pluto Press, 1977.

66. Fincher, R., Space, class, and political processes, *Progress in Human Geography*, **11,** 1987, 496–516.

67. See, for example, Miliband, R., *The State in Capitalist Society*. London: Weidenfeld & Nicholson, 1969.

68. Saunders, P., *Urban Politics: A Sociological Interpretation*. London: Hutchinson, 1979, p. 207.

69. See, for example, Offe, C., *Contradictions of the Welfare State*. London: Hutchinson, 1984.

70. Goodwin, M., S. Duncan, and S. Halford, Regulation theory, the local state, and the transition of urban politics, *Environment & Planning D: Society and Space*, **11,** 1993, 67–88; Clark, G., 'Real' regulation: the administrative state, *Environment & Planning A*, **24,** 1992, 615–627.

71. Harvey, D., Social justice, postmodernism, and the city, *International Journal of Urban and Regional Research*, 1992, 588–601.

72. The summary here follows Harvey, *Social Justice*, pp. 594–601.

73. Harvey, D., *Social Justice and the City*. London: Arnold, 1973.

74. Young, I., *Justice and the Politics of Difference*. Princeton: Princeton University Press, 1990.

Office construction, Crystal City, Virginia. Photograph by U.S. Department of Housing and Urban Development.

4 Structures of building provision and the social production of the urban environment

Housing Submarkets • Key Actors in the Social Production of the Built Environment

In this chapter, we explore another of the fundamental dimensions of the sociospatial dialectic: the intermediate-level structures and processes associated with the production of the built environment. 'Production' here is used in its widest sense – not just the construction of the built environment but also the exchange, distribution and use of the different elements and settings that provide the physical framework for the economic, social, cultural, and political life of cities. At one level, all these aspects of production can be seen in terms of the broad machinations of economics: supply and demand, working within (and interacting with) long-wave economic cycles and conditioned by the evolving institutional structures described in Chapter 3. Yet the production of the built environment is not simply a function of supply and demand played out on a stage set by broad economic and institutional forces. It is also a function of time- and place-specific social relations that involve a variety of key actors (including landowners, investors, financiers, developers, builders, design professionals, construction workers, business and community leaders, and consumers). At the same time, the state – both local and national – must be recognized as an important agent in its own right and as a regulator of competition between various actors.

These sets of relations represent *structures of building provision* through which we can understand the social production of the built environment. As Michael Ball points out, these structures of building provision need to be seen in terms of their specific linkages (functional, historical, political, social and cultural) with the broader structural elements (economic, institutional) of the political economy.[1] A comprehensive survey of the structures of building provision is beyond the scope of this book. We shall, instead, illustrate the social production of the built environment: first of all by showing how the dynamics of housing supply are socially constructed through the dynamics of the major housing submarkets and, second, by showing how some of the key actors in these submarkets are implicated in the structures of building provision.

4.1 Housing Submarkets

Much of the importance of the structures of building provision to the sociospatial dialectic has to do with the special nature of housing as a commodity. 'It is fixed in geographic space, it changes hands infrequently, it is a commodity which we cannot do without, and it is a form of stored wealth which is subject to speculative activities in the market ... In addition, the house has various forms of value to the user and above all it is the point from which the user relates to every other aspect of the urban scene.'[2] These qualities make for highly complex urban housing markets in which the needs and aspirations of different socio-economic groups are matched to particular types of housing through a series of different market arrangements. In short, there exists in each city a series of distinctive submarkets for housing. To the extent that these submarkets are localized, they have a direct expression in the residential structure of the city. At the same time, the spatial outcome of each submarket is significantly influenced by the actions of key decision-makers and mediators such as landowners, developers, estate agents and housing managers, whose motivation and behaviour effectively structure the supply of housing from which relocating households make their choices.

It is important to bear in mind that the 'housing' available in any particular submarket is a complex package of goods and services that extends well beyond the shelter provided by the dwelling itself. Housing is also a primary determinant of personal security, autonomy, comfort, well-being and status, and the ownership of housing itself structures access to other scarce resources, such as educational, medical and leisure facilities. The net utility of these services is generally referred to as the *use value* of housing. As Harvey points out, this value is fixed not by the attributes of housing alone, for utility is very much in the eyes of the beholder and will vary a good deal according to life-course, life-style, social class, and so on. The use value of housing will be a major determinant of its *exchange value* in the marketplace, although the special properties of housing as a commodity tend to distort the relationship. In particular, the role of housing as a form of stored wealth means that its exchange value will be influenced by its potential for reaping unearned income and for increasing capital.

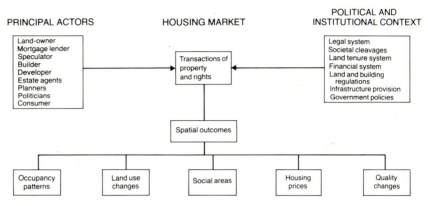

Figure 4.1
Actors and institutions in the housing market
Source: L. Bourne, *The Geography of Housing*, Arnold, London, 1981, Fig. 4.8, p. 85.

In general it is useful to think in terms of housing markets as the focus for a variety of 'actors' operating within the various constraints of political and institutional contexts, the result of which are spatial outcomes that can be identified in terms of land use changes, occupancy patterns, social area changes, housing prices and housing quality (Fig. 4.1). Traditional

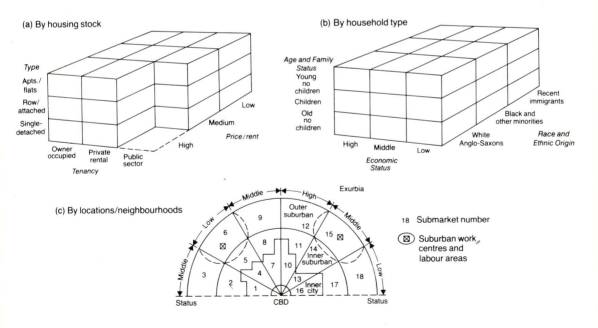

Figure 4.2
Intra-urban housing sub-markets: traditional definitions
Source: L. Bourne, *The Geography of Housing*, Arnold, London, 1981, Fig. 4.9, p. 89.

definitions of housing submarkets have been couched in terms of the attributes of housing stock (type of dwelling, type of tenancy and price), household type (family status, economic status and ethnicity), or location (Fig. 4.2). But it is unusual for housing submarkets to form such neat, discrete compartments within any given city. An example illustrates the point well.

Research undertaken in the London Borough of Southwark suggests that the interaction between various *housing groups* and *housing agencies* can be seen as the chief determinant of the structure of housing supply. Table 4.1 shows the six major housing groups identified within Southwark classified according to income, socio-economic status and national origin – variables which are used jointly as proxy measures of housing needs and

Table 4.1 Housing groups in Southwark

Housing groups	Socio-economic groups	Housing opportunities in terms of tenure	Location
1. Upper income	Primarily professional managerial and self-employed	Permanent: owner occupation, (high cost unfurnished) Temporary: furnished preceding ownership	Degree of flexiblity in location, throughout London
2. Indigenous, middle income	Skilled and semi-skilled	Permanent: owner occupation unfurnished, local authority	Owner occupied throughout London, tenants mainly inner London and locally
3. Indigenous lower income	Semi-skilled and unskilled	Permanent unfurnished, local authority, long-standing owner occupation. Temporary: furnished	Mainly Inner London, emphasis on Southwark
4. Immigrant, middle income, coloured, (West Indian, Pakistani, Greek, etc.)	Skilled and semi-skilled	Permanent: furnished, owner occupation. Temporary: furnished	London area, often in immigration community, may be temporary UK resident
5. Immigration middle income non-coloured (mainly Irish)	Skilled, semi-skilled and unskilled	Permanent: unfurnished, local authority furnished. Temporary: furnished	Mainly Inner London for jobs, may be temporary UK residents
6. Immigrant, lower income coloured and non-coloured	Semi-skilled and unskilled	Permanent: furnished, local authority, temporary: furnished	Mainly Inner London, many with their own communities

Source: London Borough of Southwark, unpublished report, Southwark Development Department, London, 1973, pp. 29–30.
Note: (a) Location preference is noted to indicate the degree to which Southwark might be subsituted for any other housing location, assuming jobs, schools, etc., to be satisfactory.
(b) Only the main housing groups and their housing opportunities are noted.

aspirations and of the 'capacity' to realize these needs and aspirations. The latter, in turn, is regarded as a product of employment status, income, capital, intelligence, education, knowledge about housing and social acceptability.[3] As indicated in Table 4.1, these characteristics lead different housing groups to seek accommodation of different kinds (distinguished chiefly by tenure) within varying geographical limits. Thus, for example, the housing opportunities of indigenous lower-income households encompass furnished and unfurnished privately-rented accommodation, publicly-rented accommodation and owner-occupation; although they were rather limited geographically.

Table 4.2 shows the major housing supply agencies operating in Southwark; and an indication of their relationship with the main housing groups is given in Fig. 4.3, which is effectively a summary of the housing submarkets within the borough. It can be seen that *each housing group enjoyed access to a different range of housing opportunities through different combinations of supply agencies offering different degrees of security of tenure*. Much of the potential choice implied in Fig. 4.3, however, is negated by competition for accommodation between housing groups and by competition between housing supply agencies for the acquisition and

Table 4.2 Housing groups in Southwark

Agency	Provision	Goal
Developers	Providing mainly new houses and flats for sale, little new renting is provided	Profit from the development process is capitalized
Landlords	Providing unfurnished and furnished lettings on a small scale, lettings often controlled or regulated	May be to retain interest, may wish to sell
Large established (estate) landlords	Providing large numbers of unfurnished lettings, concentrated in certain areas	Tradition and responsibility to community, limited profit
Small and large new landlords	Providing mainly furnished renting; (quality variable, better with larger landlords)	Profit, perhaps service to particular groups
Local authorities	Providing unfurnished lettings in new buildings or conversions	Service to the community, better environment
Housing associations	Providing unfurnished lettings	Service to the community, and professional fees
Housing societies	Providing co-ownership 'renting'	Provision of a transition tenure between renting and ownership; and professional fees
Owner occupiers	Householders seeking owner occupation are their own agency	Accommodation that is an investment

Source: London Borough of Southwark, unpublished report, Southwark Development Department, London, 1973, pp. 33.

Agencies ➡ Housing groups ⬇	Owner occupation purchase	Local authority	Housing association	Estate	Small estate landlord	New landlord
Upper income	✓					✓
Indigenous middle income	✓	✓	✓	✓	✓	✓
Indigenous lower income		✓	✓	✓	✓	
coloured middle income Immigrant	✓	✓	✓			✓
Immigrant middle income non-coloured		✓	✓		✓	✓
Immigrant lower income		✓				✓

Figure 4.3
Housing supply agencies in inner London
Source: London Borough of Southwark, unpublished report, Southwark Development Department, London, 1973, p. 40.

management of property. A more sensitive portrayal of the submarkets within this part of London therefore requires recognition of the effect of this competition. This is attempted in Figures 4.4 and 4.5, which show the major areas of effective competition between housing groups and supply agencies respectively.

In the remainder of this chapter, detailed consideration is given to the housing groups and agencies of housing supply, beginning with a summary and explanation of the major trends in the transformation of urban housing: the increase in the construction of dwellings for homeownership, the decrease in the availability of cheaper privately-rented dwellings, and the increase (in many countries) in the construction and letting of dwellings by public authorities. In doing so, we shall see that *the dynamics of housing supply are socially constructed*: they are, ultimately, a product of the interdependence of political, economic and ideological factors. Most of these factors recur throughout the Western world; but their precise composition and their inter-relationships make for significant variability between individual cities and nations.

Housing groups ➡ ⬇	Upper income	Indigenous middle income	Indigenous lower income	Immigrant middle income coloured	Immigrant middle income non-coloured	Immigrant lower income
Upper income	▓	AB	B	A	B	
Indigenous middle income	A	▓	ABC	AB	AB	B
Indigenous lower income		C	▓	C	C	C
Immigrant middle income coloured	A	AB	BC	▓	BC	BC
Immigrant middle income	C	C		C	▓	C
Owner occupier		C	C	C	C	▓

Figure 4.4
Competition between different groups for housing in inner London. A = competition for owner-occupation of similar property, B = rented property bought for owner-occupation, C = competition for the same rented property
Source: London Borough of Southwark, unpublished report, Southwark Development Department, London, 1973, p. 42.

Agencies ➡ ⬇	Developer	Small landlord	Estate landlord	New landlord	Local authority	Housing association	Owner occupier
Developer	▓	B				A	AB
Small landlord	C	▓		C	C	C	C
Estate landlord			▓	C	C		
New landlord		B		▓	A	A	A
Local authority		B	B	A	▓	A	AB
Housing association		B		A	A	▓	AB
Owner occupier	B	B				C	▓

Figure 4.5
Competition between different housing supply agencies in inner London. A = competition to buy and redevelop or convert the same property, B = one agency seeking to buy property from another, C = one agency under pressure to sell to another
Source: London Borough of Southwark, unpublished report, Southwark Development Department, London, 1973, p. 42.

The Growth of Homeownership

The growth of homeownership is characteristic of all Western countries and it has had a marked effect not only on residential differentiation but also on the whole space-economy of urbanized societies. In the United States, the overall proportion of owner-occupied dwellings rose from 20 per cent in 1920 to 44 per cent in 1940 and 65 per cent in 1990; in Britain, the proportion of owner-occupied dwellings rose steadily from 10.6 per cent in 1914 to 28 per cent in 1953, accelerated to reach 52 per cent by 1973, and stood at just under 60 per cent in 1993. There is, of course, plenty of variability within countries: individual cities can develop their own *culture of property* as part of their structures of building provision. These local cultures of property are based on distinctive sets of social institutions and patterns of social behaviour that in turn derive from local income, class and ethnic composition. Montreal, for example, developed a very distinctive culture of property that resulted in exceptionally low levels of homeownership that have carried over to influence the character and sense of place in the city.[4]

In most countries, the supply of owner-occupier housing has been *deliberately stimulated* by government policies. Part of the motivation for these policies can be attributed to the notion of giving the electorate what it wants. But homeownership has also become a key element in Keynesian macroeconomic policy. The labour-intensive nature of residential construction, together with the multiplier effects of house construction, transportation and domestic equipment, makes it an effective mechanism through which the economy can be regulated and stimulated. Political and social stabilization has also been a major motive for government intervention in promoting homeownership. As the US National Committee on Urban Problems observed, 'Homeownership encourages social stability and financial responsibility. It gives the homeowner a financial stake in society . . . It helps eliminate the "alienated tenant" psychology.'[5]

Among the various policy instruments that have been used to encourage homeownership in Britain are:

1. Grants to building societies in order to keep interest rates below market rates and to encourage the purchase of pre-1919 dwellings which were formerly rented.
2. The abolition of taxation on the imputed income from property while preserving the tax payer's right to deduct mortgage interest repayments from gross taxable income.
3. The exemption of homes from capital gains taxes.
4. The provision of mortgages by local authorities.
5. The sale of local authority dwellings to 'sitting tenants' or newly-married couples at a substantial discount from the market price.
6. The introduction of the 'option mortgage' scheme to provide cheap loans for first-time housebuyers from lower income groups.

7. The utilization of public powers of compulsory purchase to acquire development land on which owner-occupier houses could be built.
8. The underwriting of the 'voluntary sector' of housebuilding for homeownership through housing associations.
9. The discount sale of the stock of public housing.

During the 1970s, tax relief subsidies to mortgagees grew fivefold in real terms, and by the early 1990s state subsidies to owner-occupation were 40 per cent higher than to public-sector housing. Similar developments have occurred in other countries, though the policy instruments have sometimes been different. In many West European countries, for example, direct subsidies to owner-occupation have played a major role in the expansion of homeownership, with subsidized loans being made available to lower-income households. In the United States, the growth of homeownership has been encouraged by a variety of mortgage insurance programmes.

In spite of all this state protection and subsidization, homeownership has not simply become progressively easier. The reason is inflation. During the 1980s, for example, house prices rose faster than the overall rate of economic inflation, largely because of rapidly rising construction and finance costs. In the United States, new homeowners in 1989 were on average using 50 per cent more of their incomes to pay for their homes than new homeowners in 1981; and similar trends were reported throughout the Western world. Such figures, of course, obscure some very large variations within cities. The reason is that the dynamics of urban change are reflected in neighbourhood price levels. Detailed analyses of housing markets have shown that these variations are not simply a reflection of housing age, quality, or location as they are a function of the complex sociospatial dialectic of urban restructuring.[6]

Nevertheless, the overall effect of bouts of house-price inflation has *not* generally been to dampen long-term demand. On the contrary, inflation underscores for many households the urgency of participating in the potential benefits of homeownership. In general, the growth of homeownership has been sustained in three ways: (1) at the expense of households' consumption in other fields; (2) by the increasing tendency for women to re-enter the labour market after having (or having raised) children; and (3) by moves among developers to build smaller houses at higher densities in order to reduce construction costs.

There is at the same time an increasing number of households for whom house-price inflation *has* put homeownership clearly out of reach. Indeed, there is strong evidence that social *polarization* has been taking place between housing tenure categories. In Britain, for example, the rate of increase in homeownership among lower-status groups (unskilled manual) in the 1980s was less than 4 per cent, compared to growth rates of nearly 8 per cent among professionals/managers/employers and over 12 per cent among intermediate and junior non-manual workers. Conversely, unskilled and semi-skilled manual households were increasingly localized in public housing.[7] This clearly has important implications for urban social geography. In addition to the implications for residential segregation, the polarization of socio-economic groups by housing tenure raises some critical issues in relation to patterns of income and wealth, class structure and social conflict. As more and more households become outright owners (having paid off mortgages), so an important new mechanism for the *transfer of wealth* is being created. And, as more and more of these owners are drawn from the higher socio-economic groups, communities will become increasingly polarized economically: 'Disraeli's Two Nations are being perpetually recreated on a tenurial basis'.[8]

The relationships between owner-occupation and *class structure and class-consciousness* are less clear. There is a case for regarding homeownership as an instrument through which sections of the working class have been *incorporated* within the conservatism of a property-owning democracy: 'Lawns for Pawns'.[9] But although incorporation theory provides a reasonable interpretation of the effects of homeownership, it tends to overemphasize the extent to which deliberate incorporation has been the cause of expanded homeownership.[10] On the other hand, it has been argued that homeownership has intensified differences in terms of orientations towards household consumption, cutting across the traditional divisions of class. But class structure and class-consciousness are forged from the totality of life experience at both home *and* work. There are owner-occupiers and owner-occupiers:

> If you are screwed at work, the likelihood is that you are screwed in your housing construction. And being an owner-occupier does not compensate for living in a shoddily-built, high-density box in the middle of a housing estate, with the dim prospects of a real gain at the end of your housing career.[12]

Not that homeownership simply reflects and reinforces the positions that people occupy in the labour market.[13] The uneven rates of house price inflation (and, therefore, of capital gains) across neighbourhoods tends to fragment rather than to unite social groups.[14] Moreover, as different groups of owner-occupiers seek to protect and enhance the exchange value of their property, so they will inevitably come into *conflict* with one another and with other interest groups. The resolution of this conflict is part of the constant redefinition and re-creation of urban structure, both physical and social.

The Decline of Private Renting

The corollary of the growth in homeownership has been the decline of privately rented housing. In cities everywhere as recently as the 1920s, between 80 and 90 per cent of all households lived in privately-rented accommodation, whereas the equivalent figure now stands at between 25 and 35 per cent in North American cities and between 10 and 20 per cent in most European and Australian cities. Nowhere has this decline been more marked than in Britain, where just over 10 per cent of the housing stock is now rented from private landlords, compared to around 60 per cent in 1947 and 90 per cent in 1914. In general terms, this decline reflects the response by landlords to changes in the relative rates of return provided by the ownership of rental accommodation and the response by households to the artificial financial advantages associated with homeownership and (in Europe) public tenure. It is, therefore, unrelated to any decline in the demand for privately-rented accommodation as such: it is the product of wider economic and political changes.

It is not difficult to understand the landlord's desire to disinvest in rental accommodation. Before 1914, investment a rented property produced an income which was almost double the return of gilt-edged securities, even allowing for maintenance and management costs; but after the Second World War landlords in Britain could only obtain around 6 per cent on their investment, compared to the 9 per cent obtainable from long-dated government securities.[15] One of the major factors influencing the relatively low returns on investment in rental housing (thus impeding its supply) has been the existence of *rent controls*. These were introduced in many countries to curtail profiteering by landlords in the wake of housing shortages during the First World War. Once introduced, however, rent controls have tended to persist because of government fears of unpopularity with urban electorates. The effect of such controls has been to restrict the ability of landlords to extract an adequate profit while covering loan charges, maintenance and management costs. This situation has been worsened by taxation policies that do not allow landlords to deduct depreciation costs from taxes and by the introduction and enforcement of more rigorous building standards and housing codes. Meanwhile, the incomes of tenants in the privately rented sector have, in general, risen more slowly than the average. With inflation increasing landlords' costs sharply, many have responded by selling their property, either to sitting tenants or to developers interested in site redevelopment. In some inner-city neighbourhoods, the deterioration of the housing stock has reached the stage where landlords can find no buyers and so are forced to abandon their property altogether. In other areas, where there is a high level of demand for accommodation, specialist agencies have moved in to expedite disinvestment. This has been especially noticeable in London, where large numbers of purpose-built flats in interwar suburbs like Ealing, Chiswick and Streatham and in some central areas – Kensington, Chelsea and Westminster – have been sold by specialist 'break-up' companies on behalf of large landlords such as property companies and insurance companies.[16]

Overall, more than 3 million dwellings have been sold by landlords to owner-occupiers in Britain since the Second World War. Relatively little new property has since been built for private renting, so that what is left of the privately rented sector is old (about 50 per cent of the existing stock in

Britain was built before 1914) and, because of a succession of rent controls, most of it has deteriorated badly. This deterioration has itself led to a further depletion of the privately rented stock in many inner-city areas, as urban renewal schemes have demolished large tracts of housing. It is also worth noting that many European cities suffered a considerable loss of privately-rented housing through bomb damage during the Second World War.

This decline in the quantity and quality of privately rented accommodation has affected the social geography of the city in several ways:

- It has hastened the decay of inner-city areas while reinforcing the shift of a large proportion of the lower middle and more prosperous working classes to owner-occupied housing in the suburbs.
- It has led to a re-sorting and realignment of inner-city neighbourhoods and populations as the various groups requiring cheap rented accommodation are squeezed into a smaller and smaller pool of housing. These groups encompass a variety of 'short stay' households, including young couples for whom private rental accommodation is a temporary but essential stepping-stone either to owner-occupied or to public housing. In addition there are the more permanent residents who have little chance of obtaining a mortgage, saving for a house or being allocated a house in the public sector. These include some indigenous low-income households, low-income migrants, transient individuals, single-parent families, and elderly households on fixed incomes.
- Fierce competition for the diminishing supply of cheap rental housing between these economically similar but socially and racially very different groups inevitably results in an increase in social conflict which in turn leads to territorial segregation and the development of 'defended neighbourhoods'.

Finally, it should be noted that the shrinkage of the privately rented sector has been selective. In larger cities, the demand for centrally situated luxury flats has been sufficient to encourage investment in this type of property. Thus, in cities like London, Paris, Brussels and Zürich, the more expensive element of the privately rented sector has been preserved intact, if not enhanced. It must also be recognized that in some of the larger and more affluent cities of Australia and North America the privately rented sector has maintained its overall share of the housing stock through the construction of new high-income apartments for rent, at about the same rate as low-income rental accommodation has been disappearing. Shortages in the supply of land and capital in the faster-growing cities of North America has further restored the position of rental housing.

The Development of Public Housing

Like the other major changes in the long-term pattern of housing supply, the emergence of public housing is a product of wider economic and political factors rather than the result of secular changes in the underlying pattern of housing need or demand. Public housing is supplied in a variety of ways. In Britain, the bulk of all public housing is purpose-built by local authorities; in The Netherlands, Denmark and Sweden much public housing is supplied by way of cooperatives; while in Germany the public housing programme has been dominated by Neue Heimat, an adjunct of the trades union movement. But, whatever the organizational framework, the quality and extent of public housing supply is ultimately dependent upon the resources and disposition of central and local governments and public institutions. For this reason, it is difficult to make sense of trends in the provision of public housing without recourse to specific examples. Here, attention is focused on the example of public housing in the United Kingdom.

Public sector housing accounts for a large proportion of the housing stock in British cities: 25 to 30 per cent on average, rising to well over 50 per cent in Scottish cities. The provision of low-rent public housing dates from the late nineteenth century, when it emerged as part of the reformist public health and town planning movements. Nevertheless, public housing was slow to develop. The nineteenth-century legislation was permissive: local authorities could build housing for the poor but were under no obligation to do so, and there was no question of financial support from the central government. Not surprisingly, most local authorities did nothing, preferring to rely on the activities of philanthropic and charitable housing trusts. The first major step towards large-scale public housing provision came in 1919, when an acute housing shortage that had developed because of the virtual cessation of building during the war years was made even more pressing by Lloyd George's highly publicized promise of 'Homes fit for Heroes'. 'It was politically necessary to make some effort to control and organize the supply of new houses, particularly of working-class houses to let.'[17] The response was to give local authorities the responsibility and funding to provide such housing.

After the Second World War there was again a backlog of housing, this time intensified by war damage. In addition, the incoming Labour government was heavily committed to the public sector and in 1949 passed a Housing Act which removed the caveat restricting local authorities to the provision of housing for the 'working classes'. From this date, local authorities were free to gear the supply of public housing to the more general needs of the community. The immediate result was a surge in housebuilding to make up the postwar backlog – the so-called 'pack 'em in' phase. Later, with the return of the Conservatives to power, the supply of public housing was more closely tied to slum clearance programmes and the needs of specific groups such as the elderly and the poor. Subsequently, although public housing became something of a political football, the level of exchequer subsidies was steadily raised, and a succession of legislation gave local authorities increasing powers and responsibility to build public housing for a wider section of the community. By the 1960s, the housing stock of every British city had been substantially altered by the addition of large amounts of public housing.

It was not until the Thatcher government of the 1980s that this growth came to be significantly checked. Simultaneously, the stock of *existing* public housing began to be dissolved by the Conservatives' policy of encouraging the sale of local authority housing to sitting tenants at a discount of up to 60 per cent of the assessed value of the property. This retreat from public housing was part of a general 'recapitalization' instigated by the emergence of a 'New Right' in British politics. It was accompanied by cutbacks in public expenditure, reductions in taxation, and the privatization of public services. In practice, the cuts in Britain were imposed disproportionately on local government expenditures, and on housing in particular. The reason for this lopsidedness is that it would have been much more difficult to implement similar cuts in social security, defence, education or health: they would have directly undermined the political constituency of the governing Conservative party.

Sociospatial Differentiation Within the Public Sector
The legacy of these public housing policies has had a profound effect on the morphology and social geography of British cities. Tracts of public housing are to be found throughout the urban fabric, with particular concentrations in suburban locations. In general terms, and certainly in comparison with the location of public housing in North American cities, the location of public housing in British cities is remarkable for its integration with owner-occupied housing and for its occupation by a wide band of the socio-economic spectrum. The former is partly explained by the extensive planning powers of British local authorities; and the latter by standards of construction that compare favourably with those found at the lower end of the private market – a factor that is especially important when comparing the costs of renting public housing versus buying private housing. This fits conveniently with the proposition that societies with a high degree of social stratification (like Britain) require only a *symbolic distancing* of social groups, in contrast to the more overt territorial segregation of social groups required in more 'open' societies like the United States.[18] It is interesting to speculate on the role of architecture in this respect for, as many critics have pointed out, the aesthetic sterility of much local authority housing seems far in excess of any limitations on design imposed by financial constraints alone.

This image of spatial and social integration should not be taken too far, however. Public housing developments do not find a ready welcome near established owner-occupier neighbourhoods because the general perception of their morphological and social characteristics leads to fears among owner-occupiers of a fall in their existing quality of life and (perhaps more significantly) in the future exchange value of their houses. Vigorous opposition is therefore common; and, despite the legislative power of urban governments to override such opposition, it is usually deemed to be politically wiser to seek out the least contentious locations for public housing. In addition, financial pressures on local authorities tend to encourage the purchase of cheaper land whenever possible. For these reasons, many public housing developments tend to be located on extremely peripheral sites, thus effectively isolating their residents from the rest of the city, at least until residential infill and the general socio-economic infrastructure catch up with the initial housing construction.

It must also be recognized that a considerable amount of differentiation exists *within* the stock of public housing. Much of this differentiation can be explained in the context of the chronology of the supply of public housing. Six broad periods can be identified in the British case:

1. Early estates (built during the 1920s) consisted mostly of 'cottage-style' semi-detached dwellings.
2. The succeeding generation of council estates built in the 1930s was dominated by three- and four-storey walk-up flats built for slum-clearance families. These acquired a social character quite different from the earlier estates and have subsequently developed a poor reputation in the popular imagination, even if not always justified in practice.
3. A different character again was produced by the postwar boom in public housing construction. The accommodation provided at this time – in the face of waiting lists of tens of thousands in every city and in the context of strict financial constraints and a severe shortage of conventional building materials – created vast tracts of functional but austere housing on the outskirts of cities, much of it in the form of low-rise multi-family units. Because these peripheral estates were catering for those at the top of the waiting list (and who were therefore deemed to be most needy), *there developed a sequential segregation along socio-economic lines.* The first estates to be completed were thus dominated by the unskilled and semi-skilled who were the least able to compete in the private sector, and with large families whose previous accommodation was overcrowded. As these families were siphoned from the top of the waiting list, later estates were given over to relatively smaller and more prosperous families.
4. After the backlog had been cleared, architectural and planning experiments provided further differentiation of the public housing stock, leading specific housing schemes to acquire varying levels of popularity and, therefore, of status.
5. The public housing boom of the 1960s brought another set of distinctive housing environments, this time dominated by maisonettes and high-rise blocks of flats, most of which were located in inner-city areas on slum-clearance sites. The heavy emphasis on high-rise developments in the 1960s was the product of several factors. First was the infatuation of architects and planners with the 'Modern movement' in architectural design and the doctrine of high-rise solutions to urban sprawl. This was reinforced by the feeling on many city councils that large high-rise

buildings were 'prestige' developments with which to display civic pride and achievement. The pattern of central government subsidies also favoured the construction of high-density, high-rise housing schemes. Meanwhile, large construction and civil engineering companies pushed to obtain contracts for high-rise buildings in order to recoup the considerable investment they had made in 'system' building.

6. After 1968 there was a rapid retreat from this kind of development, partly as a result of the publicity given to the damaging effects of high-rise living on family and social life, partly because of shortcomings in the design and construction of high-rise buildings (the partial collapse of the Ronan Point flats in east London was crucial in this respect) and partly because the big construction firms began to turn their attention to the 'office boom' which began in the late 1960s. Instead of low-cost, high-rise, high-density living, local authorities have opted for the development of low-rise, small-scale housing schemes with 'vernacular' architectural touches and the provision of at least some 'defensible space'.

There is, therefore, a considerable stratification of the public housing

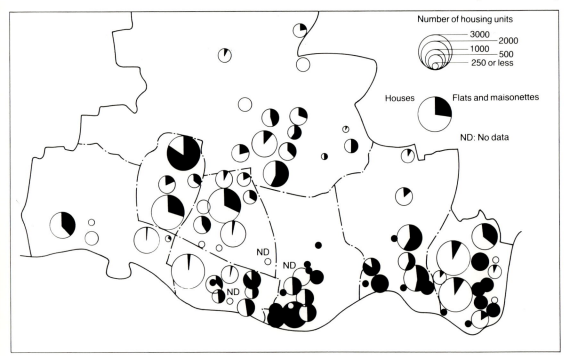

Figure 4.6
Distribution of council flats and maisonettes in Newcastle upon Tyne
Source: P. J. Taylor and H. Hadfield, in K. Cox and R. J. Johnston (eds) *Conflict, Politics, and the Urban Scene*, Longman, London, 1982, Fig. 12.2, p. 248.

stock which is reflected in the morphology of the city as a whole. In Newcastle upon Tyne, for example, the distribution of flats and maisonettes reflects the large-scale building schemes undertaken from the late 1950s to the early 1970s in the city's outer fringes and in inner city redevelopment schemes (Fig. 4.6). Morphological patterns such as these are also reflected in social patterns. Within Aberdeen, for example, there are distinctive and significant patterns of social segregation within the public sector (though they are not as marked as in the private sector), with particular concentrations of deprived, unskilled and semi-skilled manual households in the estates built under slum clearance and crowding legislation in the 1930s.[19] Such patterns form the basis for further segregation as a result of the actions of housing managers and other local authority officials (see below, pp. 145–50).

4.2 Key Actors in the Social Production of the Built Environment

Given the existence of these housing submarkets and the changing overall structure of housing supply, we now turn to the way these opportunities are shaped and constrained by various agencies and professional mediators. This focus stems largely from the view of class relations and social differentiation developed by Max Weber. Weberian analysis centres on an 'action frame of reference' which puts 'man as the actor' on the centre of the stage and seeks to explain social systems in terms of the people who make and sustain them. It seeks to describe a society 'where interest groups collide, collude and cohere in the control of institutions, where privilege and status are negotiated, where, in short, power becomes the crucial variable'.[20] Institutional arrangements and key 'actors' are therefore studied in order to explain the outcome of competition between conflicting social groups.

The development of this approach in relation to the structures of building provision can be traced to the work of Ray Pahl. In a provocative and influential essay he argued that the proper focus of urban research should be the interplay of spatial and social constraints that determine opportunities of access to housing and urban resources. Furthermore, he suggested, the key to understanding the social constraints could be found in the activities, policies and ideologies of the managers or controllers of the urban system.[21] Very broadly, this is the basis of what has become known as the *managerialist thesis*. In the context of housing, the managers of scarce resources (or the 'middle dogs' or 'social gatekeepers' as they are sometimes called) include key personnel from the following spheres:

1. *Finance capital*, e.g. building society and savings and loan association managers and others engaged in lending money for house purchase,

housing development and housing improvements.
2. *Industrial capital*, e.g. developers and builders.
3. *Commercial capital*, e.g. exchange professionals such as estate agents, lawyers and surveyors engaged in the market distribution of housing.
4. *Landed capital*, e.g. landowners and rentiers such as private landlords.
5. *State agencies*, e.g. social security agencies.
6. *Agencies of the local state* (local government). The most directly influential managers to be found within the public sector are housing managers *per se* and their related staff of lettings officers and housing visitors. To the extent that city planners control certain aspects of the housing environment they may also be regarded as 'managers' within the housing system.

What these groups have in common is a job at the interface between available resources and a client (or supplicant) population. 'It is in terms of the day-to-day decision-making of these groups that individual access to resources is determined'.[22] It is in terms of their cumulative day-to-day decision-making that sociospatial differentiation takes place, but their influence can be shown to extend beyond day-to-day decision-making. Such is the power of the institutions of housing supply that they not only shape people's actual opportunities but also their *sense of possibilities*.

It should be made clear at this point the urban managerialism is not a theory nor even an agreed perspective. It is instead a framework for study, and at this level it offers 'a useful way of penetrating into the complex of relationships that structure urban areas'.[23] A succession of empirical studies has left no doubt that there are, in every sphere of the structures of building provision, managers whose activities exert a considerable impact on the social production of the built environment – particularly in Europe, where the expansion of welfare capitalism has produced a powerful and easily-identifiable bureaucratic influence on the housing scene.

Yet it is important to set the managerialist perspective against the wider sweep of the urban political economy. It has been suggested that the managerialist approach lacks a theory of the distribution of power 'which would solve the problem of which groups are the most significant gatekeepers in given localities'.[24] This question of the relative power of gatekeepers is important, and it is essential to recognize (1) that 'managerial' decisions are themselves subject to constraints determined by the wider economic, political and ideological structure of society and (2) that there are forces completely beyond the control of the managers which exert a significant influence on urban patterns. The managerial approach, 'in concentrating on studying the allocation and distribution of "scarce resources", fails to ask why resources are in scarce supply'.[25] Urban managers, then, must be seen as actors of significant but limited importance in the context of a sociospatial dialectic in which economic, social and political processes set the limits for their activities while their professional *modus operandi* determines the detail of the resulting patterns. The following sections illustrate the influence of particular types of managers and social gatekeepers on the social production of the built environment.

Landowners and Morphogenesis

Landowners stand at the beginning of a chain of key actors and decision-makers whose activities, like the households they ultimately supply, are not always 'rational' in economic terms. The main influence that landowners can exert is through the imposition of their wishes as to the *type of development* which takes place and, indeed, whether it takes place at all. Some owners hold on to their land for purely speculative reasons, releasing the land for urban development as soon as the chance of substantial profit is presented. This can have a considerable effect on the morphology of cities, not least in the way that plots tied up in speculative schemes act as barriers to development, and in the sequence that land is released. Another example is provided by a study of suburban development which found that the manipulation of the tax system by landowners was having a distinct effect on the nature of the development.[26] Since owners were taxed less if they sold their land in small parcels over a period than if they sold it all at once, they favoured the operation of 'instalment contracts' with developers, who took up agreed portions of land at convenient intervals. This forced other developers to find land in other neighbourhoods, thus increasing what appeared to be 'random' urban sprawl.

Because of the special properties of land as a commodity, many landowners are in fact reluctant to sell at all unless they need to raise capital. For many of the 'traditional' large landholders, land ownership is steeped in social and political significance which makes its disposal a matter of some concern. When landowners do sell, they sometimes limit the nature of subsequent development through restrictive covenants, either for idealistic reasons, or, more likely, to protect the exchange value of land they still hold. Take, for example, the contrast between, on the one hand, the middle-class suburbs in North London which resulted from the insistence on high standards of construction and layout by the landowners (Eton College) and, on the other, the slums in Sheffield built on land whose owner (the Duke of Norfolk) allowed building to take place without restriction.[27] Other, well-documented examples include the close control exerted by the Fitzwilliam family on the quality and extent of residential development on their Bierlow estate in Sheffield[28] and the differential residential and commercial development within Scunthorpe resulting from the various policies of the major landowners in the town.[29]

It should also be recognized that there are different types of landowners, each with rather different priorities and time horizons. In Britain, three main types have been identified:[30]

- The biggest single group, 'former landed property', includes the Church, the Crown Estates, the landed aristocracy and the landed gentry. For this group profitability is important but is strongly mediated by social and historical ties, and strategic decisions are made with an eye to the very long term.
- The second type, 'industrial land ownership', is dominated by owner-occupier farmers, a group which is of crucial importance to the land conversion process at the urban fringe. Their decision-making typically has to balance short-term financial considerations against longer-term social ones.
- The third type, 'financial land ownership', consists of financial institutions (such as insurance companies, pension funds and banks) and property companies. The importance of the former grew very rapidly in the postwar period as they channelled savings and profits into long-term investments, often involving city centre land. The property companies, on the other hand, are less concerned with the long-term appreciation of assets and more with the exploitation of urban land markets for short- and medium-term profits.

Builders, Developers and the Search for Profit

The developer is 'a catalyst who interprets, albeit inaccurately, major forces in the urban environment; an initiator of action based on this interpretation and a challenger of public policies which obstruct such action'.[31] The profits to be made from property speculation give developers a strong incentive to insert themselves as key actors at the centre of structures of building provision. This incentive is intensified by their interest in the speed of operation (because they have to finance land preparation and construction long before receiving income from the sale of completed projects). Figure 4.7 shows that the development function is pivotal:

> It is the developers who initiate the development process – by recognising an opportunity to profit from a perceived demand for certain types of building in particular locations. They negotiate with landowners for the acquisition of development rights to sites, either purchasing a freehold or leasehold interest in the property or entering into joint development arrangements to share development profits with the site owner. It is the developers who arrange the short-term financing for construction. They commission architects to devise a scheme, within certain cost constraints, which will be acceptable to the planning authorities. It is also they who engage the builders and use estate agents to seek suitable tenants or purchasers for the completed development. ... developers might appropriately be regarded as the impresarios of the built environment.[32]

The size of the larger companies enables them to exert strong economic and political pressure on local governments. David Harvey cites the

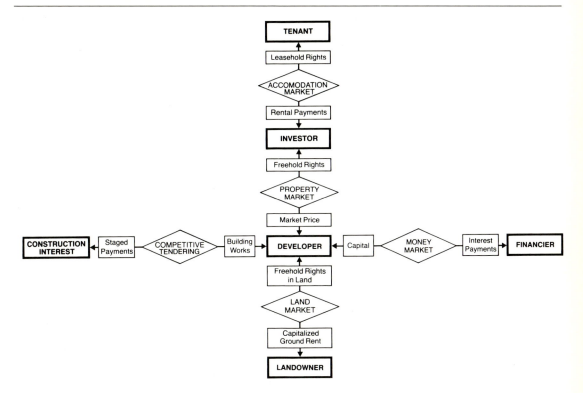

Figure 4.7
Major private sector relations within the property development industry
Source: A. MacLaran, *Dublin*, Belhaven Press, London, 1993, Fig. 7.1.

example of developers in Baltimore who, having had proposals turned down by the city Planning Board, found that their applications were approved by councilmen whose political campaign had previously been supported by large donations from the developers.[33] Large builders and developers have come to represent a powerful lobby: so powerful, in fact, that they have been able to shape the nature of many of the government programmes affecting housing and urban development.

Developers exert their most direct effect on urban structure through their selection of *sites*. For developers of suburban residential subdivisions, the overarching site criterion is that of price:

> Builders constructing lower-priced units are concerned primarily with minimizing costs. They seek to supply basic housing without frills; flat terrain with few trees is ideal. By contrast, builders of higher-priced houses look for sites with natural or social amenities. The costs of building on more rugged terrain and in denser vegetation are higher, but builders invariably find that the value of the completed house is increased by an even greater amount. When units will be sold for a higher price, builders and subdividers may create ponds out of marshes or add to the relief of an otherwise flat area by cutting streets lower and

piling excess dirt up on the building sites. Characteristics that are limiting factors to the builder of lower-priced houses therefore are considered in a positive light in the trade-off calculations of the builders of higher-priced houses.[34]

In contrast, the overarching criterion for residential development in inner city areas appears to be the availability of land.[35]

Having secured the sites they need, developers are able to exert a considerable influence on urban structure through the physical and social character of the housing they build. They build what they think the market wants, and what is easiest and safest (in marketing terms) to produce. Given their need for plentiful supplies of cheap land and for speed of construction, together with the advantages to be derived from economies of scale and standardization, the result is a strong tendency to build large, uniform housing subdivisions on peripheral sites. Moreover, the imperatives of profitability ensure that the housing is built at relatively high densities and to relatively low standards: the resultant stereotype being epitomized in Pete Seeger's song about 'little boxes made of ticky-tacky ... [that] all look just the same'. In Britain, houses at the lower end of the private market have for some time been of poorer quality and less generous space standards than the statutory minima governing public housing. Attempts by the National House Builders Registration Council to upgrade the minimum standards of private house construction have been resisted 'in the interests of the consumer', who would have to bear the extra cost. Housing opportunities for the broad spectrum of middle classes thus tend to be somewhat limited in scope. In North America, the well-tried norm of detached, single-storey, single-family dwellings has now been joined, because of the rising costs of suburban land, by suburban condominium apartment blocks. Variety is provided through deviations in façades and architectural detail: mock-Georgian doors and porticoes, mock-Tudor leaded windows and brick chimneys, and mock-Spanish colonial stucco and wrought iron. Thrown together on a single housing development, these 'customized' features can sometimes create an unfortunate Disneyland effect. In contrast, British estates tend to be uniform down to the styling of doors, windows and garden furniture.

More important from the point of view of the sociospatial dialectic, however, is the uniformity of size of house resulting from developers' interpretation of market forces. In Britain, the norm is a three-bedroom, two-storey, semi-detached or terrace house, while the lower end of the market is dominated by two-bedroom maisonettes and flats. Whole estates are built to this tried-and-trusted formula, with perhaps a sprinkling of strategically-sited larger houses in order to increase sales through raising the apparent social status of the estate. Consequently, substantial numbers of 'atypical' middle-class families – single persons and large families – are effectively denied access to the new owner-occupier submarket and so must seek accommodation either in the older owner-occupier stock or in the privately rented sector. On the other hand, 'typical' families become increasingly localized – and isolated – in suburban estates.

Finally, it should be noted that the nature of developers' activities also depends on their size and corporate organization. The typical large developer, with a compelling need to keep an extensive and specialized organization gainfully employed, will assemble 'land banks', searching out and bidding for suitable land even before it has been put on the market: a strategy known as 'bird-dogging' in the United States. Large developers are also able to purchase materials inexpensively by the wagonload, but must maintain large inventories, develop efficient subcontracting relationships, use government financial aid and housing research, and deploy mass production methods on large tracts of land. In order to achieve this, they are inevitably concerned almost exclusively with mass-market suburban development. Medium-sized companies cannot afford to take risks on land for which they might not secure permission to build, or to pay the interest on large parcels of land which take a long time to develop. When they do get sites of suitable size, they therefore seek to maximize profits either by building blocks of flats at high densities or by catering for the top end of the market, building low-density detached houses in 'exclusive' subdivisions. This leaves small firms to use their more detailed local knowledge to scavenge for smaller infill sites, where they will assemble the necessary materials and manpower and seek to build as quickly as possible, usually aiming at the market for larger, higher-quality dwellings in neighbourhoods with an established social reputation. In this context it is significant for the future pattern of housing opportunities that although the building industry in most countries tends to be dominated by small firms, the tendency everywhere is for an increasing proportion of output to be accounted for by a few large companies with regional or national operations.

Discrimination by Design: Architects and Planners

Members of the design professions have direct responsibility for the production of many aspects of the built environment, from individual buildings and detailed landscaping to land-use regulations and strategic plans for urban development. In all of these tasks, they must work within the parameters set by clients, politicians, legal codes, and so on; but to all these tasks they also bring a distinctive professional ideology and the opportunity to translate social and cultural values into material form:

> Their products, their social roles as cultural producers, and the organization of consumption in which they intervene create shifting landscapes in the most material sense. As both objects of desire and structural forms, their work bridges space and time. It also directly mediates economic power by both conforming to and structuring norms of market-driven investment, production, and consumption.[36]

The work of architects and planners can, therefore, be profitably interpreted in relation to their transcription of economic, social, cultural and political dynamics into the evolving physical settings of the city. A large literature has developed around the theme of architects and planners as both products and carriers of the flux of ideas and power relationships inherent to particular stages of urbanization.[37] We cannot consider the full scope of these issues here. We can, however, illustrate the influential role of architects and planners in the sociospatial dialectic through one of the most important (if somewhat overlooked) dimensions: the patriarchal qualities of the built environment.

As a number of feminist theorists have now established, the whole structure of contemporary cities and urban societies reflects and embodies fundamental gender divisions and conflicts. Linda McDowell, for example, has shown how urban structure reflects the construction of space into masculine centres of production and feminine suburbs of reproduction.[38] Spaces outside the home have become the settings in which social relations are *produced*, while the space inside the home has become the setting in which social relations are *re*produced. Suzanne Mackenzie has interpreted the evolution of urban structure in terms of a series of solutions to gender conflicts that are rooted in the separation of home and work that was necessary to large-scale industrialization in the nineteenth century.[39] These are important aspects of the social construction of space and place that we shall explore in greater detail in Chapter 7. Here, we are concerned with the specific roles of architects and planners as agents of gender coding within the structures of building provision. Shared systems of belief about gender roles are created and sustained, in part, at least, through every aspect of urban design.

Women's Spaces

One well-worn theme in architectural theory has been the manifestation of 'masculine' and 'feminine' elements of design. For the most part, this has involved a crude anatomical referencing: phallic towers and breast-like domes. Skyscrapers, for example, can be seen to embody the masculine character of capital (nevertheless, there are times when, as even Freud admitted, 'a cigar is just a cigar'[40]). As some feminist interpretations of architectural history have shown, however, the silences of architecture can be more revealing than crude anatomical metaphors. Thus, for example, Elizabeth Wilson has pointed to the way that Modernist architecture, self-consciously progressive, had nothing to say about the relations between the sexes.[41] It changed the shape of dwellings without challenging the functions of the domestic unit. Indeed, the Bauhaus School, vanguard of the Modern Movement, helped to reinforce the gender division of labour within households through Breuer's functional Modern kitchen.

The internal structure of buildings embodies the taken-for-granted rules that govern the relations of individuals to each other and to society just as much as the external appearance of buildings and the overall plan and morphological structure of cities. The floorplans, decor and use of domestic architecture have in fact represented some of the most important encodings of patriarchal values. As architects themselves have so often emphasized, houses cannot be regarded simply as utilitarian structures but as 'designs for living'. The strong gender coding built into domestic architecture has been demonsrated in analyses ranging from Victorian country houses to bungalows and tenements.[42] Today, the conventional interpretation of suburban domestic architecture recognizes the way that the ideals of domesticity and the wholesomeness of nuclear family living are embodied in the feminine coding given to the 'nurturing' environments afforded by single-family homes that centre on functional kitchens and a series of gendered domestic spaces: 'her' utility room, bathroom, bedroom, sitting room; 'his' garage, workshop, study. In addition (and despite the influence of Modernist precepts of design), 'beliefs about the distinctiveness of women's bodies are at work in the use of curves, and of nooks and crannies'. As Liz Bondi points out, the importance of these codings rests in the way that they present gender differences as 'natural' and thereby universalize and legitimize a particular form of gender differentiation and domestic division of labour.[43]

We must recognize, however, that even as buildings and domestic spaces are designed to symbolize and codify gender roles, their meanings become contested and unstable, particularly in relation to the complex conflicts and compromises between class and gender interests that characterize the sociospatial dialectic. Meanwhile, changes in the dynamics of household formation, in employment patterns, and in the design professions themselves, all conspire to modify continuously the received meaning of domestic design.[44]

Women's Places

City planning has a more overtly patriarchal and paternalistic ideology that has found expression in a number of ways. The key to the relationship between planning, society and urban structure can be found in the motivation, ideology and *modus operandi*, or praxis, of professional planners. The modern town planning movement grew from a coalition of sanitary reformers, garden city idealists, and would-be conservers of the countryside and architectural heritage. For all its apparent progressivism, however, it was an essentially reactionary movement, in the sense that it aimed at containing the city and maintaining a (patriarchal) social and moral order. Patrick Geddes, the visionary inspiration of the emerging planning movement in Britain, saw cities as 'sprawling man-reefs', expanding like 'ink-stains and grease-spots' over the 'natural' environment, creating nothing but 'slum, semi-slum and super-slum' with social environments that 'stunt the mind'.[45] Cities, therefore, were to be thinned out, tidied up, penned in by green belts, fragmented into 'neighbourhood units' and generally made as like traditional villages as possible.

In the subsequent struggle to establish itself as a profession with intellectual standing as well as statutory powers, city planning developed a distinctive professional ideology that now constitutes the basic operating rationale by which planners feel able to justify their own activities and to judge the claims of others. This ideology contains strands of environmentalism, aesthetics, spatial determinism and futurism as well as a strong element of paternalism and an evangelical mantle that enables practitioners to turn a deaf ear to criticism. The cumulative result has been to transform planning from an 'enabling' to a 'disabling' profession.[46]

The patriarchal strand of planning ideology can be traced back to the formative years of the profession and the threat of new metropolitan environments to the established sociocultural order. Modern cities, in short, provided women with a potential escape from patriarchal relations. Part of the task set for themselves by liberal reformers and members of the early planning movement, therefore, was to create the physical conditions not only for economic efficiency and public health but also for social stability and moral order. As a result, town planning became 'an organized campaign to exclude women and children, along with other disruptive elements – the working class, the poor, and minorities – from this infernal urban space altogether'.[47] The cumulative result has been the reinforcement and policing of the spatial separation of the 'natural', male, public domains of industry and commerce from the private, female domain of homemaking. Women were 'kept in their place' through comprehensive plans and zoning ordinances that were sometimes hostile, often merely insensitive to women's needs.[48] Consequently, the contemporary city embodies serious gender inequalities and contrasting experiences of urban and suburban living.

Mortgage Financiers: Social and Spatial Bias as Good Business Practice

The allocative decisions of mortgage finance institutions – building societies, banks, savings and loan companies, etc. – represent one of the more striking examples of gatekeeping within the sociospatial dialectic. It should be stressed at the outset that mortgage finance managers are not independent decision-makers. Much of their activity is closely circumscribed by head office policy, while many of their day-to-day decisions are dependent upon the activities of lawyers, real estate agents, surveyors, bank managers and the like. Nevertheless, mortgage finance managers enjoy a pivotal position in the 'magic circle' of property exchange professionals, and although the self-image of the trade is that of a passive broker in the supply of housing, the mortgage allocation system 'exerts a decisive influence over who lives where, how much new housing gets built, and whether neighbourhoods survive'.[49]

In order to be properly understood, the activity of mortgage finance managers must be seen against the general background of their commercial objectives. The success of mortgage companies depends upon financial growth and security and the maintenance of large reserve funds. Their chief allegiance, therefore, is to the investor rather than the borrower. Not surprisingly, they operate a fairly rigid system of rules to protect their operations and encourage an ethos of conservative paternalism among their staff. Indeed, there is some evidence to support the idea of their managers as a rather narrowly-defined breed: an 'ideal type' with a uniformity of attitudes resulting from the recruitment of a certain group (white, Anglo-Saxon, Protestant, moderately-educated family men) and the absorption of company traditions and lending policies through a career structure with a high degree of internal promotion which rewards personnel with a 'clean' record of lending decisions.[50] As a group, then, mortgage finance managers tend to have good reason to be cautious, investment oriented, and suspicious of unconventional behaviour in others. Likewise, the ground rules of lending policies are cautious, devised to ensure financial security both in terms of the 'paying ability' of potential borrowers and the future exchange value of dwellings they are willing to finance.

Bias Against People

In operating these ground rules, mortgage finance managers effectively act as social gatekeepers – wittingly or unwittingly – in a number of ways. It is normal practice to lend only 80 to 90 per cent of the total cost or valuation of a house (whichever is the less), and for the maximum loan to be computed as a multiple of the household's main income (although some institutions also take into consideration a proportion of a second income, if there is one). It is in the evaluation of potential borrowers' ability to maintain the flow of repayments that the first major stratification by mortgage finance managers takes place. Because of their desire for risk minimization, loan officers tend to give a lot of weight to the general creditworthiness of applicants. Credit register searches are used to reveal previous financial delinquency, evidence of which normally results in the refusal to advance a loan. If they pass this test, applicants are then judged principally in terms of the *stability* of their income and their future *expectations*. This, of course, tends to favour white-collar workers since their pay structure commonly has a built-in annual increment and is not subject to the ups and downs of overtime and short-time working. Conversely, several groups, including the self-employed, the low-paid and single women, will find that their chances of obtaining a mortgage are marginal. The importance of this factor has been borne out by the findings of a study of new private housing in outer London, where clerical workers were able to obtain higher mortgages, and buy more expensive houses, than skilled manual workers *whose average earnings were higher.*[51]

There is also evidence that purely subjective factors influence mortgage managers' decisions. Managers appear to categorize applicants in terms of a set of operational stereotypes ranging from bad risks to good ones, although it has proved difficult to pin down these operational stereotypes in detail and to establish their generality within the professions. It is clearly difficult even for the managers themselves to articulate something which is an unconscious activity. Nevertheless, the criteria they employ in making subjective judgements about people seem to be closely related to their values of financial caution and social conventionality. One manager, for example, is quoted as being impressed by people who had 'worked things out', suggesting that the prospective buyer who did not display this ability might be at a disadvantage in securing a loan.[52] Others have pointed out that 'I always try and assess the ability and willingness of the wife to work' and 'Those people who do not perceive that they must live an English way of life would be treated with caution.'[53] This last quote is an oblique reference to persons of colour, who seem to be particularly disadvantaged by managers' subjective judgements One loan officer in Huddersfield observed that 'From a building society point of view, they [black applicants] do not have satisfactory status;' another observed that 'whether we like it or not, the coloured people are here, and we have to be very careful. There's no doubt coloured gentlemen are good savers, but we're very careful'.[54]

While these examples reflect the most important dimension of deliberate sociospatial sorting by key actors attached to housing finance, it is important not to oversimplify. The social production of the built environment does not play itself out with clearly defined edges, producing neat cleavages between black and white, rich and poor. The sociospatial dialectic is rich and complex, and a great variety of relationships are encompassed within the structures of building provision, many of them contributing towards the mosaic of spatial differentiation. To take just one example, the social production of certain gay neighbourhoods in New Orleans has been shown to have involved an intricate and illegal appraisal-fixing scheme whereby gay entrepreneurs secured financing for the purchase and renovation of inner-city homes and then marketed these opportunities to other gays.[55]

Bias Against Property

Sociospatial sorting also takes place through managers' evaluation of the *property* for which funds are sought. With any loan, the manager's first concern is with the liquidity of the asset, so that if the borrower defaults and the company is forced to foreclose, the sale of the property will at least cover the amount advanced. The assessment of this liquidity ultimately rests with professional surveyors, but mortgage managers tend to have clear ideas as to the 'safest' property in terms of price range, size and location, and surveyors tend to anticipate these criteria in formulating their survey reports. Many managers evidently assume that market demand for properties which deviate from their ideal (a relatively new suburban house with three or four bedrooms) is very limited, and therefore regard them as greater risks and are more cautious about advancing loans for them. Managers tend to be particularly concerned with the *size* of dwellings because of the possibility of multiple occupation and the consequent problem of repossession if the borrower defaults. Their concern with *age* is related to the possibility that the property will deteriorate before the mortgage is fully redeemed; and their concern with *location* is related to the possibility of property values being undermined by changes in neighbourhood racial or social composition. Their concern with *price* reflects their anxiety that applicants should not overstretch themselves financially.

Mortgage finance managers thus effectively decide not only who gets loans but also what kinds of property they can aspire to. Households with more modest financial status, for example, will find it more difficult to buy older property even though the overall price may not be beyond their means, since loans for older property generally have to be repaid over a shorter period, thus increasing the monthly repayments.

The spatial outcome is often a dramatic contrast in lending levels for different neighbourhoods. The most striking aspect of the gatekeeping activities of loan officers in this context has been the practice of refusing to advance funds on any property within neighbourhoods which they perceive to be bad risks–usually inner-city areas, as in Birmingham (Fig. 4.8). This practice is known as *redlining* and has been well documented in a number of studies even though managers are usually reluctant to admit to redlining policies. A survey of mortgage finance managers in Bristol found that:

> All the managers had heard of redlining. . . . and said they did not practise it. One manager stated categorically 'we do not redline'. Later in the discussion he pointed to the St Paul's area on the map and said that 'there are certain areas in the city in which we won't lend'![56]

In British cities, the key indicators of 'risky' neighbourhood status seem to be the presence of black households and of students. A library assistant in Leeds, for example, was informed by the Northern Rock building society that 'it was doubtful if a mortgage would be available' on a Headingley property 'owing to the nearness of the "blue zone", i.e. high proportion of students and immigrants'.[57] In the United States, some states have passed anti-redlining laws, while federal law requires lenders to disclose their policies and lending profiles in an attempt to discourage redlining. Nevertheless, redlining continues to exist, largely through covert means: discouraging would-be borrowers with higher interest rates, higher down payments, lower loan-to-value rates and shorter loan maturity terms for property in redlined areas.

Although redlining may be an understandable and (in most countries) legitimate business practice, it has important consequences for the social geography of the city. The practice of redlining 'guarantees that property values will decline and generally leads to neighbourhood deterioration, destruction and abandonment. This process makes more credit available for the resale and financing of homes in other neighbourhoods, thus perpetuating differential neighbourhood quality, growth, decline and homeownership'.[58] This flow of capital to the suburbs, it should be noted, is closely tied to the wider operations of mortgage finance institutions; they are often heavily involved in financing and controlling the suburban activities of large construction companies. Such involvement is commonly

Figure 4.8
The 'red line' district in
Birmingham in relation to
the city's inner area
improvement programme
Source: S. Weir, *Roof,* 1,
1976, p.111.

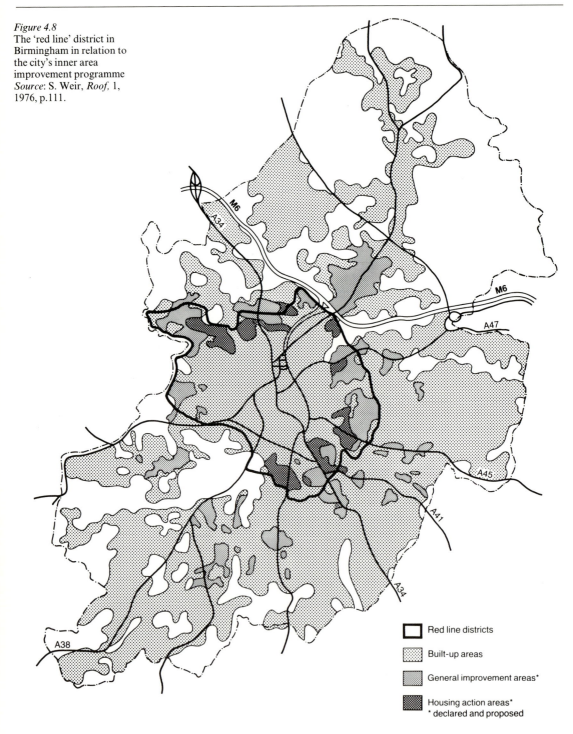

Red line districts

Built-up areas

General improvement areas*

Housing action areas*
* declared and proposed

reinforced by connections within the overall structures of building provision. Thus, for example, the Northern Rock building society in the north of England had directors in common with Bellway Holdings, a major housebuilding company, while William Leech (Builders) Ltd had directors in common with both Northern Rock and Bellway Holdings.[59] It should also be noted that a substantial proportion of the capital used to finance suburban house construction and purchase is derived from small investors in inner-city areas, so that the net effect of building society policies is to redistribute a scarce resource (investment capital) from a relatively deprived area to a relatively affluent one. In a study of Boston, for example, it was found that levels of reinvestment of savings deposits in inner-city communities were between 3 and 33 per cent, compared with levels of between 108 and 543 per cent in the outermost suburbs.[60]

Real Estate Agents: Manipulating and Reinforcing Neighbourhood Patterns

Real estate agents are responsible for a wide range of activities connected with the exchange and management of residential property. They find houses and sometimes arrange finance for buyers; they attract purchasers and transact paperwork for sellers. In addition, they may also be involved in surveying, auctioneering, valuation, property management and insurance. They have close links with mortgage financiers, collecting mortgage repayments for companies and channelling investment funds to them. The mortgage financiers reciprocate by apportioning a quota of mortgage funds to be allocated by the estate agent and by paying a small commission on investment funds received through the agent. Estate agents then use their quota of mortgage funds to expedite the sale of properties on their books. Since real estate agents' profits are derived from percentage commissions on the purchase price of houses, one of their chief concerns is to maintain a high level of prices in the market while encouraging a high turnover of sales.

In many countries of Europe and North America, estate agents account for between 50 and 70 per cent of all house sales; in Australia, the sale of houses has been almost entirely in the hands of estate agents. They are not simply passive brokers in these transactions, however; they influence the social production of the built environment in several ways. In addition to the bias introduced in their role as mediators of information, some estate agents introduce a *deliberate* bias by *steering* households into, or away from, a specific neighbourhood in order to maintain what they regard as optimal market conditions. Existing residents in a given neighbourhood represent potential clients for an agent, and if an agent is seen to be acting against their interests by introducing 'undesirable' purchasers to the area, the agent may suffer both by being denied any further listings and by any fall in prices which might result from panic selling. 'Thus the safest response is to keep like with like and to deter persons from moving to areas occupied by persons "unlike" themselves.'[61] This process was demonstrated some 40 years ago by Palmer, who seems to have coined the term 'social gatekeeper'. His study of estate agents in New Haven, Connecticut, showed that they clearly saw their role as controllers of residential opportunities. As one put it:

> People often try to get in higher class areas than they'll be accepted in. We just don't show them any houses in those areas. If they insist, we try and talk them out of it in one way or another. I've purposely lost many a sale doing just that. It pays in the long run. People in the community respect you for it and they put business your way.[62]

Palmer found that agents carefully evaluated clients' status in terms of race, ethnic origin, religion, occupation, income, education and personal appearance. Failure to satisfy the agent's notions of appropriate social attributes for a specific neighbourhood nearly always resulted in diversionary tactics, either by lying – 'it's sold' – or by warnings of unhappiness – 'you won't fit in'. Even small social handicaps could (in the 1950s) apparently disbar a person from high-status neighbourhoods. Palmer quotes one agent as saying of a person seeking a house in a high-status neighbourhood:

> What does he do for a living? Maybe he's on the road and sells – well, let's call them rubber goods for the prevention of disease . . . like a fellow who drove up here a few months ago. He didn't tell me that but I checked around and found out . . . well a man who'd fit into a top area around here just wouldn't be in that kind of business.[63]

But the most widespread discrimination undertaken by real estate agents is based on race and ethnicity. The segregation in US cities resulting from this activity has been well documented.[64] A similar process also operates on a significant scale in British cities, as revealed by interviews with estate agents:

> I would do my best to head off black buyers from a good suburban or new estate. In fact it would be my duty to do so in the interests of the community and for the sake of people who have bought houses in good faith.[65]

Manipulating Social Geographies

On the other hand, estate agents have been known to introduce black families to a white neighbourhood in the hope that whites will sell up quickly at deflated prices, allowing the agents to buy houses and then resell them to incoming black families at a much higher price: a practice known as *block busting*. In Edmondson Village, Baltimore, houses that had been purchased from departing white families were sold to incoming African-American households at a 66 per cent mark-up.[66] Because the white residents of targeted neighbourhoods can and do distinguish between middle- and lower-class black families, blockbusters have sometimes resorted to a variety of tactics in order to give the impression that the incoming households represent a 'bad element': telephone calls, door-to-door solicitations, and the posting of bogus FOR SALE signs on front lawns; even, in extreme cases, hiring outsiders to commit petty acts of vandalism or to pose as indolent 'welfare cases'. A similar process involves the purchase of older properties in prime development sites. These properties are promptly neglected and, as other residents see the neighbourhood beginning to deteriorate, more and more sell up to estate agents, who allow the properties to deteriorate along with the original 'seed' properties. 'As deterioration continues, the area becomes a fire risk, and as fire insurance companies refuse to renew insurance policies, more owners are persuaded to sell out'.[67] When a sufficient number of dwellings have been acquired, the agents themselves are able to sell out at a considerable profit to developers seeking large plots of land for redevelopment schemes.

This kind of opportunism has also been shown to have been involved in the process of *gentrification*. It has been suggested, for example, that gentrification in parts of Islington, London, can be attributed as much to the activities of estate agents as to the incomers themselves. Estate agents were often the ones who persuaded mortgage financiers to give loans for the purchase and renovation of old working-class dwellings. In addition, some agents purchased and renovated property themselves before selling to incoming young professionals. The role of estate agents in manipulating housing supply and shaping social geography in this context is well illustrated by these quotes from the *London Property Letter*, which is written by cells of estate agents:

- The fascinating thing about London is that it throws up an endless supply of new possibilities for the property pioneer and Brixton is about as near to the Klondike as you can get without actually digging.
- Nestling down at the bottom of the Archway area is a distinctly working class area which presents possibilities for reclamation.
- Grubby Kennington has been providing rich killings for sharp hunters. But the best parts of the carcass are disappearing fast leaving late comers only the bones to pick over. Where next will the South Bank hunt turn? Our money goes on the Stockwell Vauxhall sector where prices are at least starting to skip in anticipation of the Victoria Line's arrival.[68]

Public Housing Managers: Sorting and Grading

Within the public sector the principal gatekeepers are the housing managers and their staff who operate the housing authority's admissions and allocation policies. In Britain, the discretion given to local authorities in formulating and operating such policies is very broad and is encumbered by a minimum of legal regulation. There is a requirement to rehouse families displaced by clearance or other public action as well as those officially classed as overcrowded, but otherwise it is only necessary to give 'reasonable preference' to households in 'unsatisfactory' housing conditions. Since demand for public housing often exceeds supply, housing managers in most cities are in a position of considerable power and importance in relation to the spatial outcome of public housing programmes.

The rationing of available housing is carried out through a wide variety of eligibility rules and priority systems. Most local authorities operate waiting lists, although these vary in practice from a simple first-come first-served basis to sophisticated queuing systems using 'points schemes' to evaluate need for a specific type of dwelling: points may be awarded, for example, for overcrowding, ill-health or disability, substandard accommodation, marital status, length or time on the waiting list and so on, together (in some authorities) with discretionary points awarded by housing managers to enable priority to be given to 'special cases'. A general representation of the allocation process in public sector housing is shown in Fig. 4.9.

Not surprisingly, different schemes have different outcomes, and families in identical circumstances may find themselves with quite different degrees of access to council housing, depending on the local authority within whose jurisdiction they live. In general, those households with least access to public housing in British cities include young single people without dependants, newcomers to the area and former owner-occupiers. Conversely, the letting policies of most authorities tend to favour households from slum clearance and redevelopment areas, households living in overcrowded conditions, small elderly households, new households who lack their own accommodation and are living with parents or in-laws, and households with young children.

Problem Families and Dump Estates
In addition to the question of whether or not a household is offered accommodation there is the question of *what sort* of accommodation is offered, and in *what neighbourhood*. For housing managers it makes sense not only to allocate households to dwellings according to size characteristics but also to match 'good' tenants to their best housing in order to minimize maintenance costs, to ensure that the aged and 'problem families' are easily supervised, and (some would argue) to punish unsatisfactory tenants (those with records of rent arrears and unsociable behaviour in their previous accommodation) by sending them to 'dump' estates. In this situation, problem families are often doubly disadvantaged by living in low-grade property while having to pay rent at comparable levels to those paid by families in more attractive housing schemes. The localization of problem families in this way can be traced to the policy of housing 'socially weak' families in specially-designed austere and durable public housing schemes in France and The Netherlands in the 1930s. After 1945, many local authorities in Britain pursued similar, if less well-publicized, policies using obsolescent housing stock rather than purpose-built developments. By the 1960s, the segregation and localization of 'problem families' as well as grading

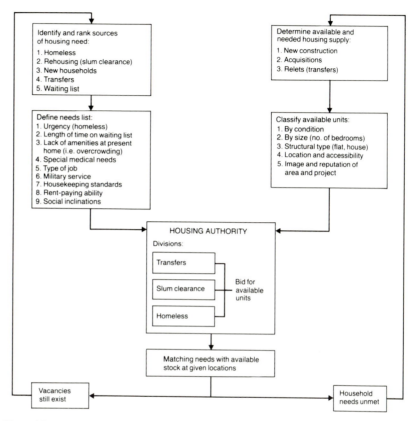

Figure 4.9
The allocation process for public sector housing
Source: L. Bourne, *The Geography of Housing*, Arnold, London, 1981, Fig. 10.2, p. 222.

of other tenants according to their worthiness for particular housing vacancies was commonplace, exciting little or no attention.[69] The 'moralistic' attitudes of local authorities were condemned (in suitably diplomatic language), however, by the Central Housing Advisory Committee:

> the underlying philosophy seemed to be that council tenancies were to be given only to those who 'deserved' them and that the 'most deserving' should get the best houses. Thus, unmarried mothers, cohabitees, 'dirty' families and 'transients' tended to be grouped together as 'undesirable'. Moral rectitude, social conformity, clean living and a 'clean' rent book . . . seemed to be essential qualifications for eligibility–at least for new housing.[70]

The process of screening tenants and allocating them to vacancies according to their 'suitability' varies somewhat from one locality to another, but central to most procedures is the housing visitor's report. It is here that the temptation to succumb to value judgements derived from impressionistic grounds is strongest, as illustrated by the following excerpts from housing investigators' reports in Hull and Bedford:[71]

- Fairly good type – suitable for post-war re-let or pre-war property
- Poor type, will need supervision – suitable for old property . . . seems to have taken over the tenancy of this house and sat back until rehoused
- A good type of applicant – this is not a long-haired person. Suitable for a post-war re-let.
- Poor, untidy and grubby: rats on premises. Even allowing for the poorness of the accommodation and his health, I would have thought he could have achieved more to make the place habitable. They have no kitchen, sink is pulled away from the wall. His effects consisted of the cot, three-piece suite (poor) and colour TV.
- Flat is very overcrowded. This was self-inflicted as they knew what problems would arise before they moved in. Would make poor tenants.
- Poor standard. A few furnishings in very poor condition. No bathroom. Children wash at school. Family sleep on floor.
- If Buckingham Palace became available she might accept.

Similarly, the grading of tenants in Glasgow has been described as 'arbitrary and subjective'. At the time of the research on which this conclusion was based, the Glasgow housing department classified its stock of housing into eight groups, ranked roughly in order of physical attractiveness, desirability to the public, and rent. At the top end were two kinds of estate: older developments which had withstood the test of desirability over time 'and now exhibit an air of embourgoisement – mature trees, well-manicured lawns, and beautifully appointed houses', and newly constructed housing (usually multi-storey flats) which remains in the top grade until such time as popular demand falls off. At the other end of the scale, Group 8 accommodation tended 'to have a blitzed, semi-derelict and thoroughly depressing appearance' and to be 'difficult to let' because of its image.[72] In order to match tenants to these carefully graded housing estates, Glasgow corporation employed seven housing visitors – all middle-aged married women – to search council records and electricity and gas board records for evidence of debt on the part of tenants and to interview them in their homes in order to inspect the house and its occupants and, subsequently, grade them. The official grading was arrived at by way of three fivefold classifications of 'cleanliness', 'furniture', and 'type of person'. Households faring best on this grading system were evidently those who were most articulate, grateful and deferential. Those who fared worst were debtors, the 'wilfully' unemployed, and previous tenants who had either done 'moonlight flits' leaving rent arrears or who had been evicted. The result, of course, is that the Group 8 estates rapidly became 'ghettos' of socially unacceptable (by middle-class standards) families. Such families included many single-parent households and families with a husband/father who was either chronically unemployed, in prison, or suffering from an incapacitating illness.

The sociospatial segregation resulting from such allocation policies is continuously reinforced by applications by existing tenants for *transfers* from one dwelling to another. This provides further opportunities for screening and grading, allowing 'deserving' and 'respectable' households to maintain or improve their housing status rather than having to remain in accommodation which may be ageing.

It is now recognized by housing managers that the localization of families in dump estates sets in motion a labelling process which results in the stigmatization of both the estate and its residents. Because of this stigmatization, accommodation in such areas becomes difficult to let. The problem is further exacerbated by societal reaction to dump estates, with media coverage helping to dramatize the situation and to reinforce 'moral panic' through the creation of sensational and sometimes distorted stereotypes. This, in turn, polarizes attitudes and behaviour both inside and outside dump estates, leading to an increase in antisocial behaviour on the part of the inhabitants, and therefore to a confirmation of the stereotypes and a further reinforcement of the area's undesirable character.

Finally, it is important to bear in mind that housing managers do not

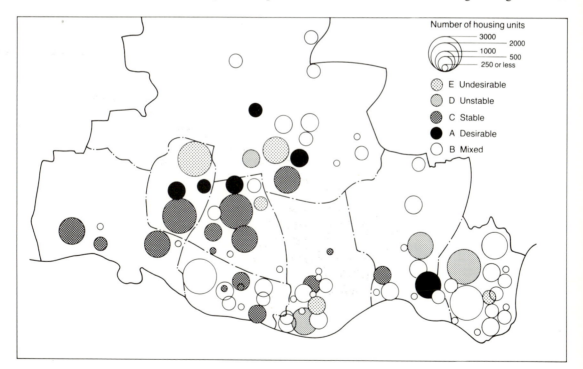

Figure 4.10
Estate quality in Newcastle upon Tyne as defined by consumers
Source: P. J. Taylor and H. Hadfield, in K. Cox and R. J. Johnston (eds) *Conflict, Politics, and the Urban Scene,* Longman, London, 1982, Fig. 12.7, p. 256.

have the power to determine the structure, form and quantity of the resources they distribute, even though they can control allocation procedures: 'No housing manager would plan to have problem estates but they have become endemic in British cities. Both tenants and managers are ultimately pawns of the system they operate in.'[73] Thus, while the basic operating principle in the public sector is 'need', families with the greatest need tend to end up in the least desirable accommodation. 'The end result is a hierarchy of council house estates in a manner not unlike the ranking of private estates by market mechanisms.'[74] Figure 4.10 illustrates the geography of this hierarchy in Newcastle upon Tyne.

SUGGESTED READING

The concept of the structures of building provision is Michael Ball's, and his original formulations can be consulted in his essay, 'The built environment and the urban question,' in *Environment & Planning D: Society and Space*, 1986, 447–464. Another useful essay on this sort of approach is by Patsy Healey and Susan Barrett: 'Structure and agency in land and property development processes', in *Urban Studies* (**27**, 1990, 89–104). A good introduction to housing submarkets, along with coverage of many of the issues dealt with in this chapter, is provided by Larry Bourne's *The Geography of Housing* (1981: Edward Arnold, London). A detailed view of the structure and processes characterizing an American metropolitan area is given by John Adams in *Our Changing Cities* (1991: J. F. Hart, ed., Johns Hopkins University Press, Baltimore). The sociospatial issues surrounding homeownership are best approached through Geraldine Pratt's work: see 'Incorporation theory and the reproduction of community fabric', in *The Power of Geography. How Territory Shapes Social Life* (1989: J. Wolch and M. Dear, eds, Unwin Hyman, London). Good sources on the role of key actors in the urban development process in America are Marc Weiss, *The Rise of the Community Builders* (1987: Columbia University Press, New York), and Joe Feagin and R. Parker, *Building American Cities* (1990: Prentice-Hall, Englewood Cliffs, NJ); on British cities, see Jeremy Whitehand, *The Making of the Urban Landscape* (1992: Basil Blackwell, Oxford). The roles of developers, planners, financiers, architects and others are also covered in *The Restless Urban Landscape* (1993: P. L. Knox, ed., Prentice-Hall, Englewood Cliffs, NJ). Liz Bondi provides a good review of the relationships between gender and urban design in her essay in *Progress in Human Geography* (**16**, 1992, 157–170). Linda McDowell provides an excellent review of the broader issues of space, place and gender relations in the same journal (**17**, 1993, pp. 157–179). More detailed sources include Leslie Weisman's *Discrimination By Design* (1992: University of Illinois Press, Urbana) and Daphne Spain's *Gendered Spaces* (1992: University of North Carolina Press, Chapel Hill).

NOTES

1. Ball, M., The built environment and the urban question, *Environment & Planning D: Society & Space*, **4,** 1986, 447–464; see also Healey, P. and S. Barrett, Structure and agency in land and property development processes, *Urban Studies*, **27,** 1990, 89–104.

2. Harvey, D., *Society, the City, and the Space-Economy of Urbanism.* Resource Paper No. 18, Commission on College Geography, Association of American Geographers, Washington, DC, 1972, p. 16.

3. London Borough of Southwark, Preliminary research, unpublished report, Planning Division, Southwark Development Department, London, 1973.

4. Choko, M., and R. Harris, The local culture of property: a comparative history of housing tenure in Montreal and Toronto, *Annals, Association of American Geographers*, **80,** 1990, 73–95.

5. US National Committee on Urban Problems, *Building the American City.* Washington, DC: US Government Printing Office, 1968, p. 401.

6. See, for example, Badcock, B., Homeownership and the accumulation of real wealth, *Environment & Planning D: Society and Space*, **7,** 1989, 69–91; and Munroe, M., and D. Maclennan, Intra-urban changes in house prices, *Housing Studies*, **2,** 1987, 65–81.

7. Hamnett, C., Housing the two nations, *Urban Studies*, **43,** 1984, 389–405.

8. *Ibid.*, p. 404. See also Hamnett, C. Consumption and class in contemporary Britain. In C. Hamnett, L. McDowell and P. Sarre (eds), *Restructuring Britain: The Changing Social Structure.* London: Sage, 1989; and Dickens, P., *One Nation? Social Change and the Politics of Locality*. London: Pluto Press, 1988.

9. Edel, M., E. Sclar, and D. Luria, *Shaky Palaces: Homeownership and Social Mobility in Boston's Suburbanization.* New York: Columbia University Press, 1984.

10. Pratt, G., Incorporation theory and the reproduction of community fabric. In J. Wolch and M. Dear (eds), *The Power of Geography. How Territory Shapes Social Life.* London: Unwin Hyman, 1989, pp. 293–315.

11. Saunders, P., Domestic property and social class, *International Journal of Urban and Regional Research*, **2,** 1978, 233–251.

12. Short, J. R., *Housing in Britain: The Postwar Experience.* London: Methuen, 1982, p. 150.

13. Pratt, G., Class analysis and urban domestic property, *International Journal of Urban and Regional Research*, **6,** 1982, 481–502.

14. Thorns, D.C., The impact of homeownership and capital gains upon class and consumption sectors, *Environment & Planning D: Society and Space*, **7,** 1989, 293–312.

15. Eversley, D., The landlords' slow farewell, *New Society*, **31,** 1975, 119–121.

16. Hamnett, C. and W. Randolph, The role of landlord disinvestment in housing market transformation: an analysis of the flat break-up market in central London, *Transactions, Institute of British Geographers*, **9,** 1984, 259–279.

17. Bowley, M., *Housing and the State.* London: Allen & Unwin, 1945, p. 9.

18. Sopher, D., Place and location: notes on the spatial patterning of culture, *Social Science Quarterly*, **52,** 1972, 321–337.

19. Twine, Y. F. and N. J. Williams, Social segregation and public sector housing: a case study, *Transactions, Institute of British Geographers*, **8,** 1983, 253–266.

20. Lambert, J., C. Paris, and R. Blackaby, *Housing Policy and the State*. London: Macmillan, 1978, p. 6.

21. Pahl, R., Urban social theory and research, *Environment & Planning A*, 1969, 143–153.

22. Norman, P., Managerialism: a review of recent work. In M. Harloe (ed.), *Proceedings of the Conference on Urban Change and Conflict*, Centre for Environmental Studies, London, 1975, p. 76.

23. Williams, P., Urban managerialism: a concept of relevance?, *Area*, **10,** 1978, 240.

24. Norman, Managerialism, p. 66.

25. Gray, The management of local authority housing. In *Housing and Class in Britain*, Political Economy of Housing Workshop, Conference of Socialist Economists, London, 1976, p. 81.

26. Harvey, R. O. and W. A. V. Clark, The nature and economics of urban sprawl, *Land Economics*, **41,** 1965, 1–9.

27. Robson, B. T., *Urban Social Areas*. Oxford: Clarendon Press, 1975.

28. Rowley, G., Landownership and the spatial growth of towns, *East Midland Geographer*, **6,** 1975, 200–213.

29. Pocock, D., landownership and urban growth in Scunthorpe, *East Midland Geographer*, **5,** 1970, 52–61.

30. Massey, D. and A. Catalano, *Capital and Land*. London: Arnold, 1978.

31. Craven, E., Private residential expansion in Kent. In R. E. Pahl (ed.), *Whose City?* Harmondsworth: Penguin, 1975, p. 124.

32. MacLaran, A., *Dublin*. London: Belhaven, 1993.

33. Harvey, D., *Society, the City, and the Space-Economy of Urbanism*. Washington, DC: Commission on College Geography, Resource Paper No. 18, Association of American Geographers, 1972.

34. Baerwald, T., The site selection process of suburban residential builders, *Urban Geography*, **2,** 1981, 351.

35. Nicholls, D. C., D. M. Turner, R. Kirby-Smith and J. D. Cullen, The risk business: developers' perception and prospects for housing in the inner city, *Urban Studies*, **19,** 1982, 331–341.

36. Zukin, S., *Landscapes of Power. From Detroit to Disney World*. Berkeley: University of California Press, 1991, p. 39.

37. See, for example, Zukin, S., The postmodern debate over urban form, *Theory, Culture and Society*, **5,** 1988, 431–446; and Knox, P. L., The social production of the built environment: architects, architecture, and the post-Modern city, *Progress in Human Geography*, **11,** 1987, 354–378.

38. McDowell, L., Towards an understanding of the gender division of urban space, *Environment & Planning D: Society and Space*, **1,** 1983, 59–72.

39. Mackenzie, S., Building women, building cities: toward gender sensitive theory in the environmental disciplines. In C. Andrew and B. Milroy (eds), *Life Spaces*. Vancouver: University of British Columbia Press, 1988, pp. 13–30.

40. Cited in Mazey, M. E. and D. R. Lee (eds), *Her Place: A Geography of Women*. Washington, DC: Association of American Geographers, 1983, p. 58.

41. Wilson, E., *The Sphinx in the City. Urban Life, The Control of Disorder, and Women*. Berkeley: University of California Press, 1991, p. 94.

42. Spain, D., *Gendered Spaces*. Chapel Hill: University of North Carolina Press, 1992; Weisman, L. K., *Discrimination by Design*. Urbana: University of Illinois Press, 1992.

43. Bondi, L., Gender symbols and urban landscapes, *Progress in Human Geography*, **16,** 1992, 157–170.

44. Madigan, R., M. Munro and S. Smith, Gender and the meaning of the home, *International Journal of Urban and Regional Research*, 1992, 625–647.

45. Geddes, P., *Cities in Evolution*. London: Williams and Norgate, 1947. First published in 1915.

46. Ravetz, A., *Remaking Cities*. London: Croom Helm, 1980.

47. Wilson, *The Sphinx in the City*, p. 6.

48. Ritzdorf, M., Regulating separate spheres. Changing gender roles and municipal land use planning, 1920–1989, *Proceedings, Society for American City and Regional Planning History*, 1989.

49. Stone, M. E., Housing mortgage lending and the contradictions of capitalism. In W. K. Tabb and L. Sawers (eds), *Marxism and the Metropolis*. New York: Oxford University Press, 1978, p. 190.

50. See, for example, Ford, J. R., The role of the building society manager in the urban stratification system: autonomy versus constraint, *Urban Studies*, **12,** 1975, 295–302.

51. Barbolet, R. H., *Housing Classes and the Socio-Ecological System*. London: Centre for Environmental Studies, Working Paper No. 4, 1969.

52. Harloe, M., R. Isacharoff and R. Minns, *The Organization of Housing*. London: Heinemann, 1974.

53. Ford, *Urban Studies*, p. 298.

54. Duncan, S. S., Self-help: the allocation of mortgages and the formation of housing sub-markets, *Area*, **8,** 1976, 310. For a recent review of financial discrimination in the United States, see Turner, M. A., R. J. Struyk and J. Yinger, *Housing Discrimination Study*. Washington, DC: The Urban Institute, 1991.

55. Knopp, L., Sexuality and the spatial dynamics of capitalism, *Environment & Planning D: Society and Space*, **10,** 1992, 651–669.

56. Bassett, K. A. and J. R. Short, Patterns of building society and local authority mortgage lending in the 1970s, *Environment & Planning A*, **12**, 286–287.

57. Weir, S., Red line districts, *Roof*, **1**, 1976, 113.

58. Darden, J., Lending practices and policies affecting the American Metropolitan System. In S. D. Brunn and J. O. Wheeler (eds), *The American Metropolitan System: Present and Future*. New York: Winston, 1980, p. 98.

59. Boddy, M., *The Building Societies*. London: Macmillan, 1980.

60. Taggart, H. and K. W. Smith, Redlining: an assessment of the evidence of disinvestment in metropolitan Boston, *Urban Affairs Quarterly*, **17**, 1981, 91–107.

61. Williams, P., *The role of financial institutions and estate agents in the private housing market*. Birmingham: Centre for Urban and Regional Studies, Working Paper 39, 1976, p. 58.

62. Palmer, R., Realtors as social gatekeepers. New Haven: Yale University, doctoral dissertation, 1955, p. 77.

63. *Ibid.*, p. 79.

64. See, for example, Downing, P. M. and L. Gladstone, *Segregation and Discrimination in Housing: A Review of Selected Studies and Legislation*. Washington, DC: Library of Congress, Congressional Research Report 89–317, 1989; Feins, J. D., and R. G. Bratt, Barred in Boston: Racial discrimination in housing, *Journal of the American Planning Association*, **49**, 1983, 344–355; James, F. J., B. I. McCummings and E.A. Tynan, *Minorities in the Sunbelt*. New Brunswick, NJ: Center for Urban Policy Research, Rutgers University, 1984.

65. Burney, E., *Housing on Trial*. Oxford: Oxford University Press, 1967, p. 39.

66. Harvey, *Society, The City, and the Space-Economy*.

67. Holmes, J. Urban housing problems and public policy. In M. Yeates and B. Garner (eds), *The North American City* 2nd edn. New York: Harper & Row, 1976, p. 411.

68. Williams, *The role of financial institutions*, p. 60.

69. Huttman, E. D., Subsidized housing segregation in Western Europe: Stigma and segregation. In E. Huttman, W. Blauw and J. Saltman (eds), *Urban Housing Segregation of Minorities in Western Europe and the United States*. Duke University Press, Durham, 1991, pp. 215–242.

70. Central Housing Advisory Committee, *Council Housing: Purposes, Procedures, and Priorities*. London: HMSO, 1969.

71. Gray, F., Selection and allocation in council housing, *Transactions, Institute of British Geographers*, **1**, 1976, 41; Skellington, R., How blacks lose out in council housing, *New Society*, **29**, January 1981, 188.

72. Damer, S. and R. Madigan, The housing investigator, *New Society*, **29**, 1974, 226.

73. Taylor, P. and H. Hadfield, Housing and the state: a case study and structuralist interpretation. In K. R. Cox and R. J. Johnston (eds), *Conflict, Politics, and the Urban Scene.* London: Longman, 1982, p. 259.

74. *Ibid.*, p. 256.

Corner bar, Milan.
Photograph by Paul Knox.

5 *The social dimensions of modern urbanism*

Urban Life in Western Culture • Urbanism and Social Theory • Social Interaction
and Social Networks in Urban Settings

An important part of the geographer's task of illuminating the nature and
causes of spatial differentiation is to lay bare the inter-relationships between
people and their environments. In urban social geography, this involves a
consideration of the complex interaction between individuals, social groups
and the diverse physical and socio-economic environments of the city. The
objective in this chapter is to provide some commentary on the theories and
ideas relevant to this task. It is based on the contention that the spatial order
of the city can only be properly understood against the background of the
underlying dimensions of social organization and human behaviour in the
city: the urban 'ultrastructure'. The suggestion is not, of course, that the
spatial order of the city is subordinate to social factors; the influence of
space and distance on individual behaviour and social organization will be
a recurring theme in this chapter as we explore the sociospatial dialectic in
close-up.

5.1 Urban Life in Western Culture

The traditional view of the overall relationship between people and their
urban environments has, for the most part, been negative. It is a view that
persists. Elizabeth Wilson, for example, claims that 'today in many cities

we have the worst of all worlds: danger without pleasure, safety without stimulation, consumerism without choice, monumentality without diversity'.[1] Public opinion and social theories about city life, together with the interpretations of many artists, writers, film-makers and musicians, tend to err towards negative impressions. They tend to be highly deterministic, emphasizing the ills of city life and blaming them on the inherent attributes of urban environments.

Evidence from attitudinal surveys, for example, suggests that most people believe city environments to be unsatisfactory. Only one in five Americans think that cities represent the best kind of environment in which to live; 30 per cent nominate suburban environments, and 44 per cent nominate small town or rural environments. Data from European surveys show a similar anti-urban leaning. Moreover, these attitudes show up not only in hypothetical residential preferences but also in evaluations of actual communities. Satisfaction with the overall 'quality of life' and with several major components of well-being tends to decline steadily with the transition from rural to metropolitan environments.[2] Such data, however, are notoriously difficult to interpret. A case in point is the apparent ambiguity of results that show people professing to prefer rural or small-town living but whose behaviour has brought them to the city, presumably in pursuit of a higher material level of living. The city thus emerges as neither good nor bad, but as a 'necessary evil'.

This lopsided ambivalence towards the city – a grudging functional attraction accompanied by an intellectual dislike – has long been reflected in the literature and art of Western society (including the idiom of popular songs). Raymond Williams, for example, showed that while British literature has occasionally celebrated the positive attributes of city life, there has been a much greater emphasis on its defects, paralleled by the persistence of a romanticist portrayal of country life. For every urban thrill and sophistication there are several urban laments and rural yearnings.[3]

Some writers have been able to demonstrate how the city has in addition been regarded as a catalyst, a challenge and a 'stage' for the enactment of human drama and personal life-style by certain schools of thought.[4] Charles Beaudelaire, writing in the mid-nineteenth century, was among the first to see in modern cities the possibility for transcending traditional values and cultural norms. He saw that the city can turn people outward, providing them with *experiences of otherness*. The power of the city to reorient people in this way lies in its diversity. In the presence of difference, people at least have the possibility to step outside themselves, even if it is just for a short while. It is this quality that makes cities so stimulating to many of us. Yet the significance of the diversity of city life goes much further. As we are exposed to otherness, so our impressions of city life and urban society and the meanings we draw from them are modified and renegotiated. In this way, our cultures (i.e. systems of shared meanings) take on a fluidity and a dynamism that is central to the sociospatial dialectic.

The cumulative image of the city has thus come to be 'a montage of mixed and clashing elements: . . . of senseless, brutal crime; of personal freedom and boundless hopes; of variety, choice, excitement; of callous and uncaring people; of social groups diverse enough to satisfy each individual's unique needs; of crass and crushing materialism; of experiment, innovation and creativity; of anxious days and frightful nights'.[6] New York, to most people, is probably the exemplar of this diversity. On the one hand it is able to prompt the horrific stereotype of urban life portrayed in Feiffer's play *Little Murders*, in which the principal character asks:

> You know how I get through the day? . . . in planned segments. I get up in the morning and think, O.K. a sniper didn't get me for breakfast, let's see if I can go for a walk without being mugged.
> O.K., I finished my walk, let's see if I can make it back home without having a brick dropped on my head from the top of a building. O.K., I'm safe in the lobby, let's see if I can go up in the elevator without getting a knife in my ribs.
> O.K., I made it to the front door, let's see if I can open it without finding burglars in the hall. O.K. I made it to the hall, let's see if I can walk into the living room and not find the rest of my family dead.[7]

On the other hand, the advantages of life in a city like New York include accessibility to a tremendous variety of opportunities. Fischer cites the reaction of a 'refugee' New Yorker living in Vermont:

> I kept hearing this tempting ad for a Czechoslovakian restaurant . . .
> When the ad went on to say that this particular place had been chosen by the critic of the *Times* out of all the Czech restaurants in New York as the very best, I could have broken down and cried. We hardly get a choice of doughnut stands in Vermont; New Yorkers idly pick and choose among Czech restaurants.[8]

Fischer suggests that it is possible to recognize four basic themes within this ambivalent imagery of cities, each expressed as polarities:

Fischer points out that there is a 'tension' in these pairings which derives from the fact that neither half is universally 'better' or 'worse' than the other. Instead, they pose dilemmas of personal choice. Depending on which horn of the dilemma they have grasped, philosophers and poets have become either pro-urbanists or (as is usually the case) anti-urbanists.

Rural		Urban
Nature	versus	Art
Familiarity	versus	Strangeness
Community	versus	Individualism
Tradition	versus	Change

These polarities are also present in the stock of social theories concerning city life. The strangeness, artificiality, individualism and diversity of urban environments have been seen by many social scientists as fundamental influences on human behaviour and social organization. This deterministic and environmentalist perspective has had a profound effect on the study of urban social geography as well as on sociology and all the cognate disciplines. It stems from the writings of European social philosophers such as Durkheim, Weber, Simmel and Tönnies, who were seeking to understand the social and psychological implications of the urbanism and urbanization associated with the Industrial Revolution of the nineteenth century.

The kernel of this classic sociological analysis is the association between the scale of society and its 'moral order'. Basically, the argument runs as follows. In pre-industrial society small, fairly homogeneous populations contain people who know each other, perform the same kind of work and have the same kind of interests: they thus tend to look, think and behave alike, reflecting a consensus of values and norms of behaviour. In contrast, the inhabitants of large cities constitute part of what Durkheim called a 'dynamic density' of population subject to new forms of economic and social organization as a result of economic specialization and innovations in transport and communications technology. In this urbanized, industrial society there is contact with more people but close 'primary' relationships with family and friends are less easily sustained. At the same time, social differentiation brings about a divergence of life-styles, values and aspirations, thus weakening social consensus and cohesion and threatening to disrupt social order. This, in turn, leads to attempts to adopt 'rational' approaches to social organization, a proliferation of formal controls and, where these are unsuccessful, to an increase in social disorganization and deviant behaviour.

The impact of these ideas on urban geography came chiefly by way of their adoption and modification in the 1920s and 1930s by researchers in the Department of Sociology in the University of Chicago under the leadership of Robert Park, a former student of Georg Simmel. Like earlier theorists, Park believed that urbanization produced new environments, new types of people and new ways of life. The net result, he suggested, was 'a mosaic of little worlds which touch but do not interpenetrate'.[9] He encouraged the 'exploration' and empirical documentation of these social worlds by his colleagues and, as a result, there developed an influential series of 'natural histories' of the distinctive groups and areas of Chicago in the 1920s: juvenile gangs, hobos, the rooming house area, prostitutes, taxi-hall dancers, the Jewish ghetto, and so on.[10] These studies represented part of an approach to urban sociology which became known as *Human Ecology*, the principles of which are discussed below.

A closely related and equally influential approach to urban sociology also sprang from Chicago a few years later: the so-called Wirthian theory of urbanism as a way of life. Wirth's ideas, although they contained much of the thinking inherent to Human Ecology, synthesized a wide range of deterministic principles relevant to individual as well as group behaviour. Wirth, like Park, had studied under Georg Simmel and was heavily influenced by Simmel's work on 'The metropolis and mental life'.[11] Putting Simmel's ideas together with subsequent work from the human ecologists, Wirth produced his classic essay, 'Urbanism as a way of life',[12] which became one of the most often quoted and reprinted articles in the literature of the city. Wirth attributed the social and psychological consequences of city life (i.e. 'urbanism') to the combined effects of three factors which he saw as the products of increasing urbanization:

1 The increased size of populations
2 The increased density of populations
3 The increased heterogeneity, or differentiation, of populations.

At the *personal* level the effect of these factors, Wirth suggested, is as follows: faced with the abundant and varied physical and social stimuli experienced in the large, dense and highly diverse city environment, the individual has to adapt 'normal' behaviour in order to cope. City dwellers thus become, for example, aloof, brusque and impersonal in their dealings with others: emotionally buffered in their relationships. Nevertheless, the intense stimuli of city environments will sometimes generate what has subsequently been dubbed a 'psychic overload', leading to anxiety and nervous strain. Furthermore, the loosening of personal bonds through this adaptive behaviour tends to leave people both *unsupported* in times of crisis and *unrestrained* in pursuing ego-centred behaviour. The net result, Wirth argues, is an increase in the incidence, on the one hand, of social incompetence, loneliness and mental illness and, on the other, of deviant behaviour of all kinds: from the charmingly eccentric to the dangerously criminal.

Wirth draws a parallel picture of *social* change associated with the increased size, density and heterogeneity of urban populations. The specialized neighbourhoods and social groupings resulting from economic competition and the division of labour result in a fragmentation of social life between home, school, workplace, friends and relatives; and so people's time and attention are divided among unconnected people and places. This weakens the social support and control of primary social groups such as family, friends and neighbours, leading to a lack of social order and an increase in 'social disorganization'. Moreover, these trends are reinforced by the weakening of social norms (the rules and conventions of proper and permissible behaviour) resulting from the divergent interests and life-styles of the various specialized groups in the city. The overall societal response is to replace the support and controls formerly provided by primary social groups with 'rational' and impersonal procedures and institutions (welfare agencies, criminal codes supported by police forces, etc.). According to Wirth, however, such an order can never replace a communal order based on consensus and the moral strength of small primary groups. As a result, situations develop in which social norms are so muddled and weak that a social condition known as *anomie* develops: individuals, unclear or unhappy about norms, tend to challenge or ignore them, thus generating a further source of deviant behaviour.

The Public and Private Worlds of City Life

One of the persistent problems associated with Wirthian theory has been that the results of empirical research have been ambivalent. Most of the available evidence comes from four kinds of research: studies of helpfulness, conflict, social ties and psychological states. In general, the first two tend to support Wirthian theory, while the second two undermine it.

Studies of *helpfulness* have typically involved field experiments designed to gauge reactions to 'strangers' who, for example, reach 'wrong' telephone numbers with their 'last' coin, who have 'lost' addressed letters, who ask for directions, and so on. The general drift of the results has been that city dwellers tend to be significantly less helpful than small-town residents.[13] Studies of *conflict* show that both group conflict – racial, social and economic – and interpersonal conflict – certain categories of crime – are disproportionately likely to occur in large communities.[14]

On the other hand, studies that have attempted to compare the number of quality of friendships or *personal relations* have generally shown no difference between different-sized communities, or have shown greater social integration among urbanites. Similarly, studies of *psychological states* such as stress and alienation show that the incidence of such phenomena is just as great, if not greater, in smaller communities.[15]

Accepting the validity of all these findings, how might they be reconciled? One way is to re-examine the idea of urban environments, recognizing the distinction between the public and the private spheres of urban life. The former consists of settings where people are strangers, in which it requires a special etiquette: reserved, careful, non-intrusive. In the public sphere, people must be – or at least appear to be – indifferent to other people. Richard Sennett contends that modern cultures suffer from having deliberately divided off subjective experience from worldly experience, that we have – literally – constructed our urban spaces in order to maintain this divide:

> The spaces full of people in the modern city are either spaces limited to and carefully orchestrating consumption, like the shopping mall, or spaces limited to and carefully orchestrating the experience of tourism. . . . The way cities look reflects a great, unreckoned fear of exposure. 'Exposure' more connotes the likelihood of being hurt than of being stimulated. . . . What is characteristic of our city-building is to wall off the differences between people, assuming that these differences are more likely to be mutually threatening than mutually stimulating. What we

make in the urban realm are therefore bland, neutralizing spaces, spaces which remove the threat of social contact: street walls faced in sheets of plate glass, highways that cut off poor neighborhoods from the rest of the city, dormitory housing developments.[17]

But avoiding 'exposure', whether through individual comportment or through urban design, is situational behaviour, not a psychological state, and says nothing about people's attitudes and actions in the private sphere. The city dweller 'did not *lose* the capacity for the deep, long-lasting, multifaceted relationship. But he *gained* the capacity for the surface, fleeting, restricted relationship'.[18] Fischer has drawn on this distinction, suggesting that urbanism is not characterized by distrust, estrangement and alienation among neighbours although it is associated with estrangement and alienation from 'other people' in the wider community. In other words, 'urbanism produces fear and distrust of "foreign" groups in the public sphere, but does not affect private social worlds'.[19] In Wirthian terminology, this means that urbanism accommodates both 'moral order' and 'social disorganization'.

The Self: Identity and Experience in Private and Public Worlds

Questions about how individuals and social groups come to identify themselves and 'others' require us to give some consideration as to how human subjects are constructed: how we come to think of our*selves* within our worlds, both public and private. At first sight, this may seem to be an issue that is somewhat removed from the concerns of geography. In fact, it is a fundamentally geographic issue: as 'knowledgeable' subjects, our intentionality and subjectivity are grounded in social relations and direct experiences that are geographically bounded. They are bounded, moreover, by spaces occupied by other 'knowledgeable subjects', which means that our 'selves' are, to a certain extent, constructed by others. As Andrew Sayer puts it, 'what you are depends not just on what you have, together with how you conceive yourself, but on how others relate to you, on what they understand you to be and themselves to be'.[20] Put another way, we have to accommodate to meanings, roles and identities imposed through the expectations of others.

In order to come to grips with this subjectivity we ought to begin with the 'unknowing subject' through psychoanalytic theory. For some social scientists, this carries the attraction of allowing us to admit human emotions such as love, desire, narcissism, anxiety, hate and suffering to our models:

> These . . . feelings are the core of our being, the stuff of our everyday lives. They are the foundations of all society. They come before symbolic meaning and value, lead us continually to reinterpret, hide from, evade and recreate thoughts and values. They inspire our practical uses of rules and they are the reasons behind our reasoned accounts. . . . Without feelings, there would be no uses for rules, ideas, or social structures; and there would be none.[21]

The case for deploying psychoanalytic theories such as those of Freud and Lacan in the context of social geography has been made by several authors,[22] though little empirical research has been carried out. Proponents of the relevance of psychoanalytic models to social geography point to the work of Alice Miller, who has shown how children repress and restructure their feelings and emotions in order to achieve a sense of safety and security amid the demands and expectations of others.[23]

Miller calls this process of repression and restructuring 'the construction of the false self'. This can be seen as the first step towards the creation of knowledgeable subjects whose personal and social identities are conditioned by various dimensions of lived experience such as family life, school, community, work and class consciousness. It follows, as Michael Watts points out, that personal and social identities have to be seen as malleable and flexible, continually subject to negotiation.[24] They are 'stories told by ourselves about ourselves' in order to cope with our experiences and to operate successfully in the urban settings in which we find ourselves. They are also part of what de Certeau calls the 'constant murmuring of secret creativity' resulting from individuals' attributing certain meanings to their relations with the world(s) around them.[25] The significance of this 'murmuring' is that it becomes embodied, in time, within cultural practices that constitute an 'upward cultural dynamics' which, in turn, engages dialectically with the cultural norms and meanings that are passed 'downward' by tastemakers, educators, and all sorts of 'experts' in science, morality and art.[26] In contemporary cities, the significance of upward cultural dynamics is widely accepted as being of increasing importance. In part, this can be attributed to the swing towards post-modern sensibilities (see p. 13); in part, it is the product, as Giddens points out, of a more open social texture and of people's ability to choose from a multiplicity of life-style options and sociocultural contexts.[27]

5.3 *Social Interaction and Social Networks in Urban Settings*

Most people are involved in several different relationships which may be inter-connected to a greater or lesser extent. We not only have friends, but know friends-of-friends; and kinfolk do not exist in isolation: we may get to know a complete stranger because he or she is a member of the same club or organization as an uncle, an aunt, or a cousin. The way in which these social linkages are structured is often very complex and, overall, they represent the foundations of social organization. Not surprisingly, therefore, the analysis of these linkages – known as *social network analysis* – has attracted a good deal of attention. Basically, social network analysis attempts to illustrate the structure of social interaction by treating persons as points and relationships as connecting lines. The analysis of social networks thus allows the researcher to 'map out the complex reality of the interpersonal worlds surrounding specific individuals',[28] and has the advantage of not being confined, a priori, to any specific level of analysis such as the family or the neighbourhood. As with the analysis of other kinds of networks – in transport geography and physical geography, for example – this approach facilitates not only the 'mapping' of the 'morphology' of networks (Fig. 5.1), but also the quantification of certain key characteristics such as their 'connectedness', 'centrality', 'proximity' and 'range'.

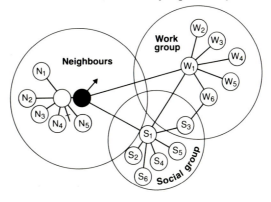

Figure 5.1
The morphology of a husband's social network
Source: C. A. Smith and C. J. Smith, *Area*, 10, 1978, p. 106.

Recent empirical research on social networks has suggested that the number of *potential* contacts for interaction in the social networks of 'typical' urbanites (defined as white, male, married, about 40 years old, with a child in elementary school) in North American cities is about 1500, with *actual* networks averaging about 400 contacts.[29] For the most part, these networks are loosely or moderately knit, with less than half of any one person's network knowing one another independently of that person. Furthermore, very few of these social ties provide significant levels of support and companionship. Wellman estimates that about 20 of the 400 in the typical network are 'active', about 10 are 'interactive', about 5 are 'intimate', and just one or two are 'confidants'.[30]

Any one person may belong to several different and non-overlapping social networks at the same time, and each of these networks may well have different properties: some may be spatially bounded while others are not; some may have dentritic structures while others are web-like, with interlocking ties, clusters, knots or sub-graphs. Early formulations of types of social networks were based on the notion of a continuum of networks ranging from *looseknit* (where few members of the network know each other independently) to *closeknit* (where most members of the network know each other); but this presents practical difficulties in operationalizing a definition of linkage. Should it extend beyond kinship and friendship to acquaintance or 'knowledge of' another person, or what? And how is friendship, for instance, to be measured? In an attempt to minimize such confusion, a typology of social situations has been proposed which incorporates the

Structure

Plexity	Dense	Looseknit	Single
Multiplex	**A**		
Simplex			
Uniplex			**B**

Figure 5.2
A typology of social situations
Source: C. R. Bell and H. Newby, in D. T. Herbert and R. J. Johnston (eds) *Social Areas in Cities*, v. 2, 1976, p. 109.

notion of the complexity as well as the structure of social networks (Fig. 5.2). The typology can be illustrated by way of the extreme and limiting cases: 'A' and 'B' in the diagram:

> A is the traditional community as normally understood: social relationships are multiplex in that, for example, neighbours are workmates are kinsmen are leisure-time companions, and the social network has a dense structure in that everyone knows everyone else. B is the situation of idealized urban anonymous anomie: social relationships are uniplex (the taxidriver and his fare), fleeting, impersonal and anonymous, and the social network structure is single-stranded in that only one person knows the others.[31]

This incorporation of the overlap and complexity of different networks brings us away from abstraction and a step nearer to reality. One person who has illustrated the practical relevance of network analysis is Christopher Smith, who has investigated the 'pro-social' behaviour of informal self-help networks which exist in modern cities.[32] Smith suggests – in contrast to the postulates of Wirthian theory – that self-help networks emerge in cities in order to provide help in many different contexts, and that their existence prevents formal welfare agencies from being swamped.

> In the mental health area, for example, help is being provided every hour of the day by people from all walks of life, including neighbours, relatives, ministers and shopkeepers. Dozens of helping hands and sympathetic ears are called on each day . . . Instead of going to an agency for help, many people prefer to search out someone in their own social network. It is quicker and cheaper; it is often more successful; and it is certainly less humiliating than going to a mental health centre.[33]

The focus of these self-help networks is often the 'natural neighbour': a person with a propensity to become involved or make himself or herself available in resolving the problems of other people, whether for self-aggrandizement, altruism, or some other motive. They are usually un-trained amateurs who may not consciously recognize their own role in helping others. Indeed, they may not actually provide any direct help themselves but act as 'brokers', putting people in touch with someone who can help. A study of neighbourhoods in the Detroit area was able to trace the patterns of helping networks used by people when high levels of expertise were not thought to be necessary (for problems related to tension or mild depression, for example, or for advice about retirement decisions, changing jobs, etc.).[34] Married persons turned most frequently to their spouse (82 per cent), while those with jobs often turned to co-workers (42 per cent). Other helpers were friends (41 per cent), relatives not living in the same household (37 per cent), neighbours (27 per cent), and a variety of professional workers such as police, clergy, doctors, counsellors and teachers (none more than 8 per cent). Except for co-workers, *most of these helpers were found within the neighbourhood.* When respondents were asked if they had been helped by a neighbour during a 'life crisis' in the previous year (e.g. personal injury, serious illness, death of a close family member, change of job, crime victimization), 56 per cent said they had.

But the study of social networks does not provide the urban social geographer with a sufficiently holistic approach: there remain the fundamental questions of the extent to which social networks of various kinds are spatially defined, and at what scales: questions that have as yet received little attention. This brings us to a consideration of the ideas of urban social ecology. Here, we must return once again to the foundational ideas of the Chicago School.

Urban Ecology as Shaper and Outcome of Social Interaction

Because the deterministic ideas of Robert Park and his colleagues in the Chicago School of urban sociology have been so influential, they merit careful consideration. The most distinctive feature of the approach adopted by the Human Ecologists is the conception of the city as a kind of social organism, with individual behaviour and social organization governed by a 'struggle for existence'. The biological analogy provided Park and his colleagues with an attractive general framework in which to place their studies of the 'natural histories' and 'social worlds' of different groups in Chicago. Just as in plant and animal communities, Park concluded, order in human communities must emerge through the operation of 'natural' processes such as dominance, segregation, impersonal competition and succession. If the analogy now seems somewhat naïve, it should be remembered that it was conceived at a time when the appeal of Social Darwinism and classical economic theory was strong. Moreover, ecological studies of plants and animals provided a rich source of concepts and a graphic terminology with which to portray the sociology of the city.

One of the central concepts was that of *impersonal competition* between individuals for favourable locations within the city. This struggle was acted out primarily through market mechanisms, resulting in a characteristic pattern of land rents and the consequent *segregation* of different types of people according to their ability to meet the rents associated with different sites and situations. Economic differentiation was thus seen as the basic mechanism of residential segregation, and the local *dominance* of a particular group was ascribed to its relative competitive power. Functional relationships between different individuals and social groups were seen as *symbiotic* and, where such relationships could be identified as being focused within a particular geographical area, the human ecologists identified *communities*, or *natural areas*: 'territorial units whose distinctive characteristics – physical, economic and cultural – are the result of the unplanned operation of ecological and social processes'.[35] As the competitive power of different groups altered and the relative attractiveness of different locations changed in the course of time, these territories were seen to shift. Once more, ecological concepts were invoked to describe the process, this time using the ideas of *invasion* and *succession* derived from the study of plant communities.

These concepts were all brought together by Burgess in his model of residential differentiation and neighbourhood change in Chicago. Observations on the location and extent of specific communities formed the basis for the identification of an urban spatial structure consisting of a series of concentric zones (Fig. 5.3). These zones were seen by Burgess as reflections of the differential economic competitive power of broad groups within society, whereas the further segregation of smaller areas within each zone – such as the ghetto, Chinatown and Little Sicily within the zone of transition – were seen as reflections of symbiotic relationships forged on the basis of language, culture and race. The model was set out in terms of dynamic change as well as the spatial disposition of different groups. Zones I to V represent, in Burgess's words, 'both the successive zones of urban extension and the types of areas differentiated in the process of expansion'.[36] As the city grew, the changing occupancy of each zone was related to the process of invasion and succession, and Burgess was able to point to many examples of this in Chicago in the early 1900s as successive waves of immigrants worked their way from their initial quarters in the zone of transition (Zone

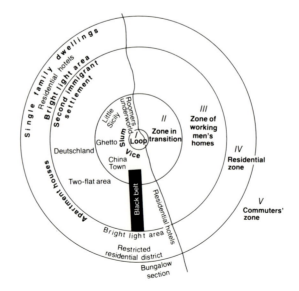

Figure 5.3
Burgess's zonal model applied to Chicago
Source: R. Park et al., *The City*, University of Chicago Press, Chicago, 1925, p. 53.

II) to more salubrious neighbourhoods elsewhere. In his diagrammatic model, some of the early immigrant groups – the Germans are explicitly noted – have already 'made it' to the area of superior accommodation in Zone III and become the dominant group, replacing second-generation American families who had moved out to colonize the outer residential zone (Zone IV).

Within this broad framework three types of study were produced by the school of Human Ecologists:[37]

1. Studies focusing on the process of competition, dominance and succession and their consequences for the spatial distribution of populations and land use. Such work is best represented by the early writings of Park, Burgess and McKenzie described above.

2. Detailed descriptions of the physical features of 'natural' areas along with the social, economic and demographic characteristics of their inhabitants. Well-known examples of this type of work include Wirth's study of *The Ghetto* (1928) and Zorbaugh's portrayal of Chicago's 'near' North Side in *The Gold Coast and the Slum* (1929).[38] Zorbaugh's work provides a good example of the intimate portrayal of individual social worlds set in the framework of broader ecological theory. The near North Side area was part of the zone in transition and contained four distinctive natural areas: the Gold Coast, a wealthy neighbourhood adjacent to the lakeshore; a rooming house area with a top-heavy demographic structure and a high population turnover; a bright-lights district – Towertown – with brothels, dance-halls and a 'bohemian' population; and a slum area containing clusters of immigrant groups. Zorbaugh showed how the personality of these different quarters related to their physical attributes – the 'habitat' they offered – as well as to the attributes and ways of life of their inhabitants. Moreover, he was also able to illustrate the dynamism of the area, charting the territorial shifts of different groups resulting from the process of invasion and succession.

3. Studies of the ecological context of specific social phenomena such as delinquency, prostitution and mental disorders. A central concern was the investigation of ecologies which seemed to generate high levels of deviant behaviour, and typical examples include the work by Shaw *et al.* on *Delinquency Areas* (1929) and Faris and Dunham's work on *Mental Disorders in Urban Areas* (1939).[39] Much of this work had a clear 'geographical' flavour since it often involved mapping exercises. It also provided the stimulus for a number of the more recent studies discussed in Chapter 8.

Criticisms of the Ecologcal Approach

Ecological research was neglected during the 1940s and 1950s following a series of theoretical and empirical critiques. The most general criticism was directed towards the biological analogies, which had been brought into great disrepute by the parallel concept of *Lebensraum*, part of the theory of geopolitics used to justify some of the territorial claims of Hitler's Third Reich. Other criticisms were more specific, centring on the excessive reliance on competition as the basis of social organization, the failure of its general structural concepts (such as the natural area and concentric zonation) to hold up under comparative examination, and its almost complete exclusion of cultural and motivational factors in explaining residential behaviour.[40]

This last criticism was perhaps the most damaging of all. The first (and therefore best-known) critic of the Chicago school, on the grounds that they overlooked the role of 'sentiment' and 'symbolism' in people's behaviour, was Walter Firey, who pointed to the evidence of social patterns in Boston where, although there were 'vague concentric patterns', it was clear that the persistence of the status and social characteristics of distinctive neighbourhoods such as Beacon Hill, The Common and the Italian North End could be attributed in large part to the 'irrational' and 'sentimental' values attached to them by different sections of the population. In short, social values could – and often did – override impersonal, economic competition as the basis for sociospatial organization. Firey's work is significant in that it directed the attention of geographers and sociologists to the importance of the subjective world in the understanding of social patterns in cities.

In fairness to the Chicago school, it should be acknowledged that they themselves did not regard their ideas on human ecology as either comprehensive or universally applicable. Park, for instance, clearly distinguished two levels of social organization: the *biotic* and the *cultural.* The former, he argued, was governed by impersonal competition whereas the latter was shaped by the consensus of social values. These cultural aspects of social organization clearly encompass Firey's notions of sentiment and symbolism, and Park and his colleagues were well aware of their influence. Park believed, however, that it was possible to study the biotic level of social organization separately, treating social values and communications as a kind of superstructure of the more basic level of the community. It is thus not so much the denial of non-biotic factors as the inadequacy of their treatment which led to the unpopularity of traditional human ecology.

Reformulations

Since the demise of traditional Human Ecology there have been several reformulations of the original ideas and concepts and, with the consequent excision of the crude mechanistic and biotic analogies, there has been a considerable revival of interest in ecological approaches. Wirth's synthesis of the effects of urban life on individual and social behaviour represented the first significant shift away from the biotic approach. Later, the concept of natural areas was reformulated by Hatt, who emphasized that natural areas, defined as discrete territories containing a homogeneous population with distinctive social characteristics, could offer a useful framework for further social analysis.[42] This is a position that has been adopted subsequently by social geographers in many avenues of investigation, even though the term 'natural area' has been abandoned in favour of less deterministic terminology such as 'social areas' or 'neighbourhood types'.

Further important contributions to the refinement of the ecological approach were made by Hawley and Schnore.[43] Hawley presented the ecological approach as the study of the form and development of community structure, emphasizing the functional inter-dependence within communities that results from the collective adaptation to competition. Schnore was able to place human ecology in perspective by elaborating in detail the preconditions and assumptions implicit in the work of Burgess and others. Schnore's own preference is for an approach in which the notion of ecology is used as a conceptual or statistical framework within which to analyse the internal structure of the city. Their work, modified sufficiently to avoid the worst shortcomings of traditional Human Ecology, was an important link with more recent work on ecological patterns in cities, e.g. Suttles's work on the Addams area of Chicago, Kearsley's attempt to

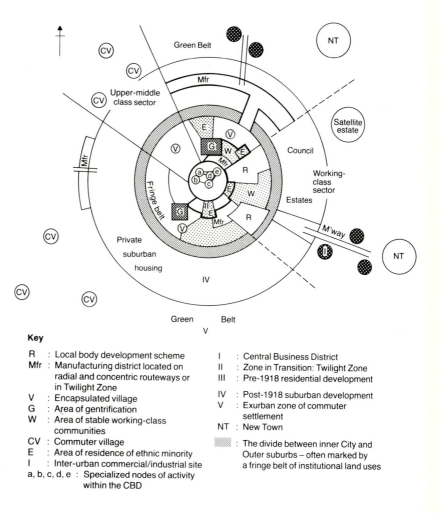

Figure 5.4
A modified Burgess model
Source: G. Kearsley, *New Zealand Journal of Geography*, 75, 1983, Fig. 1, p. 12.

Key

R : Local body development scheme
Mfr : Manufacturing district located on radial and concentric routeways or in Twilight Zone
V : Encapsulated village
G : Area of gentrification
W : Area of stable working-class communities
CV : Commuter village
E : Area of residence of ethnic minority
I : Inter-urban commercial/industrial site
a, b, c, d, e : Specialized nodes of activity within the CBD

I : Central Business District
II : Zone in Transition: Twilight Zone
III : Pre-1918 residential development
IV : Post-1918 suburban development
V : Exurban zone of commuter settlement
NT : New Town

▓ : The divide between inner City and Outer suburbs – often marked by a fringe belt of institutional land uses

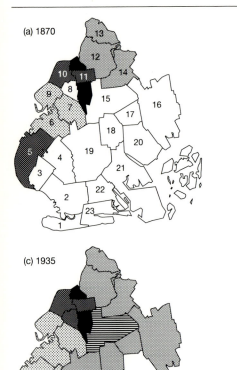

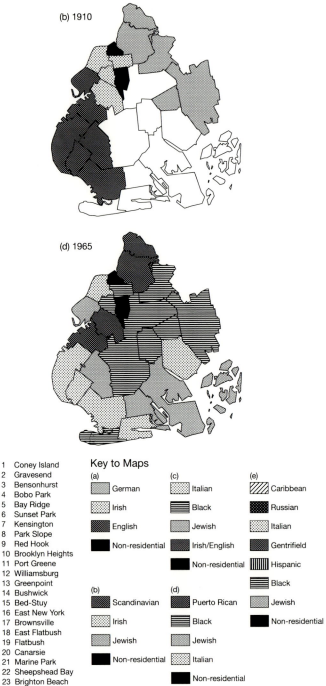

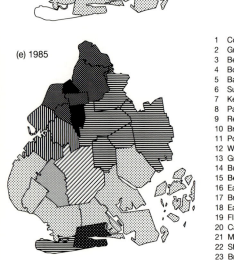

Figure 5.5 Distribution of ethnic groups in Brooklyn, 1870-1985
Source: B Warf, *Environment & Planning D: Society and Space*, 8, 1990, Figs 1-5.

modify Burgess's model of urban structure in such a way as to incorporate contemporary aspects of urbanization such as inner-city decline, gentrification and decentralization (Fig. 5.4), and Warf's reconstruction of the changing social ecology of Brooklyn (Fig. 5.5) that incorporates labour market changes and accommodates the constitutive role of culture and intentionality.[44] Meanwhile, many researchers had begun to describe and analyse the external characteristics of urban communities in ways that were divorced from any specific theoretical framework. This 'abstracted empiricism' became very well represented within urban geography – reaching its apotheosis in studies of factorial ecology (see pp. 45–57).

Social Interaction in Urban Environments

A quite different approach to the study of social organization in urban environments has developed from the pursuit of another of Georg Simmel's suggestions: that the essentials of social organization are to be found in the *forms of interaction* among individuals. At the most fundamental level, interactionist research seeks to establish the nature of non-random interaction patterns at the 'dyadic' or 'triadic' level: that is, between two or three individuals. A good deal of this research has involved the temporal and sequential characteristics of personal relationships, focusing on considerations of initiative, role and status, but it is the qualities of the *nature* and *intensity* of interaction which hold most interest for geographers.[45]

It is common for the nature of interaction to be classified according to whether it takes place in the context of primary or secondary settings. *Primary* relationships include those between kinfolk – based on ties of blood and duty – and those between friends – based on ties of attraction and mutual interest. Beyond this distinction, the nature of primary relationships may be further qualified. For example, family relationships may be differentiated according to whether the setting is a 'nuclear' unit – husband, wife and offspring – or an 'extended' unit which includes members of more than two generations. Interaction between friends may be differentiated according to whether the friendship is based on age, culture, locality, and so on.

Secondary relationships are more purposive, involving individuals who group together to achieve particular ends. Such relationships are conveniently subdivided into those in which there is some intrinsic satisfaction in the interaction involved – known as 'expressive' interaction – and those in which the interaction is merely a means of achieving some common goal – 'instrumental' interaction. Both kinds are normally set within a broad group framework. Expressive interaction, for example, is typically facilitated by voluntary associations of various kinds: sports, hobby and social clubs, and 'do-gooding' associations. Instrumental interaction, on the other hand, normally takes place within the framework of business associations, political parties, trade unions and pressure groups. In addition, some writers would include interaction between members of ethnic, religious, and even cultural groups under the label of purposive secondary relationships. It has been suggested, for example, that such relationships exist essentially to protect or advance the interests of individuals who are similarly placed on cultural, economic or political spectra.[46]

Social Distance and Physical Distance

This perspective illustrates the complexity of reality and the difficulty of pigeon-holing human behaviour. Moreover, the difficulties of conceptual and empirical classifications of different types of interaction are compounded by the fact that the propensity for, and intensity of, interaction of all kinds is strongly conditioned by the effects of distance: both *social distance* and *physical distance*. There is, however, some overlap in practice between these two concepts of distance; and a further level of complexity is introduced by the fact that patterns of interaction are not only affected by the physical and social structure of cities but that they themselves also have an effect on city structure. Unravelling the processes involved in this apparently indivisible chain of events is a central concern of urban social geography. Before proceeding to a consideration of more complex situations, however, some initial clarification of the role of social and physical distance is in order.

The idea of *social distance* has a long history, and is graphically illustrated by Bogardus's attempt to measure the perceived social distance between native-born white Americans and other racial, ethnic and linguistic groups.[47] He suggested that social distance could be reflected by a ranked scale of social relationships which people would be willing to sanction: the further up the scale, the closer the perceived distance between people:

1. to admit to close kinship by marriage;
2. to have as a friend;
3. to have as a neighbour on the same street;
4. to admit as a member of one's occupation within one's country;
5. to admit as a citizen of one's country;
6. to admit only as a visitor to one's country;
7. to exclude entirely from one's country.

It is now generally accepted that the less social distance there is between individuals, the greater the probability of interaction of some kind. Similarly, the greater the physical proximity between people – their 'residential propinquity' – the more likelihood of interaction of some kind. The exact influence of social and physical distance depends to some extent on the nature of the interaction concerned. Instrumental interaction related to trade unions or political parties, for instance, will clearly be less dependent on physical distance than instrumental interaction which is focused on a local action group concerned with the closure of a school, the construction of a power station, or the organization of a block party. In most cases, of course, the influences of social and physical distance are closely interwoven and difficult to isolate. Membership of voluntary associations, for example, tends to reflect class and life-style, with participation depending largely on social distance. Middle-class groups, in particular, have a propensity to use voluntary associations as a means of establishing and sustaining social relationships. But, because of the close correspondence between social and residential segregation, membership of such associations is also strongly correlated with locational factors.

Geographers, of course, have a special interest in the role of distance, space and location. There is, however, no real consensus on the role of propinquity in stimulating or retarding social interaction. One well-known study which is often quoted in support of the importance of distance at the micro-scale was based on the friendship patterns within two housing projects and found that friendship patterns appeared to be governed by 'the mere physical arrangement of the houses'.[48] These results, however, were based on a sample drawn from a very special case – the interaction between married engineering students studying at the Massachusetts Institute of Technology – and so their generality is doubtful. Subsequent studies have shown that the more diverse the inhabitants of housing projects, the less dominant the role of propinquity seems to be. Some writers have suggested that propinquity is only of importance during the settling-down phase of a new housing development; others have stressed that social distance and a communality of values are always the major determinants of friendship patterns.

This view was propagated by the writings of Melvin Webber and his followers who, while acknowledging the effects of propinquity, suggested that the constraints of distance are rapidly diminishing in the 'shrinking world' of modern technology and mass communications.[49] They argued that improvements in personal mobility, combined with the spatial separation of home, workplace and recreational opportunities, have released people from neighbourhood ties. More recently, it has been suggested that 'the 800 number and the piece of plastic have made time and space obsolete'.[50] But not everyone, of course, benefits from mobility to the same extent: some people are 'localites', with restricted urban realms; others are 'cosmopolites', for whom distance is elastic and who inhabit a social world without finite geographical borders.

This tendency towards an aspatial basis for social interaction has been seen by others as a result not so much of increased personal mobility as a product of modern city planning and social values. Colin Ward, for example, argues that modern housing estates have 'annihilated' community spirit and replaced it with a parental authoritarianism which restricts the outdoor activities of children and so retards the development of locality-based friendships from the earliest years of a person's life.[51] Similarly, Susan Keller has claimed that there has been a widespread decline of both organized and spontaneous neighbouring in America because of the combined effects of changes in economic organization and social values. She attributes the decline in neighbouring to four factors:

1. The presence of multiple sources of information and opinion via mass media, travel, voluntary organizations, and employment away from the local area.
2. Better transport beyond local boundaries.
3. Increased differentiation in people's interests and desires, and greater differentiation in rhythms of work, resulting in less inclination and ability, respectively, to interact with neighbours.
4. Better social services and greater economic security.

Against such arguments we must set the observation that the residential neighbourhood continues to provide much raw material for social life, especially for relatively immobile groups such as the poor, the aged, and mothers with young children. Even the more mobile must be susceptible to chance local encounters and the subsequent interaction which may follow; and most householders will establish some contact with neighbours from the purely functional point of view of mutual security. Moreover, the most telling argument in support of the role of propinquity is the way that residential patterns – whether defined in terms of class, race, ethnicity, life-style, kinship, family status or age – have persistently exhibited a strong tendency towards spatial differentiation. In a pioneering study, Duncan and Duncan showed that the residential segregation of occupational groups in Chicago closely paralleled their social distance and that the most segregated categories were those possessing the clearest rank, i.e. those at the top and the bottom of the socio-economic scale.[52] Subsequent studies of socio-economic groups elsewhere and of racial and ethnic groups in a wide variety of cities have all reported a significant degree of residential segregation. The persistence of such patterns requires us to look more closely at the socio-cultural bases of residential segregation.

SUGGESTED READING

A good introduction to the material in this chapter is provided by Claude Fischer's book *The Urban Experience* (1976: Harcourt Brace Jovanovich, New York), while a useful reference is the collection of classic essays edited by P. Sennett: *Classic Essays on the Culture of Cities* (1969: Appleton-Century-Crofts, New York). Contemporary work on the social dimensions of urbanism is represented by de Certeau's *The Practice of Everyday Life* (1985: University of Columbia Press, Berkeley), and by Anthony Giddens's *Modernity and Self-Identity. Self and Society in the Late Modern Age* (1991: Polity Press, Cambridge). An excellent review of the spatial dimensions of interpersonal relations is provided by Henry Irving in a series edited by David Herbert and Ron Johnston: *Geography and the Urban Environment* (**1**, 1978, 249–284).

NOTES

1. Wilson, E., *The Sphinx in the City. Urban Life, the Control of Disorder, and Women*. Berkeley: University of California Press, 1991, p. 9.

2. Dahman, D., Subjective assessments of neighborhood quality by size of place, *Urban Studies*, **20,** 1983, 31–45.

3. Williams, R., *The Country and the City*. London: Chatto and Windus, 1973.

4. Marx, L. The puzzle of antiurbanism in classic American literature. In L. Rodwin and R. M. Hollister (eds), *Cities of the Mind*. London: Plenum Press, 1984, pp. 163–180.

5. Baudelaire, C. *The Painter of Modern Life and Other Essays*. Trans. J Mayne. New York: Da Capo, 1986.

6. Fischer, C. S., *The Urban Experience*. New York: Harcourt Brace Jovanovich, 1976, p. 17.

7. Feiffer, J., *Little Murders*. New York: Random House, 1968, p. 88.

8. Fischer, *Urban Experience*, p. 59.

9. Park, R. E., The city: suggestions for the investigation of human behaviour in an urban environment, *American Journal of Sociology*, **20,** 1916, 608.

10. See Theodorson, G. A. (ed.), *Studies in Human Ecology*. New York: Harper & Row, 1961.

11. Simmel, G., The metropolis and mental life. In P. Sennett (ed.), *Classic Essays on the Culture of Cities*. New York: Appleton-Century-Crofts, 1969, pp. 47–60.

12. Wirth, L., Urbanism as a way of life. In R. Sennett (ed.), *Classic Essays on the Culture of Cities*. New York: Appleton-Century-Crofts, 1969, pp. 143–164. The essay was first published in 1938.

13. Korte, C., Helpfulness in the urban environment. In A. Baun *et al.* (eds), *Advances in Environmental Psychology, Volume 1: The Urban Environment*. Hilldale, NJ: Erlbaum, 1978.

14. See, for example, W. G. Skogan, The changing distribution of big-city crime, *Urban Affairs Quarterly*, **13,** 1977, 33–47.

15. See, for example, Webb, S. D. and J. Colette, Rural–urban stress: new data and new conclusions, *American Journal of Sociology*, **84,** 1979, 1446–1452.

16. Lofland, L. Social life in the public realm, *Journal of Contemporary Ethnography*, **17,** 1989, 453–482.

17. Sennett, R., *The Conscience of the Eye*. New York: Knopf, 1990, p. xii.

18. Lofland, L. *A World of Strangers*. New York: Basic Books, 1973, p. 178; emphases added.

19. Fischer, C. S., The public and private worlds of city life, *American Sociological Review*, **46,** 1981, 306–316.

20. Sayer, A., On the dialogue between humanism and historical materialism in geography. In A. Kobayashi and S. Mackenzie (eds), *Remaking Human Geography*. London: Unwin Hyman, 1989, p. 211.

21. Douglas, J., Existential sociology. In J. Douglas and J. M. Johnson (eds), *Existential Sociology*. Cambridge: Cambridge University Press, 1977, p.51. Quoted in C. Philo, De-limiting human geography: new social and cultural perspectives. In C. Philo (ed.), *New Words, New Worlds: Reconceptualising Social and Cultural Geography*. Proceedings of a conference of the Social and Cultural Geography Study Group of the Institute of British Geographers. Lampeter: Department of Geography, St David's University College, 1991, p. 20.

22. See, for example, Pile, S., Human agency and human geography revisited: a critique of 'new models' of the self, *Transactions, Institute of British Geographers*, **18,** 1993, 122–139.

23. Miller, A., *The Drama of Being a Child*. London: Virago Press, 1987.

24. Watts, M., Mapping meaning, denoting difference, imagining identity: dialectical images and postmodern geographies, *Geografiska Annaler*, **73B,** 1991, 7–16.

25. de Certeau, M., *The Practice of Everyday Life*. Berkeley: University of California Press, 1985.

26. Bassand, M., *Urbanization: Appropriation of Space and Culture*. New York: Graduate School and University Center, City University of New York, 1990.

27. Giddens, A., *Modernity and Self-Identity. Self and Society in the Late Modern Age*. Cambridge: Polity Press, 1991.

28. Smith, C. J., Self-help and social networks in the urban community, *Ekistics*, **45,** 1978, 106–115.

29. Killworth, P. D. *et al.*, Estimating the size of personal networks, *Social Networks*, **12,** 1990, 289–312; Wellman, B., *The Community Question Re-evaluated*. Research Paper No. 165, Center for Urban and Community Studies, University of Toronto, 1987.

30. Wellman, *The Community Question*.

31. Bell, C. R., and H. Newby, Community, communion, class, and community action. In D. Herbert and R. J. Johnston (eds), *Social Areas in Cities, Vol. 2: Spatial Perspectives on Problems and Policies*. Chichester: Wiley, 1976, pp. 198–199.

32. Smith, Self-help.

33. Smith, C. A. and C. J. Smith, Locating natural neighbours in the urban community, *Area*, **10,** 1978, 102.

34. Warren, D. I., *Helping Networks: How People Cope with Problems in Urban Communities*. Notre Dame: University of Notre Dame Press, 1981.

35. Burgess, E. W., Natural area. In J. Gould and W. L. Kolb (eds), *Dictionary of the Social Sciences*. New York: Free Press, 1964, p. 458.

36. Burgess, E. W., The growth of the city: an introduction to a research project, *Publications, American Sociological Society*, **18,** 1924, 88.

37. Berry, B. J. L., and J. Kasarda, *Contemporary Urban Sociology*. New York: Macmillan, 1977.

38. Wirth, L., *The Ghetto*. Chicago: University of Chicago Press, 1928; Zorbaugh, H. W., *The Gold Coast and the Slum*. Chicago: University of Chicago Press, 1929.

39. Shaw, C. R. *et al.*, *Delinquency Areas*. Chicago: University of Chicago Press, 1929; Faris, R. E. L., and H. W. Dunham, *Mental Disorders in Urban Areas*. Chicago: University of Chicago Press, 1939.

40. Entrikin, N., Robert Park's human ecology and human geography, *Annals, Association of American Geographers*, **70,** 1980, 43–58.

41. Firey, W., Sentiment and symbolism as ecological variables, *American Sociological Review*, **10,** 1945, 140–148.

42. Hatt, P., The concept of natural area, *American Sociological Review*, **11,** 1946, 423–427.

43. Hawley, A., *Human Ecology: A Theory of Community Structure*. New York: Ronald Press, 1950; Schnore, L. F., *The Urban Scene*. New York: Free Press, 1965.

44. Suttles, G., *The Social Order of the Slum. Ethnicity and Territory in the Inner City*. Chicago: University of Chicago Press, 1968; Kearsley, G., Teaching urban geography: the Burgess model, *New Zealand Journal of Geography*, **75,** 1983, 10–13; Warf, B., The reconstruction of social ecology and neighborhood change in Brooklyn, *Environment & Planning D: Society and Space*, **8,** 1990, 73–96.

45. Irving, H., Space and environment in interpersonal relations. In D. T. Herbert and R. J. Johnston (eds), *Geography and the Urban Environment*, Vol. 1. Chichester: Wiley, 1978, pp. 249–284.

46. Jones, E. and J. Eyles, *An Introduction to Social Geography*. London: Oxford University Press, 1977.

47. Bogardus, E., Social distance in the city. In E. Burgess (ed.), *The Urban Community*. Chicago: Chicago University Press, 1962, pp. 48–54.

48. Festinger, L., S. Schacter, and K. Back, *Social Pressures in Informal Groups*. New York: Harper & Row, 1950, p. 10.

49. Webber, M. M., The urban place and the nonplace urban realm. In M. M. Webber *et al.* (eds), *Explorations into Urban Structure*. Philadelphia: University of Pennsylvania Press, 1964, pp. 79–153.

50. Sorkin, M. (ed.), *Variations on a Theme Park*. New York: Noonday Press, 1992, p. xi.

51. Ward, C., *The Child in the City*. London: Architectural Press, 1978.

52. Duncan, O. D. and B. Duncan, Occupational stratification and residential distribution, *American Journal of Sociology*, **50,** 493–503.

Turkish immigrants, Berlin.
Photograph by Ruth
Rohr-Zanker.

6 *Segregation and congregation*

Social Closure, Racism and Discrimination • The Spatial Segregation of Minority Groups

There are several good reasons for sociospatial congregation and segregation within urban society. As Suttles has emphasized, the spatial segregation of different 'communities' helps to minimize conflict between social groups while facilitating a greater degree of social control and endowing specific social groups with a more cohesive political voice.[1] Another important reason for the residential clustering of social groups is the desire of members to preserve their own group identity or life-style. One of the basic mechanisms by which this segregation can be achieved is through group norms which support *marriage* within the group and oppose marriage between members of different social, religious, ethnic or racial groups. The organization of groups into different territories facilitates the operation of this mechanism by restricting the number of 'outside' contacts. Thus 'people marry their equals in social status; neighbours tend to be social equals; they marry their neighbours'.[2] There are also, of course, several negative reasons for the persistence of residential segregation. Beginning with fear of exposure to 'otherness', these extend to personal and institutionalized discrimination on the basis of class, culture, gender, sexual orientation, ethnicity and race.

6.1 Social Closure, Racism and Discrimination

'What we are talking about here,' observes Chris Philo, is 'the contest of cultures bound up in processes of socio-spatial differentiation . . '. and '. . . the clash of moralities (of differing assumptions and arguments about worth and non-worth) which are both constituted through and constitutive of a society's socio-spatial hierarchy of "winners" and "losers".'[3] One concept that is useful here is Frank Parkin's notion of social closure, whereby 'winners' are characterized by their ability to exercise power in a downward direction, excluding less powerful groups from desirable spaces and resources.[4] Parkin calls this *exclusionary closure*: an example would be the explicitly exclusionary practices of housing classes defined through membership of homeowners' associations (p. 96). It should be acknowledged, however, that there are some awkward practical and conceptual problems in attempting to rank social subgroups in terms of differential access to material resources, status, power, or cultural influence.[5]

Another means of differentiating 'winners' from 'losers' is through the social construction of racism. Peter Jackson defines racism as 'the assumption, consciously or unconsciously held, that people can be divided into a distinct number of discrete 'races' according to physical, biological criteria and that *systematic social differences automatically and inevitably follow the same lines of physical differentiation*',[6] a definition that can be extended to include cultural differences. Racism produces pejorative associations aimed both at individuals (e.g. sexuality, criminality) and at social groups (e.g. family structures, cultural pathologies). The critical point here is that racism is not a uniform or invariable condition of human nature but, rather, consists of sets of attitudes that are rooted in the changing material conditions of society. We can, therefore, identify a multiplicity of racisms within contemporary cities, depending on the particular circumstances of different places. Susan Smith has adopted this perspective in suggesting that the interaction of political culture with economic contingency produced three distinctive phases of racism in postwar Britain:[7]

1. *1945–60*: a period during which blacks and Asians, although frequently regarded as culturally backward or morally inferior, were regarded as intrinsically British, sharing equally with whites the status and privilege of Commonwealth citizenship. 'It was widely assumed that immigrant status, like the problems accompanying it, would be a temporary prelude to assimilation and absorption.'[8]

2. *1961–75*: civil unrest in the Notting Hill area of London (1958) marked the turning point at which blacks and Asians ceased to be regarded as fellow citizens and began to be depicted as alien, with alien cultures, different temperaments, backgrounds and ways of life. 'Immutable differences, indexed by colour, were overlaid on the malleable cultural boundaries previously assumed to distinguish immigrant from "host".'[9]

3. *1976– :* a period of social authoritarianism, in which neoliberal economic philosophies have defined issues of race as being insignificant to the

concerns of politics and the economy, while at the same time a resurgence of moral conservatism, in appealing to a revival of national pride, has reinforced racism, albeit in the disguised language of 'culture' or 'ethnicity'.

Smith's emphasis on the interaction of political culture and economic circumstances is particularly important to our understanding of racial segregation in societies (like Britain and America) where institutional discrimination carries racism into the entire housing delivery system. Such discrimination permeates the legal framework, government policies (those relating, among others, to urban renewal, public housing and suburban development), municipal land use ordinances and, as we saw in Chapter 4, the practices of builders, landlords, bankers, insurance companies, appraisers and real-estate agents.[10] The impersonal web of exclusionary practices that results from this institutional discrimination has reinforced the racism and discrimination of individuals to the point where segregated housing has led to *de facto* segregated schools, shopping areas and recreational facilities. All this spatial segregation, in turn, serves to reproduce racism and to sustain material inequalities between racial categories.[11]

6.2 The Spatial Segregation of Minority Groups

Given these caveats about racism and discrimination, we can interpret minority-group residential congregation and segregation as being inversely related to the process of *assimilation* with the host society, a process which is itself governed by different forms of group behaviour designed to minimize real or perceived threats to the group from outsiders. But before going on to examine this behaviour and its spatial consequences in detail, it is first necessary to clarify the meaning of terms such as 'minority group', 'host society', 'segregation' and 'assimilation'.

Issues of Definition and Measurement

The term 'minority group' is widely used to mean any group that is defined or characterized by race, religion, nationality or culture. Implicit in its use is the idea that their presence in the city stems from a past or continuing stream of in-migration. Minority groups in this sense therefore include African-Americans, Puerto Ricans, Italians, Jews, Mexicans, Vietnamese, and (Asian) Indians in American cities; Afro-Caribbeans, Asians and Irish in British cities; Algerians and Spaniards in French cities; Turks and Croats in German cities; and so on. While the host society may not be homogeneous, it always contains a *charter group* that represents the dominant matrix into which new minority groups are inserted. In North America, Australia and Britain the charter group in most cities is white, with an 'Anglo-Saxon' culture. The degree to which minority groups are spatially segregated from the charter group varies a good deal from city to city according to the group involved.

Segregation is taken here to refer to situations where members of a minority group are not distributed absolutely uniformly across residential space in relation to the rest of the population. This clearly covers a wide range of circumstances, and it is useful to be able to quantify the overall degree of segregation in some way. Several indexes of segregation are available, although the sensitivity of all of them depends on the scale of the areal units employed.[12] One of the most widely used methods of quantifying the degree to which a minority group is residentially segregated is the index of dissimilarity, which is analogous to the Gini index of inequality and which produces a theoretical range of values from 0 (no segregation) to 100 (complete segregation). Index values calculated from census tract data in US cities show that African Americans are generally the most segregated of the minorities in America. A study by Taeuber found the average index value for 109 cities to be 76 (down from an average of 82 in 1970 and 85 in 1940).[13] Over half of the 237 cities examined in another study had index values of 70 or more, with Chicago, Dallas, Fort Lauderdale, Las Vegas, Monroe (La.), Oklahoma City, Orlando (Fla.) and West Palm Beach having index values of over 90.[14] Puerto Ricans and Cubans have also been found to be very highly segregated in American cities, with index values at the tract level commonly exceeding 60; as have the new immigrant groups of the 1980s and 1990s – Mexicans and Asians.[15]

By comparison, minority-group residential segregation in European cities is relatively low. In Britain, for example, index values calculated for immigrant minority groups – Afro-Caribbeans, Pakistanis, Bangladeshis, Indians and Africans – at the enumeration district level range between 40 and 70.[16] The *Gastarbeiter* (guest worker) population of continental European cities is even less segregated: index values for Turks, Greeks, Spaniards and Portuguese in German, Dutch and Swiss cities, for example, range between 35 and 50. At more fine-grained levels of analysis the degree of segregation can be much higher, with index values of between 80 and 90 for Asians, Afro-Caribbeans, Turks and North Africans at the scale of individual streets in northwest European cities. This emphasizes the vulnerability of statistical indexes, and makes inter-city comparisons difficult.

Another practical difficulty in making precise statements about the degree of residential segregation is that minority groups may subsume important internal differences. Statements about the segregation of Asians in British cities, for instance, often overlook the tendency for Indians, Pakistanis and Bangladeshis to exist in quite separate communities, even though these communities may appear to outsiders to be part and parcel of the same community. Muslims are separated from Hindus, Gujerati speakers from Punjabi speakers, and East African Asians from all other Asians; and these segregations are preserved even within public-sector housing. Similarly, the distinctive island communities of the West Indies can be identified on the map of London:

> There is an archipelago of Windward and Leeward islanders north of the Thames; Dominicans and St Lucians have their core areas in Notting Hill; Grenadians are found in the west in Hammersmith and Ealing; Montserratians are concentrated around Stoke Newington, Hackney and Finsbury Park; Antiguans spill over to the east in Hackney, Waltham Forest and Newham; south of the river is Jamaica.[17]

What is clear enough from the available evidence, however, is that most minorities tend to be highly segregated from the charter group. Moreover, this segregation has been shown to be greater than might be anticipated from the socio-economic status of the groups concerned. In other words, the low socio-economic status of minority groups can only partially explain their high levels of residential segregation.[18] The maintenance of the minority in-migrant group 'as a distinctive social and spatial entity' will depend, as Boal observes, 'on the degree to which assimilation occurs'.[19] This process can take place at different speeds for different groups, depending on the perceived social distance between them and the charter group. Moreover, behavioural assimilation – the acquisition by the minority group of a cultural life in common with the charter group – may take place faster than structural assimilation – the diffusion of members of the minority group through the social and occupational strata of the charter group society. In general, the rate and degree of assimilation of a minority group will depend on two sets of factors: (1) external factors, including charter group attitudes, institutional discrimination, and structural effects, and (2) internal group cohesiveness. Between them, these factors determine not only the degree and nature of conflict between minority groups and the charter group, but also the spatial patterns of residential congregation and segregation.

External Factors: Discrimination and Structural Effects

Minority groups that are perceived by members of the charter group to be socially undesirable will find themselves spatially isolated through a variety of mechanisms. One of the most obvious and straightforward of these is the 'blocking' strategy by existing occupants of city neighbourhoods in order to resist the 'invasion' of minority groups. Established tightly-knit minority-group clusters tend to be the most resistant to invasion by others, actively defending their own territory in a variety of ways (ranging from social hostility and the refusal to sell or rent homes to petty violence and deliberate vandalism) against intruding members of minority groups. Perhaps the best-documented example of this is the resistance by residents of the 'Polish Principality' of Hamtramck in Detroit to the residential expansion of African Americans.[20]

Where this strategy of 'voicing' opposition is unsuccessful, or where the territory in question is occupied by socially and geographically more mobile households, the charter group strategy commonly becomes one of 'exit'. The invasion of charter group territory generally precipitates an outflow of charter group residents which continues steadily until the critical point is reached where the proportion of households from the invading minority group is large enough to precipitate a much faster exodus. This is known as the 'tipping point'. The precise level of the tipping point is difficult to establish, although it has been suggested that for whites facing 'invasion' by African Americans the tipping point may be expected to occur when African-American occupancy reaches a level of about 30 per cent.[21] The subsequent withdrawal of charter group residents to other neighbourhoods effectively resolves the territorial conflict between the two groups, leaving the minority group spatially isolated until its next phase of territorial expansion.

The spatial isolation of minority groups is also contrived through discrimination in the housing market, thus limiting minority groups to small niches within the urban fabric. Although formal discriminatory barriers are illegal, minorities are systematically excluded from charter group neighbourhoods in a variety of ways. As we have seen (pp. 138–45), the role of real-estate agents and mortgage financiers in the owner-occupied sector is particularly important, while the general gatekeeping role of private landlords also tends to perpetuate racially segregated local submarkets. There is also a considerable weight of evidence to suggest that immigrants and minorities are discriminated against in the public sector. In Britain, racial minorities have found themselves disadvantaged within the public sector in three respects. First, they have had more difficulty in gaining access to any public housing at all; second, they have often been allocated to poor-quality property, particularly older flats; and, third, they have been disproportionately allocated to unpopular inner-city housing estates, thus intensifying the localization of the non-white population in the inner city. These disadvantages are partly the result of unintentional discrimination (such as the residential requirements associated with eligibility rules), and partly the result of more deliberate discrimination through the personal prejudices, for example, of housing visitors, who may have little of no understanding of the cultural background and family life of immigrant households.[22] The effects of this type of discrimination are intensified by the discriminatory policies of city planners. Again, some of this discrimination is unintentional, as in the omission of minority neighbourhoods from urban renewal and rehabilitation schemes; but much is deliberate, as in the manipulation of land-use plans and zoning regulations in order to exclude non-whites from suburban residential areas of US cities.

The net effect of this discrimination is to render much of the housing stock unavailable to members of minority groups, thus trapping them in privately-rented accommodation and allowing landlords to charge inflated rents while providing little security of tenure. In an attempt to escape from this situation, some householders become landlords, buying large deteriorating houses and subletting part of the house in order to maintain mortgage repayments and/or repair costs. Others manage to purchase smaller dwellings that are shared with another family or a lodger, but many can only finance the purchase through burdensome and unorthodox means. Asians, in particular, have been found to exhibit a strong propensity towards home ownership in preference to tenancy, notwithstanding the extra financial costs.

The localized nature of cheaper accommodation (whether for sale or rent) is an important aspect of urban structure (sometimes referred to as a 'fabric' effect) which serves to segregate minority groups from the rest of the population by channelling them into a limited niche. Moreover, since many minority groups have an atypical demographic structure, with a predominance of young adult males and/or large, extended families, their housing needs – single-room accommodation and large dwellings respectively – can be met only in very specific locations. *In many cities, therefore, the distribution of clusters of minorities is closely related to the geography of the housing stock.* It is worth noting that this localization has a very positive side: as Louis Winnick has shown in his detailed study of Sunset Park in Brooklyn, the localization of new waves of migrants and immigrants in declining inner-city neighbourhoods brings about a demographic renewal: repopulating emptying housing, schools, and transit systems, and revitalizing local commerce.[23]

Underlying both charter group discrimination and the localization of minority groups in particular pockets of low-cost housing is their position in the overall social and economic structure of society. A study of Sparkbrook, Birmingham, for example, suggested that while some discriminatory behaviour may have been due to innate tendencies or personality disturbances, a great deal of it could be explained by Birmingham's social structure and by conflicts of interest and roles that were built into Birmingham society.[24] This approaches the Marxian analysis of race relations in Britain, which holds that

> the position of immigrants in society is not one of an 'outgroup' cut off from society by the 'factor of colour'; rather it recognizes that the subordinate, oppressed position of such groups is conditioned by their racial distinctiveness and reinforced by their concentration in the working class, leading to their super-exploitation in society.[25]

In this context, discrimination by working-class members of the charter group is related to the role attributed to minority groups in job and housing markets as competitors whose presence serves to depress wages and erode the quality of life. In short, minority groups are treated as the scapegoats for the shortcomings of the economic system.

But it is the concentration of minority groups at the lower end of the occupational structure that is the more fundamental factor in their locali-zation in poor housing. Because of their lack of skills and educational qualifications, members of minority groups tend to be concentrated in occupations that are unattractive to members of the charter group, that are often unpleasant or degrading in one way or another, and that are usually associated with low wages. The majority of such occupations are associated with the CBD and its immediate surrounds, and the dependence of minority groups on centralized job opportunities is widely cited as a prime determi-nant in the location of minority residential clusters. This factor, in turn, is reinforced by the location of inexpensive accommodation in inner-city neighbourhoods surrounding the CBD. Meanwhile, the isolation of min-ority groups in this sector of housing and labour markets has been intensified by the suburbanization of job opportunities. This effectively traps many of the poor in inner-city locations because of their inability to meet the necessary transportation costs.

Congregation: Internal Group Cohesiveness

While charter group attitudes and structural effects go a long way towards explaining residential segregation, they do not satisfactorily explain the clustering of minority groups into discrete, homogeneous territories. Such clusters must also be seen as defensive and conservative in function, partly in response to the external pressures outlined above:

> Conflict situations in cities lead people to feel threatened. This will particularly apply to recent in-migrants, who may vary culturally and indeed racially from the 'host' population. . . . The perceived threat may materialize in the form of physical violence or remain as a psychological threat. At the same time, and indeed sometimes because of the threat, the minority group may have a strong urge to internal cohesion, so that the cultural 'heritage' of the group may be retained.[26]

Four principal functions have been identified for the clustering of min-ority groups: defence, support, preservation and attack.

Clustering Together for Defence

The defensive role of minority clusters is most prominent when charter group discrimination is extremely widespread and intense, so that the existence of a territorial heartland enables members of the minority group to withdraw from the hostility of the wider society. Jewish ghettos in medieval European cities functioned in this way, while working-class Cath-olic and Protestant communities in Belfast have become increasingly segregated from one another in response to their need for physical safety. Nowhere has this phenomenon been more marked than on the Shankhill–Falls 'Divide' between the Protestant neighbourhood of Shankhill and the Catholic neighbourhood of Clonard-Springfield. Transitional between the two, and marking the Divide between the two groups, is the Cupar Street area, which had acquired a mixed residential pattern in the years up to 1968. When the 'troubles' broke out in 1969, however, the territorial boundary between the two groups took on a much sharper definition. Sixty-five households moved to the relative safety of their own religious heartland from Cupar Street alone during August/September 1969 in response to the mounting incidence of physical attacks in the district. It is estimated that within the following seven years between 35 000 and 60 000 people from the Belfast area relocated for similar reasons, thus reinforcing the segregation of Protestants and Catholics into what became known in army circles as 'tribal areas'.[27]

It should be emphasized, then, that the defensive role of minority clusters is really as much an involuntary product of external pressure (or perceived pressure) as it is a voluntary product of internal cohesiveness. A study of the Bangladeshi community in the East End of London concluded that:

> There is certain evidence . . . that one of the determinants of residential concentration of the Bangladeshi is the lack of confidence the community has in the police's ability to protect them from racial attacks which have been a dominant feature in London's East End. Certainly this is 'voluntary segregation' but inasmuch as the distinction between voluntary and involuntary segregation is related to freely determined choice, segregation as a defensive act lies more in the realm of imposed rather than self-imposed segregation.[28]

Clustering for Mutual Support

Closely related to the defensive functions of minority clusters is their role as a haven, providing support for members of the group in a variety of ways. These range from formal minority-oriented institutions and businesses to informal friendship and kinship ties. Clustered together in a mutually supportive haven, members of the group are able to avoid the hostility and rejection of the charter group, exchanging insecurity and anxiety for familiarity and strength. This 'buffer' function of minority clusters has been documented in a number of studies.[29] The existence of ethnic institutions within the territorial cluster is one of the most important factors in protecting group members from unwanted contact with the host community. Dilip Hiro, for example, has described how Sikh temples and Moslem mosques in British cities became the focus of Sikh and Pakistani local welfare systems, offering a source of food, shelter, recreation and education as well as being a cultural and religious focus.[30]

More generally, most minority groups develop informal self-help networks and welfare organizations in order to provide both material and social support for group members. At the same time, the desire to avoid outside contact and the existence of a local concentration of a minority population with distinctive, culturally-based needs serve to provide what Ulf Hannerz calls 'protected niches' for ethnic enterprise, both legitimate and illegitimate. One example given by Hannerz is the success of the Cosa

Nostra in Italian-American communities; but it is clear that minority enterprise is an important component of community cohesion in minority neighbourhoods everywhere, providing an expression of group solidarity as well as a means of economic and social advancement for successful entrepreneurs and an alternative route by which minority workers can bypass the white-controlled labour market.[31] In their classic study of the African-American community in Chicago, Drake and Cayton described the doctrine of the 'double-duty dollar', according to which members of the community should use their money not only to satisfy their personal needs but also to 'advance the race' by making their purchases in African-American-owned businesses.[32] In Britain, the most distinctive manifestations of minority enterprise are the clusters of banks, butchers, grocery stores, travel agencies, cinemas and clothing shops which have developed in response to the food taboos, specialized clothing styles and general cultural aloofness of Asian communities combined with the economic repression of British society.[33]

Clustering for Cultural Preservation
This brings us to a third major function of minority residential clustering: that of preserving and promoting a distinctive cultural heritage. Minority group consciousness sometimes results from external pressure, as in the use of Jamaican Creole by young Afro-Caribbeans in London as a private language to shut out the oppressive elements of the white world.[34] But for many groups there exists an inherent desire to maintain (or develop) a distinctive cultural identity rather than to become completely assimilated within the charter group. Residential clustering helps to achieve this not only through the operation of ethnic institutions and businesses but also through the effects of residential propinquity on marriage patterns. Many commentators have emphasized the self-segregating tendencies of Asian communities in British cities in this context, while the persistence of Jewish residential clusters if often interpreted as being closely related to the knowledge among Jewish parents that residence in a Jewish neighbourhood confers a very high probability of their children marrying a Jewish person. Other documented examples include Cypriots in British cities, and Greeks in Australian cities.[35] The residential clustering of some minority groups is also directly related to the demands of their religious precepts relating to dietary laws, the preparation of food, and attendance for prayer and religious ceremony. Where such mores form an important part of the group's culture, they are followed more easily where the group is territorially clustered. On the other hand, where group consciousness is weak and the group culture is not especially distinctive, ties between group members tend to be superficial – sentimental rather than functional – with the result that residential clustering as well as group solidarity are steadily eroded: a process which has been tellingly documented in relation to the Maltese in London.[36]

Gay neighbourhoods have also been interpreted in terms of deliberate congregation: 'liberated zones' where openly homosexual behaviour can take place and where gays can be socialized into a new culture.[37] Once established, such neighbourhoods represent important symbolic spaces – spaces of resistance to the dominant social order. Lesbian communities, on the other hand, involve less spatial congregation. This is partly because lesbians, like other women, have less access to capital, and so are more restricted in terms of their residential choices. It is also because they are more likely than gay men to be caretakers of children (and so must consider a different set of criteria in their residential preferences), and more vulnerable to male violence (thus making the idea of 'spaces of resistance' a potentially dangerous proposition).[38]

Clustering to Facilitate 'Attacks'

The fourth major function of minority spatial concentration is the provision of a 'base' for action in the struggle of its members with society in general. This 'attack' function is usually both peaceful and legitimate. Spatial concentrations of group members represent considerable electoral power and often enable minority groups to gain official representation within the institutional framework of urban politics. This has been an important factor in the political power base of African Americans in the United States, where the Black Power movement was able to exploit the electoral power of the ghetto with considerable success – to the extent that African-American politicians now constitute an important (and sometimes dominant) voice in the urban political arena. Gay neighbourhoods also represent a potentially effective electoral base. Perhaps the best-known illustration of this is is West Hollywood, where voters elected in 1984 to create a self-governing municipality and subsequently elected a city council dominated by gays.[39]

Minority clusters also provide a convenient base for illegitimate attacks on the charter group. Insurrectionary groups and urban guerrillas with minority affiliations are able to 'disappear' in their own group's territory, camouflaged by a relative anonymity within their own cultural milieu and protected by a silence resulting from a mixture of sympathy and intimidation. An obvious example of this is the way in which the IRA and Loyalist para-military organizations have taken advantage of their respective territorial heartlands in Belfast; and, indeed, the way in which the IRA has used Irish communities in Birmingham, Liverpool, London and Southampton as bases for terrorist attacks.

Colonies, Enclaves and Ghettos

The spatial expression of segregation and congregation is determined by the interplay of discrimination, fabric effects and the strength of internal group cohesion. Where the perceived social distance between the minority group and the charter group is relatively small, the effects of both charter group discrimination and internal cohesion are likely to be minimized and so minority residential clusters are likely to be only a temporary stage in the assimilation of the group into the wider urban sociospatial fabric. Such clusters may be termed *colonies*. They essentially serve as a port-of-entry for members of the group concerned, providing a base from which group members are culturally assimilated and spatially dispersed. *Their persistence over time is thus dependent on the continuing input of new minority group members*. Examples of this type of pattern include the distribution of European minority groups in North American cities during the 1920s and 1930s, of similar groups in Australasian cities during the 1950s and 1960s, and of the Maltese in London during the 1950s.

Minority clusters which persist over the longer term are usually a product of the interaction between discrimination and internal cohesion. Where the latter is the more dominant of the forces, the resultant residential clusters may be termed *enclaves*; and where external factors are more dominant, the residential clusters are generally referred to as *ghettos*. In reality, of course, it is often difficult to ascertain the degree to which segregation is voluntary or involuntary, and it is more realistic to think in terms of a continuum rather than a twofold classification. Boal has identified several distinctive spatial patterns in relation to this enclave/ghetto continuum:[40]

● The first of these is exemplified by Jewish residential areas in many cities, where an initial residential clustering in inner-city areas has formed the base for the subsequent formation of new suburban residential clusters (Fig. 6.1). The fact that this suburbanization represents a general upward shift in socio-economic status and that it is usually accompanied by the transferral of Jewish cultural and religious institutions to the suburbs suggests that this type of pattern is largely the result of voluntary segregation. It has been suggested, in fact, that congregation rather than segregation is the most appropriate term for the Jewish residential patterns.[41]

● The second distinctive expression of the enclave/ghetto takes the form of a concentric zone of minority neighbourhoods that has spread from an initial cluster to encircle the CBD. Such zones are often patchy, the discontinuities reflecting variations in the urban fabric in terms of house types and resistant social groups. The growth of African-American areas in many US cities tends to conform to this pattern, as does the distribution of Asians, Irish and Afro-Caribbeans in British cities and the distribution of Mediterraneans, Surinamers and Antilleans in Rotterdam (Fig. 6.2). It should be noted, however, that the same pattern may occur in different places for different reasons. In the case of Glasgow Asians, for example, it seems that the concentric pattern derives from a process of 'uncontested filtering' into tenement housing which has been made available by the out-migration of indigenous Glaswegians.[42] In contrast, the concentric pattern of African-American neighbourhoods

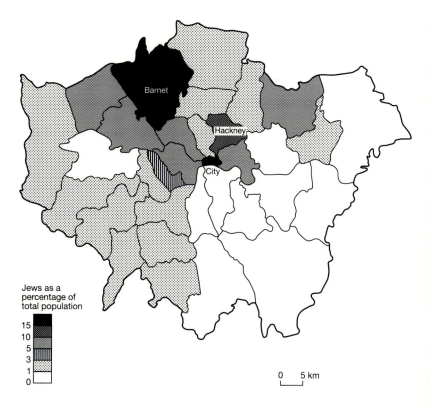

Figure 6.1
Jews as a percentage of the total population in Greater London, by boroughs, 1984
Source: S. Waterman and B. Kosmin, *Transactions, Institute of British Geographers*, 13,
1988, Fig. 1.

in certain US cities seems to be related more to twin effects of occupational status and racial discrimination. It should also be noted that the
individual clusters within such patterns may also exhibit a distinctive
morphology. Black residential clusters in south London, for example,
have been characterized as an aureole–nebula configuration (Fig. 6.3),
with successive zones of decreasing concentrations of black households.[43] This latter feature, it seems, is the result of the black clusters
being focused on sub-centres where older housing has been redeveloped
and replaced by local authority housing or non-residential land uses.

● Where a minority group continues to grow numerically, and provided
that a sufficient number of its population are able to afford better
housing, residential segregation is likely to result in a sectoral spatial
pattern. The distribution of African-Americans in many of the more
prosperous and rapidly expanding cities of the United States tends
towards this model although sectoral development is often truncated
because of economic constraints operating at the suburban margin. The
distribution of the African-American population in Oklahoma City

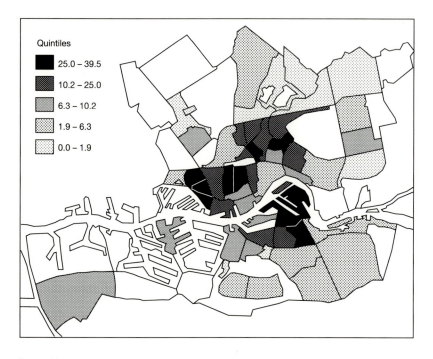

Figure 6.2
Percentage of Mediterraneans, Surinamers, and Antillians in the total population of
Rotterdam, per city district, in quintiles, 1984
Source: E. Huttman (ed.) *Urban Housing Segregation of Minorities in Western Europe and
the United States*, Duke University Press, Durham, N.C., 1991, Fig. 10.2, p. 187.

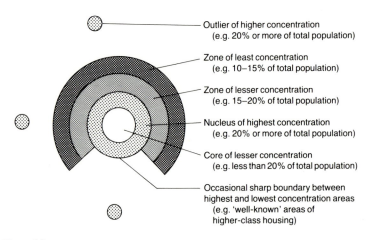

Figure 6.3
Diagrammatic representation of the morphology of black residential clusters in south
London: an aureole-nebula spatial pattern
Source: E. Baboolal, in P. Jackson and S. Smith (eds) *Social Interaction and Ethnic
Segregation*, Institute of British Geographers, London, 1981, Fig. 6, p. 75.

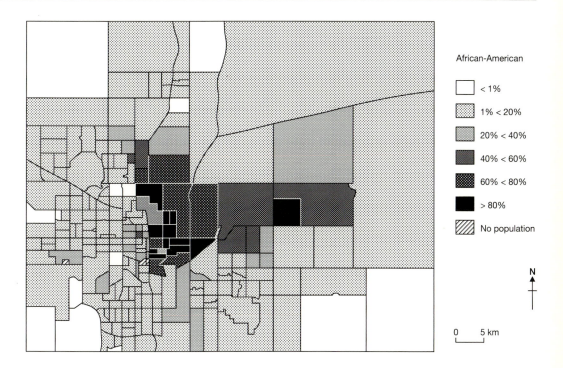

Figure 6.4
The distribution of the African-American population in Oklahoma City, 1990

provides a good example of this type of pattern. As Fig. 6.4 shows, the city's African-American population has been concentrated to the north-east of the CBD, where a contiguous sector of census tracts were more than 60 per cent African-American in 1990.

It will be clear by now that most large cities contain a variety of minorities, each responding to a different mix of internal and external factors, each exhibiting rather different spatial outcomes, and each chang-ing in different rates and in different ways. A study of Detroit's minority populations illustrates the point well.[44] On the basis of three key measures – suburbanization, clustering and segregation – for each of ten minority groups over a 30-year period, this study demonstrated how the African-American population, together with Hispanics, was characterized by centralization, clustering and segregation. Jews, Hungarians and Italians, on the other hand, were characterized by suburbanization, clustering and segregation. British and German households were characterized by subur-banization, dispersal and integration; while Polish, Irish and Russian households were characterized by the centralization of the immigrant generation and suburbanization of their descendants. Further investigation resulted in a sevenfold typology of minority communities (Table 6.1):

Table 6.1 A typology of ethnic communities

Ethnic population distribution	Clustered and segregated	Dispersed and integrated
Centralized	1. Ghetto 2. Immigrant reception centre 3. Urban village	4. Residual community
Suburbanized	5. Transplanted community 6. New suburban settlement	7. Community without neighbourhood

Source: C. Agocs, *Ethnicity*, 8, 1981, p. 132.

1. The ghetto: a single compact concentration of black households with clear boundaries, almost entirely confined to the older, deteriorating zones of the metropolitan area.
2. Recent immigrant reception centres: some located in inner-city districts (e.g. Detroit's Mexican neighbourhood); others, as a result of the chain migration process, in generationally mixed neighbourhoods in the suburbs, near industrial districts.
3. Urban villages: stable concentrations dominated by second generation immigrants, each containing a variety of supporting ethnic institutions: schools, churches, social, cultural and political organizations, and businesses. The major urban villages in Detroit were Polish (in the middle zone of older suburbs) and Hispanic (in inner-city neighbourhoods).
4. Residual communities: islands of minority-group concentration in inner-city and middle-zone neighbourhoods that had largely passed to other groups.
5. Transplanted communities: highly clustered and segregated, but located in a new setting far from earlier locations – the typical outcome of the residential dynamics of Jewish populations in American cities.
6. New suburban settlements: less compact, less dense and less well-bounded than transplanted communities, and generally a product of sectoral migration streams – best exemplified in Detroit by Hungarians, Italians and Poles.
7. Communities without neighbourhoods: dispersed and suburbanized populations – chiefly German and British – for whom community life is based less on residential propinquity than on the communication, interaction and shared activities of widely dispersed social networks and the continued (though less frequent) use of minority-group institutions in old central city neighbourhoods.

An Illustrative Example: Migrant Workers in European Cities

During the past 30 years an important new dimension has been added to the social geography of continental European cities with the arrival of tens of thousands of migrant workers, most of them from the poorer regions of the Mediterranean. Although estimates vary a good deal, there were at the beginning of the 1990s some 20 million aliens living in European countries. About half of these were young adult males who had emigrated in order to seek work, originally, at least, on a temporary basis. The rest were wives and families who had joined them. At the heart of this influx of foreign-born workers were the labour needs of the more developed regions, coupled with the demographic 'echo effect' of low birth rates in the 1930s and 1940s: a sluggish rate of growth in the indigenous labour force. As the demand for labour in more developed countries expanded, so indigenous workers found themselves able to shun low-wage, unpleasant and menial occupations; immigrant labour filled the vacuum. At the same time, the more prosperous countries perceived that foreign workers might provide a buffer for the indigenous labour force against the effects of economic cycles – the so-called *konjunkturpuffer* philosophy. The peak of these streams of immigrants occurred in the mid-1960s and early 1970s. The onset of deep economic recession in 1973, however, brought a dramatic check to the flows. Restrictions on the admission of non-EEC immigrants began in West Germany in November 1973, and within twelve months France, Belgium and The Netherlands had followed with new restrictions. By this time there were nearly two million foreign workers in West Germany, over 1.5 million in France, half a million in Switzerland, and around a quarter of a million in Belgium and Sweden.

Within each of these countries the impact of migrant labour has been localized in larger urban areas, reflecting the immigrants' role as replacement labour for the low-paid, assembly-line and service sector jobs vacated in inner-city areas by the upward socio-economic mobility and outward geographical mobility of the indigenous population. Thus, for example, more than 2 million of the 6 million aliens living in France in 1990 lived in the Paris region, representing over 15 per cent of its population. Other French cities where aliens account for more than 10 per cent of the populations include Lyons, Marseilles, Nice and St Etienne. In Germany, 25 per cent of Franfurt's population is foreign born, as is more than 15 per cent of the population of Köln, Munich, Düsseldorf and Stuttgart. In Switzerland, Basel, Lausanne and Zürich all have between 15 and 20 per cent foreign born, while Geneva (a special case) has 35 per cent.

Since nearly all of the immigrants were initially recruited to low-skill, low-wage occupations, they have inevitably been channelled towards the cheapest housing and the most rundown neighbourhoods. The position of immigrants in the labour market is of course partly self-inflicted: for many the objective has been to earn as much as possible as quickly as possible, the easiest strategy being to take on employment with an hourly wage where overtime and even a second job can be pursued. Most immigrants, however, tend to be *kept* at the foot of the economic ladder by a combination of institutional and social discrimination. The net result is reflected by the statistics for West Germany in the mid-1970s: only 1 per cent of migrant workers held non-manual jobs.

Similarly, immigrants' position in housing markets is partly self-inflicted: inexpensiveness is of the essence. But the localization of immigrants in camps, factory hostels, *hôtels meublés* (immigrant hostels), *bidonvilles* (suburban shanty towns) and inner-city tenements is also reinforced by bureaucratic restrictions and discrimination. Concentrated in such housing, immigrants find themselves in an environment which creates problems both for themselves and for the indigenous population. Trapped in limited niches of the housing stock, they are vulnerable to exploitation. A survey of housing conditions in the Ruhr, for example, found that immigrant workers were paying an average of 30 per cent more rent than German nationals, even though the latter had better accommodation.[45] One response has been the notorious 'hotbed' arrangement, whereby two or

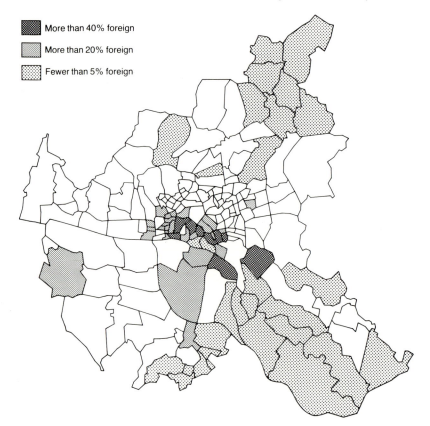

Figure 6.5
Per cent foreign born, city of Hamburg, by census tract, 1986
Source: E. Huttman (ed.) *Urban Housing Segregation of Minorities in Western Europe and the United States*, Duke University Press, Durham, N.C., 1991, Fig. 6.2, p. 132.

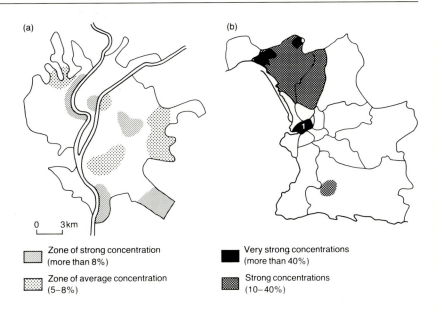

▦	Zone of strong concentration (more than 8%)	■	Very strong concentrations (more than 40%)
▦	Zone of average concentration (5–8%)	▦	Strong concentrations (10–40%)

Figure 6.6
Foreign born populations in French cities, 1982: (a) Greater Lyons, (b) Greater Marseilles
Source: E. Huttman (ed.) *Urban Housing Segregation of Minorities in Western Europe and the United States*, Duke University Press, Durham, N.C., 1991, Figs 7.3 and 7.4, pp. 148-149.

even three workers on different shifts take turns at sleeping in the same bed. In France a more common response has been to retreat to the cardboard and corrugated iron *bidonvilles*, where although there may be no sanitary facilities immigrants can at least live inexpensively among their own compatriots.

In terms of spatial outcomes, a fairly consistent pattern has emerged, despite the very different minority populations involved in different cities – Serbs, Croats and Turks in Duisburg, Frankfurt, Köln and Vienna; Algerians, Italians and Tunisians in Paris; and Surinamese and Turks in Rotterdam, for example. In short, just as the migrants are replacing the lower echelons of the indigenous population in the labour market, so they are acting as a partial replacement for the rapidly declining indigenous population in the older neighbourhoods of privately rented housing near to sources of service employment and factory jobs.[46] This typically produces the kind of spatial patterns depicted in Fig. 6.5 for foreigners in Hamburg. Quite simply, the overriding priority for migrant workers is to live close to their jobs in cheap accommodation. This applies to all national groups, so that similar spatial patterns have persisted even as (in Hamburg's case) the culturally more alien Turkish, Greek and Portuguese populations replaced older and more familiar groups such as Italians and Spaniards.[47] In some cities, a secondary pattern has developed as foreign-born workers have been allocated space in public housing projects. As in Lyons and Marseilles (Fig. 6.6), the allocation procedures of housing officials tend to result in concentrations of foreigners in dilapidated, peripheral public housing estates.

SUGGESTED
READING

There are several books that provide good resources on the topics of race, racism, and spatial segregation. These include Peter Jackson's edited volume, *Race and Racism: Essays in Social Geography* (1987: Allen and Unwin, London) and Susan Smith's *The Politics of Race and Residence* (1989: Polity Press, Cambridge). A useful introductory review essay is provided by Fred Boal in *Progress in Social Geography*, edited by Michael Pacione (1987: Croom Helm, London, pp. 90–128). Examples of detailed case studies can be found in a volume edited by Peter Jackson and Susan Smith: *Social Interaction and Ethnic Segregation* (1981: Academic Press, London). Broader theoretical issues, along with recent trends, are discussed in *Racism, the City and the State*, edited by Malcolm Cross and Michael Keith (1993: Routledge, London).

NOTES

1. Suttles, G., *The Social Construction of Communities*. Chicago: University of Chicago Press, 1972.

2. Ramsøy, N. R., Assortative mating and the structure of cities, *American Sociological Review*, **31,** 1966, 773–786.

3. Philo, C., De-limiting human geography: new social and cultural perspectives. In C. Philo (ed.), *New Words, New Worlds: Reconceptualizing Social and Cultural Geography*. Lampeter: Social and Cultural Study Group, Institute of British Geographers, 1991, p. 19.

4. Parkin, F., *Marxism and Class Theory: A Bourgeois Critique*. London: Tavistock, 1979.

5. Jackson, P., *Maps of Meaning*. London: Unwin Hyman, 1989.

6. *Ibid.*, pp. 132–133, emphasis added.

7. Smith, S. J., Political interpretations of 'racial segregation' in Britain, *Environment & Planning D: Society and Space*, **6,** 1988, 423–444.

8. *Ibid.*, p. 425.

9. *Ibid.*, p. 428.

10. See Huttman, E. D. (ed.), *Urban Housing Segregation of Minorities in Western Europe and the United States*. London: Duke University Press, 1991.

11. See, for example, S. Smith, *The Politics of Race and Residence*. Cambridge: Polity Press, 1989; Anderson, K. J., The idea of Chinatown, *Annals, Association of American Geographers*, **77,** 1987, 580–598.

12. For a discussion of these indexes, see Boal, F. W., Segregation. In M. Pacione (ed.), *Progress in Social Geography*. London: Croom Helm, 1987, 90–128.

13. Tauber, K. A., *Residence and Race: 1619 to 2019*. Working Paper 88–19, Center for Demography and Ecology, University of Wisconsin, Madison, 1988.

14. Van Valey, T. L. *et al.*, Trends in residential segregation, 1960–1970, *American Journal of Sociology*, **82,** 1977, 826–844.

15. Garcia, P., Immigration issues in urban ecology. In L. Maldonado and J. Moore (eds), *Urban Ethnicity in the United States*. Beverly Hills: Sage, 1985, pp. 73–100.

16. Phillips, D. and V. Karn, Racial segregation in Britain. In E. D. Huttman (ed.), *Urban Housing Segregation of Minorities in Western Europe and the United States*. London: Duke University Press, 1991, pp. 63–91.

17. Peach, G. C. K., The force of West Indian island identity in Britain. In C. Clarke, D. Ley and G. C. K. Peach (eds), *Geography and Ethnic Pluralism*. London: Allen & Unwin, 1984, pp. 214–230.

18. See, for example, Farley, J. *Majority–Minority Relations*. Englewood Cliffs, NJ: Prentice-Hall, 1982.

19. Boal, F. W., Ethnic residential segregation. In D. T. Herbert and R. J. Johnston (eds), *Social Areas in Cities*, Vol. 1. Chichester: Wiley, 1976, pp. 411–479.

20. Clark, D., Immigrant enclaves in cities. In C. E. Elias (ed.), *Metropolis: Values in Conflict*. Belmont, CA: Wadsworth, 1964, pp. 201–218.

21. Rose, H. M., The development of an urban sub-system: the case of the negro ghetto, *Annals, Association of American Geographers*, **60,** 1970, 1–17.

22. Phillips, D. and V. Karn, Racial segregation in Britain: patterns, processes, and policy approaches. In E. D. Huttman (ed.), *Urban Housing Segregation of Minorities in Western Europe and the United States*. London: Duke University Press, 1991, 63–91.

23. Winnick, L. *New People in Old Neighborhoods*. New York: Russell Sage Foundation, 1990.

24. Rex, J. and R. Moore, *Race, Community, and Conflict*. London: Oxford University Press, 1967.

25. Doherty, J., Race, class, and residential segregation in Britain, *Antipode*, **3,** 1973, p. 50; emphasis added.

26. Boal, Ethnic residential segregation, p. 45.

27. Boal, F. W., Territoriality on the Shankhill-Falls Divide, Belfast. In D. Lanegran and R. Palm (eds), *An Invitation to Geography*, 2nd edn. New York: McGraw-Hill, 1978, pp. 58–77.

28. Shah, S., Aspects of the geographical analysis of Asian immigrants in London. Unpublished D.Phil. thesis, University of Oxford, 1979, p. 450. Quoted in S. J. Smith, Negative interaction: Crime in the inner-city. In P. Jackson and S. Smith (eds), *Social Interaction and Ethnic Segregation*. London: Academic Press, 1981, p. 51.

29. See, for example, Deakin, N., Race and human rights in the city. In P. Cowan (ed.), *Developing Patterns of Urbanization*. Edinburgh: Oliver & Boyd, 1970, pp. 107–129.

30. Hiro, D., *Black British, White British*. Harmondsworth: Penguin, 1973.

31. Hannerz, U., Ethnicity and opportunity in urban America. In A. Cohen (ed.), *Urban Ethnicity*. London: Tavistock, 1974, pp. 37–76; Freedman, M., Urban labor markets and ethnicity: segments and shelters reexamined. In L. Maldonado and J. Moore (eds), *Urban Ethnicity in the United States*. Beverly Hills: Sage, 1985, pp. 145–166.

32. Drake, S., and H. R. Cayton, *Black Metropolis*. New York: Harper & Row, 1962.

33. See, for example, Rhodes, C. and N. Nabi, Brick Lane. In L. Budd and S. Whimster (eds), *Global Finance and Urban Living. A Study of Metropolitan Change*. London: Routledge, 1992, pp. 333–352; Carey, S. and A. Shukur, A profile of the Bangladeshi community in East London, *New Community*, **12,** 1985, pp. 405–417; Aldrich H. E., *et al.*, Business development and self-segregation: Asian enterprise in three British cities. In C. Peach, V. Robinson and S. Smith (eds), *Ethnic Segregation in Cities*. London: Croom Helm, 1981, pp. 170–190.

34. Sutcliffe, D., *British Black English*. Oxford: Blackwell, 1982.

35. Peach, G. C. K., Ethnic segregation in Sydney and intermarriage patterns, *Australian Geographical Studies*, **12,** 1974, 219–229; Immigrants in the inner city, *Geographical Journal*, **141,** 1975, 372–379.

36. Dench, G., *Maltese in London: A Case Study in the Erosion of Ethnic Consciousness*. London: Routledge & Kegan Paul, 1975.

37. M. Castells, *The City and the Grassroots*. London: Edward Arnold, 1983.

38. Adler, S. and J. Brenner, Gender and space: lesbians and gay men in the city, *International Journal of Urban and Regional Research*, **16,** 1992, 24–34.

39. Moos, A., The grassroots in action: gays and seniors capture West Hollywood, California. In J. Wolch and M. Dear (eds), *The Power of Geography*. London: Unwin Hyman, 1989, pp. 351–369.

40. Boal, Ethnic residential segregation.

41. Waterman, S. and B. A. Kosmin, Residential patterns and processes: a study of Jews in three London boroughs, *Transactions, Institute of British Geographers*, **13,** 1988, 79–95.

42. Kearsley, G. and S. R. Srivastava, The spatial evolution of Glasgow's Asian community, *Scottish Geographical Magazine*, **90,** 1974, 110–124.

43. Baboolal, E., Black residential distribution in south London. In P. Jackson and S. Smith (eds), *Social Interaction and Ethnic Segregation*. London: Academic Press, 1981, pp. 59–80.

44. Agócs, C., Ethnic settlement in a metropolitan area: a typology of communities, *Ethnicity*, **8,** 1981, 127–148.

45. Böhning, W. R., *The Migration of Workers in the United Kingdom and the European Community*. London: Oxford University Press, 1972.

46. See Leitner, H., *Gastarbeiter in der Stadtischen Gesellschaft*. Frankfurt: Campus Verlag, 1983; White, P., *The West European City: A Social Geography*. London: Longman, 1984.

47. Friedrichs, J. and H. Alpheis, Housing segregation of immigrants in West Germany. In E. D. Huttman (ed.), *Urban Housing Segregation of Minorities in Western Europe and the United States*. London: Duke University Press, 1991, pp. 116–144.

Tenement laundry lines, New York. Photograph from U.S. National Archives, American Image Collection.

7 *Neighbourhood, community and the social construction of place*

Neighbourhood and Community • The Social Construction of Urban Places • The Social Meanings of the Built Environment

---

Conceptualizations of space and place have for a long time been an important preoccupation for human geographers. For urban social geographers, one of the central issues in this preoccupation is the question of whether 'community' can be synonymous with 'neighbourhood' or 'locality', and in what circumstances. According to classic sociological theory, communities should not exist at all in cities; or, at best, only in a weakened form. This idea first entered sociological theory in the nineteenth century by way of the writings of Ferdinand Tönnies, who argued that two basic forms of human association could be recognized in all cultural systems.[1] The first of these, *Gemeinschaft*, he related to an earlier period in which the basic unit of organization was the family or kin-group, with social relationships characterized by depth, continuity, cohesion and fulfilment. The second, *Gesellschaft*, was seen as the product of urbanization and industrialization which resulted in social and economic relationships based on rationality, efficiency and contractual obligations among individuals whose roles had become specialized. This perspective was subsequently reinforced by the writings of sociologists such as Durkheim, Simmel, Sumner and, as we have seen, Wirth, and has become part of the conventional wisdom about city life: it is not conducive to 'community', however it might be defined.[2] This view has been characterized as the '*community lost*' argument.[3]

7.1 Neighbourhood and Community

There is, however, a good deal of evidence to support the idea of socially cohesive communities in cities. Writers such as Jane Jacobs have portrayed the city as an inherently human place, where sociability and friendliness are a natural consequence of social organization at the neighbourhood level.[4] Moreover, this view is sustained by empirical research in sociology and anthropology, which has demonstrated the existence of distinctive social worlds that are territorially bounded and that have a vitality that is focused on local 'institutions' such as taverns, pool halls and laundromats.[5] 'The landscape of modernity, then, is much more than the simple product of industrial relocation, the real-estate market, the architect's office, the planner's dreams, the government's regulators, and the engineer's system. It is also the product of diverse people shaping neighborhoods.'[6] Herbert Gans, following his classic study of the West End of Boston, suggested that we need not mourn the passing of the cohesive social networks and sense of self-identity associated with village life because, he argued, these properties existed within the inner city in a series of 'urban villages'.[7] This perspective has become known as 'community saved'. The focus of Gans's study was an ethnic village (the Italian quarter), but studies in other cities have described urban villages based on class rather than ethnicity. The stereotypical example of an urban village is Bethnal Green, London, the residents of which have become something of a sociological stereotype. They exhibit 'a *sense* of community . . . a feeling of solidarity between people who occupy the common territory' based on a strong local network of kinship, reinforced by the localized patterns of employment, shopping and leisure activities.[8] Similar situations have been described in a series of subsequent studies of inner-city life on both sides of the Atlantic – most recently by Thomas Jablonsky in his study of Chicago's 'Back of the Yards' neighbourhood, where 'community spirit . . . was dependent upon – indeed, was generated by – spatial forces. The *culture* of the community evolved in part from spatial habits and territorial loyalties'.[9] Although the utility of such studies is limited by their rather different objectives and by the diversity of the neighbourhoods themselves, the localized social networks they describe do tend to have common origins. In short, urban villages are most likely to develop in long-established working-class areas with a relatively stable population and a narrow range of occupations.

The importance of permanence and immobility in fostering the development of local social systems has been stressed by Margaret Stacey, who suggests that the minimum period required for the development of a distinctive locally-based social system is between 50 and 80 years, assuming the majority of the population to have been born and bred in the area;[10] and most writers agree that the relative immobility of the working classes (in every sense: personal mobility, occupational mobility and residential mobility) is an important factor. Immobility results in a strengthening of *vertical* bonds of kinship and *horizontal* bonds of friendship. The high degree of residential propinquity between family members in working-class areas not only makes for a greater intensity of interaction between kinfolk but also facilitates the important role of the matriarch in reinforcing kinship bonds. The matriarch has traditionally played a key role by providing practical support (e.g. looking after grandchildren, thus enabling a daughter or daughter-in-law to take a job) and by passing on attitudes, information, beliefs and norms of behaviour. Primary social interaction between friends is also reinforced by the residential propinquity which results from immobility. Relationships formed among a cohort of children at school are carried over into street life, courtship and, later on, the pursuit of social activities in pubs, clubs and bingo halls.

Another important factor in fostering the development of close-knit and overlapping social networks in working-class areas is the economic division of society that leaves many people vulnerable to the cycle of poverty. The shared and repeated experience of hard times, together with the cohesion and functional interdependence resulting from the tight criss-crossing of kinship and friendship networks, generates a mutuality of feeling and purpose in working-class areas: a mutuality which is the mainspring of the social institutions, ways of life and 'community spirit' associated with the urban village.[11]

The Fragility of Communality

The cohesiveness and communality arising from immobility and economic deprivation is a fragile phenomenon, however. The mutuality of the urban village is underlain by stresses and tensions that follow from social intimacy and economic insecurity, and several studies of working-class neighbourhoods have described as much conflict and disorder as cohesion and communality. The one factor that has received most attention in this respect is the stress resulting from the simple shortage of space in working-class areas. High densities lead to noise problems, inadequate play space and inadequate clothes-drying facilities and are associated with personal stress and fatigue. Children, in particular, are likely to suffer from the psychological effects of the lack of privacy, as Walter Greenwood observed so acutely in his novel *Love on the Dole*.[12]

In impoverished working-class homes, 'The only place which is private in the way that a professional worker's "study" might be, is the lavatory . . . The lavatory is the place where the man studies his wage chit, or the woman a new and daring purchase.'[13] Where even the lavatory must be shared with other households privacy is still further eroded, and stress or conflict is even more likely. As the authors of a study of a working-class neighbourhood in Nottingham drily observe: 'In St Ann's, sharing an outdoor lavatory, as did many of our respondents, may be conducive to heightened social contact, but not always in an entirely happy way.'[14] The fragility of working-class communality also stems from other sources. The Nottingham study, for example, identified three other stressors in the St Ann's area. The first was the conflict of values which arose from the juxtaposition of people from a variety of ethnic and cultural backgrounds, notwithstanding their common economic experiences. The second was the disruption of social relationships arising as one cohort of inhabitants aged, died and was replaced by younger families, who, even though they were essentially of the same class and life-style, represented an unwitting intrusion on the quieter lives of older folk. The third factor was the disruption associated with the presence of undesirable elements – 'problem families', transients and prostitutes – in the midst of an area of respectable families. It seems likely that the relative strength of these stressors may be the crucial factor in tipping the balance between an inner-city neighbourhood of the 'urban village' type and one characterized by the anomie and social disorganization postulated by Wirthian theory.

Suburban Neighbourhoods: Community Transformed

In contrast to the close-knit social networks of the urban village, suburban life is seen by many observers as the antithesis of 'community'. Lewis Mumford, for example, wrote that the suburbs represent 'a collective attempt to lead a private life', and this view was generally endorsed by a number of early studies of suburban life,[15] including the Lynds' study of Muncie, Indiana, and Warner's study of 'Yankee City' (New Haven).[16] Further sociological work such as Whyte's *The Organization Man* and Stein's *The Eclipse of Community* reinforced the image of the suburbs as an area of loose-knit, secondary ties where life-styles were focused squarely on the nuclear family's pursuit of money, status and consumer durables and the privacy in which to enjoy them.[17] Subsequent investigation, however, has shown the need to revise the myth of suburban 'non-community'. Although there is little evidence for the existence of suburban villages comparable to the urban villages of inner-city areas, it is evident that many suburban neighbourhoods do contain localized social networks with a considerable degree of cohesion: as Gans showed, for example, in his study of Levittown.[18] Suburban neighbourhoods can be thought of as 'communities of limited liability' – one of a series of social constituencies in which urbanites may choose to participate.[19] This view has been translated as '*community transformed*' or 'community liberated'. Instead of urban communities *breaking up*, they can be thought of as *breaking down* into an ever-increasing number of independent subgroups, only some of which are locality based.

It has been suggested by some that the social networks of suburban residents are in fact more localized and cohesive than those of inner-city residents, even if they lack something in *feelings* of mutuality. This perspective emphasizes the high levels of 'neighbouring' in suburbs and suggests that this may be due to one or more of a number of factors:

1. The detached house may be conducive to local social life.
2. Suburbs tend to be more homogeneous, socially and demographically, than other areas.
3. There is a 'pioneer eagerness' to make friends in new suburban developments.
4. Suburban residents are a self-selected group having the same preferences for social and leisure activities.
5. Physical distance from other social contacts forces people to settle for local contacts.

The cohesiveness of suburban communities is further reinforced by social networks related to voluntary associations of various kinds: parent–teacher associations, gardening clubs, country clubs, rotary clubs, and so on. Furthermore, it appears from the evidence at hand that suburban relationships are neither more nor less superficial than those found in central city areas.

Nevertheless, there are some groups for whom suburban living does result in an attenuation of social contact. Members of minority groups of all kinds and people with slightly atypical values or life-styles will not easily be able to find friends or to pursue their own interests in the suburbs. This often results in such people having to travel long distances to maintain social relationships. Those who cannot or will not travel must suffer a degree of social isolation as part of the price of suburban residence. The elderly provide a case in point; a study of the elderly in San Antonio, Texas, found that the further out they lived, the fewer friends they reported, the less active they were socially and the lonelier they were.[21]

The Mosaic Culture of American Suburbs

It should also be acknowledged that the nature and intensity of social interaction in suburban neighbourhoods tends to vary according to the *type* of suburb concerned. Peter Muller argues that American suburbs have become differentiated as a result of two complementary trends. The first of these is the general reorganization of 'cultural space' around different life-styles related variously to careerist orientations, family orientations, 'ecological' orientations, etc., and constrained by income and life-cycle characteristics. The second is the increasing tendency for people to want to withdraw into a 'territorially defended enclave' inhabited by like-minded people, in an attempt to find refuge from potentially antagonistic rival groups.[22] The net result of the two trends is the emergence of distinctive 'voluntary regions' in the suburbs, a process which has been reinforced by the proliferation of suburban housing types that now extend from the 'normal' detached single-family dwelling to include specialist condominium apartments, townhouse developments and exclusive retirement communities. As a result, an 'archipelago' of similar suburban communities, with outliers in every metropolitan ring, now extends from coast to coast. Muller sees this as the emergence of a 'mosaic culture', a new form of macrosocial organization consisting of a number of subcultures distinguished by sharply contrasting life-styles which, although divisive for society as a whole, produces harmonious, homogeneous communities at the local level.

Muller recognizes four major types of suburban neighbourhood, each with a rather different pattern of social interaction.

1. *Exclusive upper income suburbs*: these neighbourhoods are typically situated in the outermost parts of the city and consist of large detached houses built in extensive grounds, screened off by trees and shrubbery. This makes casual neighbouring rather difficult, and so local social networks tend to be based more on voluntary associations such as churches and country clubs.

2. *Middle-class family suburbs*: the dominant form of the middle-class American suburb is the detached single-family dwelling, and the dominant pattern of social interaction is based on the nuclear family. As in the more exclusive suburbs, socializing with relatives is infrequent, and emphasis on family privacy tends to inhibit neighbouring. Since the care of children is a central concern, much social contact occurs through family-orientated organizations such as the PTA, the Scouts and organized sports; and the social cohesion of the neighbourhood derives to a large extent from the overlap of the social networks resulting from these organizations. However, with the tendency for young people to defer marriage, for young couples to defer child rearing, and for land and building costs to escalate, there has emerged a quite different type of middle-class suburb based on apartment living. Social interaction in these neighbourhoods tends to be less influenced by local ties, conforming more to the idea of an aspatial community of interest.

3. *Suburban cosmopolitan centres*: this apparently contradictory label is given to the small but rapidly increasing number of suburban neighbourhoods which serve as voluntary residential enclaves for 'professionals, intellectuals, students, artists, writers and mutually tolerated misfits':[23] people with broad rather than local horizons, but whose special interests and life-style nevertheless generate a cohesive community through a series of overlapping social networks based on cultural activities and voluntary organizations such as bridge clubs, theatre groups and meditation classes. These neighbourhoods are very much a contemporary phenomenon, and are chiefly associated with suburbs adjacent to large universities and colleges.

4. *Working-class suburbs*: blue-collar suburban neighbourhoods have multiplied greatly in number since the 1940s to the point where they are almost as common as middle-class family suburbs in many American cities. But although these neighbourhoods are also dominated by single-family dwellings, patterns of social interaction are quite different. An intensive use of communal outdoor space makes for a high level of primary local social interaction, and community cohesion is reinforced

by a 'person-orientated' rather than a material- or status-orientated life-style. Moreover, the tendency for blue-collar workers to be geographically less mobile means that people's homes are more often seen as a place of permanent settlement, with the result that people are more willing to establish local ties.

Suburbs in West European Cities

European suburban neighbourhoods do not conform particularly well to this typology, largely because of the greater economic constraints on the elaboration of different life-styles. Exclusive upper-income suburbs are sustained by fewer cities; and there are very few examples to be found of the 'suburban cosmopolitan centre'. Moreover, the magnitude of the public housing sector in many European countries means that a large proportion of the suburbs are publicly-owned working-class neighbourhoods: altogether different from the North American suburban working-class neighbourhood.

Paul White recognizes four distinctive suburban types in continental West European cities:

1. *Industrial suburbs*, with origins that can be traced to the late nineteenth century, typically display a mixture of housing with old industrial cottages, terraces or courtyard dwellings adjacent to more recent, publicly-financed apartment blocks. These suburbs have traditionally exhibited an intimate relationship between homes and workplaces and a strong sense of community, but public housing allocation procedures, combined with the 'deindustrialization' of many cities, has disrupted this relationship. Meanwhile, many working-class households have moved to newer, peripheral, publicly-financed suburbs, leaving the industrial suburbs to the elderly and to migrant workers.

2. *Middle-class suburbs*, which are dominated by single-family dwellings, but at relatively high densities. Because of the longstanding cultural preference in continental Europe for in-town, apartment living, the middle-class suburbs of many West European cities form a relatively small proportion of the total suburban realm.

3. *Commuter villages*, which often contain a considerable mixture of social groups – working-class natives as well as middle-class newcomers. In general, they are a recent and accelerating phenomenon, with growth being dominated by private housing for more affluent social groups. They are, however, almost totally absent from Mediterranean Europe. White points out that it should not be assumed that in these settlements 'newcomer' equals 'commuter', or that 'native' can be equated with local employment: 'Continued agricultural labour shedding, coupled with increased urban employment opportunities, have conspired to encourage long-standing residents of peri-urban settlements to take urban employment, sometimes on the basis of a "worker-peasantry" retaining a smallholding as a part-time activity.'[24]

4. *New working-class suburbs*, predominantly publicly financed and typically consisting of high-rise, high-density *grands ensembles*. They are characterized by extremely large-scale developments, a high degree of homogeneity in terms of demographic and social composition (as a result of housing allocation rules), a general lack of local amenities and poor accessibility within their respective metropolitan areas.

Embourgeoisement: Social and Spatial Mobility

In Britain, such suburbs have been the focus of a great deal of sociological research, much of which was originally motivated by a concern for the effects on the extended family system and old locality-based social networks that were expected to result from the suburbanization of working-class families. This approach dovetailed nicely with the idea of *embourgeoisement*, which held that increased affluence among the working class results in conformity with the traditional norms and patterns of social interaction of the middle classes.[25] It was thus expected that the suburbanization of relatively affluent working-class families would result in a loosening of social networks of all kinds. The credibility of the *embourgeoisement* thesis has been much weakened, however, by a series of studies of the 'affluent worker' and working-class suburbs which have shown that, despite a greater relative affluence than before and despite suburban living, there is little evidence that working-class households are adopting middle-class ways of life.[26] On the other hand, it is clear that resettling working-class families in suburban estates does result in some disruption of primary social ties with the result that, for a time at least, social cohesion is reduced. An important contributory factor in this respect is the aloofness generated by status uncertainty following a move to a new and socially unknown environment. This, together with the reduction in the frequency of contact with kinfolk, leads to the development of a more home-centred way of life, so that many suburban public housing estates are characterized by low levels of neighbouring and a lack of social participation in organized activities in clubs and societies. Not every household is equally affected by status uncertainty and home-centredness, however; and not every household is of the same socio-economic status. There often emerges, therefore, a social polarization within council estates between the 'roughs' and the 'respectables'; and it is often the relationship between these two groups which determines the nature of social networks within the community. In a study of a Liverpool estate, for example, the 'rough' group dominated the area's organized social activities while the 'respectable' group withdrew from this kind of interaction; in a study of Watling, the position was reversed.[27]

Status Panic and Crisis Communality

One thing that suburban neighbourhoods everywhere seem to have in common is a lack of the mutuality, the permanent but intangible 'community spirit' that is characteristic of the urban village. An obvious explanation for this is the newness of most suburban communities: they have not had time to fully develop a locality-based social system. An equally likely explanation, however, is that the residents of suburban neighbourhoods are simply not likely to develop a sense of mutuality in the same way as urban villagers because they are not exposed to the same levels of deprivation or stress. This reasoning is borne out to a certain extent by the 'crisis communality' exhibited in suburban neighbourhoods at times when there is an unusually strong threat to territorial exclusivity, amenities, or property values. Examples of the communality generated in the wake of status panic are well documented, and the best known is probably the case of the Cutteslowe walls. In 1932 Oxford City Council set up a housing estate on a suburban site to the north of the city and directly adjacent to a private middle-class estate. The homeowners, united by their fear of a drop both in the status of their neighbourhood and in the value of their property and drawn together by their mutual desire to maintain the social distance between themselves and their new proletarian neighbours, went to the length of building an unscalable wall as a barrier between the two estates.[28] A more recent example is provided by Robson's chronicle of the Bodley barricade: a conflict which ostensibly revolved around local traffic plans but which was largely motivated by a 'hidden agenda' concerned with the socially motivated cleavage between private and public households.[29] Other documented examples have mostly been related to the threat posed by urban motorways, airports, or the zoning of land for business use.

Communities and Neighbourhoods: Definitions and Classifications

Whatever the stimulus, however, suburban communality rarely seems to survive the resolution – one way or another – of the central issue. This raises once more the problem of defining communities. As we have seen, the nature and cohesiveness of social networks vary a lot from one set of sociospatial circumstances to another, and it is not easy to say which situations, if any, reflect the existence of 'community', let alone which of these are also congruent with a discrete geographical territory. Various attempts have been made to establish the spatial expression of community social interaction. Forty years ago George Hillery unearthed over 90 definitions of 'community' in the social sciences, but found that the nearest he could get to common agreement was the presence, in most definitions, of some reference to: (1) area; (2) common ties; and (3) social interaction.[30] Since Hillery's survey there have been numerous attempts to resolve the problem and, although there is still no real consensus, it is increasingly clear that both 'community' and 'neighbourhood' should be regarded simply as general terms for a cluster of inter-related situations relating to specific aspects of social organization. The following typology of neighbourhoods postulates a continuum of neighbourhoods, the extremes of which are determined by the extent of social interaction and common ties:[31]

- At one end of the continuum are *arbitrary neighbourhoods*: general localities with definite names but imprecise limits.
- *Physical neighbourhoods* are more distinctive environments with clearer boundaries.
- *Homogeneous neighbourhoods* are distinctive *and* internally homogeneous in terms of both environmental and physical characteristics.
- *Functional neighbourhoods* are areas united by particular activity patterns – working or learning, for example.
- *Community neighbourhoods* are those which contain close-knit groups engaged in primary social interaction.

It is also possible to think in terms of a loose hierarchial relationship between neighbourhood, community and communality. Thus *neighbourhoods* are territories containing people of broadly similar demographic, economic and social characteristics, but are not necessarily significant as a basis for social interaction. *Communities* exist where a degree of social coherence develops on the basis of interdependence, which in turn produces a uniformity of custom, taste and modes of thought and speech. Communities are 'taken-for-granted' worlds defined by reference groups which may be locality-based, school-based, work-based or media-based. *Communality*, or 'communion', exists as a form of human association based on affective bonds. It is 'community experience at the level of consciousness',[32] but it requires an intense mutual involvement that is difficult to sustain and so only appears under conditions of stress.

In the final analysis, 'each neighbourhood is what its inhabitants think it is'.[33] This means that definitions and classifications of neighbourhoods and communities must depend on the geographic scales of reference used by people. In this context, it may be helpful to think of *immediate* neighbourhoods (which are small, which may overlap one another, and which are characterized by personal association rather than interaction through formal groups, institutions, or organizations), *traditional* neighbourhoods (which are characterized by social interaction that is consolidated by the sharing of local facilities and the use of local organizations), and *emergent* neighbourhoods (which are large, diverse and characterized by relatively low levels of social interaction).[34]

A rather different way of approaching neighbourhoods and communities is to focus on their *functions*. It is possible, for example, to think in terms of neighbourhoods' *existential* functions (related to people's affective bonds and sense of belonging), *economic* functions (geared to consumption), *administrative* functions (geared to the organization and use of public services), *locational* functions (relating to the social and material benefits of relative location), *structural* functions (related to the social outcomes of urban design), *political* functions (geared to the articulation of local issues) and *social reproduction* functions (related to the broader political economy of urbanization).

7.2 The Social Construction of Urban Places

'Place,' observes David Harvey, 'has to be one of the most multi-layered and multi-purpose words in our language.'[35] This layering of meanings reflects the way that places are socially constructed – given different meanings by different groups for different purposes. It also reflects the difficulty of developing theoretical concepts of place.

> There are all sorts of words such as milieu, locality, location, locale, neighbourhood, region, territory and the like, which refer to the generic qualities of place. There are other terms such as city, village, town, megalopolis and state, which designate particular kinds of places. There are still others, such as home, hearth, 'turf', community, nation and landscape, which have such strong connotations of place that it would be hard to talk about one without the other.[36]

In this context it is helpful to recognize the 'betweenness' of place: that is, the dependence of place on perspective. Places exist, and are constructed, from a subjective point of view; while simultaneously they are constructed and seen as an external 'other' by outsiders. As Nicholas Entrikin puts it, 'Our neighborhood is both an area centered on ourselves and our home, as well as an area containing houses, streets and people that we may view from a decentered or an outsider's perspective. Thus place is both a center of meaning and the external context of our actions.'[37] In addition, views from 'outside' can vary in abstraction from being in a specific place to being virtually 'nowhere' (i.e. an abstract, perspectiveless view).[38]

These distinctions are useful in pointing to the importance of understanding urban spaces and places in terms of the insider, the person who normally lives in and uses a particular place or setting.[39] Yet insideness and outsideness must be seen as ends of a continuum along which various modes of place-experience can be identified. The key argument here is that places have meaning in direct proportion to the degree that people feel 'inside' that place: 'here rather than there, enclosed rather than exposed, secure rather than threatened'.[40] One important element in the construction of place is to define the other in an exclusionary and stereotypical way. This is part of the human strategy of *territoriality*: 'a spatial strategy to make places instruments of power'.[41] Self-definition comes in relation to the *other*, the people and places outside the boundaries (real and perceived), that we establish.

Another key element in the construction of place is the existential imperative for people to define themselves in relation to the material world. The roots of this idea are to be found in the philosophy of Martin Heidegger, who contended that men and women originate in an alienated condition and define themselves, among other ways, spatially. Their 'creation' of space provides them with roots, their homes and localities becoming biographies of that creation.[42] Central to Heidegger's philosophy is the notion of 'dwelling': the basic capacity to achieve a form of spiritual unity between humans and the material world. Through repeated experience and complex associations, our capacity for dwelling allows us to construct places, to give them meanings that are deepened and qualified over time with multiple nuances. Here, though, Heidegger introduced an additional argument: that this deepening and multiple layering of meaning is subverted in the modern world by the spread of telecommunications technology, rationalism, mass production and mass values. The result, he suggested, is that the 'authenticity' of place is subverted. City spaces become inauthentic and 'placeless'[43] – a process that is, ironically, reinforced as people seek authenticity through professionally designed and commercially constructed spaces and places whose invented traditions, sanitized and simplified symbolism, and commercialized heritage all make for convergence rather than spatial identity.

Yet the construction of place by 'insiders' cannot take place independently of societal norms and representations of the world: what Larissa Lomnitz calls the 'cultural grammar' that codifies the social construction of spaces and places.[44] Both our territoriality and our sense of dwelling are informed by broadly shared notions of social distance, rules of comportment, forms of social organization, conceptions of worth and value, and so on. We see here, then, another important dialectical relationship: between social structures and the everyday practices of the 'insiders' of subjectively constructed spaces and places. We live, as noted before in this book, both *in* and *through* places. Place, then, is much more than a container or a mental construct. It is both text and context, a setting for social interaction that, among other things:[45]

1. structures the daily routines of economic and social life;
2. structures people's life paths, providing them with both opportunities and constraints;
3. provides an arena in which everyday, 'common-sense' knowledge and experience is gathered;
4. provides a site for processes of socialization and social reproduction; and
5. provides an arena for contesting social norms.

Urban Lifeworlds, Time–Space Routinization and Intersubjectivity

This dialectical relationship lends both dynamism and structure to the social geography of the city:

> The social reality of the city is not simply given. It is also constructed and maintained intersubjectively in a semiclosed world of communication and shared symbolization. The routines of daily life create a particular view of the world and a mandate for action. It is the unselfconscious, taken-for-granted character of the life-world that makes it so binding on its members, that ensures that its realities will remain secure.[46]

The crucial idea here is that of the *lifeworld*, 'the taken-for-granted pattern and context for everyday living through which people conduct their day-to-day lives without having to make it an object of conscious attention'.[47] Sometimes, this pattern and context extend to conscious attitudes and feelings: a self-conscious sense of place with an interlocking set of cognitive elements attached to the built environment and to people's dress codes, speech patterns, public comportment and material posessions. This is what Raymond Williams termed a *structure of feeling*.[48]

The basis of both individual lifeworlds and the collective structure of feeling is *intersubjectivity*: shared meanings that are derived from the lived experience of everyday practice. Part of the basis for intersubjectivity is the *routinization* of individual and social practice in time and space. As suggested by Fig. 7.1, the *temporality* of social life can be broken out into three levels, each of which is inter-related to the others.[49] The *longue durée* of social life is bound up with the historical development of institutions (the law, the family, etc.). Within the *dasein*, or life-span, social life is influenced by the life cycle of individuals and families and (interacting with the *longue durée*) by the social conditions characteristic of their particular generation. And within the *durée* of daily life, individual routines interact both with the structure of institutional frameworks and with the rhythm of their life cycle.

The *spatiality* of social life can also be broken out into three dimensions. At the broadest scale there is institutional spatial practice, which refers to the collective level of the social construction of space. 'Place' can then be thought of as related to the human consciousness and social meanings attached to urban spaces. Finally, individual spatial practice refers to the

	Longue durée	Dasein (life-span)	Durée of daily life
Longue durée	Institutional time History	Coupling of history and life history Generation	Dialectics between institutions and daily life
Dasein (life-span)		Life history, the 'I'	Relation between life strategies and daily life
Durée of daily life			Day-to-day routines (time use)

Figure 7.1
Interrelations between the dimensions of temporality
Source: K. Simonsen, *Environment & Planning D: Space and Society*, 9, 1991, Fig. 1, p. 427.

Time Space	*Longue durée*	*Dasein*	*Durée* of daily life
Institutional spatial practice	Sociospatial development (historical geography)	Life strategies in spatial context	Geographical conditioning of daily routines
Place	Local history, culture and tradition	Biography in time and space Identity	Spatially based 'natural attitudes'
Individual spatial practice	Historical conditioning of spatial practices	Relation between life strategies and spatial practices	Daily time–space routines (time–geography)

Figure 7.2
Temporality, spatiality, and social life
Source: K. Simonsen, *Environment & Planning D: Space and Society*, 9, 1991, Fig. 3.

physical presence and spatial interaction of individuals and groups. These three levels of spatiality, in turn, can be related to the three levels of temporality of social life, as depicted in Fig. 7.2. We are, thus, presented with a multi-dimensional framework within which time–space routinization is able to foster the intersubjectivity upon which people's lifeworlds depend.

The best-known element of this framework to geographers is the time–geography of daily life that has been elaborated by Torsten Hägerstrand.[50] His basic model (Fig. 7.3) captures the constraints of space and time on daily, individual spatial practices. It illustrates the way that people trace out 'paths' in time and space, moving from one place (or 'station') to another in order to fulfil particular purposes (or 'projects'). This movement is conceptualized as being circumscribed by three kinds of constraint: (1) capability constraints – principally, the time available for travelling and the speed of the available mode of transportation; (2) authority constraints – laws and customs affecting travel and accessibility; and (3) coupling constraints – resulting from the limited periods during which specific projects are available for access. The particular significance of time–geographies in the present context is that groups of people with similar constraints are thrown together in 'bundles' of time–space activity: routine patterns that are an important precondition for the development of intersubjectivity.

Structuration and the 'Becoming' of Place

These issues are central to 'structurationist' theory, which addresses the way in which everyday social practices are structured across space and time. Developed by Anthony Giddens,[51] structurationist theory accepts and elaborates Karl Marx's famous dictum that human beings 'make history,

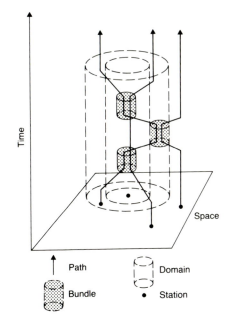

Figure 7.3
Concepts and notation of time-geography (after Hägerstrand)
Source: D. Gregory, in D. Gregory and R. Walford (eds), *Horizons in Human Geography*,
Barnes and Noble, Totowa, N.J., 1989, Fig. 1.4.4, p. 82.

but not in circumstances of their own choosing'. Reduced to its essentials,
and seen from a geographical perspective, structurationist theory holds that
human landscapes:

> are created by knowledgeable actors (or *agents*) operating within a
> specific social context (or *structure*). The structure–agency relationship
> is mediated by a series of institutional arrangements which both enable
> and constrain action. Hence three 'levels of analysis' can be identified:
> structures, institutions, and agents. Structures include the long-term,
> deep-seated social practices which govern daily life, such as law and the
> family. Institutions represent the phenomenal forms of structures,
> including, for example, the state apparatus. And agents are those
> influential human actors who determine the precise, observable
> outcomes of any social interaction.[52]

We are all actors, then (whether ordinary citizens or powerful business
leaders, members of interest groups, bureaucrats, or elected officials), and
all part of a dualism in which structures (the communicative structures of
language and signification as well as formal and informal economic, political and legal structures) enable our behaviour while our behaviour itself
reconstitutes, and sometimes changes, these structures. Structures may act
as constraints on individual action but they are also, at the same time, the
medium and outcome of the behaviour they recursively organize.

Furthermore, structurationist theory recognizes that we are all members of *systems* of social actors: networks, organizations, social classes, and so on.

Human action is seen as being based on 'practical consciousness', meaning that the way in which we make sense of our own actions and the actions of others, and the way we generate meaning in the world is rooted in routinized day-to-day practices that occupy a place in our minds somewhere between the conscious and the unconscious. Recursivity, the continual reproduction of individual and social practices through routine actions (*time–space routinization*), contributes to *social integration*, the development of social systems and structures among agents in particular *locales*. In addition, structures and social systems can be seen to develop across broader spans of space and time through *system integration*, which takes place through *time–space distanciation*: the 'stretching' of social relations over time and space as ideas, attitudes and norms are spread through print and electronic media, for example. All this recursivity and integration does not make for stasis, however, since the structurationist approach sees all human action as involving unanticipated or unacknowledged conditions and as having unintended consequences that modify or change the nature of recurrent practices (Fig. 7.4).

This kind of perspective leads us to see urban spaces and places, as Allan Pred has shown,[53] as constantly *becoming*. Place, in other words, is an historically contingent *process* in which practice and structure become one

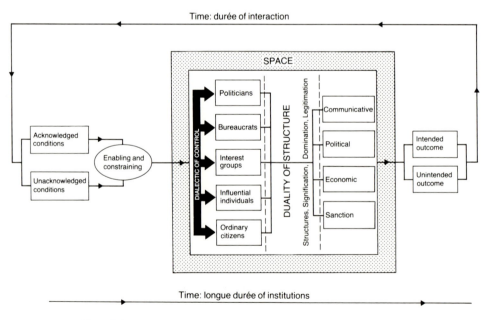

Figure 7.4
A model of the structuration of urban space
Source: A. Moos and M. Dear, *Environment & Planning A*, 18, 1986, p. 245.

another through the intertwining of recursive individual and social practices and structured relations of power. At the same time, place involves processes (socialization, language acquisition, personality development, social and spatial division of labour, etc.) through which individual biographies and collective ways of life also become one another (Fig. 7.5). As Pred puts it:

> any place or region expresses a process whereby the reproduction of social and cultural forms, the formation of biographies, and the transformation of nature and space ceaselessly become one another at the same time that power relations and time-specific path-project intersections continuously become one another in ways that are not subject to universal laws, but vary with historical circumstances.[54]

The structurationist approach has become an important influence in contemporary human geography, particularly in urban social geography because of its central concern with the sociospatial dialectic. It has, nevertheless, proven difficult to incorporate into substantive accounts of city and/or neighbourhood formation. It has also been criticized for its emphasis on recursivity (to the relative neglect of the unforeseen and the unintended), for its inattention to the role of the unconscious, for its 'anaemic' treatment of culture, and for its neglect of issues of gender and ethnicity.[55]

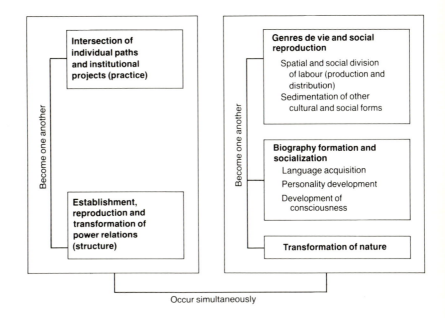

Figure 7.5
Components of place (and region) as historically contingent process
Source: A. Pred, in D. Gregory and J. Urry (eds) *Social Relations and Spatial Structures*, Macmillan, London, 1985, p. 343.

Constructing Place Through Spatial Practices

David Harvey's 'grid' of spatial practices (Table 7.1) provides one way of accommodating a broader, richer array of issues in addressing the ways in which places are constructed and experienced as material artefacts, how they are represented, and how they become used as symbolic spaces in contemporary culture. The matrix is useful in focusing our attention on the dialectical interplay between experience, perception and imagination; and in clarifying the relationships between distanciation and the appropriation, domination and production of places. It does not, though, summarize a theory: it is merely a framework across which we can interpret social relations of class, gender, community and race.

The three dimensions on the vertical axis of the grid are drawn from Lefebvre's distinction between the experienced, the perceived and the imagined:[56]

- *Material spatial practices* refer to the interactions and physical flows that occur in and across space as part of fundamental processes of economic production and social reproduction.
- *Representations of space* include all of the signs, symbols, codifications and knowledge that allow material spatial practices to be talked about and understood.
- *Spaces of representation* are mental constructs such as Utopian plans, imaginary landscapes, paintings and symbolic structures that imagine new meanings or possibilities for spatial practices.

The four dimensions across the horizontal axis of the grid on Table 7.1 have to be seen as mutually interdependent. *Accessibility and distanciation* are two sides of the same coin: the role of the friction of distance in human affairs. Distance, as we saw in Chapter 6, is both a barrier to and a defence against social interaction. Distanciation 'is simply a measure of the degree to which the friction of space has been overcome to accommodate social interaction'.[57] The *appropriation of space* refers to the way in which space is occupied by individuals, social groups, activities (e.g. land uses) and objects (houses, factories, streets). The *domination of space* refers to the way in which the organization and production of spaces and places can be controlled by powerful individuals or groups: through private property laws, zoning ordinances, restrictive covenants, gates (and implied gates), etc. The *production of space* refers to the way in which new systems of territorial organization, land use, transport and communications, etc. (actual or imagined), arise, along with new ways of representing them.

We shall draw on this grid throughout the remainder of this chapter as we examine the ways in which material and social worlds are given meaning through cultural politics, in which political and economic power is projected through urban form, and in which space and place are appropriated through symbolism and coded meanings.

Table 7.1 A 'grid' of spatial practices

	Accesiblity and distancation	Appropriation and use of space	Domination and control of space	Production of space
Material spatial practices (experience)	Flows of goods, money, people, labour, power, information, etc.; transport and communications systems; market and urban hierarchies; agglomeration	Land uses and built environments; social spaces and other 'turf' designations; social networks of communication and mutual aid	Private property in land; state and administrative divsions of space; exlusive communities and neighbourhoods; exlusionary zoning and other forms of social control (policing and surveillance)	Production of physical infrastuctures (transport and communications; built environments; land clearance, etc.); territorial organization of social infrastructures (formal and informal)
Repesentations of space (perception)	Social, psychological and physical measures of distance; map-making; theories of the 'friction of distance' (principle of least effort, social physics, range of good, central place and other forms of location theory)	Personal space; mental maps of occupied space; spatial hierarchies; symbolic repesention of spaces; spatial 'discourses'	Forbidden spaces; 'teritorial imperatives'; community; regional cultures; nationalism; geopolitics; hierachies	New systems of mapping, visual representation, communication etc.; new artistic and architectural 'discourses'; semiotics
Spaces of representation (imagination)	Attraction/repulsion; distance/desire; access/denial; transcendence 'medium is the message'	Familiarity; hearth and home; open places; places of popular spectacle (streets, squares, markets); inconography and graffiti, advertising	Unfamiliarity; spaces of fear; property and possession; monumentality and constructed spaces of ritual; symbolic barriers and symbolic capital; construction of 'tradition'; spaces of repression	Utopian plans; imaginary landscapes; science fiction ontologies and space; artists' sketches; mythologies of space and place; poetics of space spaces of desire

Source: D. Harvey, The Condition of Postmodernity, Blackwell, Oxford, pp. 220–221.

Place, Consumption and Cultural Politics

An important lesson is implicit in the grid of spatial practices outlined by Harvey: it is that we should not treat 'society' as separate from 'economy', 'politics', 'culture' or 'place'. We are thus pointed to the domain of 'cultural politics', defined by Peter Jackson as 'the domain in which meanings are constructed and negotiated, where relations of dominance and subordination are defined and contested. . . . In opposition to the unitary view of culture as the artistic and intellectual product of an elite, "cultural politics" insists on a plurality of cultures, each defined as a whole "way of life", where ideologies are interpreted in relation to the material interests they serve. From this perspective, the cultural is always, simultaneously, political'.[58] Our experiences of material and social worlds are always mediated by power relationships and culture. 'Social' issues of distinction and 'cultural' issues of aesthetics, taste and style cannot be separated from 'political' issues of power and inequality or from 'gender' issues of dominance and oppression. The construction of place is bound up, in other words, with the construction of class, gender, sexuality, power and culture. To quote Peter Jackson again, 'class relations have a cultural as well as an economic dimension and . . . patriarchy cannot be confined to questions of sexuality, marriage, or domesticity. "Home" and "work" cannot readily be separated, as relations of dominance and subordination established in one domain carry over into the other'.[59]

An important contribution to this perspective has been made by French sociologist Pierre Bourdieu. His concept of *habitus*, like Raymond Williams's concept of a 'structure of feeling', noted above, deals with the construction of meaning in everyday lifeworlds. Habitus evolves in response to specific objective circumstances of class, race, gender relations and place. Yet it is more than the sum of these parts. It consists of a distinctive set of values, cognitive structures and orienting practices: a collective perceptual and evaluative schema that derives from its members' everyday experience and operates at a subconscious level, through commonplace daily practices, dress codes, use of language, comportment and patterns of material consumption. The result is a distinctive cultural politics of 'regulated improvisations' in which 'each dimension of lifestyle symbolizes with the others'.[60]

According to Bourdieu, each group will seek to sustain and extend its habitus (and new sociospatial groups will seek to establish a habitus) through the appropriation of *symbolic capital*: consumer goods and services that reflect the taste and distinction of the owner. In this process, not every group necessarily accepts the definitions of taste and distinction set out by the élite groups and tastemakers with the 'cultural capital' to exercise power over the canons of 'good' taste and 'high' culture. In any case, such definitions are constantly subject to devaluation by the popularization of goods and practices that were formerly exclusive. The fact that symbolic capital is vulnerable to devaluation and to shifts in avant-garde taste makes it even more potent, of course, as a measure of distinction. As a result, though, dominant groups must continually pursue refinement and originality in their life-styles and ensembles of material posessions. Less dominant groups, meanwhile, must find and legitimize alternative life-styles, symbols and practices in order to achieve distinction. Subordinate groups are not necessarily left to construct a habitus that is a poor copy of others', however: they can – and often do – develop a habitus that embodies different values and 'rituals of resistance'[61] in which the meaning of things is appropriated and transformed.

All this points to the importance of *consumption* and of the aestheticization of everyday life. Consumption 'purports to dispel the dread of being in a world of strangers. Ads tell us what to expect, what is acceptable and unacceptable, and what we need to do in order to belong. They are primary vehicles for producing and transmitting cultural symbols'. Consumption 'not only produces and circulates meaning, it . . . interweaves and alters forces and perspectives, and it empowers us in our daily lives to change our culture, to transform nature, and *to create place*'.[62] Consumption is inherently spatial. The propinquity of object and place allows the former to take on the cultural authority of the latter; objects displayed beside each other exchange symbolic attributes; places become tranformed into commodities. The consumer's world consists not only of settings where things are purchased or consumed (shops, malls, amusement parks, resorts) but also of settings and contexts that are created with and through purchased products (homes, neighbourhoods). All of these settings are infused with signs and symbols that collectively constitute 'maps of meaning'.

Examples of the relationships between place, consumption and cultural politics can be drawn from a variety of scales and contexts. Gerry Pratt has shown, for instance, how the style and contents of the home can signify people's group identity as well as their individual identity. Her study of upper-class Vancouver housewives showed that women who identified with a clearly defined social group used their homes to reinforce their group identity, whereas those with little group identity used their homes and interior design as a means of personal expression.[63] David Ley, in another Vancouver study, has shown how contrasting sets of cultural values, associated with differing sociopolitical groups, have resulted in starkly different landscapes along the redeveloped north and south shores of False Creek.[64] Damaris Rose has shown how gentrification provides for the development of new patterns of consumption and new life-styles with significance for gender relations;[65] and Larry Knopp has shown how struggles over the sexual codings of space are enmeshed with issues of class, politics and economics as well as gender and sexual orientation.[66] In the remainder of this chapter, we shall explore the overall context for such relationships between place, consumption and cultural politics that is provided through the construction of social meanings associated with the built environment.

7.3 The Social Meanings of the Built Environment

At the most general level, the landscape of cities can be seen as a reflection of the prevailing ideology (in the sense of a political climate, *zeitgeist*, or 'spirit') of a particular society. The idea of urban fabric being seen – in part, at least – as the outcome of broad political, socio-economic and cultural forces has been explicit in much writing on urbanization. 'The argument, briefly, is that the political climate is determined by the dominant members of a society, that is, by the ruling classes, and that the political climate thus created in turn influences the design of urban settlements profoundly.'[67]

We can illustrate this with reference to two of the ways in which the spirit of modern capitalism has been imprinted on the fabric of cities. The first is connected with the symbolization of wealth and achievement by groups of prosperous merchants and industrialists. Early examples of this include the industrial capitalists of Victorian times, who felt the compulsion to express their achievements in buildings. The Cross Street area of central Manchester is still dominated by the imposing gothic architecture commissioned by the city's Victorian élite who, preoccupied with the accumulation and display of wealth but with a rather philistine attitude towards aesthetics, left a clear impression of their values on the central area of the city. Manchester 'was a confident city, and that confidence was expressed in bricks and mortar, in edifices built to last, to show future ages all was well'.[68] As the petite bourgeoisie of small-scale merchant and industrial capital lost ground to corporate and international capital, so the symbolization of achievement and prosperity became dominated by corporate structures. Huge office blocks such as the Prudential Building in Boston and the Pirelli Building in Paris are clearly intended as statements of corporate power and achievement, notwithstanding any administrative or speculative functions. At a more general level, of course, the whole complex of offices and stores in entire downtown areas can be interpreted as symbolic of the power of the 'central district élite' in relation to the rest of the city. Meanwhile, other institutions have added their particular statements to the palimpsest of the urban fabric. The sponsors of universities, trade union headquarters, cultural centres and the like, unable (or unwilling) to make use of the rude message of high-rise building, have generally fallen back on the combination of neoclassicism and modernism that has become the reigning international style for any building aspiring to carry authority through an image of high-mindedness rather than raw power.

A second way in which the spirit of modern capitalism can be said to have been inscribed into the fabric of cities stems from the activities of the speculative developers who have been responsible for the design and layout of a large proportion of the housing stock of cities. Their search for profit – surely the essence of the 'spirit' of capitalism – has produced, as we saw in Chapter 4, a large amount of housing that is based on a repetitive layout and characterized by uniformity of exterior design. Faced with a large but relatively impoverished market, the speculative developers of the nine-teenth and early twentieth centuries could only make a satisfactory profit by giving themselves to a high-volume, low-cost product. The latter could only be achieved by producing large tracts of standardized dwellings on rectilinear plots, taking advantage of the division of labour and economies of scale. Thus emerged the brick terraces of English cities, the tall tenements of Glasgow, Edinburgh, Paris, New York, Berlin and Genoa, the wooden 'three-deckers' of New England towns, and the two- and three-storey walk-up apartment buildings of Philadelphia, Chicago and St Louis. (Later these were joined, on the same principle, by the semi-detached and detached single-family dwellings of lower middle-class suburbs in cities everywhere.) Architecture was superseded by pattern books containing plans of known profitability, and houses were built to minimal standards, soon inducing widespread deterioration. The most profitable shape – deep, narrow buildings – allowed only minimum light and air; and the grid pattern which saved so much on survey, construction and administrative costs soon proved a hindrance to traffic as well as being unsuited to the development of centred and bounded neighbourhoods in which 'community' could flourish.

The Appropriation of Space and Place: Symbolism and Coded Meanings

While the built environment is heavily endowed with social meaning, this meaning is rarely simple, straightforward or unidimensional. To begin with, there is an important distinction between the *intended* meaning of architec-ture and the *perceived* meaning of the built environment as seen by others. This distinction is essential to a proper understanding of the social meaning of the built environment. David Harvey's study of the Sacré-Coeur in Paris, for example, demonstrates how the intended symbolism of the building – a reaffirmation of Monarchism in the wake of the Paris Commune – 'was for many years seen as a provocation to civil war',[69] and is still interpreted by the predominantly republican population of Paris as a provocative rather than a unifying symbol. At a more general level, it has been claimed that while the 'architecture of opulence' – sleek office buildings and imposing private residences – 'operates on a world-wide scale to reassure the rich, strong and self-confident', it also serves 'to provoke and radicalize the poor and the weak'.[70] Another possibility, of course, is that it reinforces feelings of deference among certain sections of the poor and the weak. The point is that much of the social meaning of the built environment depends on the audience. In turn, the concepts of audience held by the producers and managers of the built environment will help to determine the kinds of messages that are sent in the first place.

Another critical point is that the social meaning of the built environment is not static. The meanings associated with particular symbols and symbolic environments tend to be modified as social values change in response to changing life-styles and changing patterns of socio-economic organization. At the same time, powerful symbols and motifs from earlier periods are often borrowed in order to legitimize a new social order, as in Mussolini's co-opting of the symbols of Augustan Rome in an attempt to legitimize Fascist urban reorganization; and (ironically) in the adoption of a selection of motifs from the classical revival in Europe by Jefferson and the founding fathers responsible for commissioning public and ceremonial architecture in Washington, DC.

It is also clear that the style of symbolization can vary according to the intentions of the 'producers' of the built environment and the social context of the building. The 'signature of power', according to Lasswell, is manifest in two ways: (i) through a 'strategy of awe', intimidating the audience with majestic displays of power, and (ii) through a 'strategy of admiration' aimed at diverting the audience with spectacular and histrionic projects.[71] It should be recognized, however, that not everyone wishes to display power. The symbolism of the built environment may, therefore, involve 'modest' or 'low profile' architecture; or carry deliberately misleading messages for the purpose of maintaining social harmony. Nor is power the only kind of message to convey: various elements of the counter-ideology generate their own symbolic structures and environments. Similarly, there is a variety of messages which stem from the self rather than group identity. The commonest are simple 'I-am-here' messages; and these, in turn, are most frequent among the socially mobile, the nouveaux riches, new migrants and transients.[72]

How can all these observations be accommodated within a coherent framework of analysis? Let us consider first the various attempts to develop a systematic approach to the symbolic meaning of the built environment. Robert Gutman observes that the literature on architectural symbolism conventionally distinguishes three levels of symbolic meaning: 'syntactical meaning, or the meaning that an element of form or style acquires by virtue of its location in a chain of form or style elements; semantic meaning, or the meaning it acquires because of the norm, idea or attitude that it represents or designates; and pragmatic meaning, or the meaning that is understood in relation to the architect, client or social group that invents or interprets the buildings' form or style'.[73] The first of these has involved a highly abstract approach in an attempt to develop a general theory of symbols and signs: semiology. Working on the assumption that there exist innate conventions through which human artefacts convey meaning, some writers have attempted to explore the 'deep structures' of architecture and urban form.[74] Much of this work, however, is highly codified and mechanistic, deliberately and systematically abstracting symbols from their historical and social context. It has thus sustained the 'fetishism' of design, focusing attention on buildings and architects rather than on the sets of social relations that surround the production and meaning of buildings.[75]

There have been some tentative attempts to link the 'syntax' of the built environment to the wider context, moving, in Gutman's terms, towards the study of syntactical and semantic meaning. Hillier *et al.*, for example, have attempted to develop a theory relating spatial syntax and architectural form to 'social syntax': the patterns of encounters and relationships that hold within society.[76] Despite their concern with the built environment as a medium of communication, however, none of these approaches directly confronts the fundamental questions of communication by whom, to what audience, to what purpose and to what effect? These are the questions which have prompted a number of writers to build on Marxian social theory in such a way as to accommodate the social meaning of the built environment. According to this perspective, the built environment, as part of the socio-economic superstructure stemming from the dominant mode of production (feudalism, merchant capitalism, industrial capitalism, etc.), reflects the *zeitgeist* of the prevailing system; it also serves, like other components of the superstructure, as one of the means through which the necessary conditions for the continuation of the system are reproduced. One of the first people to sketch out these relationships between social process and urban form was David Harvey, who emphasized the danger of thinking in terms of simple causal relationships, stressing the need for a flexible approach which allows urbanism to exhibit a variety of forms within any dominant mode of production, while similar forms may exist as products of different modes of production.[77]

Within the broad framework sketched by Harvey, others have contributed detailed studies of the form, interior layout and exterior design of various components of the built environment as a response to the reorganization of society under industrial capitalism. To take just a few examples: Rob Shields has drawn upon Lefebvre's concepts of spaces of representation and representations of space (see Harvey's matrix of spatial practices in Table 7.1) in analysing the 'social spatialization' of the built environment, using the West Edmonton Mall as a case study; while Jon Goss and Margaret Crawford have each explored the structuration of place through the retail spaces of shopping malls.[78] Christine Boyer has described the 'commodification of history' in waterfront redevelopments; and Sharon Zukin has described the social construction of the built environment in relation to several different kinds of 'landscapes of power', including industrial neighbourhoods, malls, gentrified neighbourhoods and Disney World.[79] Barbara Rubin, in her documentation of the emergence of 'signature' structures and franchise architecture, noted that 'good taste' in urban design generally has become part of an ideology that has been used to control and exploit urban space. 'In the ideology of American aesthetics, it is understood that those who make taste make money, and those who make money make taste.'[80] This brings us back to the key role of certain actors – design professionals, in this case – within the social production of the built environment.

Architecture, Aesthetics and the Sociospatial Dialectic

The architect's role as an arbiter, creator and manipulator of style can be interpreted as part of the process whereby changing relationships within society at large become expressed in the 'superstructure' of ideas, institutions and objects. This allows us to see major shifts in architectural style as a dialectical response to the evolving *zeitgeist* of urban–industrial society – as part of a series of broad intellectual and artistic reactions rather than the product of isolated innovations wrought by inspired architects. Thus, for example, the Art Nouveau and Jugendstil architecture of the late nineteenth century can be seen as the architectural expression of the romantic reaction to what Lewis Mumford called the 'palaeotechnic' era of the industrial revolution: a reaction that was first expressed in the Arts and Crafts movement and in Impressionist painting. By 1900 the Art Nouveau style was firmly established as the snobbish style, consciously élitist, for all 'high' architecture. The dialectic response was a series of artistic and intellectual movements, beginning with Cubism, that went out of their way to dramatize modern technology, seeking an anonymous and collective method of design in an attempt to divorce themselves from 'capitalist' canons of reputability and power. Thus emerged the Constructivist and Futurist movements, the Bauhaus school and, later, Les Congrès Internationaux d'Architecture Moderne (CIAM) and the Modern Architecture Research Group (MARS), who believed that 'their new architecture and their new concepts of urban planning were expressing not just a new aesthetic image but the very substance of new social conditions which they were helping to create'.[81]

The subsequent fusion and transformation of these movements into the glib 'Esperanto' of the International Style and the simultaneous adoption of the style as the preferred image of corporate and bureaucratic conservatism, solidity and respectability provides an important example of the way in which the dominant social order is able to protect itself from opposing ideological forces. In this particular example, the energy of opposing ideological forces – idealist radicalism – has been neatly diverted into the defence of the *status quo*. The question is: how? One answer is that the professional ideology and career structure within which most practising architects (as opposed to the avant-garde) operate is itself heavily oriented towards Establishment values and sensitively tuned to the existing institutional setting and economic order. Consequently, the meaning and symbolism of new architectural styles emanating from radical quarters tend to be modified as they are institutionalized and converted into commercialism; while the core movement itself, having forfeited its raw power in the process of 'commodification', passes quietly into the mythology of architectural education and the coffee-table books of the cognoscenti. There is a direct parallel here in the way that the liberal ideology of the town planning movement was transformed into a defensive arm of urbanized capital, systematically working to the advantage of the middle-class community in general and the business community in particular.[82]

According to this perspective, architects, like planners, can be seen as unwitting functionaries, part of a series of 'internal survival mechanisms' which have evolved to meet the imperatives of urbanized capital.

Another way in which architects serve these imperatives is in helping to stimulate consumption and extract surplus value. The architect, by virtue of the prestige and mystique socially accorded to creativity, adds exchange value to a building through his or her decisions about 'design', 'so that the label "architect designed" confers a presumption of quality even though, like the emperor's clothes, this quality may not be apparent to the observer'.[83] Moreover, as one of the key arbiters of style in modern society, the architect is in a powerful position to stimulate consumption merely by generating and/or endorsing changes in the nuances of building design.

The professional ideology and career structure that reward innovation and the ability to feel the pulse of fashion also serve to promote the circulation of capital. Without a steady supply of new fashions in domestic architecture (reinforced by innovations in kitchen technology, heating systems, etc.), the filtering mechanisms on which the whole owner-occupier housing market is based would slow down to a level unacceptable not only to builders and developers but also to the exchange professionals (surveyors, real-estate agents, etc.) and the whole range of financial institutions involved in the housing market. The rich and the upper-middle classes, in short, must be encouraged to move from their comfortable homes to new dwellings with even more 'design' and 'convenience' features in order to help maintain a sufficient turnover in the housing market. One way in which they are enticed to move is through the cachet of fashionable design and state-of-the-art technology. Hence the rapid diffusion of innovations such as energy-conserving homes; and the desperate search for successful design themes to be revived and 're-released', just like the contrived revivals of haute couture and pop music. In parts of the United States, the process has advanced to the stage where many upper-middle class suburban developments resemble small chunks of Disneyland, with mock-Tudor, Spanish Colonial, neo-Georgian, Victorian gothic and log cabin de luxe standing together: style for style's sake, the *zeit* for sore eyes. And, in some cities, new housing for upper-income groups is now promoted through annual exhibitions of 'this year's' designs, much like the Fordist automobile industry's carefully-planned obsolescence in design.

But it is by no means only 'high' architecture and expensive housing which help to sustain urbanized capital. One of the more straightforward functions of architecture in relation to the structuration of class relations through residential settings is the symbolic distancing of social groups. The aesthetic sterility of most British public housing, for example, serves to distance its inhabitants from other, neighbouring, social groups. At a further level, it can be argued that the scarcity of symbolic stimuli typical of many planned, post-war working-class environments may act as a kind of intellectual and emotional straitjacket, minimizing people's self-esteem

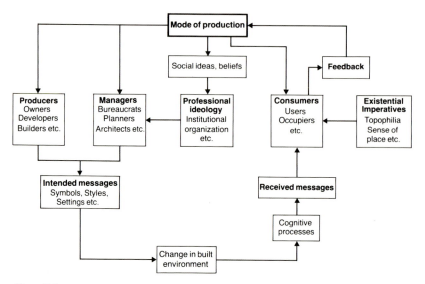

Figure 7.6
Signs, symbolism, and settings: a framework for analysis
Source: P. L. Knox, *Architecture et Comportment*, 2, 1984, 107-122.

and sense of potential while fostering attitudes of deference and defeatism. Although the process is at present very poorly understood, the role of the architect is clearly central to the eventual outcome not only in terms of the social order of the city but also in terms of the existential meaning of urban settings.

This brings us back to a final but crucial consideration: the role of the self in the interaction between society and environment. One framework that accommodates this is shown in Fig. 7.6, which is loosely based on Applyard's 'communications model' of environmental action.[84] Accepting architectural design as part of the superstructure of culture and ideas stemming from the basic socio-economic organization of society (whether as part of the prevailing ideology or as part of the counter-ideology), this framework focuses attention on (i) the intended messages emanating from particular owners/producers and mediated by professional 'managers' (architects, planners, etc.), and (ii) the received messages of environmental 'consumers' as seen through the prisms of cognitive processes and existential imperatives and the filter of the dominant ideology.

SUGGESTED READING

Good reviews of concepts of community and neighbourhood from a sociospatial perspective can be found in Barry Wellman's *The Community Question Re-evaluated* (1987: Centre for Urban and Regional Studies,

University of Toronto) and in the introductory text by Wayne Davies and David Herbert: *Communities Within Cities* (1993: Pinter, London). Further treatment of the ideas of intersubjectivity and lifeworlds can be found in Chapter 2 of Peter Jackson and Susan Smith's *Exploring Social Geography* (1984: George Allen & Unwin, London). Concepts of space and place are treated exhaustively in Nick Entrikin's *Betweenness of Place* (1991: Johns Hopkins University Press, Baltimore) and in Bob Sack's *Place, Modernity, and the Consumer's World* (1992: Johns Hopkins University Press, Baltimore). David Harvey's essay, 'From space to place and back again' (in J. Bird, ed., *Mapping the Futures. Local Cultures, Global Change*, Routledge, London, 1998, pp. 3–29), provides a good introduction to the idea of the social construction of place, while a detailed review of structurationist concepts is given in Chapter 4 of Paul Cloke, Chris Philo and David Sadler's *Approaching Human Geography* (1991: Guilford Press, London). For an introduction to the issues of place, consumption and cultural politics, see Peter Jackson's essay, 'Towards a cultural politics of consumption', in *Mapping the Futures. Local Cultures, Global Change* (cited above; pp. 207–228). Sharon Zukin's *Landscapes of Power* (1991: University of California Press, Berkeley) and Michael Sorkin's edited volume *Variations on a Theme Park* (1992: Noonday, New York) provide a lot of interesting examples of the social meanings of the built environment, while some of the theoretical aspects of symbolism and meaning are addressed in an essay by A.P. Lagopoulos (1993: *Environment & Planning D: Society and Space*, **11**, 255–278).

NOTES

1. Tönnies, F., *Community and Society*. Translated by C. P. Loomis. New York: Harper, 1963; first published in 1887.

2. Durkheim, E., *De La Division du Travail Social*. Paris: Alcan, 1893; G. Simmel, The metropolis and mental life; and Wirth, L., Urbanism as a way of life, both in R. Sennett (ed.) *Classic Essays on the Culture of Cities*. New York: Appleton-Century-Crofts, 1969, pp. 47–60 and 143–64 respectively (first published in 1905 and 1938 respectively).

3. Wellman, B., The community question, *American Journal of Sociology*, **84**, 1979, 1201–1231.

4. Jacobs, J. *The Death and Life of Great American Cities*. New York: Vintage, 1961.

5. See, for example, E. Liebow, *Tally's Corner*. Boston: Little, Brown, 1967; and Suttles, G., *The Social Order of the Slum*. Chicago: University of Chicago Press, 1968.

6. Ward, D., and O. Zunz, Introduction. In D. Ward and O. Zunz (eds), *The Landscape of Modernity*. New York: Russell Sage Foundation, 1992, p. 12.

7. Gans, H., *The Urban Villagers*. New York: Free Press, 1962.

8. Young, M. and P. Willmott, *Family and Kinship in East London*. London: Routledge and Kegan Paul, 1957, p. 89; emphasis added.

9. Jablonsky, T., *Pride in the Jungle*. Baltimore: Johns Hopkins University Press, 1993, p. 152; emphasis added.

10. Stacey, M., The myth of community studies, *British Journal of Sociology*, **20**, 134–146.

11. Jackson, B., *Working Class Community*. London: Routledge & Kegan Paul, 1968.

12. Greenwood, W., *Love on the Dole*. London: Jonathan Cape, 1933.

13. Jackson, *Working Class Community*, p. 157.

14. Coates, K., and R. Silburn, *Poverty: The Forgotten Englishmen*. Harmondsworth: Penguin, 1970, p. 94.

15. Mumford, L. *The Culture of Cities*. London: Secker & Warburg, 1940, p. 215.

16. Lynd, R. S. and H. M. Lynd, *Middletown*. New York: Harcourt, Brace, Jovanovich, 1956; Warner, W. L. and P. S. Lunt, *The Social Life of a Modern Community*. New Haven: Yale University Press, 1941.

17. Whyte, W., *The Organization Man*. New York: Doubleday, 1956; Stein, M., *The Eclipse of Community*. New York: Harper & Row, 1960.

18. Gans, H., *The Levittowners*. London: Allen Lane, 1967.

19. Connerly, C. E., The community question: an extension of Wellman and Leighton, *Urban Affairs Quarterly*, **20**, 537–556.

20. See, for example, Fischer C. S. and R. M. Jackson, Suburbs, networks, and attitudes. In B. Schwartz (ed.), *The Changing Face of the Suburbs*. Chicago: Chicago University Press, 1976, pp. 279–306.

21. Carp, F. M., Life-style and location within the city, *The Gerontologist*, **75**, 1975, 27–33.

22. Muller, P. O., *Contemporary Suburban America*. Englewood Cliffs, NJ: Prentice-Hall, 1981.

23. Muller, P. O., *The Outer City*. Resource Paper No. 22. Washington, DC: Association of American Geographers, 1976, p. 17.

24. White, P., *The West European City: A Social Geography*. London: Longman, 1984, p. 225.

25. Parsons, T., *The Social System*. London: Tavistock, 1951.

26. Goldthorpe, J. H. *et al.*, The affluent worker and the thesis of embourgeoisement: some preliminary research findings, *Sociology*, **1**, 1967, 11–31.

27. Lupton, J. and G. D. Mitchell, *Neighbourhood and Community*. Liverpool: Liverpool University Press, 1954; Durant, R., *Watling: A Survey of Social Life on a New Housing Estate*. London: King, 1959.

28. Collinson, P., *The Cutteslowe Walls*. London: Faber & Faber, 1963.

29. Robson, B., The Bodley barricade: social space and social conflict. In K. R. Cox and R. J. Johnston (eds), *Conflict, Politics, and the Urban Scene*. London: Longman, 1982, pp. 45–61.

30. Hillery, G., Definition of community: areas of agreement, *Rural Sociology*, **20**, 1955, 111–123.

31. Blowers, A., The neighbourhood: exploration of a concept. In *The City as a Social System*. Milton Keynes: Open University, 1973, pp. 49–90.

32. Bell, C. R. and H. Newby, Community, communion, class, and community action. In D. T. Herbert and R. J. Johnston (eds), *Social Areas in Cities*, vol. 2, *Spatial Perspectives on Problems and Policies*. Chichester: Wiley, 1976, p. 197.

33. US National Commission on Neighborhoods, *People, Building Neighborhoods*. Washington, DC: USGPO, 1968, p. 7.

34. Hojnacki, W. P., What is a neighbourhood? *Social Policy*, **10**, 1979, 47–52.

35. Harvey, D. W., From space to place and back again: Reflections on the condition of postmodernity. In J. Bird *et al.* (eds), *Mapping the Futures. Local Cultures, Global Change*. London: Routledge, 1993, p. 4.

36. *Ibid.*

37. Entrikin, N., *The Betweenness of Place*. Baltimore: Johns Hopkins University Press, 1991, p. 7.

38. Sack, R., *Place, Modernity, and the Consumer's World*. Baltimore: John Hopkins University Press, 1992.

39. Buttimer, A., Grasping the dynamism of the life-world, *Annals, Association of American Geographers*, **66**, 1976, 227–292.

40. Relph, E., *Place and Placelessness*. London: Pion, 1976.

41. Sack, *Place, Modernity and the Consumer's World*, p. 83.

42. Heidegger, M., *Poetry, Language, Thought*. New York: Harper & Row, 1971; Samuels, M. S., An existential geography. In M. E. Harvey and B. P. Holly (eds), *Themes in Geographic Thought*. London: Croom Helm, 1981.

43. Relph, E., *Place and Placelessness*. London: Pion, 1976.

44. Lomnitz, L. and R. Díaz, Cultural grammar and bureaucratic rationalization in Latin American cities. In R. Morse and J. Hardoy (eds), *Rethinking the Latin American City*. Washington, DC: Woodrow Wilson Center Press, 1992, pp. 179–192.

45. See, for example, Thrift, N., Flies and germs: a geography of knowledge. In D. Gregory and J. Urry (eds), *Social Relations and Spatial Structures*. Basingstoke: Macmillan, 1985, pp. 366–403.

46. Ley, D., *A Social Geography of the City*. New York: Harper & Row, 1983, p. 203.

47. Seamon, D., *A Geography of the Lifeworld*. New York: St Martin's, 1979.

48. Williams, R. *The Country and the City*. London: Chatto & Windus, 1973.

49. Simonsen, K., Towards an understanding of the contextuality of mode of life, *Environment & Planning D: Society and Space*, **9,** 1991, 417–431.

50. For an introduction to time–geography, see T. Carlstein, D. Parkes, and N. Thrift (eds), *Human Activity and Time Geography*. London: Edward Arnold, 1978.

51. Giddens, A., *Central Problems in Social Theory*. London: Macmillan, 1979; *The Constitution of Society: Outline of the Theory of Structuration*. Cambridge: Polity Press, 1984; *A Contemporary Critique of Historical Materialism* (3 volumes). Cambridge: Polity Press, 1981, 1985, 1989. See also C.G.A. Bryant and D. Jary (eds), *Giddens's Theory of Structuration: A Critical Appreciation*. London: Routledge, 1991.

52. Dear, M. and J. Wolch, How territory shapes social life. In M. Dear and J. Wolch (eds), *The Power of Geography*. Boston: Unwin Hyman, 1989, p. 6; emphasis added.

53. Pred, A., Structuration, biography formation and knowledge, *Environment & Planning D: Society and Space*, **2,** 1984, 251–275; The social becomes the spatial, the spatial becomes the social; enclosures, social change and the becoming of place in the Swedish province of Skäne. In D. Gregory and J. Urry (eds), *Social Relations and Spatial Structures*. London: Macmillan, 1985.

54. Pred, The social becomes the spatial, p. 344.

55. See, for example, Gregson, N., Structuration theory: some thoughts on the possibilities for empirical research, *Environment & Planning D: Society and Space*, **5,** 1987, 73–91; Thrift, N., The arts of living, the beauty of the dead: anxieties of being in the work of Anthony Giddens, *Progress in Human Geography*, **17,** 1993, 111–121; and Bryant and Jary, *Giddens's Theory*.

56. Lefebvre, H., *The Production of Space*. Oxford: Blackwell, 1991.

57. Harvey, D. W., *The Condition of Postmodernity*. Oxford: Blackwell, 1989, p. 222.

58. Jackson, P., Mapping meanings: a cultural critique of locality studies, *Environment & Planning A*, **23,** 1991, 219.

59. Jackson, P., *Maps of Meaning*. London: Unwin Hyman, 1989, p. 115.

60. Bourdieu, P., *Distinction: A Social Critique of the Judgement of Taste*. London: Routledge & Kegan Paul, 1984, p. 173.

61. Hall, S. and T. Jefferson (eds), *Resistance through Rituals: Youth Subcultures in Postwar Britain*. London: Hutchinson, 1976; see also Jackson, *Maps of Meaning*, pp. 59–65.

62. Sack, *Place, Modernity, and the Consumer's World*, p. 102, emphasis added, and p. 128.

63. Pratt, G., The house as an expression of social worlds. In J. Duncan (ed.), *Housing Identity: Cross-Cultural Perspectives*. London: Croom Helm, 1981.

64. Ley, D., Styles of the times: liberal and neo-conservative landscapes in inner Vancouver, 1968–1986, *Journal of Historical Geography*, **13,** 1987, 40–56.

65. Rose, D., Rethinking gentrification, *Environment & Planning D: Society and Space*, **2**, 1984, 47–74.

66. Knopp, L., Sexuality and the spatial dynamics of capitalism, *Environment & Planning D: Society and Space*, **10**, 1992, 651–669.

67. Curl, J. S., *European Cities and Society*. London: Leonard Hill, 1970, p. 1.

68. Kennedy, M., *Portrait of Manchester*. Manchester: Hale, 1970, p. 86.

69. Harvey, D. W., Monument and myth, *Annals, Association of American Geographers*, **69,** 1979, 362.

70. Lasswell, H., *The Signature of Power*. New Brunswick, NJ: Transaction Books, 1979, p. 57.

71. *Ibid.*

72. See, for example, Duncan, J. S. and N. G. Duncan, Housing as presentation of self and the structure of social networks. In G. T. Moore and R. Golledge (eds), *Environmental Knowing*. Stroudsburg, PA: Dowden, Hutchinson and Ross, 1976, pp. 247–253.

73. Gutman, R., *People and Buildings*. New York: Basic Books, 1972, p. 299.

74. See, for example, Eco, U., Function and sign: the semiotics of architecture. In G. Broadbent *et al.* (eds), *Signs, Symbols and Architecture*. Chichester: Wiley, 1980, pp. 11–69.

75. For a review of this literature, see Duncan, J. S., Review of urban imagery: urban semiotics, *Urban Geography*, **8,** 1987, 473–483.

76. Hillier, B. *et al.*, *Social Logic and Space*. Cambridge: Cambridge University Press, 1981.

77. Harvey, D., Labour, capital, and the class struggle around the built environment. In K. Cox (ed.), *Urbanization and Conflict in Market Societies*. London: Methuen, 1978, pp. 9–37.

78. Shields, R., Social spatialization and the built environment: the West Edmonton Mall, *Environment & Planning D: Society and Space*, **7,** 1989, 147–164; Goss, J., The 'Magic of the Mall': an analysis of form, function and meaning in the contemporary retail built environment, *Annals, Association of American Geographers*, **83,** 1993, 18–47; Crawford, M., The world in a shopping mall. In M. Sorkin (ed.), *Variations on a Theme Park*. New York: Noonday, 1992, pp. 3–30.

79. Boyer, C., Cities for sale: merchandising history at South Street Seaport. In M. Sorkin (ed.), *Variations on a Theme Park*. New York: Noonday, 1992, pp. 181–204; Zukin, S., *Landscapes of Power. From Detroit to Disney World*. Berkeley: University of California Press, 1991.

80. Rubin, B., Aesthetic ideology and urban design, *Annals, Association of American Geographers*, **69,** 1979, 360.

81. Carter, E., Politics and architecture: an observer looks back at the 30s, *Architectural Review*, November 1979, 324.

82. Knox, P. L. and J. D. Cullen, Town planning and the internal survival mechanisms of urbanized capitalism, *Area*, **13,** 1981, 183–188.

83. Darke, R. and J. Darke, Towards a sociology of the built environment, *Architectural Psychology Newsletter*, **11,** 1981, 12.

84. Appleyard, D., The environment as a social symbol, *Journal of the American Planning Association*, **45,** 1979, 143–153.

Informal public space: steps
of the Paris Opera.
Photograph by Paul Knox.

8 Environment and behaviour in urban settings

Theories about Deviant Behaviour • Cognition and Perception

Geographers have for a long time been interested in the relationships between urban settings and certain aspects of people's behaviour. As we know well enough by now, these relationships are *reciprocal*: 'a neighbourhood takes its character from the values and life-styles of its residents; however, reciprocally, its personality is also a context that acts to reinforce and narrow a range of human responses'.[1] The emphasis of most research in this area, though, has been on the way in which the 'personality' of urban settings influences individual and group behaviour and, in particular, the way in which 'deviant' behaviour is related to urban settings. It should be very clear at the outset that this sort of approach can easily fall into a deterministic frame of thinking, where 'space' is a cause. 'Behavioural geography has its roots in the classic observed-stimulus→observed-response behaviouralism of psychologist J.B. Watson.'[2] The sophistication of contemporary behavioural geography is that behaviour is no longer described solely in terms of stimulus and reaction. Rather, stimuli are thought of in terms of information (of any kind) that is filtered through the elements of cognition, reflection and consciousness before provoking behavioural responses (Fig. 8.1). Within these theoretical terms, 'human behaviour is explained as responses to stimuli, selectively received from the social and physical environment, which have been cognitively processed into information'.[3]

Central to this whole perspective is the idea of *environmental conditioning*. A classic example is provided by Newson and Newson's work on patterns of infant care.[4] Impoverished neighbourhoods, they argued, are

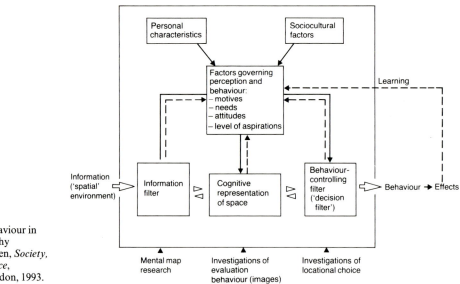

Figure 8.1
A model of behaviour in
human geography
Source: B. Werlen, *Society,
Action, and Space*,
Routledge, London, 1993.

characterized by a poverty of sensory stimulation, by crowded environments that inhibit play, and by unenlightened attitudes towards child rearing. The net result, they concluded, is that the environmental conditioning experienced by children growing up in such settings produces 'under-socialized' individuals with a competitive nature attuned only to the immediate social group, leaving them ill equipped to cope with the more subtle forms of competition which prevail in the world beyond. By extension, it was argued that this kind of environmental conditioning tends to curtail creativity, adaptability and flexibility. The result is doubly disadvantaged individuals who, on the one hand, seek short-term gratification and are weakly attuned to the established norms and rules of society at large and on the other hand are unable to articulate a coherent alternative or opposition to these norms and rules.

This kind of argument begs all sorts of questions about the mechanisms and processes involved. How, for example, are distinctive local values sustained in local settings; and to what extent do localized values and attitudes affect the incidence of particular patterns of behaviour? How important is the built environment? And what is the role of broader, class-based factors? As we shall see from an examination of ideas about deviant behaviour, there is a broad spectrum of theories.

8.1 Theories about Deviant Behaviour

The notion of deviance covers a multitude of social sins, but geographers have been most interested in behaviour with a distinctive pattern of intra-urban variation, such as prostitution, suicide, truancy, delinquency and drug addiction. In fact, most aspects of deviant behaviour seem to exhibit a definite spatial pattern of some sort, rather than being randomly distributed across the city. But, whereas there is little disagreement about the nature of the patterns themselves, theory and research in geography, sociology and environmental psychology are less conclusive about explanations of the patterns. Some writers, for instance, see deviant behaviour as a pathological response to a particular social and/or physical environment. Others argue that certain physical or social attributes act as environmental cues for certain kinds of behaviour; others still that certain environments simply attract certain kinds of people. Until quite recently, almost all the theorizing about spatial variations in deviant behaviour shared a common element of environmental determinism, usually traceable to the determinists of the Chicago School. In this section the more influential aspects of this theory are outlined before going on to examine briefly the intra-urban geography of one kind of deviant behaviour – crime and delinquency – as an illustration of the complexity of the actual relationships between urban environments and human behaviour.

Determinist Theory

There is no need to reiterate at length the relationships between urban environments and deviant behaviour postulated by adherents to Wirthian theory (see pp. 160–2). The general position is that deviant behaviour is a product either of adaptive behaviour or maladjustment to city life, or to life in certain parts of the city. Thus the aloofness and impersonality that are developed in response to the competing stimuli and conflicting demands of different social situations are thought to lead to a breakdown of interpersonal relationships and social order and to an increase in social isolation, which in turn facilitates the emergence of ego-centred, unconventional behaviour and precipitates various kinds of deviant behaviour.

Evidence to support these tenets of determinist theory has been assembled on several fronts. The idea of psychological overload resulting from complex or unfamiliar environments has been investigated by environmental psychologists and popularized by Toffler, who suggested that the need to 'scoop up and process' additional information in such situations can lead to 'future-shock'; the human response to over stimulation.[5] The nature of this response has been shown by psychologists to take several forms: 'Dernier's strategy', for example, involves the elimination from perception of unwelcome reality, and in an extreme form can result in the construction of a mythological world which becomes a substitute for the real world and in which deviant behaviour may be seen by the person concerned as 'normal'. Another response is for people to 'manage' several distinct roles or identities at once.[6] According to determinist theory, this is characteristic of urban environments because of the physical and functional separation of the 'audiences' to which different roles are addressed: family, neighbours, co-workers, club members, and so on. Thus, people tend to be able to present very different 'selves' in different social contexts. Again, the extreme form of this behaviour may lead to deviancy. The city, with its wide choice of different roles and identities becomes a 'magic theatre', an 'emporium of styles', and the anonymity afforded by the ease of slipping from one role to another clearly facilitates the emergence of unconventional and deviant behaviour. It has also been suggested that *further* deviancy or pathology may result from the strain of having to sustain different and perhaps conflicting identities over a prolonged period.[7]

Most interest, however, has centred on the *impersonality* and *aloofness* that apparently result from the *psychological overload* associated with certain urban environments. There are many manifestations of this impersonality, the most striking of which is the collective paralysis of social responsibility that seems to occur in central city areas in crisis situations. Perhaps the best known example is the murder of Catherine Genovese, who was stabbed to death in a respectable district of Queens in New York, the event evidently witnessed by nearly 40 people, none of whom attempted even to call the police. Other evidence of the lack of 'bystander intervention' and of an unwillingness to assist strangers comes from experiments contrived by psychologists.[8] Such behaviour is itself deviant to some extent, of course; but its significance to determinist theory is in the way in which it fosters the spread of more serious forms of deviancy by eroding social responsibility and social control.

The overall result of these various forms of adaptive behaviour is thus a weakening of personal supports and social constraints and a confusion of behavioural norms. This, in turn, gives a further general impetus to deviant behaviour. Feelings of isolation among the 'lonely crowd' are associated with neurosis, alcoholism and suicide;[9] and the anomic state induced by the weakening of behavioural norms and intensifying levels of incivility is associated with various forms of crime and delinquency.[10] Academic opinion, however, is by no means unanimous as to the utility of determinist theory in explaining patterns of deviant behaviour. It is difficult to establish either proof or refutation of the connections between stress, adaptive behaviour, social isolation, social disorganization, anomie and deviancy because of the difficulty of controlling for the many intervening variables such as age, class, education and personality. Nevertheless, many investigations of intra-urban variations in deviant behaviour have found it useful to invoke determinist theory in at least partial explanation of the patterns encountered. The geography of looting during electricity blackouts in New York City (Fig. 8.2), for example, was closely correlated with patterns of poverty. 'Apparently, people excluded from effective participation in the

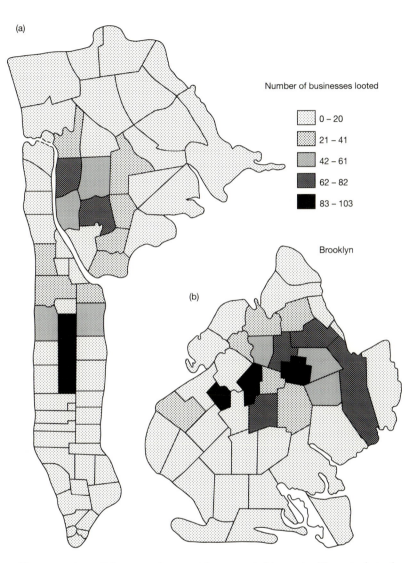

(a)

Number of businesses looted

0 – 20
21 – 41
42 – 61
62 – 82
83 – 103

Brooklyn

(b)

Figure 8.2
Looting in New York:
businesses approved for
Reestablishment Grants by
the mayor's Emergency Aid
Commission
Source: E. H. Wohlenberg,
Economic Geography, 58,
1982, Fig. 2, p. 36.

affluent society did not, and cannot be expected to, act with restraint when the enforcement of law and order is immobilized.'[11] To the extent that determinist theory is founded on the effects of urbanism on human behaviour, the inference must be that some parts of the city are more 'urban' (in the Wirthian sense) than others, with more social disorganization, a greater incidence of anomie and, consequently, a higher incidence of deviant behaviour.

Crowding Theory

There is now a considerable literature linking high residential densities, irrespective of other characteristics of urbanism, with a wide range of deviant behaviour.[12] High densities and a sense of crowding, it is argued, create strains and tensions which can lead to aggression, withdrawal or, if these strategies are unsuccessful, mental or physical illness. The initial link between crowding and stress is attributed by many to an innate sense of *territoriality*. This idea has been popularized by ethologists who believe that humans, like many other animals, are subject to a genetic trait that is produced by the species' need for territory as a source of safety, security and privacy. Territoriality is also seen as satisfying the need for stimulation (provided by 'border disputes') and for a physical expression of personal identity. These needs are believed to add up to a strong 'territorial imperative': a natural component of behaviour that will clearly be disrupted by crowding.[13]

This approach draws heavily on behavioural research with animals, where the links between crowding, stress and abnormal behaviour can be clearly established under laboratory conditions. Calhoun, for example, in his celebrated studies of rat behaviour, showed that crowding led to aggression, listlessness, promiscuity, homosexuality and the rodent equivalent of juvenile delinquency.[14] Projecting these ideas directly to human behaviours leads to the idea of crowded urbanites as 'killer apes'. One sociologist, for example, writes that 'We have caged ourselves in zoos of our own creation; and like caged animals we have developed pathological forms of behaviour.'[15] Critics of crowding theory have emphasized the obvious dangers involved in extending animal behaviour to humans: people are not rats; it is by no means certain that humans possess any innate sense of territoriality; and in any case even the most crowded slums do not approach the levels of crowding to which experimental animals have been subjected.

It is difficult, however, to establish conclusively whether or not there is any connection between territoriality, crowding and deviant behaviour in human populations. Territoriality may exist in humans through cultural acquisition even if it is not an innate instinct, since territoriality in the form of property rights does provide society with a means of distinguishing social rank and of regulating social interaction. Moreover, there is a considerable body of evidence to support the idea of territorial behaviour in urban men and women, whatever the source of this behaviour may be. Individuals' home territory represents a *haven*, and an expression of identity. At the group level, gang 'turfs' are rigorously and ceremonially defended by gang members. More complex and sophisticated social groups also seem to exhibit territorial behaviour, as in the 'foreign relations' of different social groups occupying 'defended neighbourhoods' in American inner-city areas;[16] and in the extreme territoriality that exists in the area around the Shankhill/Falls divide in Belfast, where aggression between members of rival Catholic and Protestant communities has resulted in complete segregation.[17]

Accepting that humans do acquire some form of territoriality, it does seem plausible that crowding could induce stress and so precipitate a certain amount of deviant behaviour. The evidence, however, is ambiguous. Some studies report a clear association between crowding and social and physical pathology, others report contradictory findings, and the whole debate continues to attract controversy in all of the social and environmental disciplines.

Design Determinism

In addition to the general debate on crowding theory, a growing amount of attention has been directed towards the negative effects of architecture and urban design on people's behaviour. In broad terms the suggestion is that the design and configuration of buildings and spaces sometimes creates micro-environments that discourage 'normal' patterns of social interaction and encourage deviant behaviour of various kinds. A considerable amount of evidence has been accumulated in support of this idea. The inhibiting effects of high-rise and deck-access apartment dwellings on social interaction and child development, for example, have been documented in a number of different studies;[18] and from these it is a short step to studies which point to the correlation between certain aspects of urban design and the incidence of particular aspects of deviancy such as mental illness and suicide.

The nature of these relationships is not entirely clear. One interesting proposition was put forward by Peter Smith, who suggested that the configuration of buildings and spaces creates a 'syntax' of images and symbolism to which people respond through a synthesis of 'gut reactions' and intellectual reactions.[19] Environments that are dominated by an unfamiliar or illogical visual language are thus likely to appear threatening or confusing: qualities that may well precipitate certain aspects of malaise or deviant behaviour. This, however, requires more empirical investigation before its utility can be confirmed.

A better known and more thoroughly examined link between urban design and deviant behaviour is Oscar Newman's concept of 'defensible space'. Newman suggested that much of the petty crime, vandalism, mugging and burglary in modern housing developments is related to an attenuation of community life and a withdrawal of local social controls caused by the inability of residents to identify with, or exert any control over, the space beyond their own front door. This, he argued, was a result of the 'designing out' of territorial definition and delineation in new housing developments, in accordance with popular taste among architects. Once the space immediately outside the dwelling becomes public, Newman suggested, nobody will feel obliged to 'supervise' it or 'defend' it against intruders.[20] Newman's ideas have been supported by some empirical work and enthusiastically received in the professions concerned with urban design, where they have created a new conventional wisdom of their own: defensible space is now an essential component in the praxis of urban design. On the other hand, Newman's work has been heavily criticized for the quality of his statistical analysis and for his neglect of the interplay of physical and social variables.[21]

Alienation

The concept of alienation is a central construct of Marxian theory, where it is seen as a mechanism of social change contributing towards the antithesis of the dominant mode of production; it also has wider sociopolitical connotations, however, with some relevance to the explanation of deviant behaviour. In its wider sense, alienation is characterized by feelings of powerlessness, dissatisfaction, distrust, and a rejection of the prevailing distribution of wealth and power. These feelings usually stem from people's experience of some aspect of social, political or economic system. Some people may be alienated because they feel that the structure of these systems prevents their effective participation; others may be alienated because they disagree with the very nature of the systems – perhaps because of their ineffectiveness in satisfying human needs.

Whatever the source, such feelings are clearly experience based and therefore spatially focused, to a certain extent, on people's area of residence. This makes alienation an attractive explanatory factor when considering spatial variations in people's behaviour, as the early deterministic theorists were quick to note. The major interest in this respect has been the relationship between alienation and political behaviour, but it has also been suggested that certain aspects of deviant behaviour may be related to feelings of alienation. Such behaviour may be manifested in apathy: mildly unconventional in itself but more significant if it is prevalent enough to erode social order. Alternatively, alienation may precipitate deviance directly through some form of activism – which can range from eccentric forms of protest to violence and terrorism.

Compositional Theory

Compositional theory is the product of another school of thought which has developed out of the writings of the Chicago determinists. Compositionalists emphasize the cohesion and intimacy of distinctive social worlds based on ethnicity, kinship, neighbourhood, occupation, or life-style, rejecting the idea that these social networks are in any way diminished by urban life.[22] They also minimize the psychological effects of city life on people's behaviour, suggesting, instead, that behaviour is determined largely by economic status, cultural characteristics, family status, and so on: the same attributes that determine which social worlds they live in.

Compositional theory is not framed explicitly to analyse deviant behaviour, but it does offer a distinctive perspective on the question. Deviancy, like other forms of behaviour, is seen as a product of the composition of local populations, with the social mores, political attitudes and cultural traits of certain groups being more productive of unconventional or deviant behaviour than others. The pattern of sexually transmitted disease in London serves to illustrate this compositionalist perspective. The incidence of this particular manifestation of deviant behaviour had for many years a very marked peak in the bed-sitter land of West-Central London, especially around Earls Court. The explanation, in compositionalist terms, is the high proportion of young transients in the area – mostly young single people living in furnished rooms – whose sexual mores are different from those of the rest of the population and whose vulnerability to VD and other sexually transmitted diseases is increased by the presence of a significant proportion of young males who have themselves been infected before arriving in London. According to London's urban folklore, much of the blame in this respect is attached to Australians who arrive in London having visited Bangkok.

Subcultural Theory

Subcultural theory is closely related to compositional theory. Like the latter, subcultural theory subscribes to the idea of social worlds with distinctive sociodemographic characteristics and distinctive life-styles which propagate certain forms of behaviour. In addition, however, subcultural theory holds that these social worlds, or subcultures, will be *intensified* by the conflict and competition of urban life; and that *new* subcultures will be spawned as specialized groups, generated by the arrival of immigrants and by the structural differentiation resulting from industrialization and urbanization, reach the 'critical mass' required to sustain cohesive social networks. Fischer suggests that

> Among the subcultures spawned or intensified by urbanism are those
> which are considered to be either downright deviant by the larger
> society – such as delinquents, professional criminals, and homosexuals;
> or to be at least 'odd' – such as artists, missionaries of new religious
> sects, and intellectuals; or to be breakers of tradition – such as life-style
> experimenters, radicals and scientists.[23]

What is seen as deviancy by the larger society, however, is seen by the members of these subcultural groups as a normal form of activity and part of the group's internal social system.

Subcultural theory does not in itself carry any explicitly spatial connotations but the continued existence of subcultural groups depends to a large extent on avoiding conflict with other groups. Conflict may be avoided by implicit *behavioural* boundaries beyond which groups 'promise' not to trespass: a kind of social contract; but the most effective means of maintaining inter-group tolerance is through *spatial* segregation. This idea makes subcultural theory attractive in explaining spatial variations in deviant behaviour. It has proved useful, for example, in studies of delinquent behaviour.

Subcultural theory also fits in conveniently with the idea of *cultural transmission*, whereby deviant norms are passed from one generation to another within a local environment. This process was identified over 130 years ago by Mayhew (1862) in the 'rookeries' of London, where children were 'born and bred' to the business of crime; and it was given prominence by Shaw and McKay in their classic study of delinquency in Chicago.[24]

Another concept relevant to the understanding of deviant behaviour within a localized subculture is the so-called *neighbourhood effect*, whereby people tend to conform to what they perceive as local norms in order to gain the respect of their local peer group. Empirical evidence for this phenomenon has been presented in a number of studies. One well-known example comes from a study of attitudes towards education in different parts of Sunderland, where 'No matter what the area, the attitudes of individual families were more familiar to those prevailing around them than to those of their objective social class.'[25] Many aspects of people's behaviour seem to be directly susceptible to a neighbourhood effect. The paradoxical syndrome of 'suburban poverty' in new owner-occupier subdivisions, for example, can be seen as a product of neighbourhood effects which serve to impose middle-class consumption patterns on incoming families, many of whom have incomes which are really insufficient to 'keep up with the Jones's' but who nevertheless feel obliged to conform with their neighbours' habits. There is also evidence that many deviant attitudes and deviant forms of behaviour are subject to neighbourhood effects, though the evidence is by no means clear-cut.[26]

Structuralist Theory

This perspective, based on a Marxian interpretation of urban society, views the rules of social behaviour and the definitions of deviant behaviour as part of society's *superstructure*, the framework of social and philosophical organization that stems from the economic relationships on which society is based (see p. 100). Definitions of deviance, it is argued, protect the interests of the dominant class, thereby helping that class to continue its domination. In modern society, deviant behaviour can be seen as a direct result of stresses associated with the contradictions that are inherent to the operation of the economic system. One major contradiction in this context involves the necessary existence of a 'reserve army' of surplus labour that is both vulnerable, in the sense of being powerless, but at the same time dangerous, because its members represent a potentially volatile group. The need to maintain this reserve army and to defuse unrest among its members explains the substantial social expenditure of modern welfare states; while the need to control the behaviour of its members explains the rules and definitions attached to many aspects of 'deviant' behaviour associated with the stress of unemployment and the repression and degradation of being supported at a marginal level by the welfare state.

Another important contradiction, it is argued, is that while capital accumulation requires fit and healthy workers, it also tends to debilitate them through the effects of the stresses that result from the various controls that are exerted on the labour force. Examples of these controls include the patterns of socialization that are part of the superstructure of society, in which individuals are rewarded for being competitive but not too individualistic, and in which they are encouraged to spend their rewards on the acquisition of material possessions:

> These sources of stress are endemic in the capitalist system, but they are unequally allocated between the classes; workers experience more than their share of the costs or stresses, and less than their share of the benefits. It is no surprise, therefore, that the working classes are disproportionately represented in the prevalence data for mental illness, drug and alcohol abuse, and crime.[27]

Multi-factor Explanations: The Example of Crime and Delinquency

The difficulty of reconciling the apparently conflicting evidence relating to these different theories has, inevitably, led to a more flexible approach in which multi-factor explanations of deviant behaviour are admitted without being attached to a specific theoretical perspective. This is common to all branches of social deviance research, although it is probably best illustrated in relation to crime and delinquency. Empirical studies of spatial variations in crime and delinquency have lent support, variously, to theories of crowding, social disorganization, anomie, design determinism and deviant subcultures; but it is difficult to assemble evidence in support of any one theory in preference to the rest. In the absence of any alternative all-embracing theoretical perspective, an eclectic multi-factor approach thus becomes an attractive framework of explanation.

Data Problems

The evidence that can be drawn from studies of spatial variations in crime and delinquency is, like much social geographical research, subject to important qualifications relating to the nature of the data and methods of research which have been employed. It is, therefore, worth noting some of the difficulties and pitfalls involved in such research before going on to illustrate the complexity of inter-relationships between environment and behaviour suggested by the results of empirical research.

One of the most fundamental problems concerns the *quality of data*. Most research has to rely on official data derived from law enforcement agencies, and these data are usually far from comprehensive in their coverage. Many offences do not enter official records because they are not notified to the police; and data on offenders are further diluted by the relatively low detection rate for most offences. More disconcerting is the possibility that the data which are recorded do not provide a representative sample. Many researchers have argued that official data are biased against working-class offenders, suggesting that the police are more likely to allow parental sanctions to replace legal sanctions in middle-class areas, that working-class areas are more intensively policed, and that crime reporting by adults is similarly biased. Conversely, 'white-collar' crimes – fraud, tax evasion, expense account 'fiddles', and so on – tend to be under-reported and are more difficult to detect, even where large amounts of money are involved. Some critics have suggested that this bias has been compounded by the predilection in empirical research for data relating to blue-collar crimes. This may be attributable in part to the differential availability of data on different kinds of offence, but it also seems likely that data on white-collar crimes have been neglected because they are, simply, less amenable to deterministic hypotheses.

Because data for many important crime-related variables are only available for groups of people rather than individuals, many studies have pursued an ecological approach, examining variations in crime between territorial groups. Such an approach is inherently attractive to geographers but it does involve certain limitations and pitfalls. The chief limitation of ecological studies is that they cannot provide conclusive evidence of causal links. Thus, although certain categories of offenders may be found in crowded and/or socially disorganized areas, their criminal behaviour may actually be related to other causes – alienation or personality factors, for example – and the ecological correlation may simply result from their gravitation to a certain kind of neighbourhood. The chief pitfall associated with ecological studies is the so-called *ecological fallacy*: the mistake of drawing inferences about *individuals* on the basis of correlations calculated for areas. One pertinent example is the frequently encountered association within British cities between crime rates and neighbourhoods containing large numbers of immigrants. The inference drawn by many is that immigrants and their subcultures are particularly disposed towards crime and delinquency; but research at the level of the individual has in fact shown that 'immigrants are very much less involved in the crime and disorder that surround them in the areas where they live than their white neighbours'.[28]

The Geography of Urban Crime

Bearing these limitations in mind, what conclusions can be drawn from empirical studies about the factors which precipitate crime and delinquency? It is not possible to do justice to the extensive literature on criminology and the geography of crime in a text such as this: the serious student should consult the large volume of specialist work on the subject.[29] Nevertheless, it is possible to give some indication of the issues involved. First, following David Herbert,[30] it is useful to distinguish between factors influencing the pattern of *occurrence* of crime and delinquency and those influencing the pattern of *residence* of offenders.

Most cities exhibit very distinctive areas where the occurrence of crime and delinquency is well above average. An analysis of police call data in Minneapolis, for example, found that just 3.3 per cent of addresses and intersections in the city generated 50 per cent of all calls to the police for which cars were dispatched.[31] In many cities, the pattern conforms to the archetypal distribution identified in Chicago in the 1920s, with low rates in the suburbs increasing steadily to a peak in the inner city and CBD. The most notable exceptions are in European cities, where substantial numbers of low-income, 'problem' households have become localized in suburban public housing estates: as in the example of Aberdeen (Fig. 8.3).

In detail, however, patterns of occurrence vary considerably by the *type of offence*. In Cleveland, Ohio, for example, the geography of murder differs considerably from the geography of assault, while the geography of larceny is different from both (Fig. 8.4). Ecological analyses of occurrence patterns for different offences provide some clues as to the relationships between crime and urban environments, and there are several studies that are useful in this context.

In his pioneering study of crime in Seattle, Schmid demonstrated the concentration of shoplifting and cheque fraud offences in the CBD, of larceny and burglary in suburban areas, and of robbery and female drunkenness in the 'skid row' area of the city.[32] In a later study of the same city, the dominant pattern of crime occurrence was found to be associated with inner-city areas of low social cohesion, where there was a concentration of burglary, car theft and handbag snatching.[33] Studies of other cities have demonstrated a similar general association between the occurrence of crime and poverty, and detailed ecological analysis has revealed a distinct association between low-income neighbourhoods and crimes of violence, including murder, rape and assault.[34] There is also evidence to suggest that transitional areas – with a high proportion of land devoted to manufacturing and wholesaling, a decaying physical environment and an ageing population – are associated with a separate and equally distinctive concentration of offences which includes larceny, robbery and car theft as well as assault and murder.[35] Other important relationships to emerge from these studies are the correlation between property crimes – burglary, larceny and car theft – and stable, mid- and upper-income suburban neighbourhoods, and between violent crimes and black neighbourhoods. A *compositional* perspective is useful in interpreting these various patterns: the idea here being that communities move through 'life cycles' or 'careers' in their experience of criminality as the demographic composition of their population changes in response to neighbourhood deterioration and family life-cycle changes. Because the peak years for offence rates are the teens and

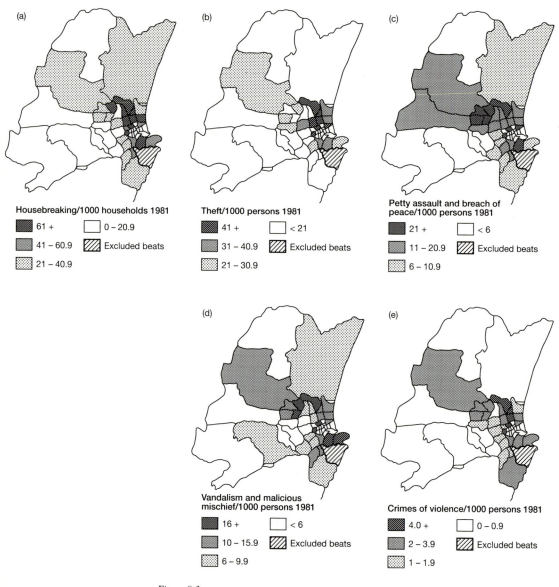

Figure 8.3
Patterns of crime in Aberdeen, Scotland
Source: N. J. Williams, *Scottish Geographical Magazine,* 101, 1985, Fig. 3.

early twenties, neighbourhoods with high proportions of youths of this age can be expected to exhibit high levels of criminality, especially if the neighbourhood is caught in a spiral of economic decline and physical decay that heightens youths' feelings of relative deprivation.[36]

The compositional perspective has been developed into what has become known as the *routine activities* theory of crime, in which demographic or

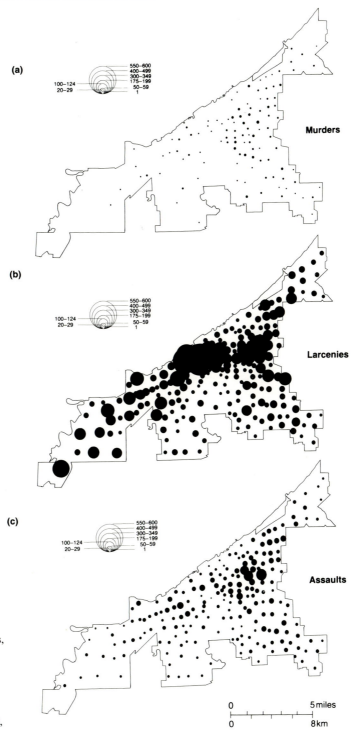

Figure 8.4
The distribution of murders,
larcenies and assaults in
Cleveland, Ohio
Source: G. F. Pyle, in J.
Adams (ed.) *Urban
Policymaking and
Metropolitan Dynamics,*
Ballinger, Cambridge, 1976,
pp. 273, 275.

social class characteristics lead to certain activity routines that bring together the three prerequisites for crime: the presence of a motivated offender, a suitable target and the absence of a capable guardian. Spatial variations in *opportunities* for crime have been shown to be critical in studies of occurrence patterns of several different kinds of offences in St Louis[37] and Sheffield.[38] In the Sheffield study, for example, a marked relationship between property values and house-breaking offences was revealed. The ecology of other offences also seemed to confirm the general importance of opportunity factors, although the evidence was not always conclusive, partly because of the scale of analysis: ecological studies are simply not able to reflect the environmental nuances which influence the exact location of offences. The importance of the micro-environment was emphasized by the US National Commission on the Causes and Prevention of Violence, which concluded that accessibility, visibility, control of property, residential density and state of physical repair are the most significant aspects of the micro-environment of violent crime.[39] Other studies have illustrated the importance of micro-environmental features in explaining other kinds of offence. The incidence of burglary in Tallahassee, for example, has been shown to be higher in the peripheral blocks of housing projects, where burglars could benefit from the weaker social control of 'anonymous' boundary areas.[40] And the occurrence of abandoned and stripped cars in Philadelphia, which appeared to have a random spatial distribution at the 'micro' scale, was found to be closely related to vacant land, doorless sides of buildings and institutional land use.[41] Also relevant at this scale, of course, is Newman's concept of defensible space. For example, the uneven micro-pattern of burglary victims in Newcastle under Lyme (Fig. 8.5) is explained by the distribution of open and recreational space, playgrounds, garage space and disused railway lines that give rear access to properties.[42]

In summary, 'There are qualities attached to the offence location which relate to the *built* environment – its design, detailed land use – and to the *social* environment – status, local activity patterns, local control systems.'[43] Figure 8.6 represents an attempt to capture this, emphasizing sociodemographic composition, routine activities and opportunities.

Patterns of *residence* of offenders are subject to a much wider range of explanatory factors although, like patterns of occurrence, they display a consistent social order and clustering which makes them suitable for ecological analysis. Although there are variations by type of offence and age of offender, the classic pattern is the one described by Shaw and McKay for Chicago and other American cities: a regular gradient, with low rates in the suburbs and a peak in the inner city.[44] Such gradients have typified not only North American cities, but virtually all Western cities for which evidence is available. Recently, however, departures from this pattern have become more apparent as the spatial structure of the Western city has changed. Many cities have experienced an outward shift of offenders' residences with changes in residential mobility and housing policies. British studies, in particular, have identified localized clusters of offenders in

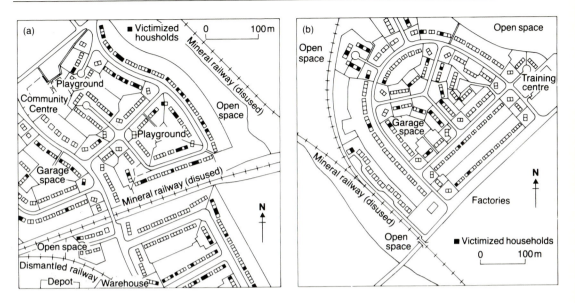

Figure 8.5
Distribution of burglary victims in two study areas, Newcastle-under-Lyme, 1978-81
Source: D. Evans and G. Oulds, *Tijdschrift voor Economische en Sociale Geografie*, 75, 1984, Fig. 5, p. 349.

peripheral local authority housing estates, which suggests that the social environment is at least as important as the physical environment in explaining offenders' patterns. In Cardiff, for example, the residences of juvenile delinquents tend to be localized not only among inner-city terrace areas around the docks and in middle-ring rooming-house areas, but also in certain suburban local authority housing estates (Fig. 8.7).

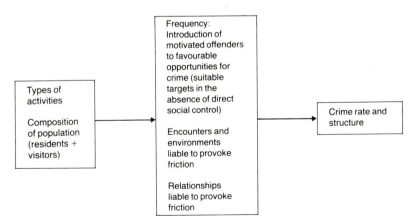

Figure 8.6
Variation in crime (offence rate) and structure in the urban environment
Source: A. Bottoms and P. Wiles, in D. Evans et al. (eds) *Crime, Policing, and Place*, Routledge, London, 1992, Fig. 1.1.

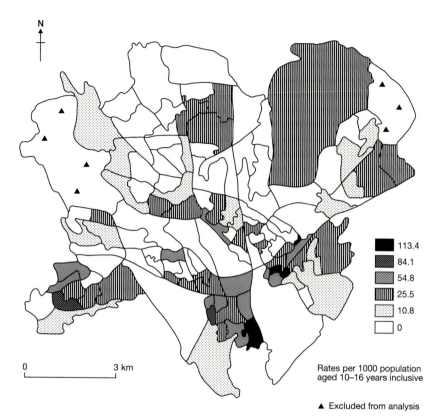

Figure 8.7
Juvenile delinquency: offenders' residences in Cardiff, 1977
Source: D. Evans, *Geographical Perspectives on Juvenile Delinquency*, Gower Westmead, Farnborough, 1980, Fig. 25, p. 18.

Ecological analyses have been useful in specifying the social and environmental contexts of crime and delinquency residence areas, although it should be emphasized that few studies have been able to incorporate, or control for, all of the factors which might affect individual behaviour. Most geographical research has set aside the possible influence of personal factors (such as physical and mental make-up) and factors associated with the family, school and workplace in order to concentrate on the social and physical context provided by the neighbourhood. From these studies *there is an overwhelming weight of evidence connecting known offenders with inner-city neighbourhoods characterized by crowded and substandard housing, poverty, unemployment and demographic imbalance.* In Seattle, for example, crime areas 'are generally characterized by all or most of the following factors: low social cohesion, weak family life, low socioeconomic status, physical deterioration, high rates of population mobility and personal disorganization'.[45] This general finding has been confirmed in subsequent studies of the city and has been replicated in studies of other cities. In cities where peripheral clusters of offenders are found, there appears to be an additional syndrome linking offenders with public housing developments containing high proportions of families of particularly low social and economic status, many of whom have been dumped in problem estates through the housing allocation mechanisms of public authorities.

A few studies have followed up this general ecological approach with an examination of the less tangible local factors that may be related to crime and delinquency: the dominant values and attitudes associated with different areas. Susan Smith, for example, has argued that the distribution of crime reflects the life-style and activity patterns of a community and that the effects of crime, in turn, help to shape these *routine urban behaviours*.[46] Work on juvenile delinquency in Cardiff has attempted to illustrate the ways in which attitudes and values actually vary between neighbourhoods. By administering a questionnaire survey to residents of several 'delinquent' neighbourhoods and several 'non-delinquent' neighbourhoods, researchers were able to show that 'spatial order in the incidence of delinquency is underlain by systematic variations in related attitudes and behaviour.'[47] Significant differences were found in the way in which people 'labelled' areas in their own mind as either delinquent or non-delinquent. Differences between delinquent and non-delinquent areas were also found in relation to people's conception of what amounts to delinquent behaviour: residents of the former were much less disposed towards reporting petty theft and damage to public property than were residents of non-delinquent areas. Similarly, parents in non-delinquent areas were much more inclined to administer sanctions in the home when it came to dealing with misbehaviour. Parents in delinquent areas tended to refer truancy to school authorities, for example, rather than deal with the issue themselves. It has been concluded that these results tend to support subcultural theory more than any other.[48]

But, while it is tempting to cite evidence such as this in support of particular theories and concepts, past experience shows that it is possible to find support for quite different theories within the same pool of evidence. In this situation it seems sensible to accept a multi-factor explanation. David Herbert has provided a useful framework within which to subsume the various factors which appear to be involved (Fig. 8.8). Areas of crime and delinquency are linked to several local environmental contexts and generally related to a nexus of social problems. Poverty is the central focus of the model, and is seen as the product of structural factors which, through differential access to educational facilities and employment opportunities, produce an 'impersonal social environment' (i.e. local population) consisting of 'losers' – the aged, the unemployed, misfits and members of minority groups:

> . . . poverty limits individuals to particular types of built environment; at worst to the most disadvantaged housing classes, at best to local

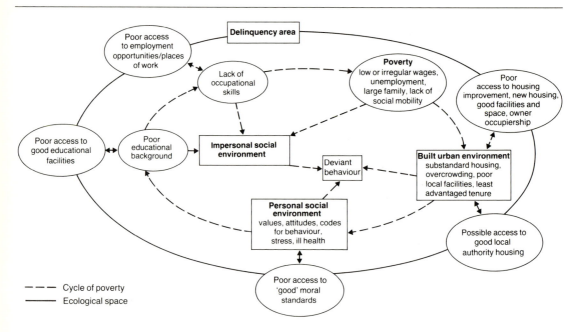

Figure 8.8
Delinquency residence: the cycle of disadvantage and its spatial connotations
Source: D. Herbert, *Progress in Human Geography*, 1, 1977, p. 277.

authority tenure; both may mean inadequate spatial access to facilities. Disadvantages of the impersonal *social* environment may be compounded by a poor *personal* social environment in which the prevalence of 'unfavourable' values and attitudes may have deleterious effects.[49]

8.2 *Cognition and Perception*

Interest in the perceived environment can be traced back to the publication in the early 1960s of papers by Lowenthal and Kirk that demonstrated the utility of perception studies to a geographical audience.[50] Since then a large number of geographers have become involved in the increasingly inter-disciplinary field of environmental perception, and there now exists a significant body of scientific research on the perception of the urban environment by its inhabitants. This interest was reinforced by the emergence within geography of a school of thought stemming from the phenomenological tradition of Husserl and giving a central position on the experiential 'sense of place' associated with different urban environments.[51] The effect was to provide a powerful antidote to the impression that cities are populated by land uses and pathologies rather than people, and an enlightening background to the behavioural patterns which contribute so much to the 'objective' geography of the city.

Central to the whole approach are the images, inner representations, mental maps and schemata derived from people's perception of the environment. These are the result of processes in which personal experiences and values are used to filter the barrage of environmental stimuli to which the brain is subjected, allowing the mind to work with a partial, simplified (and often distorted) version of reality. It follows that the same environmental stimuli may evoke different responses from different individuals, with each person effectively living in his or her 'own world'. Nevertheless, it is logical to assume that certain aspects of imagery will be held in common over quite large groups of people because of similarities in their socialization, past experience and present urban environment.

What are these images like? What urban geographies exist within the minds of urbanites, and how do they relate to the objective world? It is possible to give only tentative answers to these questions. It is clear, though, that people do not have a single image or mental map which can be consulted or recalled at will. Rather, we appear to possess a series of latent images that are unconsciously operationalized in response to specific behavioural tasks. In this context, a useful distinction can be made between the following two aspects:

1. The *designative* aspects of people's imagery which relate to the mental or cognitive organization of space necessary to their orientation within the urban environment.
2. The *appraisive* aspects of imagery which reflect people's feelings about the environment and which are related to decision-making within the urban environment.

Designative Aspects of Urban Imagery

The seminal work in this field was Kevin Lynch's book *The Image of the City*, published in 1960 and based on the results of lengthy interviews with (very) small samples of middle- and upper-class residents in three cities: Boston, Jersey City and Los Angeles.[52] In the course of these interviews, respondents were asked to describe the city, to indicate the location of features which were important to them, and to make outline sketches, the intention being to gently tease out a mental map from the subject's consciousness. From an examination of the resultant data, Lynch found that people apparently structure their mental image of the city in terms of five different kinds of elements: *paths* (e.g. streets, transit lines, canals), *edges* (e.g. lakeshores, walls, steep embankments, cliffs, *districts* (e.g. named neighbourhoods or shopping districts), *nodes* (e.g. plazas, squares, busy intersections) and *landmarks* (e.g. prominent buildings, signs, monuments).

As Lynch pointed out, none of these elements exists in isolation in people's minds. Districts are structured with nodes, defined by edges, penetrated by paths and sprinkled with landmarks. Elements thus overlap and pierce one another, and some may be psychologically more dominant than others.

Lynch also found that the residents of a given city tend to structure their mental map of the city with the same elements as one another, and he produced ingenious maps with which to demonstrate the collective image of Boston (Fig. 8.9), using symbols of different boldness to indicate the proportion of respondents who had mentioned each element. Another important finding was that, whereas the collective image of Boston was structured by a fairly dense combination of elements, those of Los Angeles and Jersey City were much less complex. Lynch suggested that this reflected a difference in the *legibility* or imageability of the cities resulting from differences in the 'form qualities' of the built environment. These, he argued, include the clarity and simplicity of visible form, the continuity and 'rhythm' of edges and surfaces, the dominance (whether in terms of size, intensity of interest) of one morphological unit over others, and the presence or absence of directional differentiation in terms of asymmetries, gradients and radial features.

Although Lynch's work has been criticized for its intuitive approach to the identification of image elements, and the validity of attempting to aggregate the imagery of people with quite different backgrounds and experience has been questioned,[53] his techniques have found wide application, and results from these studies provide an intriguing pool of information about the way different groups of people in different places structure their image of the city. Amsterdam, for example, was found to be much more legible to its inhabitants than were Rotterdam or The Hague to theirs, apparently because of its striking spider-web pattern of concentric canals and its strong linear core incorporating the Mint Square, the Central Station and The Dam – a great square containing the Royal Palace. The same study, however, found evidence to suggest that although environments with salient paths and nodes tend to be most legible, people also like *illegible* environments, possibly because of abstract qualities such as 'quaintness'.[54] A comparison of Milan and Rome found that both cities are highly legible, but in different ways: the mental maps of Milanese are structured by a clearly connected set of paths relating to their city's radial street pattern, whereas Romans' mental maps exhibit a greater diversity of content and tend to be structured around the landmarks and edges associated with their city's historic buildings, its hills, and the course of the Tiber.[55]

The same study was also able to demonstrate the differences that exist between the social classes in their image of the city. Basically, middle-class residents held a more comprehensive image than lower-class residents, covering a much wider territory and including a larger number and greater variety of elements. A similar conclusion can be drawn from the maps compiled from respondents living in different neighbourhoods in Los

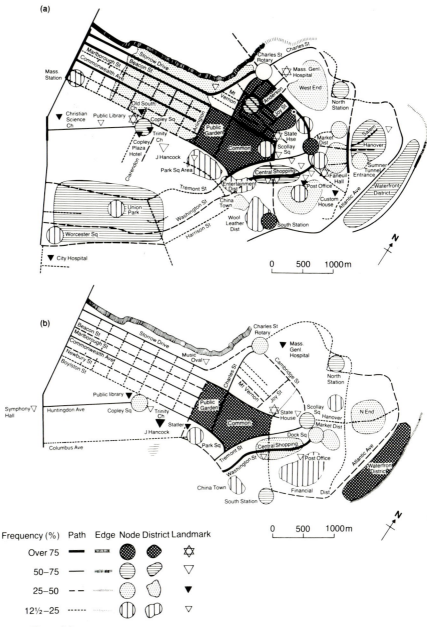

Figure 8.9
Designative images of Boston: (a) as derived from verbal interviewing, (b) as derived from sketch maps
Source: K. Lynch, *The Image of the City*, M.I.T. Press, Cambridge, Mass., 1960, p. 146.

Angeles, where ethnicity is closely associated with socio-economic status. The high-status, white residents of Westwood (a 'foothills' neighbourhood situated between Beverly Hills and Santa Monica) have a well-formed, detailed and generalized image of the entire Los Angeles Basin (Fig. 8.10a), whereas the middle-class residents of Northridge (a suburb in the San Fernando Valley) have a less comprehensive image which is oriented away from the city proper (Fig. 8.10b):

> As a sign on the Ventura Freeway proclaims: 'Topanga Plaza (in the [San Fernando] Valley) is downtown for over a million people.' Thus, although they have a reasonably detailed image of the San Fernando Valley extension of the city, the Santa Monica mountain chain effectively segregates Northridge residents from the rest of this sprawling metropolis.[56]

At the other end of the socio-economic ladder, residents of the black ghetto neighbourhood of Avalon, near Watts, have a vaguer image of the city which, in contrast to the white images which are structured around the major east–west boulevards and freeways, is dominated by the grid-iron layout of streets between Watts and the city centre (Fig. 8.10c). Reasons for these differences are not hard to find. The greater wealth and extended education of higher-status whites confers a greater mobility, a greater propensity to visit other parts of the city and a tendency to utilize a wider range of information sources. In contrast, the less mobile poor, with a shorter journey to work, and with less exposure to other sources of environmental information, will naturally tend to have a local rather than a metropolitan orientation: something which will be buttressed by racial or ethnic segregation. Where language barriers further reinforce this introversion, the likely outcome is an extremely restricted image of the city, as in the Spanish-speaking neighbourhood of Boyle Heights (Fig. 8.10d).

One aspect of Lynch's technique which has been pursued separately for its own sake is the use of sketch maps. Although they do not lend themselves to the compilation of a composite image, sketch maps do help to illuminate the way in which people perceive the city. Images of New York portrayed in Figures 8.11 and 8.12 show very clearly how each person structures the city quite differently, with the organization and content of their sketch reflecting their own life-style and emotional concerns. These two sketches are part of the sample of 332 derived from a questionnaire in *New York* magazine and organized by Stanley Milgram, who found that, in addition to the idiosyncratic aspects of the sketches, many were drawn from the perspective of the individual's immediate neighbourhood (as in Fig. 8.12). On the other hand, many respondents made Manhattan the central feature, even though they lived and worked in one of the city's other boroughs.[57]

It has been suggested that the kinds of map people draw can be categorized according to their *accuracy* and the *type of element* emphasized, with a basic division between those who emphasize 'sequential' elements (such as roads and pathways) and those who emphasize 'spatial' elements (such as individual buildings, landmarks and districts). Empirical studies suggest that the overall tendency is for a sequential structuring, with working-class and female respondents tending to draw the least sophisticated maps. Most

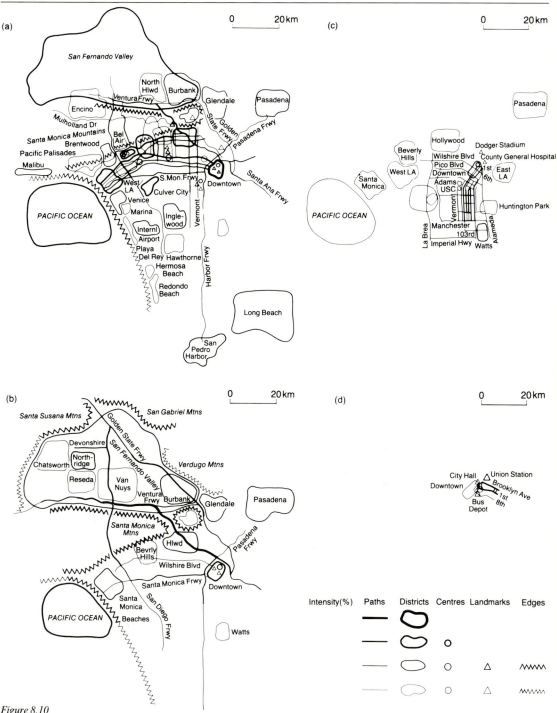

Figure 8.10
Designative images of Los Angeles: (a) as seen by residents of Westwood; (b) as seen by residents of Northridge; (c) as seen by residents of Avalon; (d) as seen by residents of Boyle Heights
Source: P. Orleans, in R. Downs and D. Stea (eds) *Image and Environment*, Aldine, Chicago, 1973, pp. 120-123.

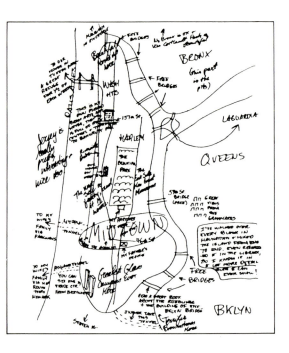

Figure 8.11
A mental map of New York City drawn by a 29-year-old writer from the West Side
Source: S. Duncan, *New York Magazine*, December 19, 1977, p.53. © News Group
Publications Inc.

researchers have also noted, like Milgram, the tendency for people's mental maps to be oriented around the home neighbourhood or city centre, along with the tendency for people to 'better' the environment, recording a structure more uniform and less haphazard than the real world – a tendency which evidently increases with familiarity with the city concerned.

Cognitive Distance

Underlying the organization of people's mental maps is the cognitive distance between image elements, and this is another aspect of imagery which has been shown to exhibit interesting and important regularities. Cognitive distance is the basis for the spatial information stored in cognitive representations of the environment. It is generated from a variety of mechanisms which includes the brain's perception of the distance between visible objects, the use-patterns and structure of the visible environment, and the impact of symbolic representations of the environment such as maps and road signs. For the majority of people, intra-urban cognitive distance is generally greater than objective distance, regardless of city size and their usual means of transport, although there is evidence to suggest that this overestimation declines with increasing physical distance.

It has been suggested that people's images and cognitive distance

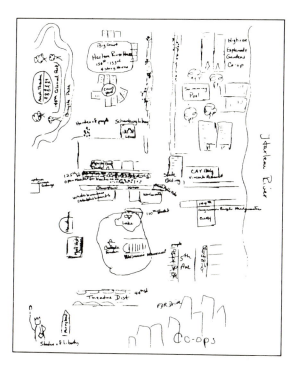

Figure 8.12
A mental map of New York City drawn by a teacher in her forties and living in Harlem
Source: S. Duncan, *New York Magazine*, December 19, 1977, p.53. © News Group
Publications Inc.

estimates are a function of the number and type of environmental stimuli,
or *cues*, they encounter along the paths, or *supports*, that they normally use,
and that the actual form of the city is of greater importance in determining
the cue selection process than any personal characteristics, including length
of residence. It is also suggested that different types of urban structure will
result in the selection of different cues, thus generating a different metric of
cognitive distance and producing different kinds of mental maps. Residents
of concentrically zoned cities might be expected to respond more to changes
in land use, for example, than residents of sectorally structured cities, who
might be expected to respond more to traffic-related cues along the typical
path from suburb to city centre and back.[58]

   Another interesting feature of cognitive distance is that it appears to be
dependent upon orientation in relation to the city centre. A study of
Cambridge housewives' imagery, for example, led to the conclusion that
the 'schema of the whole city includes a *focal* orientation, built up by the
satisfactions of the centre. These satisfactions ... have a dynamic effect on
the perceptual process, causing a foreshortening of perceived distances in
the inward direction'.[59] This tendency is consistent with research findings
from other studies which have related cognitive distance to the

characteristics of 'origins' and 'destinations' in mental maps: cognitive distance tends to shrink with the perceived utility or attractiveness of the 'destination'. Thus a general survey of neighbourhood characteristics in Baltimore, Maryland, revealed that desirable elements such as parks, post offices and libraries were felt to be closer to respondents' homes than they actually were, while less desirable elements such as parking lots and express-way interchanges were thought to be further away than they actually were.[60] Similarly, socially desirable neighbourhoods are often felt to be nearer than they really are; and the attractions of shopping centres tend to foreshorten the real distance between the home and the shop.

Given the distorting effect of the values attached to different 'origins' and 'destinations', it seems likely that people possess a basic image of the city consisting of the branching network of their 'action space' which undergoes topological deformation, perhaps hourly, as they move about the city from one major node – home, workplace, city centre – to another. 'Who, for instance, has not experienced a homeward trip to be shorter than the identical outward journey?'[61] The relationship of such a cognitive structure to the more general Lynch-type image of the city has not yet been properly explored, but it seems logical to expect that most people will possess an interlocking hierarchy of images that relates directly to the different geographical scales at which they act out different aspects of their lives.

Appraisive Aspects of Urban Imagery

In many circumstances it is not so much the structural aspects of people's imagery which are important so much as the meaning attached to, or evoked by, the different components of the urban environment in their mental map. Behaviour of all kinds obviously depends not only on *what* people perceive as being *where* but also on how they *feel* about these different elements. A specific node or district, for example, may be regarded as attractive or repellent, exciting or relaxing, fearsome or reassuring or, more likely, it may evoke a combination of such feelings. These reactions reflect what have been called the *appraisive* aspects of urban imagery.[62]

In overall terms, the appraisive imagery of the city is reflected by the desirability or attractiveness of different neighbourhoods as residential locations. This is something that can be measured and aggregated to produce a map of the collective image of the city which can be regarded as a synthesis of all the feelings, positive and negative, which people have about different neighbourhoods. A good example of this approach is provided by a study in which respondents in Los Angeles were asked to indicate the three neighbourhoods they would most like to live in, bearing in mind their family income. Figure 8.13 shows their first-choice prefer-ences, revealing an interesting geography which is by no means a simple reflection of the 'objective' socio-economic geography of the city. Thus,

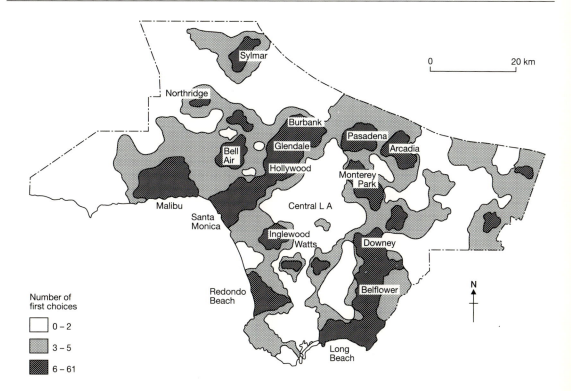

Figure 8.13
Residential desirability of Los Angeles neighbourhoods
Source: W. A. V. Clark and M. T. Cadwallader, *Environment & Planning A*, 5, 1973, p. 697.

while the widespread popularity of communities such as Santa Monica, Westwood Village, Beverly Hills and Hollywood could be accounted for in terms of their physically attractive environment, the presence of several well-developed employment centres, and a wide variety of shopping and entertainment facilities, and the popularity of 'beach' communities such as Redondo Beach could be related to their life-style, the widespread preference for communities in the eastern portion of the Los Angeles basin – Pasadena, Monterey Park, Alhambra and Arcadia – is 'less easily understood'.[63] The inclusion of large parts of the San Fernando Valley in the least-preferred category is also paradoxical, since it has been one of the most rapidly growing residential regions of the Los Angeles metropolitan area.

The Cognitive Dimensions of the Urban Environment
Given that people are able to make these overall evaluations of residential desirability, the question arises as to their derivation. In other words, what are the components of people's overall evaluation of a given place or neighbourhood, and how do they feel about these particular aspects of the

environment? Johnston, in an attempt to explain the process of neighbourhood evaluation, investigated the perceived attributes of 11 different suburbs in Christchurch, New Zealand.[64] His analysis suggested that neighbourhood preferences are based on three underlying evaluative dimensions which are invariant with area of residence in the city:

1. The 'impersonal environment', composed mainly of the physical attributes of the neighbourhood.
2. The 'interpersonal environment', composed mainly of the social attributes of the neighbourhood.
3. The locational attributes of the neighbourhood.

Another analysis of the cognitive dimensions of the urban environment that asked respondents to consider the relevance of 100 different items to their *own* neighbourhood (in the San Francisco Bay area) found as many as 20 'meaningful' dimensions. These include the following:

1. Aspects related to the *aesthetics* of the neighbourhood – its general appearance, tidiness, colourfulness, and level of maintenance, and the 'spaciousness' and general level of service provision in the area.
2. Aspects related to *neighbours* – their friendliness, helpfulness, or snobbishness; and the feelings of contentment, happiness, pride, power, loneliness and safety which stem from living among them.
3. Aspects related to *noise* – these include noise from the immediate environment (neighbours' children or lawnmowers, for example) as well as noise from aircraft and trains.
4. Aspects related to *safety* – these centred on two distinctive dimensions, one related to danger from traffic and the other to the safety and security of people and property.
5. Aspects related to *accessibility* and mobility – these include accessibility to freeways, neighbourhood parking conditions, and accessibility to public transport.
6. Aspects regarded as *annoyances*, such as the lack of privacy, the incidence of door-to-door salesmen, and the presence of animal nuisances.[65]

Generalizations such as these should be treated with caution, however. Both the Christchurch and San Francisco studies were based on analyses of data that were aggregated across different neighbourhoods. Martin Cadwallader, using a methodology similar to Johnston's in an analysis of Madison, Wisconsin, found the evaluative dimensions associated with different neighbourhoods were in fact 'far from identical', although there was some evidence that similar neighbourhoods evoked similar cognitive responses and that Johnston's three main evaluative dimensions were 'generally identifiable' in people's feelings about different neighbourhoods.[66]

There clearly remains a good deal of investigation to be undertaken before the composition of appraisive imagery in cities can be fully understood. There are many facets to the dialectic between places and people's

perceptions of them. Research on residents of Bath found that their appraisive imagery tended to contrast places which were liked and beautiful
(especially the Georgian areas of the city) with those which were disliked
and ugly (mainly the working-class, industrialized areas of the lower Avon
valley). A second dimension was found to contrast places in which respondents were involved (the city centre and the middle-class residential areas)
with places where they felt out of place (notably the Georgian areas); while
a third dimension contrasted places with a wide significance and which had
been known for a long time with recently discovered places of only local
significance.[67] In addition to this layering of imagery, we must recognize
that both people and neighbourhoods are continually changing. In this
context, it is interesting that an attempt to come to grips with residents'
perceptual responses to change found that *neighbourhood stability* was the
dominant cognitive concern.[68]

Other, more specific aspects of appraisive imagery have been elicited by
researchers pursuing particular themes. David Ley, for instance, illustrated
the local geography of perceived danger in an inner-city neighbourhood in
Philadelphia, showing how most people recognized – and avoided – the
danger points near gang hang-outs, abandoned buildings and places where
drugs were peddled.[69] The imagery of fear is often time-dependent: public
parks, for example, may be felt to be tranquil and safe places by day but
might induce quite different feelings at night. It is also gender dependent,
women being subject to fear of crime and harassment in a much greater
range of settings and to a much greater degree than men. This is an
important (but under-researched) topic, since the spatial patterns of
women's perceptions of risks, of the actual risks they are exposed to and of
their behavioural responses, have implications for their equal participation
in society.[70]

Another important aspect of appraisive imagery is the way in which
some areas of larger cities become *stigmatized*, their inhabitants being
labelled as 'work-shy', 'unreliable', or 'troublesome', thus making it difficult for them to compete in local housing and job-markets. Another
concerns the role of clothes and personal objects (rather than buildings and
social characteristics) in contributing towards our feelings about different
parts of the city. Many of our material objects are used, consciously or not,
to communicate what we like or believe in: the pair of shoes, the book, the
wall poster and the cut of a pair of jeans become briefly exhibited signs and
badges which not only help their owners to say something about themselves
but which also help others to attach meaning and significance to their
owners and to *their owners' environment*. Here is one reaction to the people
encountered on different Underground routes in London:

> People who live on the Northern Line I take to be sensitive citizens; it is
> a friendly communication route where one notes commuters reading
> proper books and, when they talk, finishing their sentences. But the
> Piccadilly Line is full of fly-by-nights and stripe-shirted young men who
> run dubious agencies, and I go to elaborate lengths to avoid travelling

on it. It is an entirely irrational way of imposing order on the city, but it does give it a shape in the mind, takes whole chunks of experience out of the realm of choice and deliberation, and places them in the less strenuous context of habit and prejudice.[71]

Images of the Home Area

Just as individual personality is reflected in home and possessions, so collective personality and values are translated into the wider environment of 'cultural landscapes'. The existence of such relationships between places and people leads to the idea of a 'sense of place', which incorporates aspects of imageability, the symbolic meaning of places, and 'topophilia' – the affective *bond* between people and place.[72] In the specific context of urban social geography, the most important aspect of this sense of place is probably the attachment people feel to their *home area*. There is no doubt that the immediate physical and social environment is crucially important in the early psychological and social development of the individual, and it seems that this generates a strong bond – often amounting almost to reverence – for the territorial homeland: a phenomenon which Yi-Fu Tuan calls 'geopiety'.[73] Such feelings are clearly related to the idea of territoriality (see p. 00), and there is plenty of evidence to suggest that they exist as a kind of latent 'neighbourhood attachment' in most people who have lived in a particular area for any length of time. The most striking evidence of such feelings emerges after people have been forced to leave their home neighbourhood in the cause of redevelopment or renewal schemes, when many report feelings of grief at the loss of their old neighbourhood. This is because 'It is not only the built environment that is razed but also the contextual environment, the symbol of life's experience: part of people's roots, part of *themselves* is lost.'[74]

Most people seem to have an attachment to a home area which they mentally 'recognize' and identify with. Evidence for this comes from the Royal Commission on Local Government in England which contracted Research Services Ltd to carry out a survey of a carefully stratified sample of 2000 in order to ascertain the most appropriate size of local government units. One of the questions asked in the study was: 'Is there an area around here, where you are now living, which you would say you belonged to, and where you feel "at home"?' Approximately 80 per cent of the respondents claimed to possess some feelings of attachment to a 'home' community area, and this tendency tended to increase with length of residence. Similar findings have emerged from a survey of Los Angeles residents, where it was also found that the size and orientation of husbands' and wives' home areas tended to differ, largely as a result of their differential use of space around the home.[75] In addition, it seems that subjectively-defined local areas exhibit a high degree of stability over time.[76]

The home area thus seems to exist and to be closely related to people's 'activity space' around the home. Here is one person's description of his own 'home area':[77]

The Greater London Council [was] responsible for a sprawl shaped like a rugby ball about twenty-five miles long and twenty miles wide; my city is a concise kidney-shaped patch within that space, in which no point is more than about seven miles from any other. On the south, it is bounded by the river, on the north by the fat tongue of Hampstead Heath and Highgate Village, on the west by Brompton cemetery and on the east by Liverpool Street station. I hardly ever trespass beyond those limits and when I do I feel I'm in foreign territory, a landscape of hazard and rumour. Kilburn, on the far side of my northern and western boundaries, I imagine to be inhabited by vicious drunken Irishmen; Hackney and Dalston by crooked car dealers with pencil moustaches and goldfilled teeth; London south of the Thames still seems impossibly illogical and contingent, a territory of meaningless circles, incomprehensible one-way systems, warehouses and cage-bird shops. Like any tribesman hedging himself in a stockade of taboos, I mark my boundaries with graveyards, terminal transportation points and wildernesses. Beyond them, nothing is to be trusted and anything might happen.

The constrictedness of this private city-within-a-city has the character of a self-fulfilling prophecy. Its boundaries, originally arrived at by chance and usage, grow more not less real the longer I live in London. I have friends who live in Clapham, only three miles away, but to visit them is a definite journey, for it involves crossing the river. I can, though, drop in on friends in Islington, twice as far away as Clapham, since it is within what I feel to be my own territory.

But how typical is this imagery, and how might it relate to people's social behaviour? Terence Lee, a psychologist, made a major contribution to this issue. He suggested that people build up a mental model, or *schema*, of the area in which their daily lives are played out – their home area. In order to elaborate this idea, Lee developed a technique in which respondents were asked to 'please draw a line around the point which you consider acts as your neighbourhood or district', and applied it to a representative sample of the residential areas of Cambridge, England.[78] While it can be argued that such instructions predispose an obliging respondent to construe his or her world in a way that may be alien or unnatural, it should be emphasized that the technique was used only after a large number of pilot interviews had suggested that some kind of neighbourhood structuring of the city was widespread, and that people described their area mainly by delineating its boundaries in a variety of ways. As in the Royal Commission survey, Lee found that about 80 per cent of the people could delineate a home area. What is interesting, however, is that these turned out to be highly personal and idiosyncratic, with a map of superimposed home areas resembling 'a plate of spaghetti'. Nevertheless, there were also several interesting and significant regularities in the data. First, the *area* covered by people's schemata tended to be fairly consistent: about 100 acres (40 ha). Second, it was found that this size was quite unrelated to changes in population density, so that the home areas or schemata of suburban residents tend to extend over the same amount of territory as the home areas of inner-city residents. Lee suggested that this is probably because the home area is dependent on an action space based on walking distance. From a closer examination of the 165 schemata produced by his respondents, Lee also proposed a typology of neighbourhoods:

1. The *social acquaintance neighbourhood*: a small area in which people 'keep themselves to themselves' and where the main support in times of trouble is from kin rather than neighbours. This kind of neighbourhood is much more a function of people than locality. That is, it could be found in a variety of localities but only among a certain kind of person.
2. The *homogeneous neighbourhood*: here the schema includes greater awareness of physical aspects of the environment as well as people. An underlying principle is that the neighbourhood is comprised not only of 'people like us' but also of 'people who live in houses like ours'.
3. The *unit neighbourhood*: a territory which approximates to planners' conceptions of 'neighbourhood' – larger, with a heterogeneous population and a balanced range of amenities.

Further analysis of people's schemata was achieved by computing a 'neighbourhood quotient' that measured the size and complexity (in terms of the content of houses, shops and amenities) of neighbourhoods while holding constant the physical area in which they were drawn. The mean quotients for a particular social or spatial group thus reflects its overall level of 'sociophysical involvement' in the locality, while the range of values serves as a measure of that group's agreement or, as Lee called it, 'consentaneity'. Using this technique, Lee found evidence to support the classic planning axiom that a neighbourhood with well-defined boundaries will have a high level of social participation.

The very existence of these schemata, of course, is highly relevant to the debate on communities and neighbourhoods outlined in Chapter 6, and several researchers have attempted to relate functional neighbourhoods (based on patterns of social interaction and economic behaviour) to the perceived neighbourhood or home area. Annette Buttimer, for example, demonstrated the rather variable relationship between the size and orientation of people's 'micro-service' activity spaces, 'macro-service' activity spaces, 'social participation' spaces and perceived home areas in different parts of Glasgow;[79] while John Everitt demonstrated the broad congruence between the perceived home areas of a sample of Los Angeles residents and their activity patterns in relation to workplace, friends' residences, and clubs.[80] Perhaps the most useful work in this context is the re-analysis by Brian Berry and John Kasarda of the Royal Commission data. They found that community sentiments, including the ability to identify a 'home area', are primarily influenced by participation in local social networks, and that this participation, in turn, is influenced mainly by length of residence in the area.[81] This relationship held true even when population size, density, socio-economic status and life-cycle factors were held constant, suggesting that the 'systemic model' of community organization – based on length of residence and the strength of local social networks – is more appropriate than the 'linear development' model based on population size and density and stemming from the ideas of Tönnies and Wirth.

SUGGESTED
READING

A good place to get started with an introduction to behavioural geography is D. J. Walmsley's *Urban Living: The Individual in the City* (1988: Longman, Harlow). Also useful as introductory reviews are John Gold's *An Introduction to Behavioural Geography* (1980: Oxford University Press, Oxford), and Reg Golledge and R. Stimson's *Analytical Behavioural Geography* (1987: Croom Helm, London). A review of geographical approaches to social deviance in the city is provided by David Herbert in his essay in Mike Pacione's edited volume, *Social Geography: Progress and Prospect* (1987: Croom Helm, London); while Pacione himself reviews a wide range of behavioural literature in his essay on urban livability (*Urban Geography*, **11,** 1990, 1–30). The relationships between urban settings and criminality are dealt with in several accessible sources: David Evans and David Herbert (eds), *The Geography of Crime* (1989: Routledge, London), Susan Smith, *Crime, Space, and Society* (1986: Cambridge University Press, Cambridge), and Ralph Taylor's chapter on urban communities and crime in *Urban Life in Transition* (1991: M. Gottdiener and C. Pickvance, eds, Sage, Newbury Park, CA). Anthony Bottoms and Paul Wiles provide a structurationist perspective on crime and place that is useful in bridging the behavioural emphasis of this chapter with the material covered in the previous two chapters: their essay, 'Explanations of crime and place', is in *Crime, Policing and Place*, edited by David Evans, Nicholas Fyfe and David Herbert (1992: Routledge, London, pp. 11–35). On mental maps, perception and the cognitive dimensions of urban settings, see Douglas Pocock and Ray Hudson's *Images of the Urban Environment* (1978: Macmillan, London).

NOTES

1. Ley, D., *A Social Geography of the City*. New York: Harper & Row, 1983.

2. His classic paper was 'Psychology as the behaviouralist views it' *Psychological Review*, **XX,** 1913, 158–177.

3. Werlen, B. *Society, Action, and Space. An Alternative Human Geography*. London: Routledge, 1993, p. 9.

4. Newson, J. and E. Newson, *Patterns of Infant Care in an Urban Community*. Harmondsmith: Penguin, 1965.

5. Toffler, A., *Future Shock*. London: The Bodley Head, 1970.

6. See, for example, Goffman, E., *The Presentation of Self in Everyday Life*. New York: Doubleday, 1959.

7. Goffman, E., *Relations in Public*. New York: Basic Books, 1971.

8. See, for example, Korte, C., Helpfulness in the urban environment. In A. Baun *et al.* (eds), *Advances in Environmental Psychology, Vol. 1: The Urban Environment*. Hillsdale, NJ: Erlbaum, 1978.

9. Riesman, I., *The Lonely Crowd*. New Haven: Yale University Press, 1950.

10. See, for example, Skogan, W.G., *Disorder and Decline. Crime and the Spiral of Decay in American Neighborhoods*. Berkeley: University of California Press, 1992; and Herbert, D. T., Neighbourhood incivilities and the study of crime in place, *Area*, **25,** 1992, 45–54.

11. Wohlenberg, E. The geography of civility revisited: New York blackout looting, *Economic Geography*, **58,** 1982, 29–44.

12. See, for example, Galle, O. and W. Gove. Overcrowding, isolation, and human behavior. In M. Baldassare (ed.), *Cities and Urban Living*, New York: Columbia University Press, 1983, pp. 215–241.

13. Sack, R., Human territoriality: a theory, *Annals, Association of American Geographers*, **73,** 1983, 55–74.

14. Calhoun, J. B., Population density and social pathology, *Scientific American*, **206,** 1962, 139–148.

15. van den Berghe, P., Bringing beasts back in: toward a biosocial theory of aggression, *American Sociological Review*, **39,** 1974, 777–788.

16. Suttles, G., *The Social Order of the Slum: Ethnicity and Territory in the Inner City*. Chicago: University of Chicago Press, 1968.

17. Boal, F., Territoriality on the Shankhill–Falls Divide, Belfast. In D. Lanegran and R. Palm (eds), *An Invitation to Geography*. New York: McGraw-Hill, 1978, pp. 58–77.

18. See, for example, Jephcott, P., *Homes in High Flats*. Edinburgh: Oliver and Boyd, 1971.

19. Smith, P. F., *The Syntax of Cities*. London: Hutchinson, 1977.

20. Newman, O., *Defensible Space*. New York: Macmillan, 1972.

21. See, for example, Gold, J. R., Territoriality and human spatial behaviour, *Progress in Human Geography*, **6,** 1982, 44–67.

22. See, for example, Gans, H. J. *The Urban Villagers*. New York: Free Press, 1962.

23. Fischer, C., *The Urban Experience*. New York: Harcourt, Brace, Jovanovich, 1976.

24. Shaw, C. R. and H. D. McKay, *Juvenile Delinquency and Urban Areas*. Chicago: University of Chicago Press, 1942.

25. Robson, B. T., *Urban Analysis*. Cambridge: Cambridge University Press, 1969.

26. See, for example, Jencks, C. and S. E. Mayer, The social consequences of

growing up in a poor neighborhood. In L. E. Lynn and M. G. H. McGreary (eds), *Inner City Poverty in the United States*. Washington, DC: National Academy Press, 1990, pp. 68–186; and Crane, J, The epidemic theory of ghettos and neighbourhood effects on dropping-out and teenage childbearing, *American Journal of Sociology*, **96,** 1991, 1226–1259.

27. Smith, S., Economic determinism and the provision of human services. In A. Kirby, P. Knox and S. Pinch (eds), *Public Service Provision and Urban Development*. London: Croom Helm, 1984, p. 194.

28. Lambert, J. R., *Crime, Police, and Race Relations*. London: Oxford University Press, 1970, p. 124.

29. See, for example, Taylor, R. B., Urban communities and crime. In M. Gottdiener and C. G. Pickvance (eds), *Urban Life in Transition*. Newbury Park, CA: Sage, 1991, pp. 106–134; Smith, S. *Crime, Space, and Society*. Cambridge: Cambridge University Press, 1986; Evans, D. J. and D. T. Herbert, (eds) *The Geography of Crime*. London: Routledge, 1989; and Davidson, N; *Crime and Environment*. London: Croom Helm, 1981.

30. Herbert, D. T., Social deviancy in the city: a spatial perspective. In D. T. Herbert and R. J. Johnston (eds), *Social Areas in Cities*, **2**, London: Wiley, 1976, pp. 89–121.

31. Sherman, L. W., P. R. Gartin, and M. E., Buerger. Hot spots of predatory crime: routine activities and the criminology of place, *Criminology*, **27,** 1989, 27–55.

32. Schmid, C. F., Urban crime areas, *Sociological Review*, **25,** 1960, 527–542, 655–678.

33. Schmid, C. F. and S. E. Schmid, *Crime in the State of Washington*. Olympia: Law and Justice Planning Office, Washington State Planning and Community Affairs Agency, 1972.

34. See, for example, Pyle, G., Geographic perspectives on crime and the impact of crime legislation. In J.S. Adams, (ed.), *Urban Policymaking and Metropolitan Dynamics*. Cambridge, Mass.: Ballinger, 1976, pp. 257–292.

35. *Ibid.*

36. See, for example, Bottoms, A.E. and P. Wiles, Housing markets and residential crime careers. In D. J. Evans, N. R. Fyfe and D. T. Herbert (eds), *Crime, Policing, and Place*. London: Routledge, 1992, pp. 118–144; and Chilton, R., Age, sex, and arrest trends for 12 of the nation's largest central cities. In J. M. Byrne and R. J. Sampson (eds), *The Social Ecology of Crime*. New York: Springer, 1986, pp. 102–115.

37. Boggs, S. L., Urban crime patterns, *American Sociological Review*, **30,** 1965, 899–908.

38. Baldwin, J., A. E. Bottoms and M. A. Walker, *The Urban Criminal*. London: Tavistock, 1976.

39. US National Commission on the Causes and Prevention of Violence, *Report*. Washington, DC: USGPO, 1969.

40. Brantingham, P. L. and J. Brantingham, Residential burglary and urban form, *Urban Studies*, **12,** 1975, 273–284.

41. Ley, D. and R. Cybriwsky, The spatial ecology of stripped cars, *Environment & Behavior*, **6,** 1974, 63–67.

42. Evans, D., and G. Olds, Geographical aspects of the incidence of residential burglary in Newcastle-under-Lyme, UK. *Tijdschrift voor Economische en Sociale Geografie*, **75,** 1984, 344–355.

43. Herbert, D. T., Crime, delinquency, and the urban environment, *Progress in Human Geography*, **1,** 1977, 224.

44. Shaw and Mckay, *Juvenile Delinquency.*

45. Schmid, Urban crime areas, p. 678.

46. Smith, *Crime, Space, and Society.*

47. Herbert, D.T., The study of delinquency areas: a social geographical approach, *Transactions, Institute of British Geographers*, **1,** 490.

48. Evans, D. J., *Geographical Perspectives on Juvenile Delinquency.* Farnborough: Gower Westmead, 1980.

49. Herbert, D.T., Crime, delinquency and the urban environment, pp. 226–227.

50. Lowenthal, D., Geography, experience, and imagination: towards a geographic epistemology, *Annals, Association of American Geographers*, **51,** 1961, 241–260; Kirk, W., Problems in geography, *Geography*, **48,** 1963, 357–371.

51. Tuan, Y-F., *Topophilia.* Englewood Cliffs, NJ: Prentice-Hall, 1974; Relph, E., *Place and Placelessness.* London: Pion, 1976.

52. Lynch, K., *The Image of the City.* Cambridge, Mass.: MIT Press, 1960; see also Lynch, K., Reconsidering 'The Image of the City'. In R. M. Hollister and L. Rodwin, (eds), *Cities of the Mind*, New York: Plenum, 1984.

53. See, for example, my review of his work: *Environment & Planning D: Society and Space.* **10,** 1992, 231–233.

54. de Jonge, D., Images of urban areas: their structure and psychological foundations, *Journal of the American Institute of Planners*, **28,** 1962, 266–276.

55. Francescato, D., and W. Mebane, How citizens view two great cities. In R. Downs and D. Stea, (eds), *Image and Environment*, Chicago, Aldine, 1973, pp. 131–147.

56. Orleans, P. Differential cognition of urban residents: effects of social scale on mapping. In Downs and Stea, *Image and Environment*, pp. 118–119.

57. Duncan, S. Mental maps of New York, *New York Magazine*, 19 December 1977, 51–72.

58. Golledge, R. and G. Zannaras, Cognitive approaches to the analysis of human spatial behavior. In W. H. Ittelson, (ed.), *Environmental Cognition*. New York: Seminar Press, 1973.

59. Lee, T., Perceived distance as a function of direction in the city, *Environment & Behaviour*, **20,** 1970, 41.

60. Lowery, R. A., A method for analysing distance concepts of urban residents. In Downs and Stea, *Image and Environment*, pp. 338–360.

61. Pocock, D. and R. Hudson, *Images of the Urban Environment*. London: Macmillan, 1978, p. 57.

62. *Ibid.*

63. Clark, W. A. V. and M. Cadwallader, Residential preferences: an alternate view of intra-urban space, *Environment & Planning A*, **5**, 1973, 693–703.

64. Johnston, R. J., Spatial patterns in suburban evaluations, *Environment & Planning A*, **5**, 1973, 385–395.

65. Carp, F. M., R. T. Zawadski and H. Shokrkon, Dimensions of urban environmental quality, *Environment & Behaviour*, **8**, 1976, 239–264.

66. Cadwallader, M., Neighborhood evaluation in residential mobility, *Environment & Planning A*, **11**, 1979, 393–401; see also Unger, D. G. and A. Wandersman, The importance of neighbours: the social, cognitive, and affective components of neighbouring, *American Journal of Community Psychology*, **13**, 1985, 139–169.

67. Harrison, J. A. and P. Sarre, Personal construct theory in the measurement of environmental images: problems and methods, *Environment & Behaviour*, **3**, 1971, 351–374.

68. Aitken, S., Local evaluations of neighbourhood change, *Annals, Association of American Geographers*, **80**, 1990, 247–267.

69. Ley, D., *The Black Inner City as Frontier Outpost*. Washington, DC: Association of American Geographers, 1974.

70. Pain, R., Space, violence and social control: integrating geographical and feminist analyses of women's fear of crime, *Progress in Human Geography*, **15**, 1991, 415–431; Smith, S. J., Social relations, neighbourhood structure, and fear of crime in Britain. In D. Evans and D. T. Herbert (eds), *The Geography of Crime*, Routledge, London, 1989, pp. 193–227.

71. Raban, J., *Soft City*. London: Fontana, 1975, p. 168.

72. Tuan, *Topophilia*; Relph, *Place and Placelessness*.

73. Tuan, Y-F., Geopiety: a theme in man's attachment to nature and place. In D. Lowenthal and M. J. Bowden (eds), *Geographies of the Mind*. London: Oxford University Press, 1976, pp. 11–39.

74. Pocock and Hudson, *Images of the Urban Environment*, p. 85.

75. Everitt, J. and M. Cadwallader, Local area definition revisited, *Area*, **9**, 1977, 175–176.

76. Pacione, M., The temporal stability of perceived neighbourhood areas in Glasgow, *Professional Geographer*, **35**, 1983, 66–73.

77. Raban, *Soft City*, pp. 166–167.

78. Lee, T., Urban neighbourhood as a socio-spatial schema, *Human Relations*, **21**, 1968, 241–268.

79. Buttimer, A., Social space and the planning of residential areas, *Environment & Behaviour*, **4**, 1972, 279–318.

80. Everitt, J., Community and propinquity in a city, *Annals, Association of American Geographers*, **66,** 1976, 104–116.

81. Berry, B. J. L. and J. Kasarda, *Contemporary Urban Sociology*. New York: Macmillan, 1977.

Neighbourhood transition:
the Bronx, New York.
Photograph by U.S.
Department of Housing and
Urban Development.

9 Residential mobility and neighbourhood change

Although it is widely accepted that the shaping and reshaping of urban social areas is a product of the movement of households from one residence to another, the relationships between residential structure and patterns of residential mobility are only imperfectly understood. This is a reflection of the complexity of these relationships. While migration creates and remodels the social and demographic structure of city neighbourhoods, it is also conditioned by the existing ecology of the city: a classic example of the sociospatial dialectic. Moreover, the process is undergoing constant modification, as each household's decision to move (or not to move) has repercussions for the rest of the system. Chain reactions of vacancies and moves are set off as dwellings become newly available, and this movement may itself trigger further mobility as households react to changes in neighbourhood status and tone.

The basic relationship between residential mobility and urban structure is outlined in Fig. 9.1, which emphasizes the circular and cumulative effects of housing demand and urban structure on each other. Mobility is seen as a product of *housing opportunities* – the new and vacant dwellings resulting from suburban expansion, inner-city renewal and rehabilitation, etc., – and the housing *needs* and *expectations* of households, which are themselves a product of income, family size and life-style. Meanwhile, as Fig. 9.2 shows, residential mobility can also be interpreted within the frame of broader structural changes.

Given a sufficient amount of mobility, the residential structure of the city will be substantively altered, resulting in changes both to the 'objective'

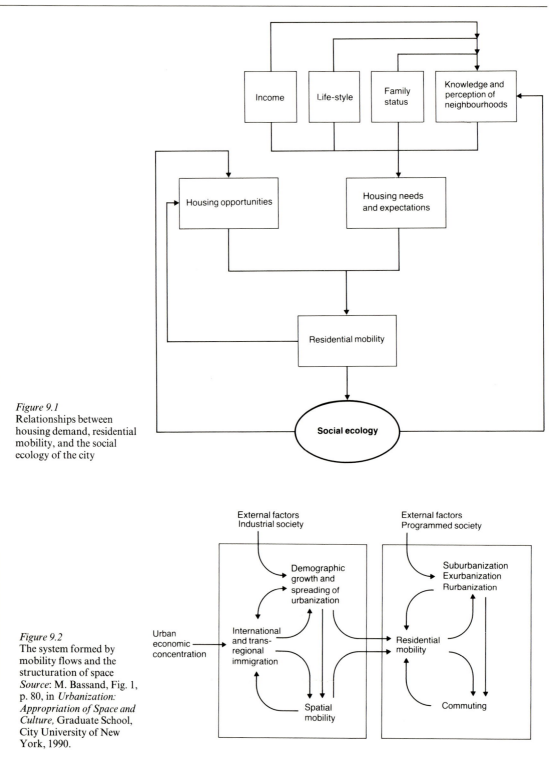

Figure 9.1
Relationships between housing demand, residential mobility, and the social ecology of the city

Figure 9.2
The system formed by mobility flows and the structuration of space
Source: M. Bassand, Fig. 1, p. 80, in *Urbanization: Appropriation of Space and Culture,* Graduate School, City University of New York, 1990.

social ecology and to the associated neighbourhood images that help to attract or deter further potential movers. *Households, then, may be seen as decision-making units whose aggregate response to housing opportunities is central to ecological change.* It therefore seems logical to begin the task of disentangling the relationship between movement and urban structure by seeking to establish the fundamental parameters of household mobility. How many households do actually move in a given period? Do particular types of households have a greater propensity to move than others? And are there any spatial regularities in the pattern of migration?

9.1   *Patterns of Household Mobility*

In fact, the amount of movement by households in Western cities is considerable. In Australia, New Zealand and North America, between 15 and 20 per cent of all urban households move in any one year. Having said this, it is of course important to recognize that some cities experience much higher levels of mobility than others. Cities in the fast-growing West, South and Gulf Coast of the United States – Reno, Colorado Springs, Las Vegas and Anaheim/Santa Ana/Garden Grove, for instance – have an annual turnover of population which is double that of the likes of Scranton, Johnstown and Wilkes-Barre/Hazeltown in the slow-growing North East. In Europe, rates of mobility also vary a good deal, but in general they range between 5 and 10 per cent per year (Table 9.1).

Table 9.1 Intra-urban migration rates, 1980 (or latest available year), selected European cities

	Movers per 1000 population		Movers per 1000 population
Aberdeen	73.8	Lisbon	39.9
Amsterdam	93.3	Lyons	71.9
Berlin (West)	116.3	Manchester	66.4
Brussels	57.0	Munich	72.9
Copenhagen	116.0	Newcastle	70.9
Cork	21.3	Oporto	39.9
Dijon	70.3	Paris	59.9
Dublin	20.3	Rome	70.5
Geneva	100.6	Tampere	120.7
Gothenburg	97.1	Turku	113.5
Hamburg	85.9	Sheffield	70.5
Helsinki	119.4	Stockholm	57.5
Köln	83.0	Vienna	48.8
Lausanne	109.4	Zurich	103.1
London	76.2		

Source: Derived from P. White, *The West European City: A Social Geography*, Longman, London, 1984, Table 2.

It is also important to recognize that the magnitude of this movement stems partly from economic and social forces that extend well beyond the housing markets of individual cities. Some of the most important determinants of the overall level of residential mobility are the business cycles that are endemic to capitalist economies. During economic upswings the increase in employment opportunities and wages leads to an increase in the effective demand for new housing which, when completed, allows whole chains of households to change homes. Changes in social organization – particularly those involving changes in family structure and the rate of household formation, dissolution and fusion – also affect the overall level of mobility by exerting a direct influence on the demand for accommodation. Long-term changes in the structure of the housing market itself are also important. In many European countries, for example, the expansion of owner-occupied and public housing at the expense of the privately rented sector has led to a general decrease in mobility because of the higher costs and longer delays involved in moving. An analysis of the factors affecting mobility rates in nine European cities found that, in addition to the composition of housing markets, mobility was chiefly related to the local balance between housing construction and population growth, the presence of foreign workers, and population density.[1]

Notwithstanding these general factors, it is clear that residential mobility is a selective process. Households of different types are not equally mobile. Some have a propensity to move quite often; others, having once gained entry to the housing system, never move at all, thus lending a degree of stability to the residential mosaic. This basic dichotomy between 'movers' and 'stayers' has been identified in a number of studies, and it has been found that the composition of each group tends to be related to the life-style and tenure characteristics of households. In particular, younger households have been found to move more frequently than older households; and private renters have been found to be more mobile than households in other tenure categories.[2] People can also be conceptualized as 'locals' or 'cosmopolitans', depending on the type and intensity of their attachments to their immediate social environments, and this distinction has been shown to have a significant bearing on intra-urban mobility.[3]

In addition, there appears to be an independent duration-of-residence effect whereby the longer a household remains in a dwelling the less likely it is to move. This has been termed the principle of 'cumulative inertia', and is usually explained in terms of the emotional attachments that develop towards the dwelling and immediate neighbourhood and the reluctance to sever increasingly strong and complex social networks in favour of the unknown quantity of the pattern of daily life elsewhere. In contrast, the actual experience of moving home probably reinforces the propensity to move. Movers 'are more oriented to future mobility than are persons who have not moved in the past and are better able to actualize a moving plan and choice'.[4]

It is important to recognize that these differentials are all structured by broader dimensions of the sociospatial dialectic, and in this context it is useful to follow Feitelson's conceptualization of a hierarchy of household segmentation (Fig. 9.3).[5] According to this schema, the likelihood of residential mobility resulting in a significant change in a household's housing situation depends, first, on societal constraints (based on economic and social status, race and ethnicity). Second, groups facing similar constraints are stratified according to the basic life-style choices made by households. Third, households are stratified according to their current situation (domestic needs, financial resources, etc.).

Spatial regularities in the migration patterns of movers have proved difficult to establish, however, partly because of the problems involved in obtaining and analysing migration data. Census data, although reliable, rarely include sufficient information about the origin of migrants; and few countries outside The Netherlands and Scandinavia have registers of households that can be used to plot household movements. Questionnaire surveys provide an obvious alternative, but they involve the expenditure of a large amount of time and money in order to obtain a sufficiently large sample of migrants. In North America, many researchers have resorted to data based on changes of address worked out from telephone directories; but European researchers, faced with large numbers of households who do not have telephones, have often had to rely on town directories and electoral lists, both of which are known to be rather incomplete sources of information. Difficulties have also been experienced in analysing migration data. In

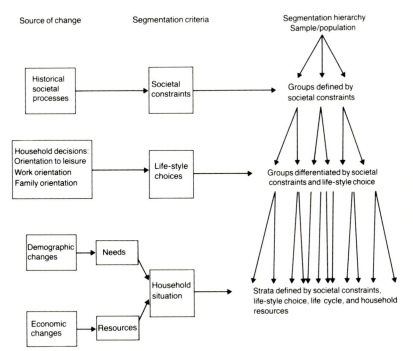

Figure 9.3
Hierarchical segmentation of
residential demand
Source: E. Feitelson,
Environment & Planning A,
25, 1993, Fig. 3, p. 557.

addition to the pitfalls of the ecological fallacy, these include the statistical problem of multi-collinearity and the practical problems involved in handling the large, complex data sets associated with migration studies.[6]

Patterns of In-migration

Nevertheless, it is possible to suggest a number of important regularities in people's migration behaviour. At this stage, it is useful to distinguish between the spatial behaviour of intra-urban movers and that of in-migrants from other cities, regions and countries. Furthermore, in-migrants can be usefully divided into high- and low-status movers. The latter were particularly influential in shaping the residential structure of cities earlier this century. There are some cities, however, where low-status in-migrants continue to represent a significant component of migration patterns, as illustrated by population movements in London, for example, where in-migrants from foreign countries and from Scotland and Ireland (the majority of whom can safely be assumed to have been of low socio-economic status) have continued to make a significant contribution to the city's residential structure, with large numbers moving to cheap housing in the western sector of the inner city.[7]

Substantial flows of low-status in-migrants have also been shown to be directed to fairly narrowly-defined inner-city districts in other cities: Cincinnati, for example, where the in-migrants are mainly poor whites from Appalachia; Australian cities such as Melbourne and Sydney, where the in-migrants are mainly foreign born; and some European cities, where the in-migrants are *gastarbeiter*. As we saw in Chapter 6, the impact of these in-migrants on urban social ecology is often finely tuned in relation to the national and regional origins, religion and ethnic status of the migrants involved.

High-status in-migrants are similar to low-status in-migrants in that the majority are drawn into the city in response to its economic opportunities. Their locational behaviour, however, is quite different. The majority constitutes part of a highly mobile group of the better-educated middle classes whose members move from one city to another in search of better jobs or career advancement. Some of these moves are voluntary and some are made in response to the administrative fiat of large companies and government departments. The vast majority, though, follow the same basic pattern, moving to a rather narrowly defined kind of neighbourhood: newly established suburban developments containing housing towards the top end of the price range. Such areas are particularly attractive to the mobile élite because the lack of an established neighbourhood character and social network minimizes the risk of settling among neighbours who are unfriendly, too friendly, 'snobbish' or 'common': something that may otherwise happen very easily, since out-of-town households must usually search the property market and make a housing selection in a matter of days. Moreover, housing in such areas tends to conform to 'conventional' floor and window shapes and sizes, so that there is a good chance that furnishings from the previous residence will fit the new one. Nevertheless, once established in the new city, it is common for such households to make one or more follow-up or 'corrective' moves in response to their increasing awareness of the social ambience of different neighbourhoods and the quality of their schools and shops.

Intra-urban Moves

This brings us conveniently to the general category of intra-urban moves that makes up the bulk of all residential mobility and which therefore merits rather closer consideration. Indeed, a good deal of research effort has been devoted to the task of searching for regularities in intra-urban movement in the belief that such regularities, if they exist, might help to illuminate a key dimension of the sociospatial dialectic: the relationships between residential mobility and urban ecology.

One of the most consistent findings of this research concerns the *distance moved*. In virtually every study, the majority of moves has been found to be relatively short, although the distances involved clearly depend to a certain extent on the overall size of the city concerned. In a national sample of US movers, almost 45 per cent had moved within the same central city, with half of these moves taking place within the same neighbourhood.[8] Results from studies of individual cities are consistent with these findings. Within Minneapolis, for example, the longest moves made by relocating households in 1970–71 were over 20 miles (32 km); but the modal distance moves were nearer to one mile (1.6 km) and about 30 per cent of all the moves involved distances of less than one mile.[9] This tendency for short moves notwithstanding, variability in distance moved is generally explained best by income, race and previous tenure, with higher-income, white, owner-occupier households tending to move furthest.

Directional bias has also been investigated in a number of migration studies, but with rather less consistent results. While it is widely recognized that there is a general tendency for migration to push outward from inner-city neighbourhoods towards the suburbs, reverse flows and cross-currents always exist to complicate the issue. The most significant regularities in intra-urban movement patterns, however, relate to the relative *socio-economic status* of origin and destination areas. The vast majority of moves – about 80 per cent in the United States – take place within census tracts of similar socio-economic characteristics. A parallel and related tendency is for a very high proportion of moves to take place within tenure categories. In other words, relocation within 'community space' and 'housing space' usually involves only short distances. Where transitions do occur between tenure categories, a great deal depends on the ecology of housing supply.[10] It follows from these observations that, while intra-urban mobility may have a significant impact on the spatial express-ion of social and economic cleavages, the overall degree of residential segregation tends to be maintained or even reinforced by relocation processes.

Putting together these empirical regularities in an overall spatial context, we are presented with a threefold zonal division of the city. The innermost zone is characterized by high levels of mobility, which are swollen by the arrival of low-status in-migrants. Similarly, high levels of mobility in the outermost zone are supplemented by the arrival and subsequent follow-up mobility of higher-status in-migrants. Between the two is a zone of relative stability containing households whose housing needs are evidently satisfied. Here, turnover is low simply because few housing opportunities arise, either through vacancies or through new construction. It is probably the existence of such a zone which accounts for longer-distance moves and which helps to explain the sectoral 'leap-frogging' of lower-middle-class and working-class households to new suburban subdivisions and dormitory towns.

In an attempt to throw further light on these patterns, several researchers have undertaken analyses of the spatial correlates of mobility rates. In general, however, the results of such studies have been inconclusive. The most rigorous and systematic analysis of the ecological relationships ex-hibited by rates of residential mobility is that undertaken by Martin Cadwallader. In a study of Canton, Des Moines, Knoxville and Portland, he was able to establish that housing type (i.e. tenure and size charac-teristics) is consistently the single most important determinant of residential mobility, with the lowest rates being associated with neighbourhoods dominated by owner-occupied and single-family dwelling units.[11]

The generalizations made here must be qualified in cities where there is a significant amount of public sector housing, since the entry and transfer rules for public housing are completely different from those in the rest of the housing market. In general this does not distort the overall pattern of household movement, although it is likely that different elements of the pattern will be linked to particular sectors of the housing market. In Glasgow, for example, where the privately rented and owner-occupied sectors are truncated by a massive public sector (in 1993, well over 55 per cent of the city's households lived in publicly owned dwellings), the overall pattern of residential mobility still exhibits the 'typical' components of short distance relocation within the neighbourhood of origin and of out-ward sectoral movement over larger distances. But a closer examination of migration flows reveals that these components are derived in composite fashion from the various flows within and between the main tenure categor-ies. Thus, while short-distance moves dominate both the owner-occupied and public sector (see Figs 9.4 and 9.5), the longer-distance sectoral movements stem from the following:

1. Outward flows of owner-occupiers and council tenants from first-tier suburban neighbourhoods toward peripheral locations outside the city boundary.

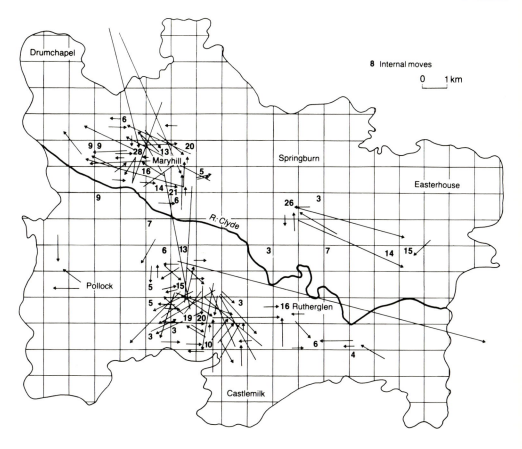

Figure 9.4
Moves within the owner-occupied sector of Glasgow District involving three or more
households, 1974
Source: J. Forbes and I. M. L. Robertson, conference paper, annual meeting of the Institute
of British Geographers, Glasgow, 1978.

2. Outward flows of households from inner-city slum-clearance areas to
    suburban public housing estates.
3. A smaller, inward flow of households moving from public housing to
    older, owner-occupier tenement property nearer the centre of the city.[12]

The Determinants of Residential Mobility

If the outward configuration of intra-urban mobility is difficult to pin
down, its internal dynamics can be even more obscure. The flows of
mobility that shape urban structure derive from aggregate patterns of
demand for accommodation which in turn spring from the complex deliber-
ations of individual households. An understanding of how these

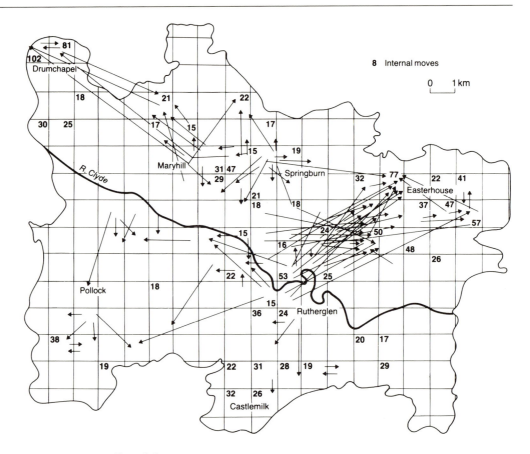

Figure 9.5
Moves into and within public housing in Glasgow District involving 15 or more
households, 1974. Numbers represent the number of internal moves in each grid square
Source: J. Forbes and I. M. L. Robertson, conference paper, annual meeting of the Institute
of British Geographers, Glasgow, 1978.

delibertions are structured is thus likely to provide some insight into the
relocation process, and a considerable amount of attention has therefore
been given by geographers to two important aspects of household behaviour:

1. The decision to seek a new residence.
2. The search for and selection of a new residence.

This two-stage approach is adopted here. First, attention is focused on the
personal, residential and environmental circumstances that appear to precipitate the decision to move, and a conceptual model of the decision to
move is outlined. Subsequently, attention is focused on how this decision
is acted upon, highlighting the bias imposed on locational behaviour by
differential access to, and use of, information.

Reasons for Moving

In any consideration of migration it is important to make a distinction between *voluntary* and *involuntary* moves. As Rossi showed in his classic study of migration in Philadelphia, involuntary moves make up a significant proportion of the total. In Philadelphia, almost a quarter of the moves were involuntary, and the majority of these were precipitated by property demolitions and evictions.[13] Similar findings have been reported from studies of other cities, but remarkably little is known about the locational behaviour of affected households. In addition to these purely involuntary moves is a further category of 'forced' moves arising from marriage, divorce, retirement, ill-health, death in the family, and long-distance job changes. These frequently account for a further 15 per cent of all moves, leaving around 60 per cent as voluntary moves.

Survey data show that the decision to move home voluntarily is attributed to a number of quite different factors. It must be acknowledged, however, that the reasons given for moving in the course of household interviews are not always entirely reliable. Some people have a tendency to rationalize and justify their decisions, others may not be able to recollect past motivations; and most will inevitably articulate reasons that are simpler and more clear-cut than the complex of factors under consideration at the time of the move. Nevertheless, survey data are useful in indicating the major elements which need to be taken into consideration in explaining movement behaviour. Table 9.2 presents the reasons given for moving – both voluntarily and involuntarily – by a large sample of recently moved British households, revealing a mixture of housing, environmental and personal factors. Among the more frequently cited housing factors associated with voluntary moves are complaints about dwelling and garden space, about housing and repair costs and about style obsolescence. Environmental factors encompass complaints about the presence of noxious activities such as factories, about noisy children, and about the incidence of litter, garbage and pet dogs. Personal factors are mostly associated with forced moves, but some voluntary moves are attributed to personal factors, such as a negative reaction to new neighbours. These generalizations tend to hold true for sample populations in North America, Australia and New Zealand, as well as Britain. Figure 9.6 illustrates a general classification of the reasons for household relocation.

Of the more frequently cited reasons for moving, it is generally agreed that the most important and widespread is related to the household's need for dwelling space. More than half of the movers in Rossi's study cited complaints about too much or too little living space as contributing to their desire to move (with 44 per cent giving it as a primary reason). Subsequent surveys have confirmed the decisive importance of living-space in the decision to move and, furthermore, have established that the crucial factor is not so much space *per se* but the relationship between the size and composition of a household and its *perceived* space requirements.[14] Because both of these are closely related to the family life-course,[15] it is widely

Table 9.2 Reasons for wishing to move: British Households, 1976

	%
Housing reasons	
Too large	6
Too small	16
Poor amenities or standard/poor repair	8
Condemned/due for demolition	3
Too expensive	4
Other	10
Total	47
Environmental reasons	
Job/study reasons (change of job, etc.)	21
Other	7
Personal reasons	
Ill health	3
To join relatives/friends	5
Retirement and other	4
Total	12
Other reasons	
To be nearer work	3
Been asked to leave (by landlord)	2
To buy a house/flat	4
Other	3
Total	12
Base (= 100%)	1040

Source: Office of Population Censuses and Surveys, *General Household Survey, 1976*, HMSO, London, p. 164

believed that life-course changes provide the foundation for much of the residential relocation within cities. Moreover, the attractions of the family life-course as an explanatory variable are considerably reinforced by its relationships with several other frequently cited reasons for moving, such as the desire to own (rather than rent) a home and the desire for a change of environmental setting. Changes in household structure and the fragmentation of life-styles in contemporary cities make it difficult, however, to generalize about relationships between residential mobility and family life-course in the way that was possible in the 1960s.[16]

We can say, though, that a marked residential segregation tends to emerge as households at similar stages in their life-course respond in similar ways to their changing domestic and material circumstances. This, of course, fits conveniently with the results of the many descriptive studies (including factorial ecology studies) which have demonstrated a zonal pattern of family status. The generally accepted sequence to these zones runs from a youthful inner-city zone through successive zones of older and middle-aged family types to a zone of late youth/early middle-age on the periphery. It must be acknowledged, however, that such a pattern may be

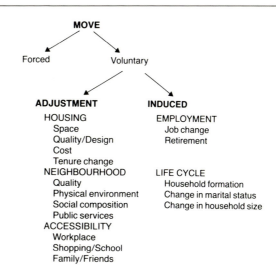

Figure 9.6
A classification of reasons
for household relocation
Source: W. A. V. Clark and
J. L. Onaka, *Urban Studies*,
20, 1983, Fig. 2, p. 50.

the result of factors other than those associated directly with the dynamic of household life-courses. 'Households often undergo changes in their family status at the same time as they experience changes in income and social status,'[17] so it is dangerous to explain mobility exclusively in terms of one or the other. Quite different factors may also be at work. Developers, for example, knowing that many households prefer to live among families similar to their own age and composition as well as socio-economic status, have reinforced family status segregation by building apartment complexes and housing estates for specific household types, with exclusionary covenants and contracts designed to keep out 'non-conforming' residents. It is thus quite common for entire condominiums to be inhabited by single people or by childless couples. The extreme form of this phenomenon is represented by Sun City, a satellite suburb of Phoenix, Arizona, where no resident under the age of 50 is allowed, and where the whole townscape is dominated by the design needs of the elderly, who whir along the quiet streets in golf caddy-cars, travelling from one social engagement to the next. In contrast, much of the family status segregation in British cities with large amounts of public housing can be attributed to the letting policies of local authorities, since eligibility for public housing is partly a product of household size (see pp. 145–9).

The Decision to Move

The first major decision in the residential mobility process – whether or not to move home – can be viewed as a product of the *stress* generated by discordance between a household's needs, expectations and aspirations on the one hand and its actual housing conditions and environmental setting on the other (Fig. 9.7). While the nature of the stresses associated with

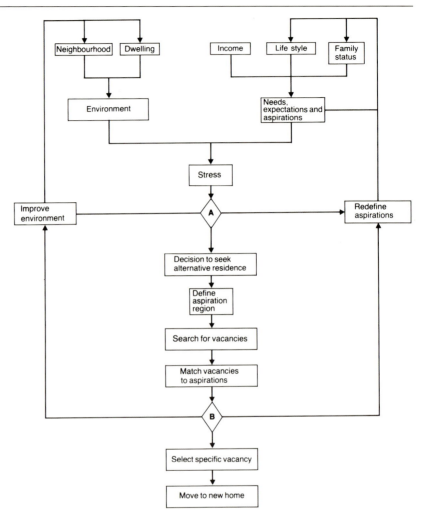

Figure 9.7
A model of residential
mobility
Source: B. Robson, *Urban Social Areas*, 1975, p.33.

housing and environmental conditions should be clear, it is necessary at this point to elaborate upon the idea of people's housing *expectations* and *aspirations*. Basically, these are thought by behaviouralists to stem from the different frames of reference that people adopt in making sense of their lives and, in particular, in interpreting their housing situation. These frames of reference are the product of a wide range of factors which includes age, class background, religion, ethnic origin, and past experience of all aspects of urban life. What they amount to is a series of *life-styles* – privatized, familistic, cosmopolitan, and so on – each with a distinctive set of orientations in relation to housing and residential location. We can recognize three traditional life-style orientations in urban cultures: family, career and consumption.[18]

Family-oriented people are also home-centred and tend to spend much of their spare time with their children. As a result, their housing orientations are dominated by their perceptions of their children's needs for play space, a clean, safe environment, proximity to child clinics and school, and so on. Bell found that 83 per cent of the households in his sample who had moved to suburban locations in Chicago had done so 'for the sake of the children'.

Careerists have a life-style centred on career advancement. Since movement is often a necessary part of this process, careerists tend to be highly mobile; and since they are, by definition, status-conscious, their housing orientations tend to be focused on prestige neighbourhoods appropriate to their jobs, their salary and their self-image.

Consumerists are strongly oriented towards enjoying the material benefits and amenities of modern urban society, and their housing preferences are therefore dominated by a desire to live in downtown areas, close to clubs, theatres, art galleries, discothèques, restaurants, and so on.

Bell's typology can be criticized for its middle-class tenor, since it overlooks the 'life-style' of the large number of households whose economic position reduces their housing aspirations to the level of survival. Many working-class households view their homes as havens from the outside world rather than as platforms for the enactment of a favoured life-style. This limitation, however, is allowed for by the behaviouralist model outlined in Fig. 9.7. Quite simply, households with more modest incomes are expected to aspire only to housing which meets their minimum absolute needs. The latter are generally held to be a function of family size, so that the idea of life-course-related mobility plugs in conveniently to the behaviouralist model without equating stress automatically with mobility.

Whatever the household's expectations and aspirations may be, the crucial determinant of the decision to move is the intensity of the stress (if any) generated as a result of the difference between these and its actual circumstances. The point where tolerable stress becomes intolerable strain will be different for each household but, once it is reached (at point 'A' on Fig. 9.7) the household must decide between three avenues of behaviour:

1. *Environmental improvement*: this embraces a wide range of activities, depending on the nature of the stressors involved. Small dwellings can be enlarged with an extension, cold dwellings can have central heating, double glazing and wall cavity insulation installed, dilapidated dwellings can be rewired and redecorated, and over-large dwellings can be filled by taking in lodgers. Neighbourhood or 'situational' stressors can also be countered in various ways: inaccessibility to shops and amenities, for example, can be tackled through the purchase of a car or by petitioning the local authority to provide better bus services. Environmental degradation and intrusive land-users can be tackled through residents' associations and action committees; and undesirable neighbours can be harassed or ostracized. As with other aspects of residential behaviour, these strategies vary in their appeal according to household circumstances. Owner-occupiers, for example, are much more likely to opt for neighbourhood activism than renters.

2. *Lowering aspirations*: this is an alternative means of coming to terms with existing housing conditions. It appears to be a common strategy, since survey data show that for every household that moves there are two or three more who report that they would like to move if they could. Lowering aspirations may involve a change in life-style or a reformulation of plans: the decision to have children may be deferred, for example. More commonly it is simply a psychological matter of 'dissonance reduction' – learning to like what one has and to become indifferent to what one knows one cannot get. Not surprisingly, the older people get, the more proficient they become at dissonance reduction.

3. *Residential relocation*: this, as we have seen, is the course chosen by a large minority of households. The decision to move, however, leads to a second important area of locational behaviour: the search for and selection of a new residence.

The Search for a New Residence

Whether the decision to move is voluntary or involuntary, all relocating households must go through the procedure of searching for suitable vacancies and then deciding upon the most appropriate new home. The chief interest of geographers in this procedure lies in the question of whether it is spatially biased and, if so, whether it is biased in different ways for different groups of households. In other words, do spatially biased search procedures contribute to the changing social ecology? Although information on the way people behave in looking for a new home is rather fragmentary, the general process is conveniently encompassed within the decision-making framework of Brown and Moore's behavioural model (Fig. 9.7). Accordingly, it is useful to break down household behaviour into three stages:

1. The specification of criteria for evaluating vacancies.
2. The search for dwellings which satisfy these criteria.
3. The final choice of a new dwelling.

Specifying the Desiderata of a New Home

In behaviouralist terms, the household's first step in coping with the problem of acquiring and organizing information about potential new dwelling is to define, consciously or subconsciously, its *aspiration region*. Quite simply, this is a conception of the limits of acceptability which a household is prepared to entertain as an alternative to its current accommodation. These limits may be defined in terms of the desired *site* characteristics – attributes of the dwelling itself – and/or the desired *situational* characteristics – the physical and social environment of the neighbourhood, its proximity to schools, shops, etc. The lower limits of the aspiration region are commonly defined by the characteristics of the dwelling the household wants to leave, while the upper limits are set by the standards to which the household can reasonably aspire. In many cases these will be determined by income constraints, but there are important exceptions: some householders, for example, may not want to take on a large garden, regardless of house price; others may rule out affordable dwellings in certain areas because the neighbourhood does not conform with their desired life-style.

In general, the criteria used by households in specifying their aspiration region reflect their motivations in deciding to move. We can thus expect living-space, tenure, dwelling amenities, environmental quality and social composition to be among the more frequently used criteria. This is confirmed by Table 9.3, which compares the reasons given for moving with those given for selecting a new residence by a sample of Toronto households. But, in addition to the broad correspondence between the two, it is worth noting that some of the criteria used in evaluating the new residence are largely unrelated to the problems encountered in the previous residence. Interior aspects of the dwelling, the social characteristics of the neighbourhood and accessibility to various facilities are more important in attracting people to a new home than in propelling them away, for example. It also appears that movers of different types tend to differ quite a lot in the criteria they use. In Toronto, households moving to houses were more likely to be concerned with situational characteristics than those moving to apartments. Furthermore, those moving to suburban houses tended to be particularly concerned with the layout of the dwelling and its potential as an investment, whereas for those moving to downtown houses the aesthetics of dwelling style and the neighbourhood environment tended to be a

Table 9.3 Motivations associated with intra-urban mobility, Toronto

Reasons*	For move away from current home (%)	For a choice of a new residence (%)
Unit interior size and layout	17.0	23.7
Unit interior features	3.1	4.7
Exterior setting	16.8	17.3
Dwelling unit	20.2	10.2
Neighbourhood	12.4	19.0
Access	7.1	17.4
Family composition	15.0	1.3
Interaction with people	1.1	0.2
Leisure activities	0.6	0.4
Fiscal considerations	8.0	6.0
Other	0.8	0.1
Total reasons	2658	4019

*Up to but not necessarily four reasons per person
Source: W. Michelson, *Environmental Choice, Human Behaviour and Residential Satisfaction*, Oxford University Press, New York, 1977, pp. 115 and 112.

more important criterion.[19] The existence of differently conceived aspiration regions is, of course, a function of the different needs and aspirations which prompt households to move in the first place. Their significance to the relocation process lies not only in the consequent variability in the evaluation of particular housing opportunities, but also in the fact that households set out from the very start to look for vacancies with quite different housing goals in mind.

Searching for Vacancies

The general objective of the search procedure is to find the right kind of dwelling, at the right price, in the time available. It must be acknowledged that there are some households that do not have to search deliberately because their decision to move has come after accidentally discovering an attractive vacancy. These 'windfall' moves may account for as many as 25 per cent of all intra-urban moves. The majority of movers, though, must somehow organize themselves into finding a suitable home within a limited period of deciding to relocate. Most households organize the search procedure in locational terms, focusing attention on particular neighbourhoods which are selected on the basis of their perceived *situational* characteristics and the household's evaluation of the probability of finding vacancies satisfying their *site* criteria. Moreover, faced with the problem of searching even a limited amount of space, it is natural that households will attempt to reduce further both effort and uncertainty by concentrating their search in areas which are best known and most accessible to them.[20]

The upshot is that households concentrate their house-hunting activities within a limited *search space* that is spatially biased by their familiarity with different districts. In behaviouralist terminology, this search space is a subset of a more general *awareness space*, which is usually regarded as a product of:

- people's *activity space* or *action space* (the sum of all the places with which people have regular contact as a result of their normal activities), and
- information from secondary sources such as radio, television, newspapers, and even word-of-mouth.

Both elements are subject to a mental filtering and coding that produces a set of imagery that constitutes the operational part of the individual's awareness space. The subset of this space that constitutes the search space is simply the area (or areas) that a household feels to be relevant to its aspiration region, and it is spatially biased because of the inherent bias in both activity spaces and mental maps. It follows that *different subgroups of households, with distinctive activity spaces and mental maps, will tend to exhibit an equally distinctive spatial bias in their search behaviour*. In particular, we may expect the more limited activity spaces and more localized and intensive images of the home area to limit the search space of low-income households to a relatively small area centred on the previous home, while more mobile, higher-income households will have a search space which is more extensive but focused on the most familiar sector of the city between home and workplace.

The *information sources* used to find vacant dwellings within the search space can also exert a significant spatial bias. Moreover, since different types of households tend to rely on different sequences and combinations of sources, there results a further process of sociospatial sorting. Overall, the most frequently used sources of information about housing vacancies are newspaper advertisements, real-estate agents, friends and relatives, and personal observation of 'for sale' signs, although their relative importance and effectiveness seems to vary somewhat from one city to another. Although little research has been done on these information sources, it is clear that each tends to be biased in a different way. Personal observation, for example, will be closely determined by personal activity space, while the quantity and quality of information from friends and relatives will depend a lot on social class and the structure of the searcher's social networks. Real-estate agents also exert a considerable spatial bias in their role as mediators of information. This has been shown to operate in two ways: first, each business tends to specialize in limited portions of the housing market in terms of both price and area; second, while most estate agents have a fairly accurate knowledge of the city-wide housing market, they tend to over-recommend dwellings in the area in which they are most experienced in selling and listing accommodation and with which they are most familiar. As a result, 'households which are dependent on realty salesmen for information . . . are making use of a highly structured and spatially limited information source'.[21]

The critical issue in the present context, however, is the *relative importance and effectiveness of different information sources for different households*. Again, empirical evidence is rather patchy, but survey data do suggest a marked variation in the emphasis that different movers put on different sources. In Toronto, for example, several sharp differences emerged. Newspaper advertisements were a much more effective source of information for households searching for an apartment than for those searching for a house. Conversely, real-estate agents were consulted mainly about houses, proving a very effective source (in the sense that a high proportion of movers eventually found their new homes as a result of information obtained from estate agents rather than from other sources), particularly for housing in the downtown area. Personal observation (in the form of 'driving around'), on the other hand, was a more popular and effective source of information for suburban house-hunters.[22]

Accessibility to information channels is also related to another important issue affecting residential behaviour: the problem of *search barriers*. There are two important aspects of this problem: barriers that raise the costs of searching or gathering information, and barriers that explicitly limit the choice of housing units or locations available to households.[23] Factors related to search costs include, for example, lack of transportation for searching and lack of child care facilities while searching, as well as lack of knowledge about specific information channels. Factors that limit housing choice include financial constraints, discrimination in the housing market and the housing quality standards of rent assistance programmes.

Time Constraints

This differential use and effectiveness clearly serves to increase the degree of sociospatial sorting arising from residential mobility, while at the same time making it more complex. Another important compounding factor in this sense is the constraint of *time* in the search procedure. Both search space and search procedures are likely to alter as households spend increasing amounts of time and money looking for a new home. When time starts to run out, the search strategy must change to ensure that a home will be found. Anxiety produced by a lack of success may result in a modification of the household's aspiration region, a restriction of their search space and a shift in their use of information sources; and the pressure of time may lead people to make poor choices. On the other hand, the longer the search goes on, the greater the household's knowledge of the housing market. Each household therefore has to balance the advantages of searching and learning against the costs – real and psychological – of doing so. This dilemma is analogous to the so-called 'marriage problem', which has been stated (from a male point of view) as follows:

> A known number, *n*, of ladies are presented to you one at a time in random order. After inspecting any number *r* (1≤ *r* ≤ *n*) of them you are able to rank them from best to worst and this order will not be changed if the (*r* + 1)th lady is inspected; she will merely be inserted into the order. At any stage of the 'game' you may either propose to the lady *then being inspected* (there is no going back!), when the game stops, or inspect the next lady; however, if you reach the last lady you have to propose. All proposals are accepted. What is the optimum strategy?[24]

Statistical probability models have been developed in order to devise the optimal 'stopping rule' for this type of problem. Evidently the optimal strategy in the marriage problem is to pass by all opportunities of marriage until the age of 26, and then propose to the first person who compares favourably with the best of those encountered before. The probability of marrying the 'best' possible partner in this way is, rather dauntingly, estimated at just over 36 per cent.[25] No such bold conclusions have yet been derived for house-hunting, although the bases of a relatively sophisticated stopping-rule model for house-hunting have been outlined.[26] One of the difficulties in operationalizing such models, however, is the variability of personality and psychological factors in decision-making. Conservative households, for example, may tend to take an acceptable vacancy instead of pushing on to find a better deal.

Survey data in fact show a consistent tendency for the majority of households to consider seriously only a few vacancies (usually, only two or three) before selecting a new home, an observation which may appear to undermine the utility of developing elaborate models and theories of search behaviour. Nevertheless, this phenomenon can itself be explained with a behaviouralist framework: households are able to reduce the element of uncertainty in their decision-making by restricting serious consideration to only a few vacancies. Moreover, most households begin with an aspiration region that is quite narrowly defined (either because of income constraints or locational requirements), so that what appears to be an inhibited search pattern is in fact a logical extension of the decisions formulated in the preceding stage of the search procedure.

Choosing a New Home
Households that find two or more vacancies within their aspiration region must eventually make a choice. Theoretically, this kind of choice is made on the basis of household *utility functions* that are used to give a subjective rating to each vacancy. In other words, vacancies are evaluated in terms of the weighted sum of the attributes used to delineate the aspiration region. These weights reflect the relative importance of the criteria used to specify the aspiration region, and so they will vary according to the preferences and predilections of the household concerned. Difficulties arise, however, in attempting to operationalize the theory for more than one household at a time, when non-transitive preferences and the 'paradox of majority rule' wreak havoc with the theoretical elegance of utility functions.[27]

Nevertheless, it is clear that some criteria are given greater weight than others. A national survey of US movers, for example, discovered an overall tendency:

- for people to value neighbourhood quality more than housing quality and accessibility;
- to value interior style and appearance more than the exterior style and appearance of a dwelling;
- to prefer neighbourhoods with better-than-average schools and relatively high local taxes to those with lower taxes but poorer schools.[28]

What is not properly known, though, is the nature of differences in the housing preferences of different demographic and socio-economic groups. Without this kind of information, few inferences can be made about the nature of sociospatial outcomes, if any, associated with the choice of housing. It has been suggested that the constraints of time, coupled with the limitations of human information-processing abilities and a general lack of motivation, mean that a real choice of the kind implied in behaviouralist theory is seldom made: people are happy to take any reasonable vacancy, so long as it does not involve a great deal of inconvenience.[29]

It should also be noted that the basic behavioural model allows for those households that are unable to find vacancies within their aspiration region in the time available to them (point 'B' on Fig. 9.7) to change their strategy to one of the two options open to them at point 'A' on the diagram: environmental improvement or a redefinition of aspirations.

Finally, we must recognize that there are many households in every city whose residential location is constrained to the point where behavioural approaches are of marginal significance. The most obvious subgroup here is low-income households. Larry Bourne has suggested that at least one-third of all households in most cities have little or no choice in their housing. 'These people may be the real working poor, the elderly, the very young, the unemployed, or the transient. In any case, their numbers are large.'[30] Other subgroups whose residential choice is heavily constrained include households who have special needs (e.g. large families, single-parent families, non-married couples, former inmates of institutions and 'problem' families); households who cannot relocate because of personal handicaps, family situations or medical needs; and households who are unwilling to move because of the psychological stress of moving from familiar environments.

9.2 Residential Mobility and Neighbourhood Change

Although the behavioural approach provides important insights into the spatial implications of mobility, the emphasis on individual decision-making tends to divert attention from the aggregate patterns of neighbourhood change which result 'as like individuals make like choices'.[31] In this section, therefore, some consideration is given to the macro-scale generalizations which have been advanced about processes of mobility and neighbourhood change.

One scheme that has already been introduced and discussed is the zonal patterning of socio-economic status associated with the sequence of invasion–succession–dominance postulated by Burgess in his model of ecological change (see pp. 167–9). The dynamic of this model, it will be recalled, was based on the pressure of low-status in-migrants arriving in inner-city areas. As this pressure increases, some families penetrate surrounding neighbourhoods, thus initiating a chain reaction whereby the residents of each successively higher status zone are forced to move further out from the centre in order to counter the lowering of neighbourhood status. Notwithstanding the criticisms of ecological theory *per se*, with its heavy reliance on biotic analogy, the concept of invasion–succession–dominance provides a useful explanatory framework for the observed sequence of neighbourhood change in cities where rapid urban growth is fuelled by large-scale in-migration of low-status families. The classic example, of course, was Chicago during the 1920s and 1930s, although many of the industrial cities in Britain had undergone a similar process of neighbourhood change during the nineteenth century. More recently, the flow of immigrants to London, Paris and larger Australian cities such as Melbourne and Sydney and the flow of *gastarbeiter* to the industrial cities of northwestern Europe has generated a sequence of change in some neighbourhoods which also fits the invasion/succession model. Nevertheless, this model is of limited relevance to most modern cities, since its driving force – the inflow of low-status migrants – is of diminishing importance; the bulk of in-migrants is now accounted for by middle-income families moving from a suburb in one city to a similar suburb in another.

High-status Movement, Filtering and Vacancy Chains

An alternative view of neighbourhood change and residential mobility stems from Homer Hoyt's model of urban growth and socio-economic structure. Hoyt's ideas were derived from a detailed study of rental values in 142 US cities which was undertaken in order to classify neighbourhood types according to their mortgage lending risk.[32] This study led him to believe that the key to urban residential structure is to be found in the behaviour of high-status households. These, he argued, pre-empt the most desirable land in the emerging city, away from industrial activity. With urban growth, the high-status area expands axially along natural routeways, in response to the desire among the well-off to combine accessibility with suburban living. This sectoral movement is reinforced by a tendency among 'community leaders' to favour non-industrial waterside sites and higher ground; and for the rest of the higher-income groups to seek the social cachet of living in the same neighbourhood as these *prominenti*. Further sectoral development occurs when dissatisfaction with their existing housing prompts a move outwards to new housing in order to maintain standards of exclusivity. In the wake of this continual outward movement of high-status households, the housing they vacate is occupied by middle-status households whose own housing is in turn occupied by lower-status households. At the end of this chain of movement, the vacancies created by the lowest-status groups are either demolished or occupied by low-status in-migrants. Subsequently, as other residential areas also expand outwards, the sectoral structure of the city will be preserved, with zonal components emerging as a secondary element because of variations in the age and condition of the housing stock.

The validity of Hoyt's sectoral model has been much debated. Empirical studies of the emerging pattern of élite residential areas and tests of the existence of sectoral gradients in socio-economic status have provided a good deal of general support for the spatial configuration of Hoyt's model, although the relative dominance of sectoral over zonal components in urban structure is by no means a simple or universal phenomenon.

It is the *mechanism* of neighbourhood change implied in Hoyt's model which is of interest here, however. The basis of this mechanism is the chain of moves initiated by the construction of new dwellings for the wealthy, resulting in their older properties *filtering* down the social scale while individual households *filter up* the housing scale. In order for this filtering process to operate at a sufficient level to have any real impact on urban structure, there has to be more new construction than that required simply to replace the deteriorating housing of the élite. According to Hoyt, this will be ensured by the *obsolescence* of housing as well as its physical deterioration. For the rich, there are several kinds of obsolescence which may trigger a desire for new housing. Advances in kitchen technology and heating systems and the innovation of new luxury features such as swimming pools, saunas and jacuzzis may cause 'functional obsolescence', while more general social and economic changes may cause obsolescence of a different kind: the trend away from large families combined with a relative increase in the cost of domestic labour, for example, has made large free-standing dwellings something of a white elephant.

Changes in design trends may also cause obsolescence – 'style obsolescence' – in the eyes of those who can afford to be sensitive to architectural fads and fashions. Finally, given a tax structure that allows mortgage repayments to be offset against taxable income (as in Britain and many other Western countries), dwellings may become 'financially obsolescent' as increases in household income and/or inflation reduce the relative size of mortgage repayments (and therefore of tax relief). Driven on to new housing by one or more of these factors, the wealthy will thus create a significant number of vacancies which the next richest group will be impelled to fill through a desire for a greater quantity and/or quality of housing. This desire can be seen not only as the manifestation of a general preference for better housing but also as a result of the influence of changing housing needs associated with the family life cycle. In addition, the social and economic pressures resulting from proximity to the poorest groups in society may prompt those immediately above them to move as soon as the opportunity presents itself, either by moving into vacancies created by the construction of new housing for others or by moving out into subdivisions specially constructed for the lower-middle classes.

Obstacles to Filtering

In practice, however, the dynamics of the housing market is rather more complex than this. To begin with, vacancy chains may start in other ways than the construction of new housing. A substantial proportion of vacancies arise through the subdivision of dwelling units into flats and the conversion of non-residential property to residential uses. Even more occur through the death of a household, through the move of an existing household to share accommodation with another, and through emigration outside the city. Similarly, vacancy chains may be ended in several ways other than the demolition of the worst dwellings or their occupation by poor in-migrants. Some vacancies are rendered ineffective through conversion to commercial use, while others may be cancelled out by rehabilitation or conversion schemes which involve knocking two or more dwellings into one. Vacancy chains will also end if the household which moves into a vacant dwelling is a 'new' one and so leaves no vacancy behind for others to fill. This may arise through the marriage of a couple who had both previously been living with friends or parents, through divorced people setting up separate homes, or through the splitting of an existing household with, for example, a son or daughter moving out to his or her own flat.

A closer examination of the filtering process between the start and finish of vacancy chains also reveals a certain amount of complexity. This is not helped by the lack of agreement on how to measure the process, despite a lengthy and often bitter debate in the literature. Among the more straight-forward definitions of filtering is that proposed by Grigsby, who suggests that 'filtering only occurs when value declines more rapidly than quality so that families can obtain either higher quality and more space at the same price or the same quality and space at a lower price than formerly'.[33] This clearly comes close to the conception of filtering in Hoyt's model. It is also useful in emphasizing the role of filtering not just as a mechanism of intra-urban mobility but also as a means of facilitating a general improvement of housing conditions as new houses filter down the social scale.

This aspect of filtering has attracted more attention than any other because of its policy implications, since it can be argued that facilitating new housebuilding for higher income groups will result in an eventual improvement in the housing conditions of the poor through the natural process of filtering, without recourse to public intervention in the housing market. This argument has a long history, dating to the paternalistic logic of nineteenth-century housing reformers who used it to justify the construction of model housing for the 'industrious' and 'respectable' working classes rather than the poorest sections of society to whom their efforts were ostensibly directed. Subsequently, it became the central plank of government housing policy in many countries. Up to the 1930s, Britain relied almost entirely on the filtering process to improve the housing conditions of the working classes, while it still remains the basis of US housing strategy.

Vacancy Chains

The general validity of the filtering concept is not disputed, apart from the obvious exception of movement into and within the public sector. Many of the once-fashionable quarters of the rich, now subdivided into flats and bed-sitters, can be seen to be occupied by distinctly less prosperous families, students, single-person households and the aged. What is not clear, however, is the impact of this process on different social groups and different neighbourhoods. Relatively few studies have been able to furnish detailed empirical evidence, and their results are rather inconclusive. One of the most comprehensive analyses of vacancy chains so far undertaken is that by Lansing, Clifton and Morgan in the United States. They sought to answer a series of questions, including 'what is the economic level of people who move into new housing? If rich people move into new housing, do poor people benefit directly by moving into vacancies further along in the sequence? Or do the sequences stop before they reach low income people?'[34]

An examination of over 1100 vacancy chains generated by the construction of new dwellings showed that while the average sequence of moves thus initiated was 3.5, those resulting from the construction of more expensive houses were roughly twice as long as those resulting from the construction of cheaper houses and rental units. It was also found that a majority of the families moving into a dwelling had a lower income and socio-economic status than the previous occupants. At the same time, almost two-thirds of the moves resulted in an increase in dwelling space. It is also interesting to note in relation to both Hoyt's model and the household life-course model that the average distance from the centre of the city was found to decrease with each successive link in the chain, and that whereas over 40 per cent of the households moving into a house were at an 'earlier' stage in the life-course than families moving out, only 28 per cent were at a later stage.

These results seem to suggest that an upward filtering of households does arise from the construction of new homes for the wealthy. Nevertheless, closer inspection of the results shows that the benefits to poor families (in terms of vacant housing opportunities) are not in proportion to their numbers, *suggesting that filtering is unlikely to be an important agent of neighbourhood change in poor areas.* Moreover, the fact that a large proportion of the vacancy chains ended through the formation of 'new' households while only a small proportion ended through demolitions also suggests that the filtering mechanism rarely penetrates the lower spectrum of the housing market to any great extent.

In summary, filtering offers a useful but nevertheless partial explanation of patterns of neighbourhood change. Among the factors that can be identified as inhibiting the hypothesized sequence of movement arising from new high-status housing are:

1. The failure of high income housing construction to keep pace with the overall rate of new household formation and in-migration.
2. The structure of income distribution which, since higher-income groups constitute a relatively small class, means that the houses they vacate in preference for new homes are demanded by a much larger group, thus maintaining high prices and suppressing the process of filtering.
3. The inertia and non-economic behaviour of some households. This includes many of the behavioural patterns discussed above, although the most striking barrier to the filtering process is the persistence of élite neighbourhoods in symbolically prestigious inner-city locations.
4. The existence of other processes of neighbourhood change – related to invasion/succession, household life courses, gentrification, etc.[35] – whose dynamic is unrelated to the construction of new, high-income housing.

SUGGESTED
READING

A thorough review of the issues covered in this chapter is provided by Martin Cadwallader in his book, *Migration and Residential Mobility* (1992: University of Wisconsin, Madison; see especially Chapters 5 and 6), which also provides a discussion of the overall theoretical frameworks within which residential mobility can be understood. Useful literature reviews can be found in M. Munro's chapter in Michael Pacione's edited volume, *Social Geography: Progress and Prospect* (1987: Croom Helm, Beckenham), and in Patricia Gober's review of the literature on urban housing demography (1992: *Progress in Human Geography*, **16**, 171–189). Coverage of behavioural models and analyses is provided by W.A.V. Clark's edited volume, *Modelling Housing Market Search* (1982: Croom Helm, Beckenham).

NOTES

1. White, P. Levels of intra-urban migration in Western European cities: A comparative analysis, *Espaces, Populations, Societies*, **1**, 1985, 129–137.

2. Hamnett, C., The relationship between residential migration and housing tenure in London, 1971–1981: a longitudinal analysis, *Environment & Planning A*, **23**, 1991, 1147–1162; Poot, J., Estimating duration-of-residence distributions: age, sex, and occupational differentials in New Zealand, *New Zealand Geographer*, **43**, 1987, 23–32.

3. See, for example, Dahman, D., *Locals and Cosmopolitans. Patterns of Spatial Mobility during the Transition from Youth to Early Adulthood.* Research Paper 204. Chicago: University of Chicago, Department of Geography, 1982.

4. Van Arsdol, M.D., Jr *et al.*, Retrospective and subsequent metropolitan residential mobility, *Demography*, **5**, 1968, 266.

5. Feitelson, E., An hierarchical approach to the segmentation of residential demand: theory and application, *Environment & Planning A*, **25**, 1993, 553–569.

6. Clark, W.A.V. and E. Moore, *Population Mobility and Residential Change.* Northwestern University Studies in Geography, No. 25. Evanston, Illinois, 1978.

7. Johnston, R. J., Population movements and metropolitan expansion, *Transactions, Institute of British Geographers*, **46**, 1969, 69–91.

8. Butler, E. W. *et al.*, *Moving Behavior and Residential Choice: A National Survey.* National Co-operative Highway Research Program Report no. 81, Highway Research Board, Washington, DC, 1969.

9. Nordstrand, E. A., Relationships between intra-urban migration and urban residential social structure. M.A. Thesis, University of Minnesota, 1973.

10. Duerloo, M. C., W. A. V. Clark and F. M. Dieleman, Choice of residential environment in the Randstad, *Urban Studies*, **27**, 1990, 335–351.

11. Cadwallader, M., A unified model of urban housing patterns, social patterns, and residential mobility, *Urban Geography*, **2**, 1981, 115–130.

12. Forbes, J. and I. M. L. Robertson, Intra-urban migration in Greater Glasgow. Paper given to the Population Studies Group of the Institute of British Geographers, Glasgow, September, 1978.

13. Rossi, P. *Why Families Move*, 2nd edn. Glencoe, IL: Free Press, 1980.

14. Clark, W. A. V. *et al.*, Housing consumption and residential mobility, *Annals, Association of American Geographers*, **74,** 1984, 29–43.

15. Clausen, J. A., *The life course: A Sociological Perspective*. Englewood Cliffs, NJ: Prentice-Hall, 1986.

16. The original formulation of the 'family life-cycle' model can be found in Abu-Lughod, J. and M. M. Foley, Consumer strategies. In N. Foote *et al.* (eds) *Housing Choices and Constraints*. New York: McGraw-Hill, 1960, pp. 387–447. For a more contemporary perspective, see Gober, P., K. E. McHugh and N. Reid, Phoenix in flux: household instability, residential mobility, and neighborhood change, *Annals, Association of American Geographers*, **81,** 1991, 80–88.

17. Adams, J. S. and K, Gilder, Household location and intra-urban migration. In D. T. Herbert and R. J. Johnston (eds), *Social Areas in Cities*, Vol. 1, *Spatial Processes and Form*. Chichester: Wiley, 1976, p. 165.

18. Bell, W., The city, the suburb, and a theory of social choice. In S. Greer *et al.* (eds), *The New Urbanization*. New York: St Martin's, 1968, pp. 132–168.

19. Michelson, W., *Environmental Choice, Human Behaviour, and Residential Satisfaction*. New York: Oxford University Press, 1977.

20. Huff, J. O., Geographic regularities in residential search behavior, *Annals, Association of American Geographers*, **76,** 1986, 208–227.

21. Palm, R., The role of real estate agents as mediators in two American cities, *Geografiska Annaler*, **58B,** 1976, 28.

22. Michelson, *Environmental Choice*.

23. Weisbrod, G. and A. Vidal, Housing search barriers for low-income renters, *Urban Affairs Quarterly*, **16,** 1981, 465–482.

24. Lindley, D. V., Dynamic programming and decision theory, *Applied Statistics*, **10,** 1961, 47.

25. *Ibid.*

26. See, for example, Flowerdew, R., Search strategies and stopping rules in residential mobility, *Transactions, Institute of British Geographers*, **1,** 1976, 47–57; Clark, W. A. V., *Modelling Housing Market Search*. New York: St Martin's; Phipps, A. G. and W. H. Laverty, Optimal stopping and residential search behavior, *Geographical Analysis*, **15,** 1983, 187–204.

27. Arrow, K. J., *Social Choice and Individual Values*. New York: Wiley, 1951.

28. Butler *et al.*, *Moving Behaviour*.

29. Lyon, S. and M. E. Wood, Choosing a house, *Environment & Planning A*, **9,** 1977, 1169–1176.

30. Bourne, L. S., *The Geography of Housing*. London: Edward Arnold, 1981, p. 143.

31. Rees, P., Concepts of social space. In B. J. L. Berry and F. Horton (eds), *Geographic Perspectives on Urban Systems*. Englewood Cliffs, NJ: Prentice-Hall, 1970, p. 313.

32. Hoyt, H., *The Structure and Growth of Residential Neighborhoods in American Cities*. Washington, DC: Federal Housing Administration, 1939.

33. Grigsby, W. G., *Housing Markets and Public Policy*. Philadelphia: University of Pennsylvania Press, 1963, p. 97.

34. Lansing, J. B., C. W. Clifton, and J. N. Morgan, *New Homes and Poor People: A Study of Chains of Moves*. Ann Arbor: University of Michigan Institute for Social Research, 1969.

35. See, for example, Beauregard, R., Trajectories of neighbourhood change: the case of gentrification, *Environment & Planning A*, **22,** 1990, 855–874.

Infill offices and apartments,
Alexandria, Virginia.
Photograph by Paul Knox.

10   *Urban change and conflict*

Accessibility to Services and Amenities • Urban Restructuring: Inequality and Conflict

Much of the stress that is central to behaviouralists' approaches to urban social geography derives from households' desire to maximize the net *externalities* of urban life. Externalities, sometimes called 'spillover' or 'third-party' effects, are unpriced by-products of the production or consumption of goods and services of all kinds. An externality effect exists if the activity of one person, group or institution impinges on the welfare of others. The classic example is the factory which pollutes local air and water supplies in the course of its operations, bringing *negative* externalities to nearby residents. In contrast, well-kept public parks produce *positive* externalities for most nearby residents. The behaviour of private individuals also gives rise to externality effects. These can be divided into 'public behaviour' externalities and 'status' externalities. The former include people's behaviour in relation to public comportment (e.g. quiet, sobriety and tidiness), the upkeep of property and the upbringing of children. Status externalities relate to the 'reflected glory' (or otherwise) of living in a distinctive neighbourhood. Externality effects therefore can take a variety of forms. They are, moreover, very complex in operation. Consider, for example, the behaviour of a household in adding an imitation stone façade to the exterior of their house, adding new coach lamps as finishing touches to their work. For one neighbour this activity may generate a positive externality in the form of improved environmental quality; but for another, with different tastes in design, it may produce an equally strong negative externality effect.

For the geographer, much of the significance of externality effects stems from the fact that their intensity is usually a function of relative location. In other words, externalities may be regarded as having a spatially limited 'field'. Figure 10.1 shows the example of two types of externality fields surrounding a sports stadium located in the middle of a residential area. Note that the noise nuisance is much more localized than the nuisance of parked cars, and that the latter does not exhibit a simple distance gradient from the stadium. David Harvey makes a useful distinction between the *price of accessibility* to desirable urban amenities and the *costs of proximity* to the unwanted aspects of urban life.[1] Both, however, are a product of relative location, and it is clear that the spatial organization of social groups in relation to one another and to the urban infrastructure therefore determines the net intensity of the externality effects which they enjoy. As a general rule, of course, those with the greatest wealth, the most power and the best knowledge will be best placed to reap the benefits of positive externalities and to fend off activities which generate negative externalities. 'The unequal distribution of power, wealth and prestige created by the occupational structure may be simply reinforced in a given locality – so that the less privileged are made even more "less privileged" by differential access to facilities.'[2] The location of public facilities such as transport routes, hospitals, and sports centres is often intended to ameliorate the regressive nature of locational advantage resulting from private competition but the 'hidden mechanisms' of group conflict tend to ensure that the inhabitants of the richest and most powerful neighbourhoods enjoy a large net benefit as a result of decisions affecting the location of public goods and the organization of public services.

It is clear, then, that the pattern of externality fields can exert a powerful influence on people's welfare. Because of this, many commentators regard the social geography of the city as the outcome of conflicts which are worked out in society as a whole between unequally endowed groups seeking to obtain more or less exclusive access to positive externalities and to deflect negative externality fields elsewhere: 'much of what goes on in a city . . . can be interpreted as an attempt to organize the distribution of externality effects to gain income advantages'. Harvey is particularly concerned to show that the form, location and focus of such conflict depends, ultimately, on long-term urban structure changes and broader class conflicts:

> Because changes to the urban fabric introduce new sources of positive and negative externalities, they are potential generators of local conflicts. In the face of such proposed changes, the main protestors are usually those with most to lose: property owners, who perceive possible falls in land values, and parents, who identify potential deterioration in an area's schools. In general, it is the more affluent property owners who have the most to lose, and who, because of their ability to purchase legal and technical advice and their greater knowledge of, and links to, the political systems within which such conflicts are adjudicated, are most likely to prevent changes likely to injure their interests. Such

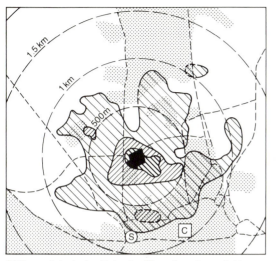
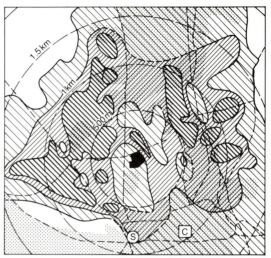

(a) The spatial extent and intensity of the noise nuisance field.   (b) The spatial extent and intensity of the parked cars nuisance

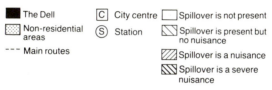

■ The Dell
▨ Non-residential areas
--- Main routes

Ⓒ City centre
Ⓢ Station

☐ Spillover is not present
◩ Spillover is present but no nuisance
▨ Spillover is a nuisance
◪ Spillover is a severe nuisance

Figure 10.1
Negative externality fields around a soccer stadium ('The Dell', Southampton)
Source: Humphreys *et al.*, *Geoforum*, 14, 1983, Figs 4 and 5, p. 405.

> conflicts are usually played out locally, but *their existence is part of the dynamic of capitalist cities*. Alterations in land use are needed if investors are to achieve profits, and if the losers in the conflicts over changes are the less affluent, then the price paid for those changes is substantially carried by them. *Local conflicts are part of the general contest between classes within capitalist society*.[3]

In the long run, one of the principal outcomes of the resolution of locational conflicts is the creation of a set of *de facto* territories on the basis of income and ethnicity as people respond by relocating to neighbourhoods where they can share their positive externalities with one another and are able to avoid, as much possible, those who impose negative externalities. The residents of such territories also attempt to improve and preserve their quality of life through collective action: competing through formal and informal neighbourhood groups and local political institutions to attract the utility-enhancing and keep out the utility-detracting. As we have seen, one of the most common community strategies in this context is that of *voicing* claims over a particular issue, whether by organizing petitions, lobbying politicians and bureaucrats, writing to newspapers, forming local resident groups, picketing, or distributing handbills and posters. This strategy can sometimes extend to illegal activities, such as personal violence, damage to property, sit-ins and deliberate violations of anti-discrimination laws. Alternatively, some communities are able to use formal channels of participation as a profitable strategy when they find themselves in conflict with other communities or institutions. Another 'strategy' available to communities is that of resignation to the imposition of negative externalities. This is especially common where communities feel that voicing strategies are regularly ignored or overruled and that participation is ineffective. Many people who disapprove of city plans, for example, simply resign themselves to the 'inevitable' because they feel unable, individually or collectively, to exert any real influence on policy-makers. The final strategy is that of relocation, or 'exit', which is a household rather than a community strategy, and which brings us back to the idea of a continually evolving geography of *de facto* territories.

10.1 *Accessibility to Services and Amenities*

In every city there is a large number and a great variety of services and amenities – parks, schools, restaurants, theatres, libraries, fire stations, shops, doctors' clinics, hospitals, day care centres, post offices, riverside walks, and so on – that are tied to specific locations and which therefore exhibit externalities with *tapering effects* (i.e. decreasing intensity with distance from a fixed point). To these we must add certain place-specific disamenities and the noxious activities associated with some services: refuse dumps and crematoria, for example; and we must recognize that what constitutes an amenity to some (a school, or a soccer stadium, for example) may represent a disamenity to others. From another perspective, it is clear that some externalities apply only to users while others apply to whole neighbourhoods. In addition, we must recognize that each individual service or amenity may generate several different types of externality effect, as in the example of the soccer stadium (Fig. 10.1). Finally, we must recognize that the *intensity* of the externality effects will also vary according to people's preferred distance from particular services or amenities (Fig. 10.2). We are thus faced with a very complex set of phenomena.

The externalities associated with physical proximity to services, amenities and disamenities not only prompt competition and conflict between households within different housing markets but also precipitate collective political strategies, including the formation of coalitions between different institutions and organizations and the propagation of distinctive *de facto* communities whose mutuality involves life-styles which are dependent to some extent on accessibility to specific amenities.

These coalitions and communities represent the major protagonists in much of the conflict over the preservation and fortification of the relative quality of life in different urban settings. It should be noted, however, that

Figure 10.2
Preferred residential distance from different public facilities
Source: C. J. Smith, in D. Herbert and R. J. Johnston (eds) *Geography and the Urban Environment*, v. 3, Wiley, Chichester, 1980.

overt conflicts associated with neighbourhood activism have become more frequent with the extension of owner-occupation and as larger-scale housing and construction projects have replaced smaller-scale activities as the dominant aspect of urban development. It follows that a good deal of neighbourhood activism is directly associated with construction and development activity around the urban fringe. A study of Columbus, Ohio, suggested that it is those with the greatest stakes in a particular local setting, or 'turf' (i.e. owner-occupiers and parents of school-aged children), who are most likely to become involved in neighbourhood activism, and that the dominant types of conflicts tend to be associated with the public regulation of privately-initiated patterns of urban development, with publicly-initiated construction projects (e.g. new highways, street widenings and urban renewal projects), and with the quality of public services.[4] More generally, neighbourhood activism has been categorized in terms of four types, according to the aims and strategies of the neighbourhood groups involved:

- Defensive and exclusionary.
- Demand-aggregating and articulation.
- Resource allocation.
- Concession-seeking and supportive.[5]

Finally, we must acknowledge that understanding patterns of service delivery and amenity location is not simply a matter of competition and conflict over which households win proximity to the most desirable services and amenities and which communities are able to 'capture' new services and amenities. The geography of many services and amenities is also a product of other factors: the 'fabric' effects of the urban environment; the internal organization and politics of particular professions and service-delivery agencies; and the functional linkages that exist between certain services and other activities, for example. This, of course, means that aggregate patterns of service and amenity provision rarely exhibit clear or unambiguous relationships with urban social ecology. Nevertheless, it is clear that the general tendency is for the most affluent, most powerful and most active communities to capture a disproportionate share of the positive externalities associated with urban services and amenities. In the following sections, this tendency is illustrated, first in terms of patterns of medical care in cities generally, and then in terms of a spectrum of services and amenities in one particular city. Attention is then turned to the implications of such patterns for the political economy of cities.

Accessibility to Medical Care

Patterns of accessibility to medical care facilities provide a particularly good example of the way in which the location of amenities can affect the quality of neighbourhood life and so serve as the focus for competition and conflict between households and communities. In countries like the United States and Australia, where medical care delivery systems are essentially run on *laissez-faire* principles, wide variations have come to exist between neighbourhoods in the availability and quality of medical care. In general, the spatial arrangement of hospital services tends to follow the intra-urban commercial hierarchy, except that there is rarely the same degree of suburbanization of facilities. As a result, there tends to be an excess of capacity in the central city and a shortage in the suburbs, especially the less prosperous black and working-class suburbs. Such a pattern has been demonstrated in a number of studies. In Adelaide, South Australia, for example:

> the overall pattern is one of a marked hierarchical system of hospital provision . . . with high concentration of facilities in the inner city

locations . . . with lower order facilities, almost always of the private type, located in the higher status areas or at locations that are old settlement nodes . . . As a result, patients and the friends and relatives visiting them will have relatively long journeys to make to gain access to a hospital.[6]

The spatial organization of primary care in cities also tends to be regressive. In addition to the important limitations on people's accessibility to primary care imposed by income constraints and sociopsychological barriers, home-to-office distance is especially important because of its repercussions on local patterns of health and well-being, due to the deterrent effect of distance in relation to 'therapeutic behaviour' – the seeking of medical advice. In cities where large sectors of the population are still without private transport, the actual distance from home to the family doctor's office is particularly critical. About 0.75 kilometres – 'stroller-pushing distance' – is often regarded as the upper limit for mothers with pre-school children and for the elderly; and travelling much more than this by public transport may involve a long wait or a change of bus unless both home and office lie conveniently near a bus route. Class differences in car ownership are also exacerbated by the time constraints of the working classes, who are normally subject to much more inflexible working hours than the middle classes. The disutility of travelling to the office can thus act as a substantial barrier to proper care, influencing therapeutic behaviour just as educational, religious and class-related barriers do.[7] Patients living further away will tend to make light of symptoms and put up with discomfort, gambling that their condition is not serious rather than making the effort to travel to their doctor. Distance has been shown to have a marked negative effect on consultation rates, and it seems reasonable to suppose that this will eventually exercise a direct effect on local patterns of morbidity and mortality. It is also worth noting that blue-collar workers are, in general, less inclined to consult family doctors and much less concerned than white-collar workers with preventive medicine, with the likely result that distance will affect the delivery of medical care differentially by social class, notwithstanding class differences in personal mobility.

In this context, intra-urban variations in the provision of primary care are alarming. Where primary care is provided on a competitive fee-for-service basis – as in Australia and North America – the locational behaviour of general practitioners is influenced primarily by local effective demand and the propensity for people to want (rather than need) medical care. Other factors that have been identified as influencing the location of surgeries include neighbourhood ethnicity, the availability of office space, the proximity of specialist hospital facilities, the availability of manpower to cover illness and vacations, the approval of the neighbourhood by the doctor's spouse, and the pull of local family ties. The result is a gross imbalance between medical needs and resources, with physicians tending to be clustered around hospitals and nodes of commercial activity and in affluent white suburbs.[8] These outcomes are rooted in the pattern of service delivery that evolved during the urban transition of the late nineteenth century, when the professional specialization of orthodox medicine co-incided with the sociospatial realignment of cities, with the result that medical care ceased to be a ubiquitous, neighbourhood-oriented service.

Even in countries such as the United Kingdom and New Zealand, where nationalized health services make adequate health care a legitimate expec-tation for all, the maldistribution of general medical practictioners (i.e. family doctors, or GPs) within cities has given cause for concern. In Britain, the locational inertia of GPs has meant that their distribution is much as it was at the inception of the National Health Service (NHS) in 1948, with a polarized, localized pattern that had emerged, as in the United States, during the urban transition in response to the interactions of professional realignment and urban restructuring.[9] This pattern has been characterized by a concentration of surgeries in the older and more central neighbour-hoods, particularly those of higher socio-economic status where large dwellings can be used to incorporate both office and residence. Although controls and incentives have been introduced under the NHS in order to regulate the spatial distribution of GPs, these policies have rarely operated at a scale below that of whole towns or cities, so that these intra-urban disparities have been reinforced by the natural tendency for family doctors to live and work in well-established high-status areas where there often exists the possibility of earning extra income with fees from private patients.[10]

At the same time, the structure and ideology of the medical profession in Britain has discouraged the location of GPs in working-class areas, since not only is working in blue-collar neighbourhoods held to be unglamorous and unsatisfactory, but time spent in general practice in such areas is regarded as almost certain disqualification for any further career advance-ment. Having said this, however, it is important to point out that the locational behaviour of GPs has also been influenced by 'fabric' effects, which have tended to reinforce the relative advantages enjoyed by older middle-class neighbourhoods. There is, for instance, an almost complete lack of accommodation suitable for use as doctors' surgeries in the large housing estates – both public and speculatively built – which have encircled most British cities since 1945. The net result is maldistribution of medical resources which is part of what has been called the *inverse care law*: the tendency for medical care to vary inversely with the need of the population served.[11]

This tendency is evident in the distribution of primary care resources in Edinburgh (Fig. 10.3), although the pattern does not conform exactly with the notion of an inverse care law – the localization of surgeries in the older central areas of the city tending to favour several of the more deprived inner-city neighbourhoods as well as the prestigious Georgian neigh-bourhoods of the city centre. The regressive nature of these patterns is rather more apparent when local variations in car ownership are taken into account. Figure 10.4 shows the results of an index which takes into account the relative size and location of general practitioner services, local levels of

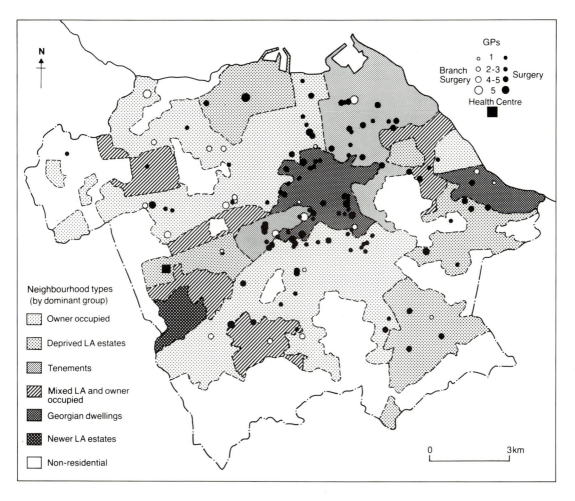

Figure 10.3
The distribution of general medical practitioners in Edinburgh, 1973

car ownership, and the relative speed of public and private transport. Scores of more than 100 on the index indicate that a neighbourhood has more than its fair 'share' of accessibility to the city's primary care facilities. In general, accessibility corresponds systematically and inversely to the social geography of the city.

Physical inaccessibility to GPs, however, is only one aspect of medical deprivation in urban areas, and other aspects of the geography of primary care lend still more support to the idea of an inverse care law, with the deprived areas of the inner-city emerging as the worst off in terms of the quality, if not the availability, of primary care facilities. The reality of primary care in the Vauxhall area of Liverpool has been described in daunting terms:

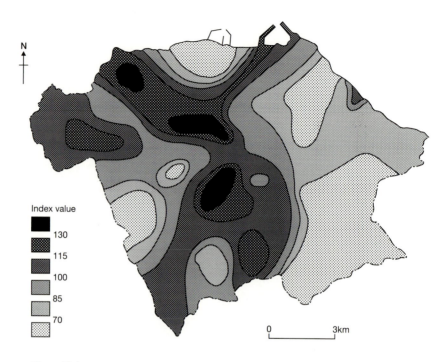

Index value

130

115

100

85

70

Figure 10.4
Accessibility to primary medical care in Edinburgh, 1973

> There are no chairs [in the waiting room]. From the ceiling a large piece of wallpaper hangs down limply. Unshaded light bulbs, coated in grime, hang among drooping coils of lighting flex. Nearby, three GPs hold their surgeries in a converted pair of shops. The windows are boarded up and one of the few panes of glass is smashed. The waiting area smells damp. It contains chairs–red plush, former cinema seats, torn and losing their stuffing, and wooden benches arrayed around the walls.[12]

Complaints by patients of cursory and unsympathetic treatment by doctors are rife. In such areas it is the conditions in which primary care is presented – their dehumanizing ambience – that constitutes the major barrier to therapeutic behaviour, and not distance between home and office. Nevertheless, there are many patients who are subject to both deterrents. Patients who move out – or are moved – to suburbs as part of urban renewal schemes are often forced to remain on the list of the GP in the area from which they were rehoused. As a result, many patients must face journeys of over 30 minutes by car each way; or a total of a least four bus journeys.

Aggregate Patterns of Accessibility: The Example of Oklahoma City

When we examine a wider range of services and amenities, do we find that there are certain neighbourhoods that suffer from poor accessibility on the whole spectrum of facilities? Or are there, for example, distinctive constellations of facilities which give rise to different 'packages' of accessibility/inaccessibility in different parts of a city? An analysis of accessibility to 17 different services and amenities (including the location of job opportunities) in Oklahoma City suggests that there are in fact distinctive variations in the type as well as the level of accessibility enjoyed by different communities.[13] Patterns of accessibility to each of the facilities (ambulance services, banks, community centres, day nurseries, dentists, elementary schools, family doctors, fire stations, golf courses, hospitals, libraries, managerial jobs, post offices, public parks, service jobs,

Table 10.1 Factor structure of accessibility variables

Factor I:	'central city/suburbs' (variance explained = 56.1%)	
	Variable	*Loading*
	Managerial jobs	–0.98
	Service jobs	–0.91
	Public parks	–0.74
	Hospitals	0.68
	Department stores/variety stores	–0.51
Factor II:	'public services' (variance explained = 17.8%)	
	Variable	*Loading*
	Libraries	0.74
	Post offices	0.73
	Elementary schools	0.69
	Ambulance services	0.68
	Community centres	0.64
	Fire stations	0.51
Factor III:	'personal services' (variance explained = 10.9%)	
	Variable	*Loading*
	Banks	0.95
	Day nurseries	0.93
	Dentists	0.87
	General medical practitioners	0.61
Factor IV:	'outdoor amenitites' (variance explained = 6.2%)	
	Variable	*Loading*
	Golf courses	0.56
	Public parks	0.54

Source: P.L. Knox, in K. Cox and R.J. Johnson (eds), *Conflict, Politics, and the Urban Scene*, Longman, 1982, Table 8.3, p.76.

Service sector jobs

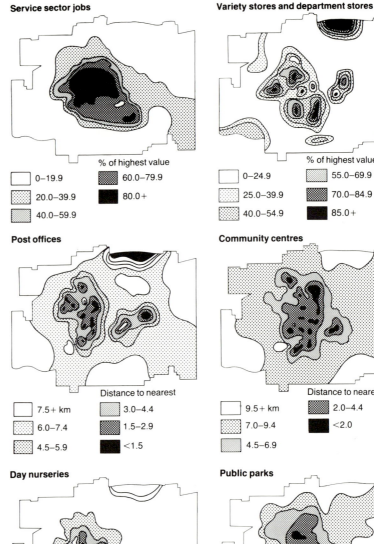

% of highest value

☐ 0–19.9	▨ 60.0–79.9
▨ 20.0–39.9	■ 80.0+
▨ 40.0–59.9	

Variety stores and department stores

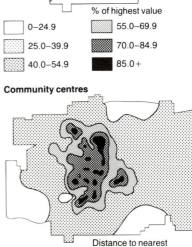

% of highest value

☐ 0–24.9	▨ 55.0–69.9
▨ 25.0–39.9	▨ 70.0–84.9
▨ 40.0–54.9	■ 85.0+

Post offices

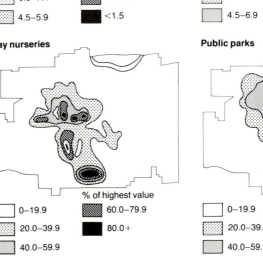

Distance to nearest

☐ 7.5+ km	▨ 3.0–4.4
▨ 6.0–7.4	▨ 1.5–2.9
▨ 4.5–5.9	■ <1.5

Community centres

Distance to nearest

☐ 9.5+ km	▨ 2.0–4.4
▨ 7.0–9.4	■ <2.0
▨ 4.5–6.9	

Day nurseries

% of highest value

☐ 0–19.9	▨ 60.0–79.9
▨ 20.0–39.9	■ 80.0+
▨ 40.0–59.9	

Public parks

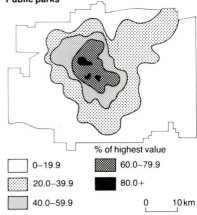

% of highest value

☐ 0–19.9	▨ 60.0–79.9
▨ 20.0–39.9	■ 80.0+
▨ 40.0–59.9	

0   10 km

Figure 10.5 Accessibility surfaces in Oklahoma City
Source: P. L. Knox, in K. Cox and R. J. Johnston (eds) *Conflict, Politics, and the Urban Scene*, Longman, London, 1982, Fig. 4.3, p. 78.

unemployment offices and variety stores) were factor analysed, resulting in the identification of four major dimensions of differentiation which between them accounted for over 87 per cent of the total variance (Table 10.1). The first factor alone accounts for more than 50 per cent of the total variance. As shown by the factor loadings in Table 10.1, it is strongly associated with patterns of accessibility to jobs (both managerial and service-sector), shopping opportunities, parks and hospitals. Essentially, this factor has identified a dichotomy between the central city – with high levels of accessibility to concentrations of employment, shops and parks – and suburban districts, which have poor accessibility to these facilities but rather better accessibility to hospitals. The individual accessibility surfaces for service-sector jobs and department stores, for example (see Fig. 10.5), both exhibit a basic central city/suburban contrast, although they differ somewhat in local detail.

The remaining three factors are each associated with distinctive types of facilities. Factor II is strongly associated with patterns of accessibility to public services, with particularly high loadings on variables measuring accessibility to libraries, post offices, elementary schools, community centres and fire stations, as well as to the (privately organized) ambulance services. The third factor is equally distinctive in that it is clearly associated with a specific group of facilities relating to personal services of various kinds, including banks, day nurseries and the offices of dentists and general practitioners. Finally, factor IV suggests a distinctive dimension of accessibility associated with outdoor amenities such as public parks and golf courses.

Given these distinctive dimensions, the question arises as to how they relate to the social ecology of the city. Figure 10.6 represents an attempt to answer this question. It is a regionalization of the city's census tracts based on a cluster analysis of the 17 accessibility variables together with 25 socio-economic variables. As might be expected from an analysis including so many distance-based variables, there is a good deal of coherence and contiguity to the map. Located in the centre of the inner city are type 1 census tracts. These represent a core area of deprivation on socio-economic indicators, and they are characterized by high levels of accessibility to concentrations of employment and to public parks but very poor accessibility to community centres, libraries, hospitals and ambulance services. To the north and south of its district are extensive areas of type 2 census tracts, which exhibit similar (though less extreme) characteristics of poverty and deprivation and which are similarly deficient in accessibility to health care facilities and community centres. To the east of the CBD and adjacent to these neighbourhoods is a relatively compact district of type 3 census tracts. This coincides with the heart of the city's African-American ghetto. In addition, it is characterized by a high incidence of poverty, of single males and single-parent families, and of people employed in service-sector jobs. Although the area enjoys relatively high levels of accessibility to public parks, it is particularly deficient in accessibility to elementary schools, community centres and health care facilities.

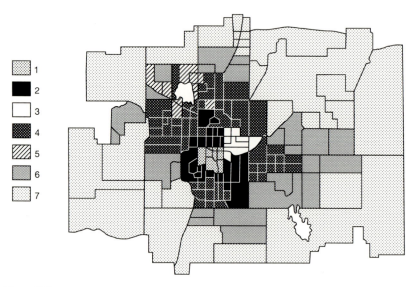

Figure 10.6
Community types in the Oklahoma City SMSA
Source: P. L. Knox, in K. Cox and R. J. Johnston (eds) *Conflict, Politics, and the Urban Scene*, Longman, London, 1982, Fig. 4.4, p. 79.

Forming an almost continuous zone around these three inner city community types is a large number of type 4 census tracts. While these neighbourhoods are of average prosperity, they do not enjoy particularly good accessibility. Indeed, they are significantly deficient in physical accessibility to several public services, including elementary schools, post offices, libraries and community centres. To the northwest of the city is a small enclave of type 5 census tracts containing an affluent and high status population which, in terms of accessibility to facilities, is particularly well placed in relation to parks, golf courses and general practitioners' offices. Type 6 census tracts, located in a series of neighbourhoods in the northern, western and southeastern suburbs of the city, are also relatively affluent. As a group, they tend to be occupied by large households with a young age structure and to have experienced a high level of population turnover. Although they enjoy better-than-average accessibility to hospitals and ambulance services, they are poorly served by the location of the city's jobs, parks and shopping opportunities. Finally, there are the peripheral type 7 census tracts. Although fairly prosperous, these outlying areas contain a high proportion of crowded dwellings and large numbers of people with relatively low levels of educational achievement. They are also characterized by low levels of accessibility to jobs, public parks, shopping opportunities and hospitals. Such patterns provide an essential backcloth for the understanding of past conflict and competition between communities and households; they also help to illuminate the major dimensions of accessibility which are likely to form the basis of future conflict as different groups attempt to improve or enhance the net benefits conferred by the present accessibility structure of the city.

The Aggregate Effects of Aggregate Patterns

We have seen that much of what takes place within the urban arena involves the resolution of conflicts over spatial organization and the relative location of certain 'goods' and 'bads'. The question remains, however, as to the relationships between, on the one hand, the outcome of these conflicts (segregated communities, *de facto* and *de jure*, with access to different 'packages' of services and externalities) and, on the other, the overall process of urban differentiation and change.

At the beginning of this chapter, it was suggested that the richest and most powerful neighbourhoods will enjoy a cumulative net benefit as a result of the outcome of conflict and competition over the organization and location of services and amenities. The implication of this is that urban development is dominated by marginal adjustments in social ecology as new developments are made to fit the mould of the *status quo*. Many of the examples we have examined can be interpreted as supporting this proposition; but it is also clear that it is a crude generalization. Indeed, it is legitimate to ask why there is not a closer correspondence between community status and the geography of externality effects. Several studies of the intra-urban distribution of services and amenities have in fact stressed the 'unpatterned' nature of the disparities that exist,[14] attributing the lack of correspondence between community status and the spatial organization of services and amenities to a combination of idiosyncratic events and bureaucratic decision rules or to the typical spatial structure of Western cities, whose geometry is such that low-income groups are inevitably favoured, notwithstanding the ability of more affluent communities to exert a disproportionate influence on the outcome of conflict and competition.

Other studies point not so much to the idea of unpatterned inequality as to patterns that are a little more complex than we might expect, given the inequalities of income and power implicit in the social ecology of cities. A study of municipal expenditures in New York City, for example, found that expenditures on some services (fire, sanitation) did match socio-economic gradients while others (health, welfare, education) did not.[15] Similarly, a study of the distribution of 16 different kinds of facilities in a cross-section of 12 West German cities found that some facilities (secondary schools, health facilities, public open space, nursery schools) favoured middle-class neighbourhoods, some (leisure centres, sports facilities, sheltered housing) were evenly distributed, and some (day care centres, day centres for the elderly, playgrounds) favoured working-class neighbourhoods in inner-city or extreme peripheral locations that were very poorly served in relation to most facilities.[16] It thus seems that what may appear to be an 'unpatterned' or 'complex' distribution of services and amenities is in fact likely to be the aggregate of two very different sets of patterns – the essentially regressive patterns of property-related services and amenities and the more regressive patterns of 'compensatory', welfare-related services – both of which may, in detail, be conditioned by idiosyncratic effects, bureaucratic decision rules and the constraints imposed by the geometry of the city. In this context, we should note the work of Jennifer Wolch, who has illuminated the spatial linkages which underpin the progressive patterns of many compensatory services. She attributes the localization of the service-dependent poor and their support services in the inner city to the following causes:

1. The dominance of housing and transportation-to-services costs in the locational decisions of service-dependent households.
2. The desire of service facility administrators to minimize clients' transportation costs.
3. The budgetary constraints of both clients and services, which dictate low-rent, inner-city locations.[17]

Finally, we must consider the implications of aggregate patterns of service and amenity location not just in relation to the way that they intensify or ameliorate socio-economic differentiation but also in relation to the broader sociospatial dialectic. What is at issue here is the way that the economic and class relationships inherent to capitalism are perpetuated in cities through ecological processes. From this perspective, we can see that the ecology of cities provides some of the conditions necessary for the *reproduction* of the necessary relationships between labour and capital and for the stabilization and *legitimation* of the associated social formation. Thus we find 'a white collar labour force being "reproduced" in a white collar neighbourhood, a blue collar labour force being reproduced in a blue collar neighbourhood, and so on'.[18] An essential factor in this reproduction is the differential access to scarce resources – especially educational resources – between neighbourhoods, since it helps preserve class and neighbourhood differences in 'market capacity' (the ability to undertake certain functions within the economic order) from one generation to another. At the same time, the locations of 'compensatory' services and amenities not only helps to reproduce and maintain a ready population of workers (at the expense of taxpayers rather than employers) but also helps to defuse the discontent that their position might otherwise foster.

We must accept that the conceptual and empirical distinctions between the accumulation and legitimation functions of services are sometimes difficult to make, and that the politics of service provision rarely relate in overt or explicit ways to functional notions of accumulation or legitimation.[19] Because public service provision is contingent on a variety of sociopolitical factors involving different time frames and periodicities, it is useful to think in terms of services arrayed along a continuum with the accumulation function at one end and the legitimation function at the other (Fig. 10.7).

PURE LEGITIMATION

Housing and community development
Libraries
Parks and recreation
Health and hospitals

Education
Police protection

Fire protection
Sanitation
Sewerage
Water
Highways

PURE ACCUMULATION

Figure 10.7
A conceptual ranking of
services
After L. Staeheli, *Urban
Geography*, 10, 1989, p. 242.

Services located on the accumulation end of the continuum can be thought of as important for the accumulation of capital and are provided primarily in keeping with the needs of capital; roads, water and sewer systems are typical accumulation services because they allow the initial development of land and preserve its subsequent exchange value. . . . As such, their provision is greatly influenced by higher levels of government and by the needs of large, mobile capital. This influence . . . is a smoothing effect on the distribution of accumulation services. . . . In contrast, legitimation services have a larger discretionary component. Parks and libraries, for instance, are generally provided for the benefit of the general, 'classless' public; their amenity value to capital is real, but indirect and possibly will accrue over a longer time span. Because such services are provided for the public, it is common for small groups and individuals to be involved in the decisionmaking process; the politics of consumption characterize this process. The variable cast of characters and concerns involved in the provision of legitimation services means that the demand for these services is likely to be uneven. . . . Finally, some services blend accumulation and legitimation concerns, and are therefore situated in the middle of the continuum. These services are necessary for the accumulation of capital, and so certain aspects of their provision will be similar in most municipalities. However, services in the middle of the continuum, such as police protection and local schools, also have a large discretionary element that may lead to more variability.[20]

Patterns of service and amenity provision, then, are at once the product of the social formation and an element in its continuing survival.

10.2 Urban Restructuring: Inequality and Conflict

As we saw in Chapter 1, cities throughout the developed world have recently entered a new phase – or, at least, begun a distinctive transitional phase –

in response to changing economic, political, social and cultural conditions. The continual restlessness of urbanization has been accentuated by the imperatives of restructuring cities in order not only to accommodate to these changing conditions but also to exploit new technologies and new sociocultural forces. Among the chief features of this restructuring have been the decentralization of jobs, services and residences from traditional city centres to suburban settings and 'edge cities' within expanded metropolitan frameworks; the decline of traditional inner-city employment bases in manufacturing, docks, railways, distribution and warehousing; the recentralization of high-level business services in CBDs; the gentrification of selected inner-city neighbourhoods; the localization of residual populations of marginal and disadvantaged groups and of unskilled migrants and immigrants in other inner-city neighbourhoods; the emergence of a 'new politics' of fiscal conservatism; the emergence of a new politics of race; the emergence of a 'new culture' of material consumption and differentiated life-styles; the feminization of poverty; and the intensification of economic and social polarization. Meanwhile, the need to accommodate a new mix of industry and employment within the fabric of a pre-existing built environment has led to localized conflicts over development and land conversion processes.[21] It is beyond the scope of this book to deal systematically with these issues, or to do justice in depth to any one of them. It must suffice, therefore, to illustrate just a few aspects of the sociospatial consequences of urban change and restructuring.

Decentralization and Accessibility to Services and Amenities

The restructuring of metropolitan form in response to the ascendancy of the automobile has brought to an end the traditional notion that jobs, shops, schools, health services and community facilities will be within ready walking distance of homes. Even by 1960, over 90 per cent of the households in the most recently developed parts of metropolitan California had at least one car, and between 40 and 45 per cent had two or more. By 1970, comparable levels of car ownership had been achieved in most other metropolitan areas of the United States, while in Europe the spread of car ownership was at last beginning to accelerate rapidly. One result of this trend has been that employers, retailers and planners have tended to make their location decisions on the assumption of perfect personal mobility. The prime example of this is the ascendancy of suburban shopping centres and shopping malls. Their magnetic power has rearranged not only the commercial geography of urban areas but also the whole social life of the suburbs. Malls have become the most popular gathering places for suburban teenagers, and adults use them to stroll and promenade, much as continental Europeans have used their city centres on Sundays. Americans now spend more time at shopping malls than anywhere outside their homes and workplaces.

The benefits of increased personal mobility are enjoyed disproportionately by the middle-class, the middle-aged and the male population, however. In the United States, for example, although the overall ratio of motor vehicles to households increased from 1.3 to nearly 2.3 between 1960 and 1993, only the more affluent households actually had an increase in car ownership. Less affluent households, as a group, were worse off in 1993 than in 1960. Indeed, surveys have shown that, despite the advent of the 'automobile age', around three out of ten urban residents lack direct personal access to a motor vehicle. Many of these individuals are old, poor or black, and a good many are inner-city residents.

Women are also significantly deficient in access to motor vehicles for, although their household unit may own a car, its use by other members of the household is likely to render it unavailable for much of the time. In a study of San Francisco households, six or seven out of every ten women were unable to claim direct personal access to a motor vehicle. And, where this gender constraint was compounded by age and low household income, levels of car availability dropped to only two in every ten women. In contrast, nine out of every ten males in moderately affluent households did have direct access to a car.[22] Furthermore, the urban form which the automobile has triggered – low-density development spread over a wide area – has made it very difficult to provide public transport systems which are able to meet the needs of car-less suburban women, the elderly and the poor.

Women are particularly vulnerable to constraints on locational accessibility. Labour-market changes that have concentrated women in a limited range of occupations are compounded by the spatial concentration of female-dominated jobs and by the constraints of gender roles in contemporary society.[23] Even affluent suburban housewives with access to a car are limited in their opportunities because of the limited time available between their fixed 'duties' as homemakers: providing breakfast for the family and driving the children to school, preparing lunch, picking up the children from school, chauffeuring them to sporting or social engagements and preparing dinner. In addition, homemakers may have to be at home to accept deliveries, supervise repair workers or care for a sick child. Women without cars, of course, suffer much greater restriction on their quality of life. As we have seen, women do not, in general, enjoy very good levels of accessibility to cars, even in the United States. As Pred and Palm put it, the daily routine of the car-less suburban housewife:

> is restricted to those opportunities which can be reached on foot or by the use of a bus service (which in many suburbs is inconvenient and in some non-existent) . . . Even routine shopping becomes a chore. Socializing is limited to the neighbourhood in which she lives. . . . With children under school age she is virtually locked into a world of very limited physical space because of coupling constraints and societal expectations concerning her family role. Viewed from a time-geographic perspective, she has the greatest number of leisure hours and yet little opportunity to invest leisure time in personal fulfilment.[24]

Some of the most severe accessibility problems arising from urban decentralization are experienced by suburban single parents:

> lone parents must inevitably have lifestyles which differ from those of two-parent families. They have much less flexibility in employment and in recreation, for example, having to dovetail their activities to the time schedules of their children. Those parents with school-age children may find full-time employment impossible without after-school and holiday care facilities, while those with pre-school children are dependent on crèches and day nurseries. In both cases the proximity of relatives and friends is often critical. Late opening of commercial and other enterprises is also vital if a single parent is to incorporate visits to shops, banks, libraries and offices in the weekly activity pattern.[25]

Among single-parent households, those living in the deprived, peripheral public housing estates of British cities must have a strong claim to the worst problems of all. In Glasgow, where Isobel Robertson investigated the time–geographic aspects of single-parent life-styles, one in six of the households allocated to peripheral estates is a single-parent family. In parts of one neighbourhood (Drumchapel) studied by Robertson, the time requirements for fundamental activity sequences common to single parents were extremely high. For some, the return journey (on foot, for lack of any alternatives) to the nearest day care centre took over an hour and a half. A visit to the nearest unemployment office also took an hour and a half from some parts of Drumchapel; and so on. Moreover, Robertson found that most of the single-parent households were located in the very districts with the worst locations in terms of 19 different activity sequences typical of single-parent households.[26]

As Linda McDowell and others have pointed out, the predicament of suburban women is not simply a consequence of urban decentralization.[27] It is intimately related to a whole nexus of the trends outlined at the beginning of this book. The intersection of economic, demographic, social and cultural trends, for example, has allocated to women a pivotal role in the consumption-oriented suburban life-styles that dominate the logic of contemporary urbanism. In short, women are trapped economically, socially and culturally, as well as ecologically. Meanwhile, the suburban environment has evolved in ways that reinforce inequality between the sexes, contributing, among other things, to emotional strain and the erosion of 'community'.

Redevelopment and Renewal

One of the longest-running aspects of urban restructuring has been the physical redevelopment and renewal of worn-out and outmoded inner-city environments. In excising the most inefficient factories and the worst slums from city centres, urban renewal has undoubtedly contributed not only to economic regeneration but also to the 'common good' in terms of environmental quality and public health. But in rehousing the residents of clearance areas and replacing the built environment, planners have managed to preside over some spectacular débâcles. The principal charge against them in this context is the dismantling of whole communities, scattering their members across the city in order to make room for luxury housing, office developments (including, in many instances, new accommodation for the urban bureaucracy), shopping areas, conference centres and libraries. A secondary charge – urban blight – stems from the discrepancy between the ambitions of planners and what can actually be achieved within a reasonable future. During the intervening period, neighbourhoods scheduled for renewal are allowed to slide inexorably down a social and economic spiral. No landlord will repair a condemned house if he can help it; tenants who can afford it will move out; shopkeepers will close and drift away; and the city council, waiting for comprehensive redevelopment, will meanwhile defer any 'unnecessary' expenditure on maintenance. Schools, public buildings, roads and open space become rundown, matching the condition of the remaining population of the poor and the elderly.[28] This dereliction has been extensive in many cities. Combined with the actual demolition of condemned property, the result has been that large areas have been laid waste and thousands of families have been displaced. Moreover, the problem has been compounded since, as the worst parts of the cities' housing stock have been cleared, the bureaucratic offensive has gone on to condemn housing that was relatively sound, turning slum clearance from a beneficent if blunt instrument into a bureaucratic juggernaut.

By removing the structure of social and emotional support provided by the neighbourhood, and by forcing people to rebuild their lives separately amid strangers elsewhere, slum clearance has often imposed a serious psychological cost upon its supposed beneficiaries. At the same time, relocatees typically face a steep increase in rents because of their forced move 'upmarket': the median rent of the families in Hartman's early study of Boston's West End rose by over 70 per cent.[29] In Britain, most slum clearance families are rehoused in the public sector, but this also brings disadvantages which may outweigh the attractions of more modern accommodation at subsidized rents. Slum clearance families must face the vicissitudes of a housing bureaucracy whose scale and split responsibilities tend to make it insensitive to their needs. Since they are 'slum dwellers', the new accommodation which is offered to them is likely to be in low-status estates. Even the offer of accommodation in new maisonettes or high-rise apartments may compare unfavourably with the tried-and-tested environment of old inner-city neighbourhoods. The open spaces, pedestrian pathways and community centres regarded as major advantages by planners may seem of minor importance to their users; while some such 'amenities' serve only as focal points of vandalism, souring the whole social atmosphere. Moreover, because much new residential planning has been guided by the objective of fostering 'community' feelings, problems of a different nature can be precipitated by the lack of privacy on new estates.

Apartments and maisonettes tend to be worst in this respect, since common stairways, lifts and desk access mean that interaction with uncongenial neighbours is unavoidable. On the other hand, the planned and regulated environment of new estates has little of the richness of opportunity associated with older neighbourhoods. Finally, it is worth noting that not everyone from clearance areas ends up being relocated in sound accommodation, let alone satisfactory or desirable housing. Hartman's study of rehousing in Boston, for example, found that over 25 per cent of families displaced from slum clearance areas were not properly rehoused. Furthermore, it transpires that renewal sometimes creates new slums (especially in North American cities where the public housing stock is so small) by pushing relocatees into areas and buildings which become overcrowded and therefore deteriorate rapidly. This has principally been the case with African-American families, who, because of both economic constraints and racial discrimination, have been forced to double up in other ghettos.[30]

The chief *beneficiaries* of urban renewal are the dominant political and economic élite of the city. The former benefit from the existence of a much more lucrative tax base with which to finance public services, as well as the feelings of civic pride generated by redevelopment schemes and the symbolization of power they represent. One particularly well-documented example of this is Newcastle upon Tyne, where a unique Victorian townscape, as well as the less appealing housing of the terraced streets off the Scotswood Road, was replaced by a city centre which earned the leader of the council the title of 'man of the year' from the *Architect's Journal* and led the city's politicians proudly to boast of the city as the 'Brasilia of the North'.[31] The dominant business élite, meanwhile, benefits in much more tangible ways. In his book, *The Rape and Plunder of the Shankhill*, for example, Wiener has shown how the redevelopment of Belfast city centre has served to benefit monopoly capital by wiping out small retailers, thus giving the big stores and large supermarkets the market they require.[32] But it is the speculative developers of property whose interests have been best served by urban renewal. Obtaining sites which have been cleared at public expense, they have been encouraged by planners to develop them for 'higher' uses–offices, hotels, conference centres and shopping precincts. The planners' 'Reconquest of Paris', for example, has resulted in the replacement of deteriorating housing (but not the worst housing, which did not happen to occupy prime sites), public facilities and public open space with large-scale commercial installations and office blocks.[33] Such developments have been highly lucrative, and it is therefore not surprising to find that, in many cities, developers have 'worked' the planning system in order to secure ever greater profits.[34]

Service Sector Restructuring

In parallel with the restructuring and reorganization of industrial production that has transformed the economic base of cities everywhere (see pp. 8–11), there have been some interdependent changes in the structure of national and local welfare systems that have resulted in significant changes to the geography of urban service provision. The combination of economic recession and the globalization of manufacturing and of financial and business services has led to a retreat from the public provision of welfare services, an increase in public–private cooperation, and an emphasis on accumulation-oriented services that enable cities to compete more effectively within an international urban system.

This is an area that has not been systematically researched, though it is clear that there has been a great deal of substitution between different forms of service provision (i.e. domestic, voluntary, commercial, subsidized commercial, community-based, city-based, state-based, etc.), which has in turn resulted not only in new patterns of service provision and relative accessibility but also, in some instances, in new sociospatial phenomena. Perhaps the best-known example is the way that the deinstitutionalization of mental health services has contributed to urban homelessness.[35] Public services, meanwhile, have not only been cut back in extent but geared more to yardsticks of cost-efficiency and flexibility than need or equity. Moreover, just as private-sector services have restructured in response to changing economic circumstances, changing technologies, and new managerial strategies, so have public-sector services (Table 10.2). As Steven Pinch points out, a very wide spectrum of change has been imprinted on to the geography of public service provision, including partial self-provisioning, intensification, capitalization, rationalization, subcontracting, substituting expensive employees with cheaper ones, centralization, materialization, domestication and spatial relocation.[36] What remain to be established, however, are the sociospatial outcomes of this change, in terms of who gets what, where.

Social Polarization

Social polarization and the spatial segregation of the poor is of course a well-worn theme in urban social geography. As Manuel Castells has noted, 'the existence in 1980s Los Angeles of $11 million condominium apartments, sold with a complimentary Rolls Royce, and 50 000 homeless wandering the beaches of the Californian dream', was simply 'an extreme manifestation of an old urban phenomenon, probably aggravated in the 1980s by the removal of the welfare safety net in the wake of neoconservative public policies'.[37] It is clear, however, that economic restructuring and social polarization, in tandem with social and demographic changes, have heightened economic inequality along class and racial cleavages: 'The

Table 10.2 Forms of service sector restructuring

Private sector	Public sector
1 Partial self-provisioning	
Self-service in retailing	Child care in the home
Replacement of services with goods	Care of elderly in the home
Videos, microwave ovens, etc.	Personal forms of transport
	Household crime-prevention strategies, neighbourhood watch, use of anti-theft devices, vigilante patrols
2 Intensification: increases in labour productivity via managerial or organizational changes with little or no investment or major loss of capacity	
Pressure for increased turnover per employee in retailing	The drive for efficiency in the health service
	Competitive tendering over direct labour operations, housing maintenance, refuse collection
	Increased numbers of graduates per academic in universities
3 Investment and technical change: capital investment into new forms of production often with considerable job loss	
The development of the electronic office in private managerial and producer services	Computerization of health and welfare service records
	Electronic diagnostic equipment in health care
	Distance learning systems through telecommunications video and computers
	Larger refuse disposal vehicles, more efficient compressed loaders
4 Rationalization: closure of capacity with little or no new investment or new technology	
Closure of cinemas	Closure of schools, hospitals, day-care centres for under fives, etc.
	Closure or reduction of public transport systems
5 Subcontracting: of parts of the services sector to specialized companies, especially of producer services	
Growth of private managerial producer services	Privatization or contracting out of cleaning, laundry, and catering within the health service
	Contracting out of refuse disposal, housing maintenance, public transport by local government
6 Replacement of existing labour input by part-time, female or non-white labour	
Growth of part-time female labour in retailing	Domination of women in teaching profession?
	Increased use of part-time teachers
7 Enhancement of quality through increased labour input, better skills, increased training	
In some parts of private consumer services	Retraining of British Rail personnel
	Community policing?
8 Materialization of the service function so that the service takes the form of a material product that can be bought, sold, and transported	
Entertainment via videos and televisions rather than 'live' cinema or sport	Pharmaceuticals rather than counselling and therapy?

Table 10.2 Continued

Private sector	Public sector
9 Spatial relocation	
Movement of offices from London into areas with cheaper rents	Relocation from larger psychiatric hospitals into decentralized community-based hostels
	Relocation of offices from London to realize site values and to reduce rents and labour costs
10 Domestication: *the partial reelocation of the provision of the functions within forms of household or family labour*	
Closure of laundries	Care of the very young and elderly in private houses after reductions in voluntary and public service
11 Centralization: *the spatial centralization of services in larger units and the closure or reduction of the number of smaller units*	
Concentration or retailing into larger units	Concentration of primary and secondary hospital care into larger units, that is, the growth of large general hospitals and group general practices
Closure of corner shops	

Source: S. Pinch, *Environment & Planning A*, **21**, 1989, p.910.

differential reassignment of labor in the process of simultaneous growth and decline results in a sharply stratified, segmented social structure that differentiates between upgraded labor, downgraded labor, and excluded people.' The latter 'share an excluded space that is highly fragmented, mainly in ethnic terms, . . . reservations for displaced labor, barely maintained on welfare'.[38]

The 'new poor', in other words, represent a distinctive component of the new urban geography that has been produced by restructuring. Most striking among the polarized landscapes of contemporary cities are 'impacted ghettos', spatially isolated concentrations of the very poor, usually (though not always) racial minorities that have been drained of community leaders and positive role models and that are dominated numerically by young unmarried mothers and their children.[39] Less visible, but more decisively excluded, are the 'landscapes of despair' inhabited by the homeless: micro-spaces that range from vest-pocket parks and anonymous alleyways to squalid shelters and hostels.[40]

These phenomena raise a wide variety of conceptual, theoretical and practical issues. Though it is beyond our scope to pursue them all, one issue that should be raised here is that of attributing causality to the deprivation inherent to social polarization. Table 10.3 outlines six main explanations of deprivation, ranging from the concept of a 'culture of poverty' – which sees urban deprivation as a pathological condition – to the concept of an 'underclass' of households that have become detached from the formal labour market.

The idea of a *culture of poverty* is seen as being both an adaptation and a reaction of the poor to their marginal position in society, representing an effort to cope with the feelings of helplessness and despair which develop from the realization of the improbability of achieving success within a capitalist system. In short, it results in a vicious cycle of lack of opportunity and lack of aspiration. There is, however, considerable room for debate as to whether culture is more of an effect than a cause of poverty and, indeed, whether the values, aspirations and cultural attributes of the poor in Western cities really are significantly different from those of the rest of society.

The idea of *transmitted deprivation* is really concerned with explaining why, despite long periods of full employment and the introduction of improved welfare services, problems of deprivation persist. According to this model, the answer lies in the cyclical process of transmission of social maladjustment from one generation to another. Thus, while it is acknowledged that low wages, poor housing and lack of opportunity are important factors, the emphasis is on the inadequacies of the home background and the upbringing of children.

The idea of *institutional malfunctioning* shares some common ground with the managerialist school of thought, since the behaviour of bureaucrats is given a central role in explaining the persistence of deprivation. Here, however, it is not so much the 'gatekeeping' role of bureaucrats which is emphasized as the administrative structure within which they work. Thus, it is argued, the formulation of public policy in separate departments concerned with housing, education, welfare, planning and so on is

Table 10.3 Differing explanations of urban deprivation

Theoretical model	Explanation	Location of the problems
1. Culture of poverty	Problems arising from the internal pathology of deviant groups	Internal dynamics of deviant behaviour
2. Transmitted deprivation (cycle of deprivation)	Problems arising from individual psychological handicaps and inadequacies transmitted from one generation to the next	Relationships between individuals, families and groups
3. Institutional malfunctioning	Problems arising from failures of planning, management or administration	Relationship between the 'disadvantaged' and the bureacracy
4. Maldistribution of resources and opportunities	Problems arising from an inequitable distribution of resources	Relationship between the underprivileged and the formal political machine
5. Structural class conflict	Problems arising from the divisions necessary to maintain an economic system based on private profit	Relationship between the working class and the political and economic structure
6. Underclass	Minority groups isolated from formal labour market and from mainstream society	Spatial mismatch of jobs and labour; feminization of poverty; suburbanization of role models

inevitably ineffective in dealing with the interlocking problems of deprivation. Moreover, such organizational structures are vulnerable to inter-departmental rivalries and power struggles which can only reduce their overall effectiveness.

The idea of a *maldistribution of opportunities and resources* can be accommodated within pluralist political theory, with deprivation being seen as the result of failures of participation and representation of certain interests in the political process.

The idea of *structural inequality* sets problems of deprivation as inevitable results of the underlying economic order and of structural changes in labour markets, etc., that are attached to the overall restructuring of the economy and of the built environment.

The idea of an *underclass* borrows from several of these perspectives, emphasizing the effects of economic restructuring and sociospatial change in isolating racial minorities not only from the economic mainstream but also from the social values and behavioural patterns of the rest of society. The existence of large numbers from minority groups with only weak connections to the formal labour force is attributed largely to the spatial mismatch between people and jobs that has intensified as many of the low-skill jobs traditionally found in inner-city areas have been relocated, to

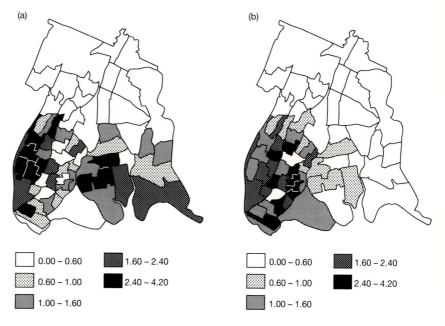

Figure 10.8
The Bronx, New York: (a) Annual number of drug-related deaths, by quintiles; (b) AIDS deaths per 100 000 population, cumulative to 1988
Source: R. Wallace and M. T. Fullilove, *Environment & Planning A*, 21, 1989, pp. 1707, 1708.

be replaced mainly by jobs requiring higher skills.[41] The development of a distinctive context of values and attitudes is attributed largely to the feminization of poverty resulting from an increase in teenage unwed mothers (itself a product of a combination of economic and social trends), combined with the suburbanization of more affluent, better-skilled households. It has proven difficult, however, to establish the nature of the linkages between labour markets, poverty, migration, household structure, race, gender, attitudes, and behaviour; while the term 'underclass' itself has been criticized because of the way it has been used as a pejorative label for the 'undeserving' poor by some commentators.

All this leaves us some way short of a clear and comprehensive explanatory framework for deprivation and social polarization. What is clear,

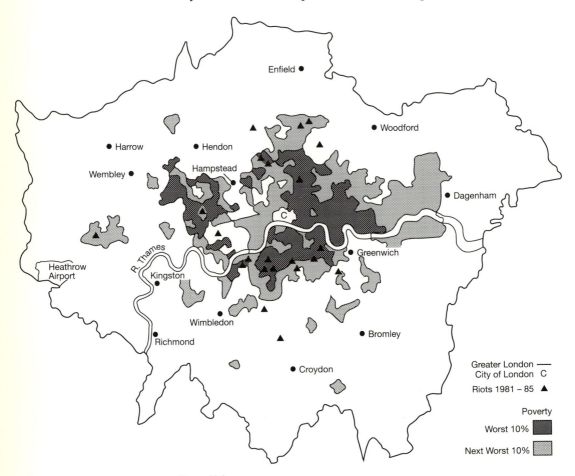

Figure 10.9
Poverty and urban riots, Greater London
Source: D. Diamond, in R. Bennett and R. Estall (eds) *Global Change and Challenge*,
Routledge, London, 1991, p. 218.

however, is that the *degree* of sociospatial polarization in contemporary cities has brought a disturbing dimension of urban social geography to a new prominence. Riots, civil disorder, social unrest and social disorganization are by no means new to cities, but they appear to have developed to unprecedented levels. Take, for example, the inner-city neighbourhoods of the Bronx, where relict and dilapidated neighbourhoods (Fig. 2.13a) have come to represent 'burnt out' settings where social disintegration has fostered extremely high levels of poverty, substance abuse (Fig. 10.8a), violent deaths, low birthweight infants, and deaths from AIDS (Fig. 10.8b).[42] The combination of such aetiologies with continuing discrimination and a newly-racialized politics[43] has begun to precipitate rebellion, as manifested by rioting (Fig. 10.9). Thus we enter a new round of the sociospatial dialectic, with events such as the Los Angeles riot of April 1992, which accounted for 52 deaths and between $785 million and $1 billion in property damage,[44] leading to a widespread 'hardening' of the built environment, with 'fortress' and 'bunker' architecture, the loss of public urban spaces, the 'militarization' of social control, intensified surveillance, gated streets, private security forces, and intensified sociospatial segregation.[45]

SUGGESTED READING

An excellent introduction to the geography of urban public service provision is provided by Steven Pinch's text: *Cities and Services: The Geography of Collective Consumption* (1985: Routledge, London). Alternatively, see Paul Knox, 'Collective consumption and sociospatial change' in *Social Geography: Progress and Prospect*, edited by Michael Pacione (1987: Croom Helm, Beckenham) and Lynn Staeheli, 'Accumulation, legitimation, and the provision of public services' (*Urban Geography*, **10**, 1989, 229–250). On urban restructuring, inequality and conflict, see Robin Law and Jennifer Wolch, 'Social reproduction in the city: restructuring in time and space' in *The Restless Urban Landscape*, edited by Paul Knox (1993: Prentice-Hall, Englewood Cliffs, NJ); this extended essay provides an excellent overview of the interdependence of economic restructuring, the restructuring of households, of communities, and of the welfare state, relating them all to changing urban activity patterns. Useful empirical studies of various aspects of restructuring can be found in edited volumes by John Mollenkopf (*Power, Culture, and Place*: 1988, Russell Sage Foundation, New York – see especially Chapters 7–12), Susan Fainstein, Ian Gordon and Michael Harloe (*Divided Cities: New York and London in the Contemporary World*: 1992, Blackwell, Oxford), and John Mollenkopf and Manuel Castells (*Dual City. Restructuring New York*: 1991, Russell Sage Foundation, New York).

NOTES

1. Harvey, D. W., *Social Geography and the City*. Oxford: Blackwell, 1973.

2. Pahl, R. E., *Whose City?* London: Longman, 1970, p. 113.

3. Johnston, R. J., *City and Society*, 2nd edn. London: Hutchinson, 1984, p. 171; emphasis added.

4. Cox, K. R. and J. J. McCarthy, Neighborhood activism in the American city: behavioral relationships and evaluation, *Urban Geography*, **1**, 1982, 22–38.

5. Rich, R., The roles of neighbourhood organizations in urban service delivery, *Urban Affairs Papers*, **1**, 1979, 81–93; Burnett, A. D. and D. Hill, Neighbourhood organizations and the distribution of public-service outputs in Britain. In R. C. Rich (ed.), *The Politics of Urban Public Services*. Lexington, Mass.: Lexington Books, 1982, pp. 189–206.

6. Cleland, E. A., R. J. Stimpson and A. J. Goldsworthy, *Suburban Health Care Behaviour in Adelaide*. Adelaide: Centre for Applied and Survey Research, Flinders University, 1973, p. 50.

7. Mechanic, D., *Medical Sociology: A Selective View*. New York: Free Press, 1968; Phillips, D. R., Public attitudes to general practitioner services: a reflection of an inverse care law in intra-urban primary medical care? *Environment & Planning A*, 1979, 315–324.

8. Rosenberg, M., Accessibility to health care: a North American perspective, *Progress in Human Geography*, **7**, 1983, 78–87; Gober, P. and R. J. Gordon, Intraurban physician location: a case study of Phoenix, *Social Science and Medicine*, **14D**, 1980, 407–417.

9. Knox, P. L., The geography of medical care: an historical perspective, *Geoforum*, **13**, 1982, 245–251.

10. Knox, P. L. and M. Pacione, Locational behaviour, place preferences, and the inverse care law in the distribution of primary medical care, *Geoforum*, **11**, 1980, 43–55.

11. Hart, J. T., The inverse care law, *Lancet*, **i**, 1971, 405–412.

12. Phillips, M., Health gap in a class of its own, *The Guardian*, 20 October 1978, p.3.

13. Knox, P. L., Residential structure, facility location, and patterns of accessibility. In K. Cox and R. J. Johnston (eds), *Conflict, Politics, and the Urban Scene*. London: Longman, 1982, pp. 62–87.

14. See, for example, Rich, R. C., The political economy of urban service distribution. In R. C. Rich (ed.), *The Politics of Urban Public Services*. Lexington, Mass.: Lexington Books, 1982, pp. 1–16.

15. Boyle, J. and D. Jacobs, The intracity distribution of services: a multivariate analysis, *American Political Science Review*, **76**, 1982, 371–379.

16. Göschel, A. *et al.*, Infrastructural inequality and segregation, *International Journal of Urban and Regional Research*, **6**, 1982, 503–531.

17. Wolch, J. R., The location of service-dependent households in urban areas, *Economic Geography*, **57**, 1981, 52–67.

18. Harvey, D. W., Class structure in a capitalist society and the theory of residential differentiation. In R. Peel *et al.* (eds), *Processes in Physical and Human Geography: Bristol Essays*. London: Heinemann, 1975, p. 363.

19. Staeheli, L., Accumulation, legitimation, and the provision of public services in the American metropolis, *Urban Geography*, **10**, 1989, 229–250.

20. *Ibid.*, p. 243.

21. See, for example, Fainstein, N. I. and S. S. Fainstein, Economic restructuring and the politics of land use planning in New York City, *Journal of the American Planning Association*, **53**, 1987, 237–248; Berry, M. and M. Huxley, Big build: property capital, the state and urban change in Australia, *International Journal of Urban and Regional Research*, 1993, 35–59.

22. Foley, D. L., Accessibility for residents in the metropolitan environment. In A. H. Hawley and V. P. Rock (eds), *Metropolitan America in Contemporary Perspective*, New York: Halsted Press, 1975.

23. See Wekerle, G. R. and B. Rutherford, The mobility of capital and the immobility of female labor: responses to economic restructuring. In J. Wolch and M. Dear (eds), *The Power of Geography. How Territory Shapes Social Life*. London: Unwin Hyman, 1989, pp. 139–172; Bromley, R. F. and C. J. Thomas, The retail revolution, the careless shopper, and disadvantage, *Transactions, Institute of British Geographers*, **18**, 1993, 222–236; England, K. Suburban pink collar ghettos: The spatial entrapment of women? *Annals, Association of British Geographers*, **83**, 1993, 225–242.

24. Pred, A. and R. Palm, The status of American Women: a time–geographic view. In D. A. Lanegran and R. Palm (eds), *An Invitation to Geography*, 2nd edn. New York: McGraw-Hill, 1978, p. 108.

25. Robertson, I. M. L., Single parent lifestyle and peripheral estate residence, *Town Planning Review*, **55**, 1984, 198.

26. *Ibid.*

27. McDowell, L., Towards an understanding of the gender division of urban space, *Environment & Planning D: Society and Space*, **1**, 1983, 59–72.

28. Ravetz, A. *Remaking Cities*. Beckenham: Croom Helm, 1980.

29. Hartman, C., The housing of relocated families, *Journal of the American Institute of Planners*, **30**, 1964, 266–286.

30. *Ibid.*

31. Davies, J. G., *The Evangelistic Bureaucrat*. London: Tavistock, 1972.

32. Wiener, R., *The Rape and Plunder of the Shankhill*. Belfast: Notaems Press, 1976.

33. Castells, M., *City, Class, and Power*. London: Macmillan, 1978.

34. See, for example, Feagin, J. and R. Parker, *Building American Cities. The Urban Real Estate Game*, 2nd edn. Englewood Cliffs, NJ: Prentice Hall, 1991.

35. Dear, M. and J. Wolch, *Landscapes of Despair*. Princeton, NJ: Princeton University Press, 1989.

36. Pinch, S., The restructuring thesis and the study of public services, *Environment & Planning A*, **21**, 1989, 905–926.

37. Castells, M., *The Informational City*. Oxford: Blackwell, 1989, p. 224.

38. *Ibid.*, pp. 225, 227.

39. See, for example, Hughes, M., Formation of the impacted ghetto. Evidence from large metropolitan areas, 1970–1980, *Urban Geography*, **11**, 1990, 265–284; Wilson, W. J., *The Truly Disadvantaged: The Inner City, the Underclass, and Public Policy*. Chicago: University of Chicago Press, 1987.

40. Dear, M. and J. Wolch, *Landscapes of Despair*; Law, R., and J. Wolch, Homelessness and economic restructuring, *Urban Geography*, **12**, 1991, 105–136.

41. Holzer, H. J., The spatial mismatch hypothesis, *Urban Studies*, **28**, 1991, 105–122; Kasarda, J. D., Structural factors affecting the location and timing of urban underclass growth, *Urban Geography*, **11**, 1990, 234–264.

42. Wallace, R. and M. T. Fullilove, AIDS deaths in the Bronx, 1983–1988: spatiotemporal analysis from a sociogeographic perspective, *Environment & Planning A*, **23**, 1991, 1701–1723.

43. See, for example, Omi, M. and H. Winant, The Los Angeles 'Race Riot' and Contemporary US Politics. In R. Gooding-Williams (ed.), *Reading Rodney King. Reading Urban Uprising*. New York: Routledge, 1993, pp. 97–114.

44. Oliver, M. L., J. H. Johnson, Jr and W. C. Farrell, Jr, Anatomy of a rebellion: A political–economic analysis. In R. Gooding-Williams (ed.), *Reading Rodney King. Reading Urban Uprising*. New York: Routledge, 1993, pp. 117–141.

45. Davis, M., Fortress Los Angeles: The militarization of urban space. In M. Sorkin (ed.), *Variations on a Theme Park*. New York: Noonday Press, 1992, pp. 154–180.

Index